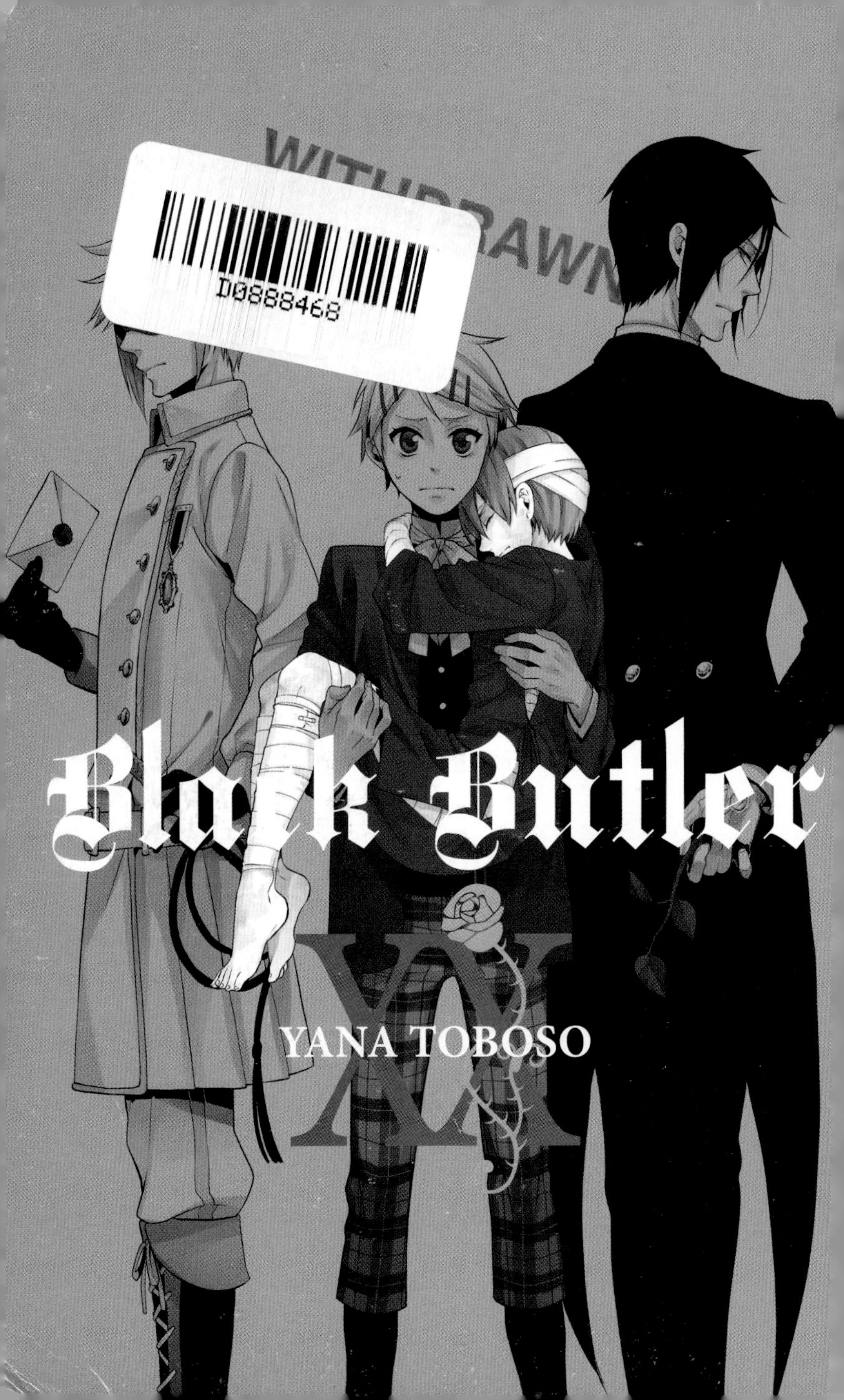
Black Butler
XX
YANA TOBOSO

Contents

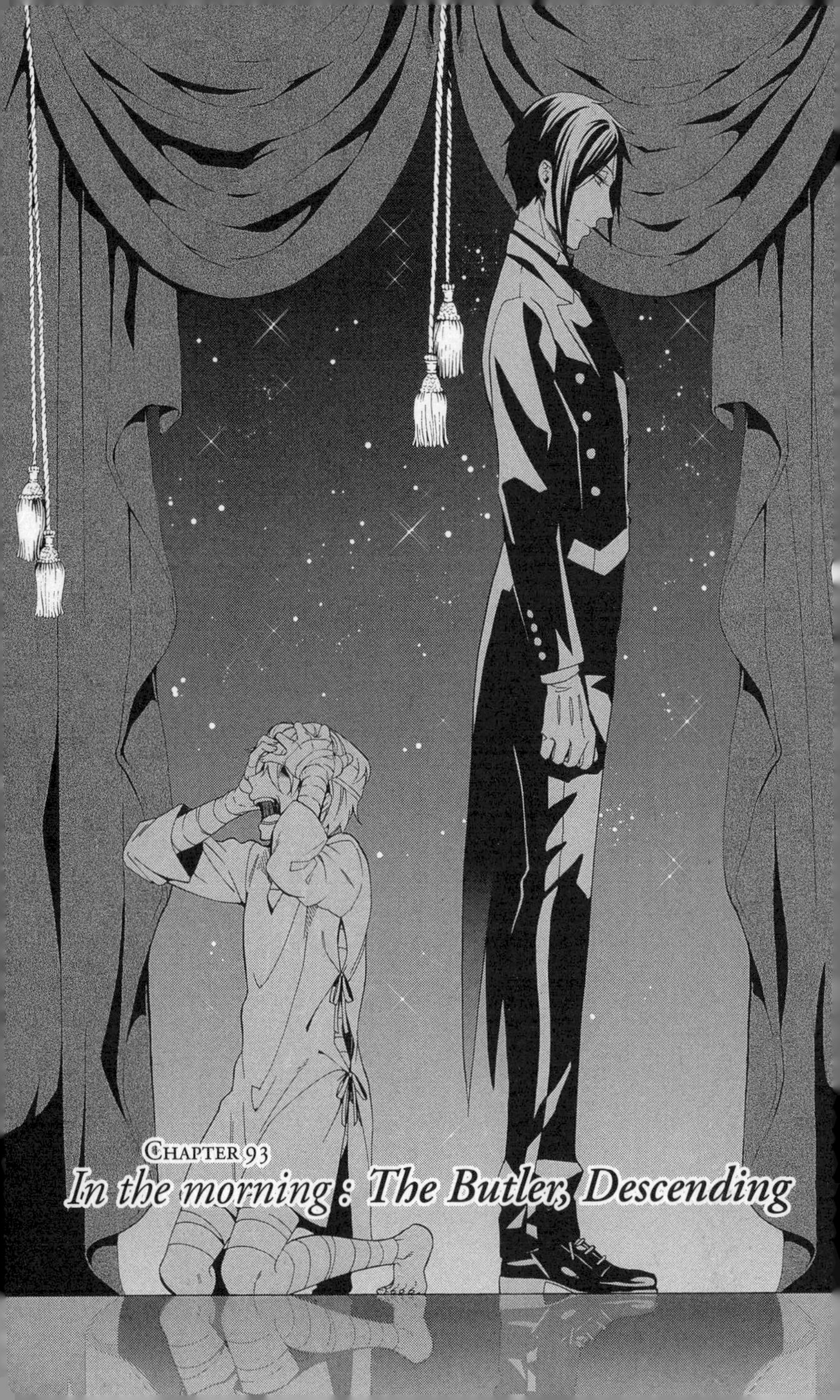
Chapter 93
In the morning : The Butler, Descending

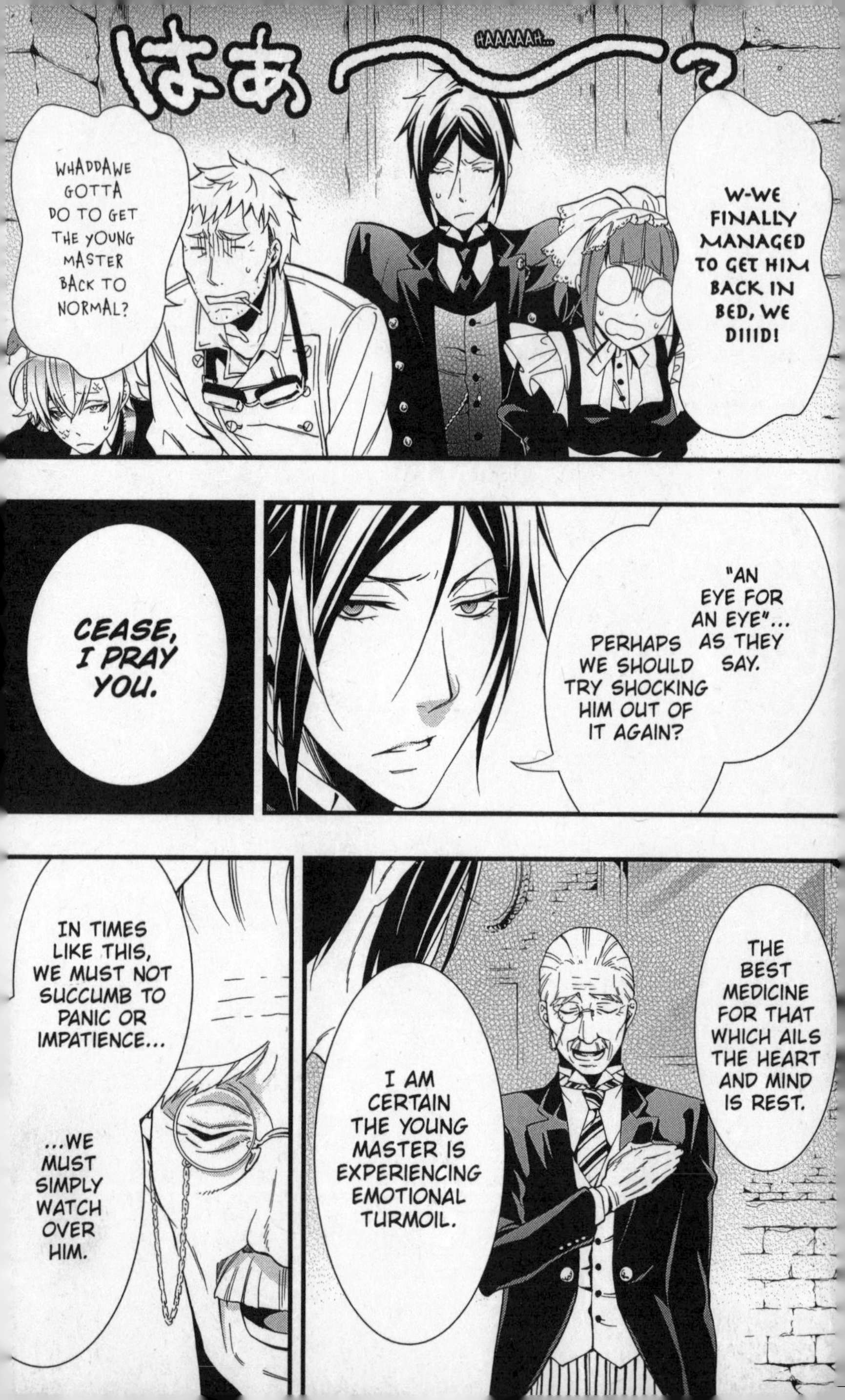
はあ〜っ
HAAAAAH...
W-WE FINALLY MANAGED TO GET HIM BACK IN BED, WE DIIID!
WHADDAWE GOTTA DO TO GET THE YOUNG MASTER BACK TO NORMAL?
"AN EYE FOR AN EYE"... AS THEY SAY.
PERHAPS WE SHOULD TRY SHOCKING HIM OUT OF IT AGAIN?
CEASE, I PRAY YOU.
THE BEST MEDICINE FOR THAT WHICH AILS THE HEART AND MIND IS REST.
I AM CERTAIN THE YOUNG MASTER IS EXPERIENCING EMOTIONAL TURMOIL.
IN TIMES LIKE THIS, WE MUST NOT SUCCUMB TO PANIC OR IMPATIENCE...
...WE MUST SIMPLY WATCH OVER HIM.

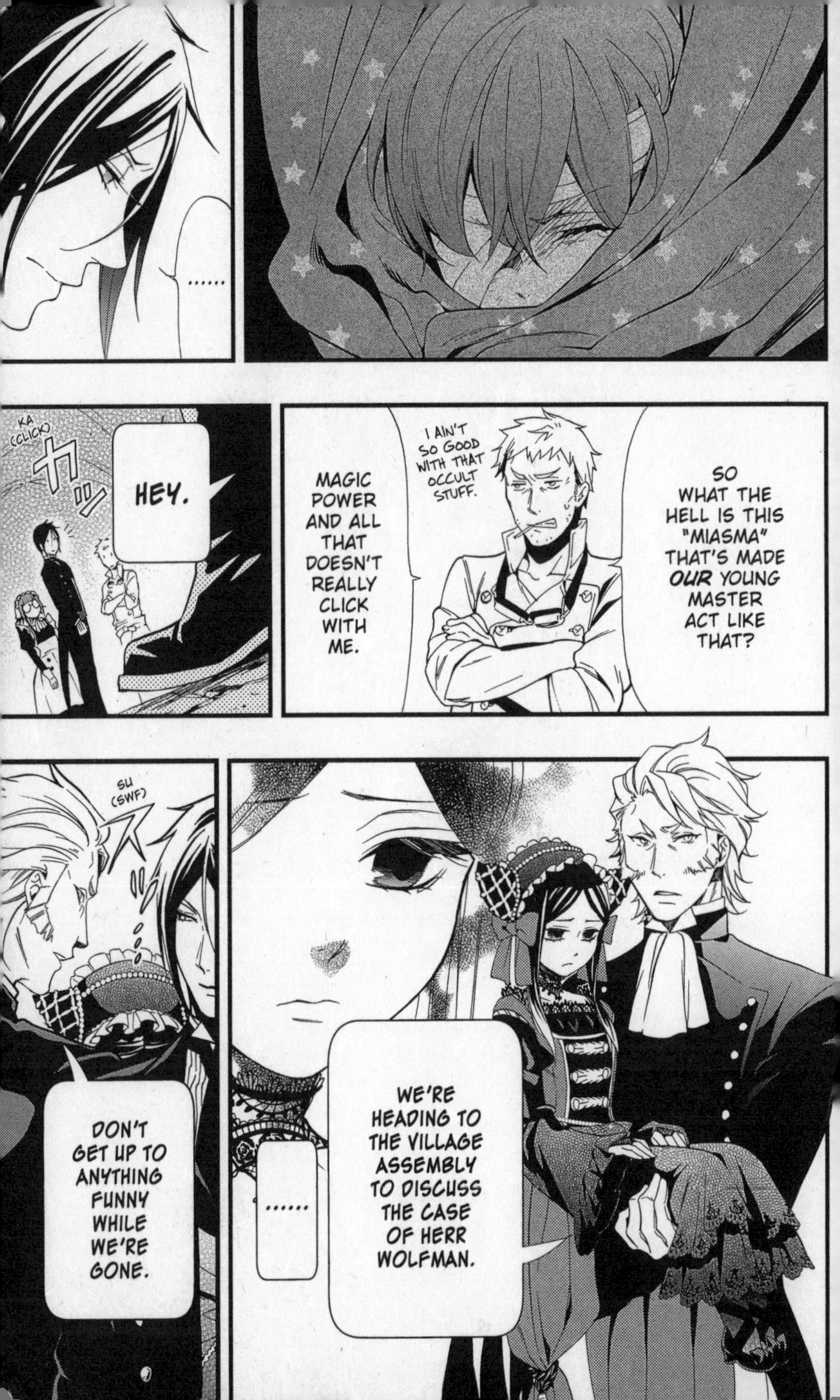

……
SO WHAT THE HELL IS THIS "MIASMA" THAT'S MADE OUR YOUNG MASTER ACT LIKE THAT?
I AIN'T SO GOOD WITH THAT OCCULT STUFF.
MAGIC POWER AND ALL THAT DOESN'T REALLY CLICK WITH ME.
KA (CLICK)
HEY.
WE'RE HEADING TO THE VILLAGE ASSEMBLY TO DISCUSS THE CASE OF HERR WOLFMAN.
……
SU (SWF)
DON'T GET UP TO ANYTHING FUNNY WHILE WE'RE GONE.

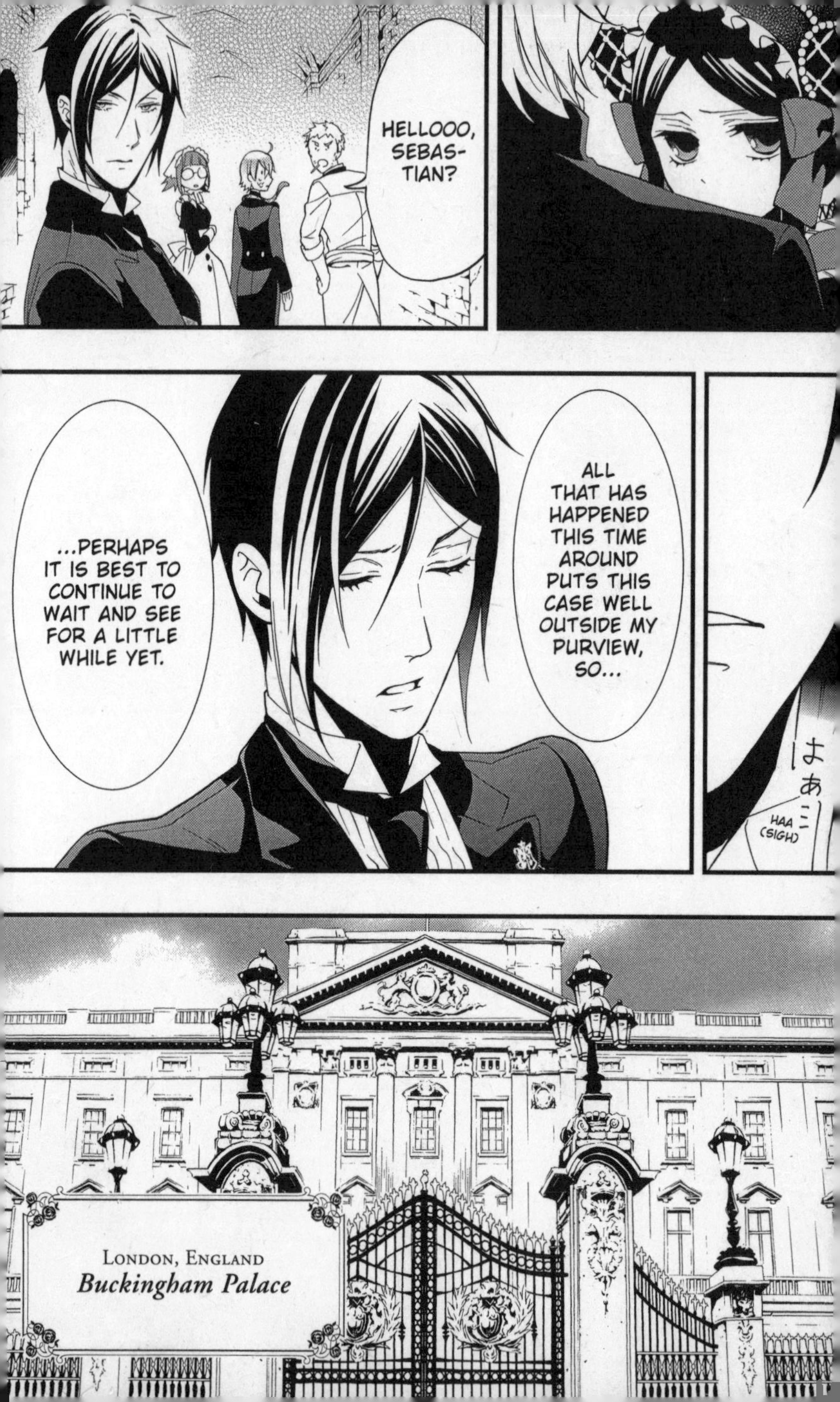
HELLOOO, SEBAS-TIAN?
HAA (SIGH)
ALL THAT HAS HAPPENED THIS TIME AROUND PUTS THIS CASE WELL OUTSIDE MY PURVIEW, SO...
...PERHAPS IT IS BEST TO CONTINUE TO WAIT AND SEE FOR A LITTLE WHILE YET.
LONDON, ENGLAND
Buckingham Palace

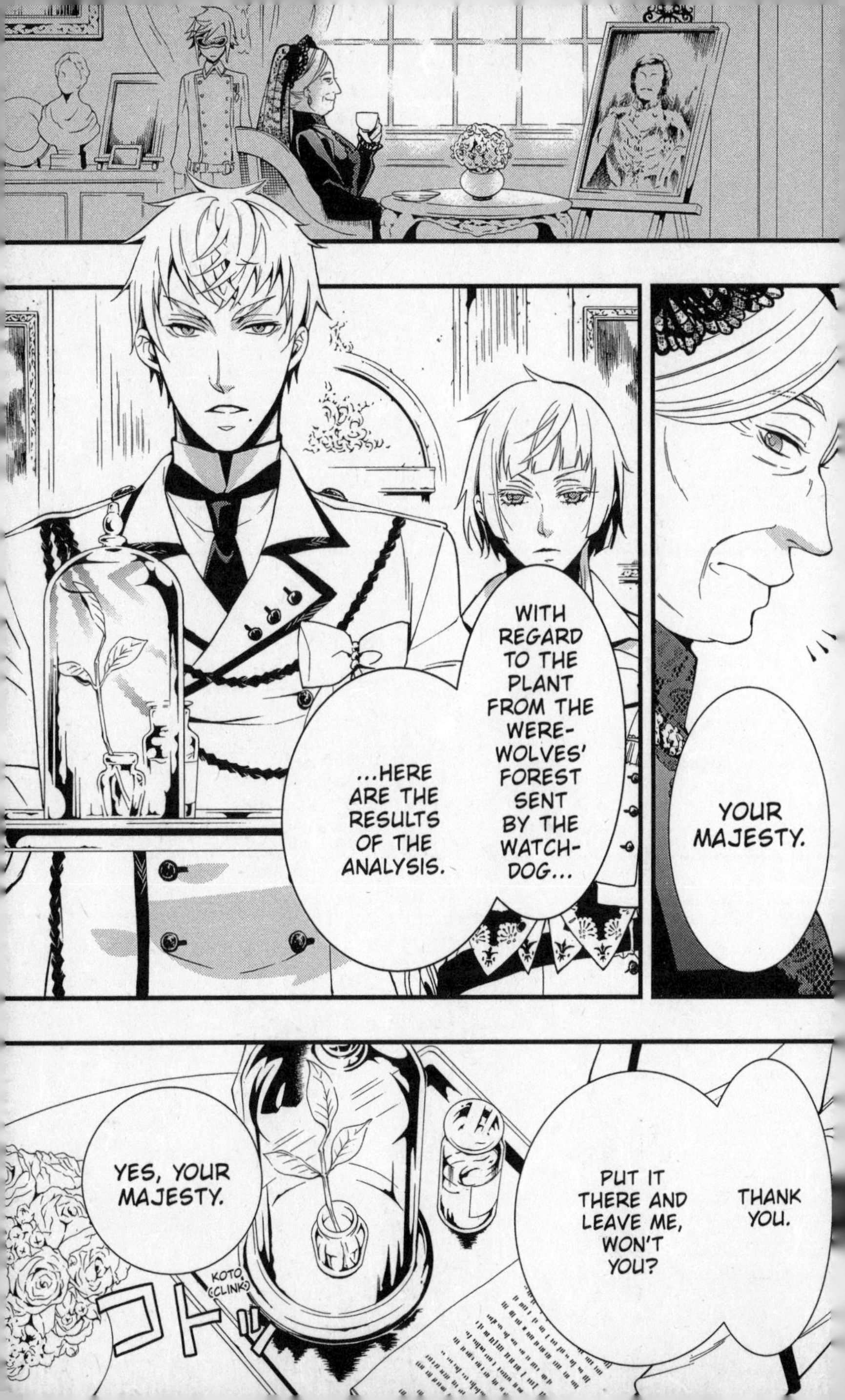
YOUR MAJESTY.
WITH REGARD TO THE PLANT FROM THE WERE-WOLVES' FOREST SENT BY THE WATCH-DOG...
...HERE ARE THE RESULTS OF THE ANALYSIS.
THANK YOU.
PUT IT THERE AND LEAVE ME, WON'T YOU?
YES, YOUR MAJESTY.
KOTO (CLINK)

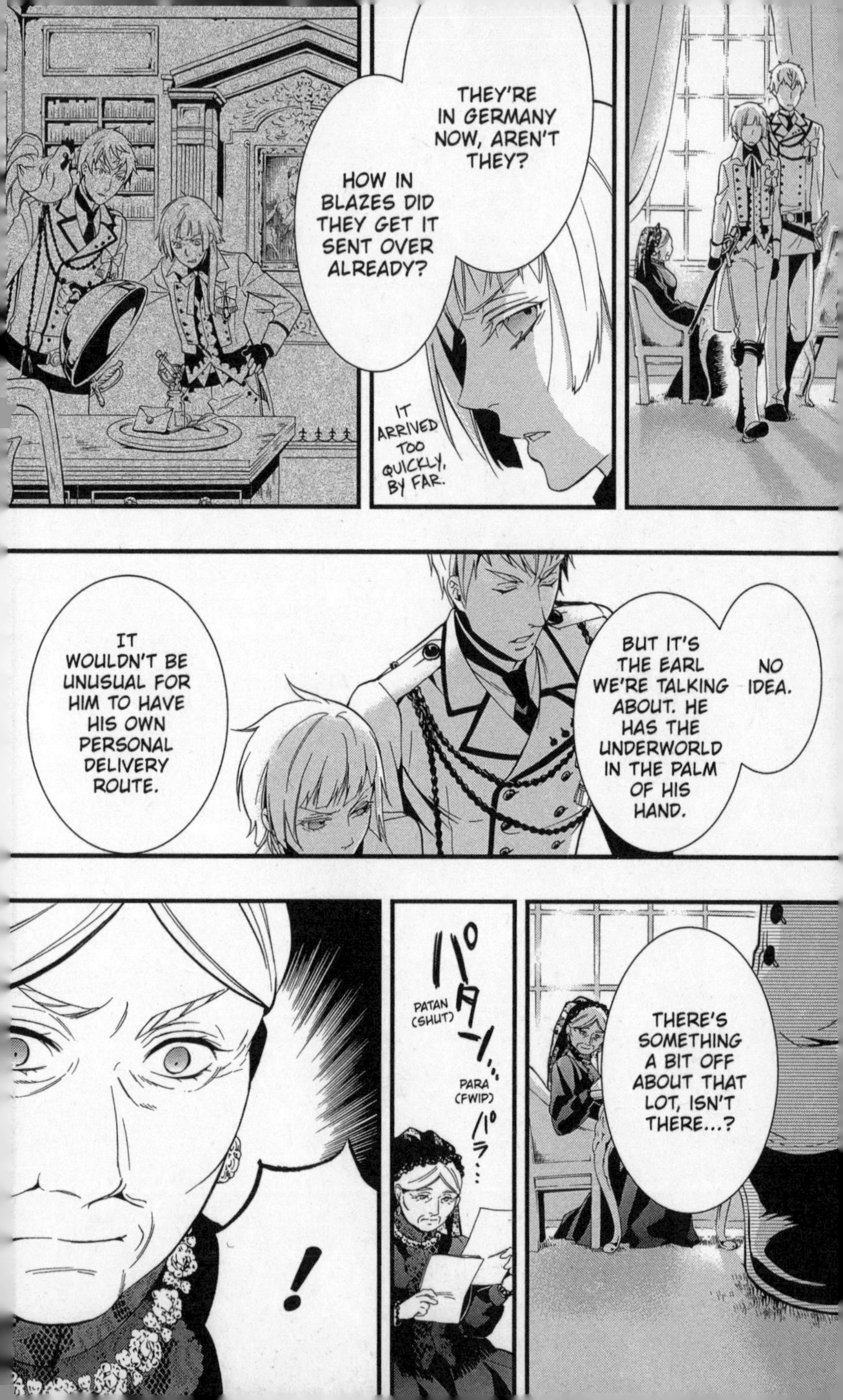
THEY'RE IN GERMANY NOW, AREN'T THEY?
HOW IN BLAZES DID THEY GET IT SENT OVER ALREADY?
IT ARRIVED TOO QUICKLY, BY FAR.
NO IDEA.
BUT IT'S THE EARL WE'RE TALKING ABOUT. HE HAS THE UNDERWORLD IN THE PALM OF HIS HAND.
IT WOULDN'T BE UNUSUAL FOR HIM TO HAVE HIS OWN PERSONAL DELIVERY ROUTE.
THERE'S SOMETHING A BIT OFF ABOUT THAT LOT, ISN'T THERE...?
パタン
PATAN (SHUT)
PARA (FWIP)
パラ…
!

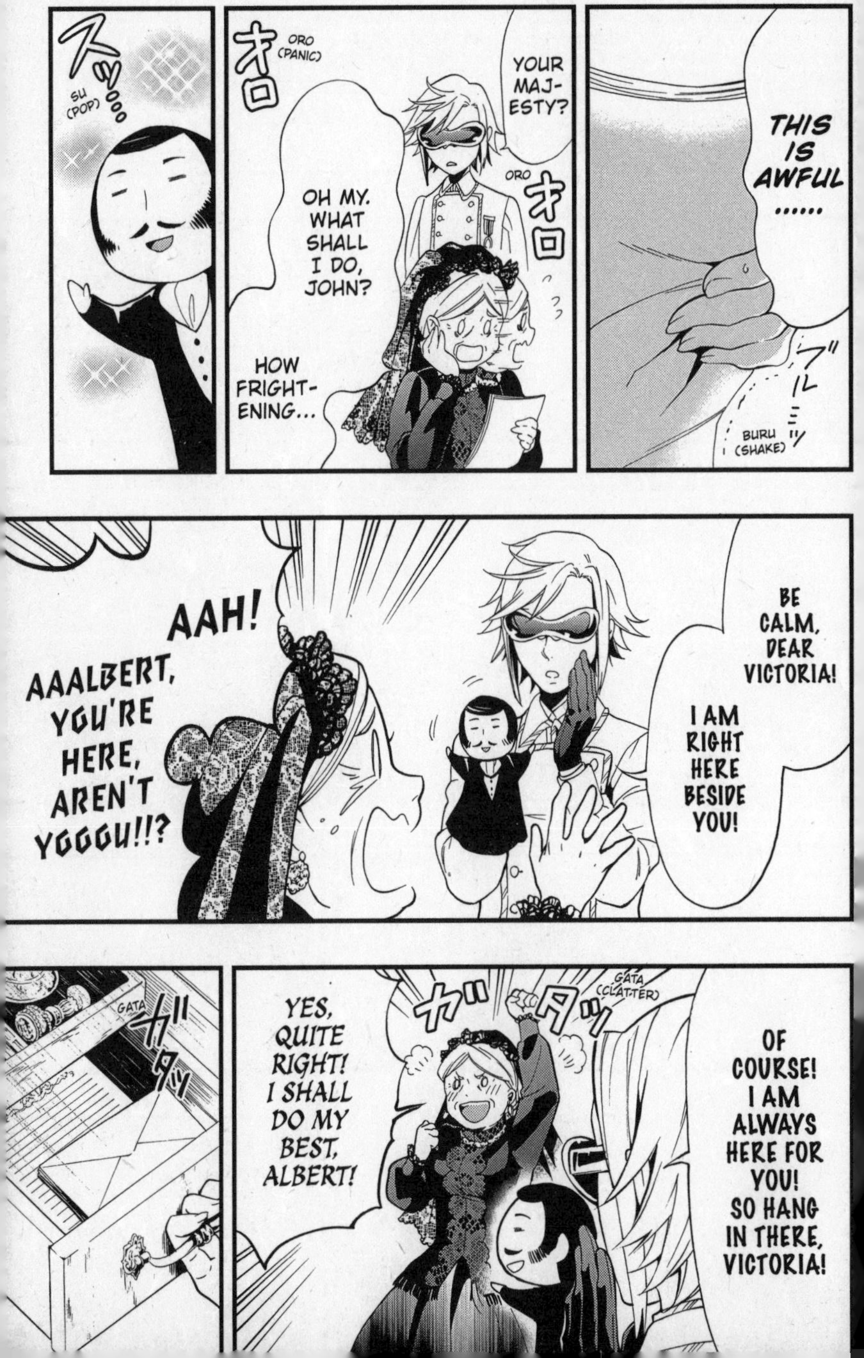
THIS IS AWFUL......
ブル
BURU (SHAKE)
YOUR MAJ-ESTY?
オロ
ORO (PANIC)
ORO
オロ
OH MY. WHAT SHALL I DO, JOHN?
HOW FRIGHT-ENING...
スッ
SU (POP)
BE CALM, DEAR VICTORIA!
I AM RIGHT HERE BESIDE YOU!
AAH!
AAALBERT, YOU'RE HERE, AREN'T YOOOU!!?
OF COURSE! I AM ALWAYS HERE FOR YOU! SO HANG IN THERE, VICTORIA!
GATA (CLATTER)
ガタッ
YES, QUITE RIGHT! I SHALL DO MY BEST, ALBERT!
GATA
ガタッ

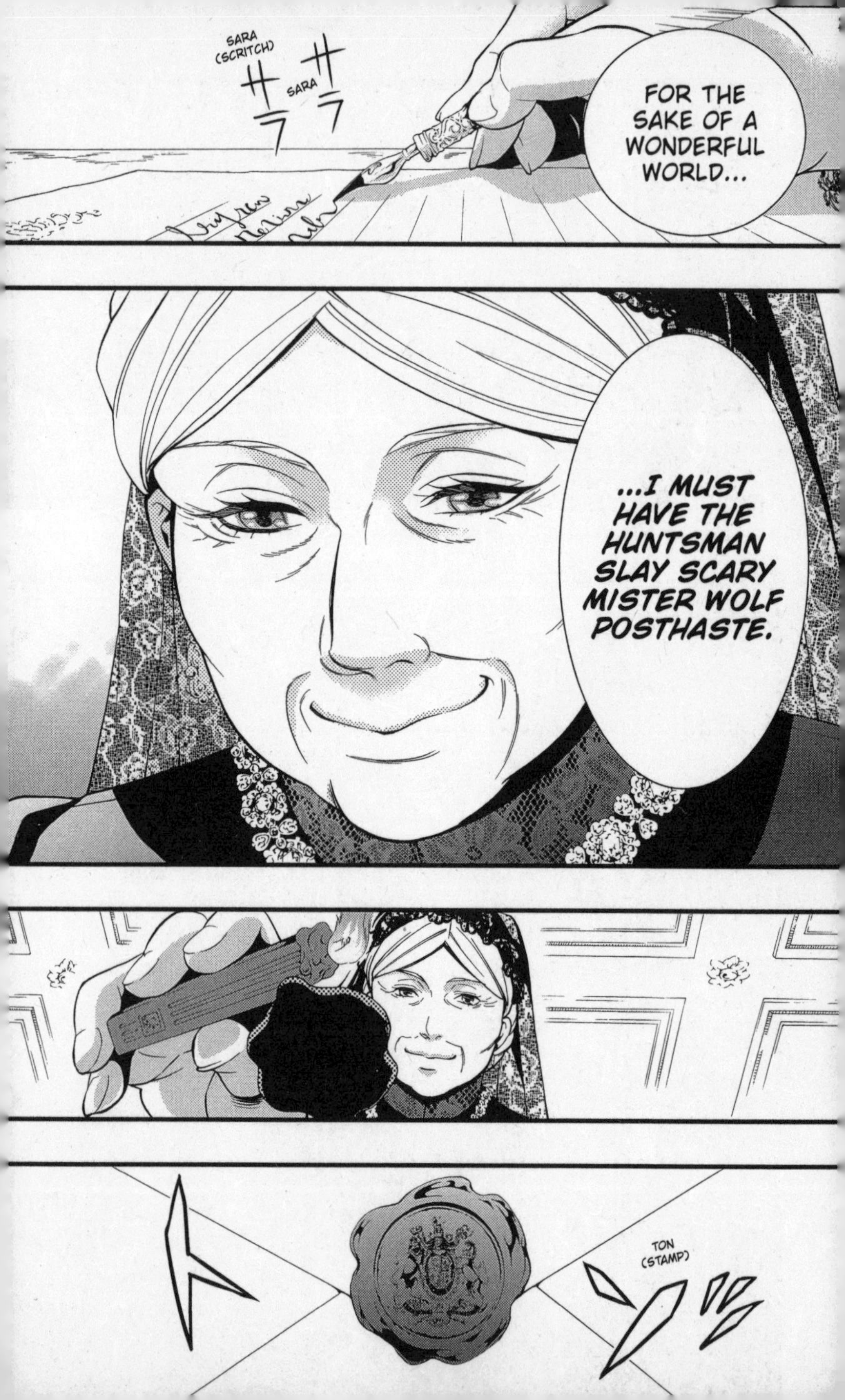
FOR THE SAKE OF A WONDERFUL WORLD...
SARA
SARA (SCRITCH)
...I MUST HAVE THE HUNTSMAN SLAY SCARY MISTER WOLF POSTHASTE.
TON (STAMP)

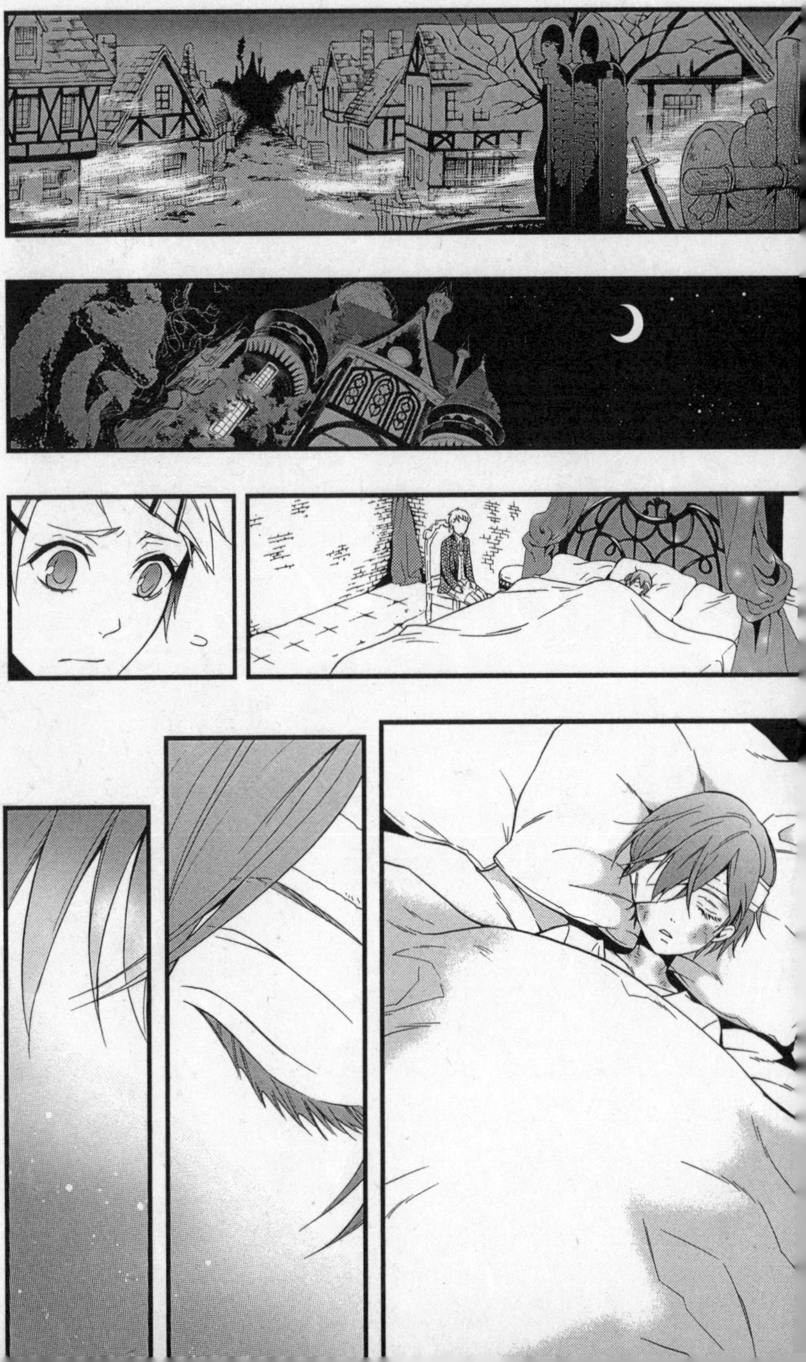

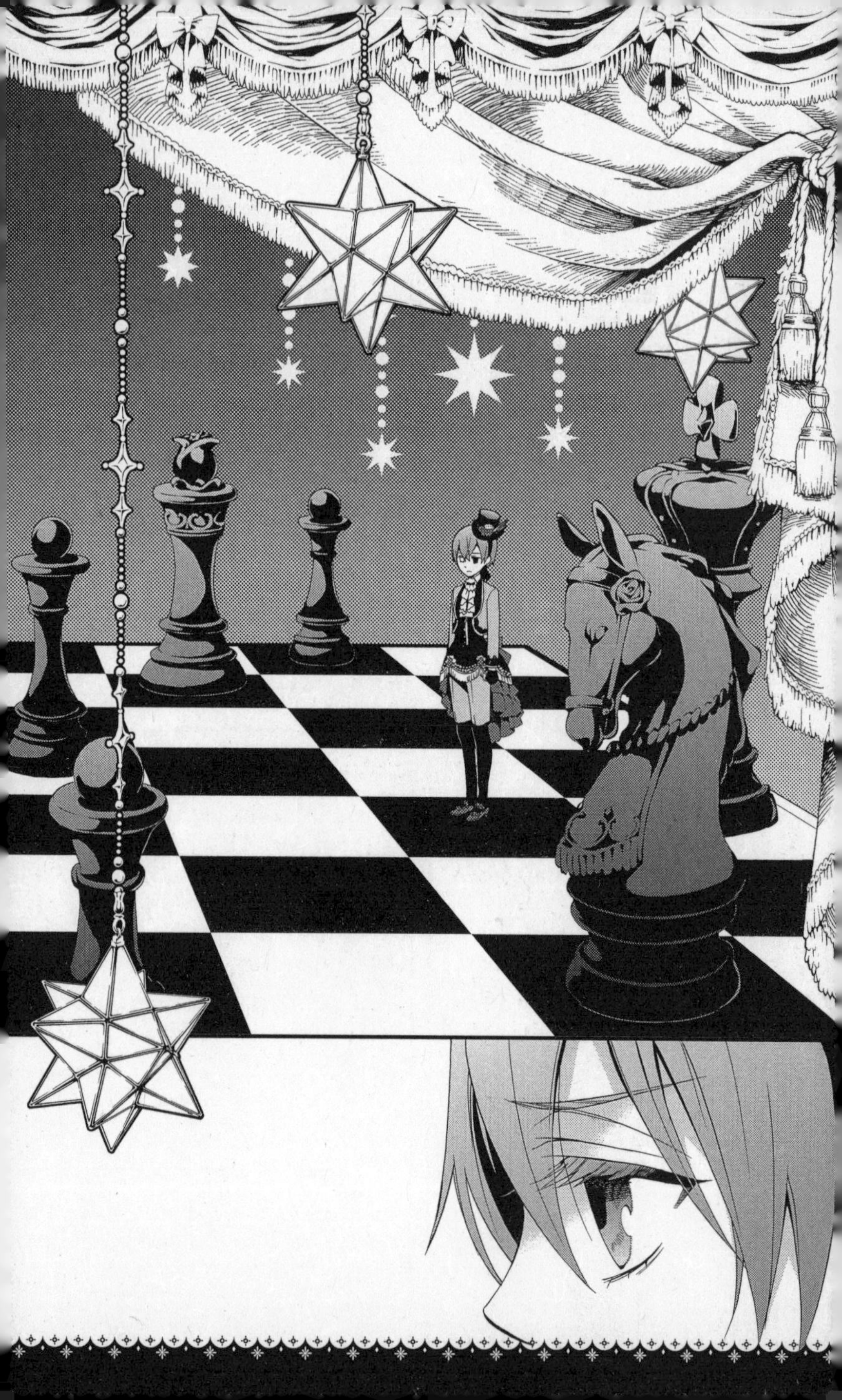

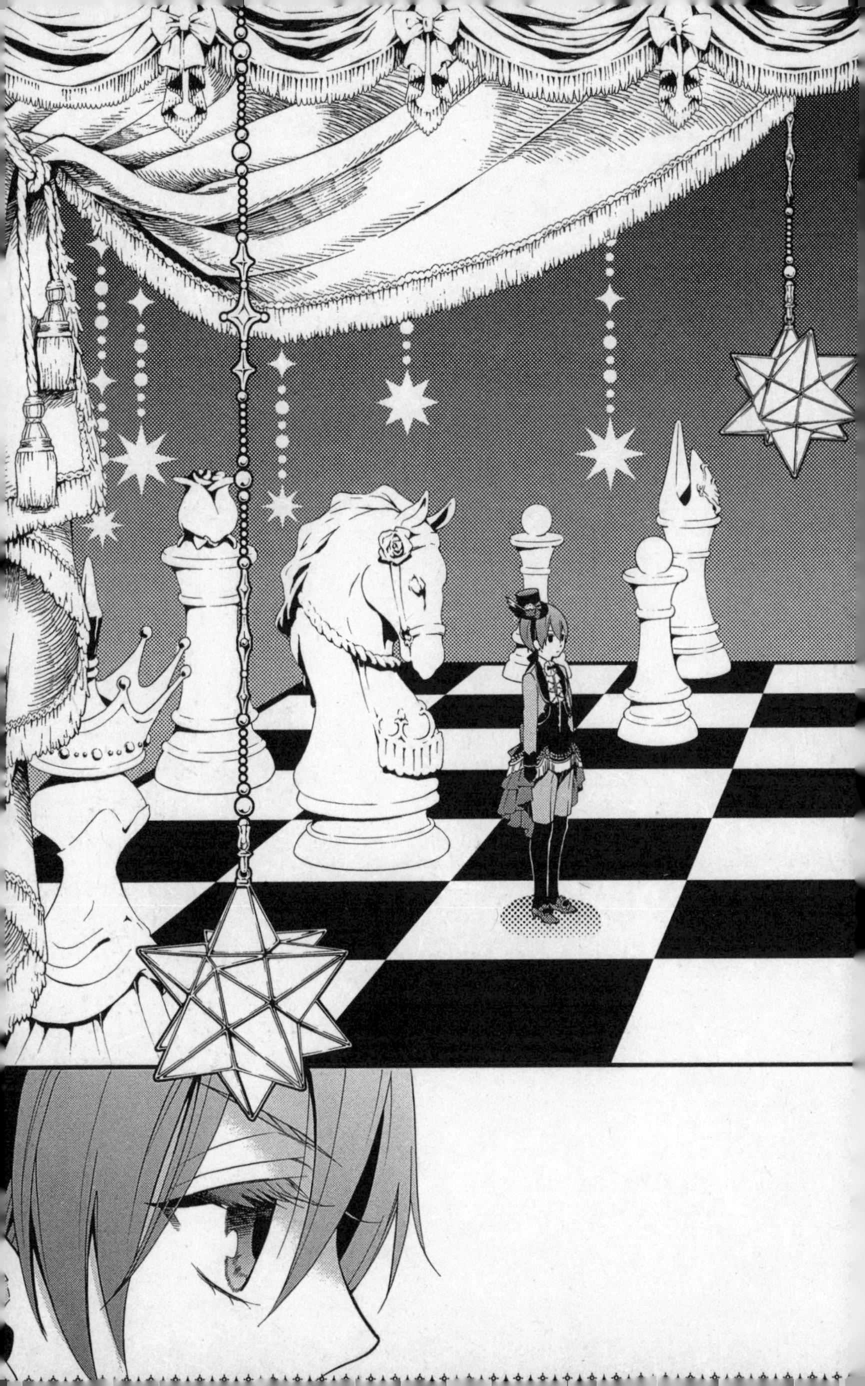

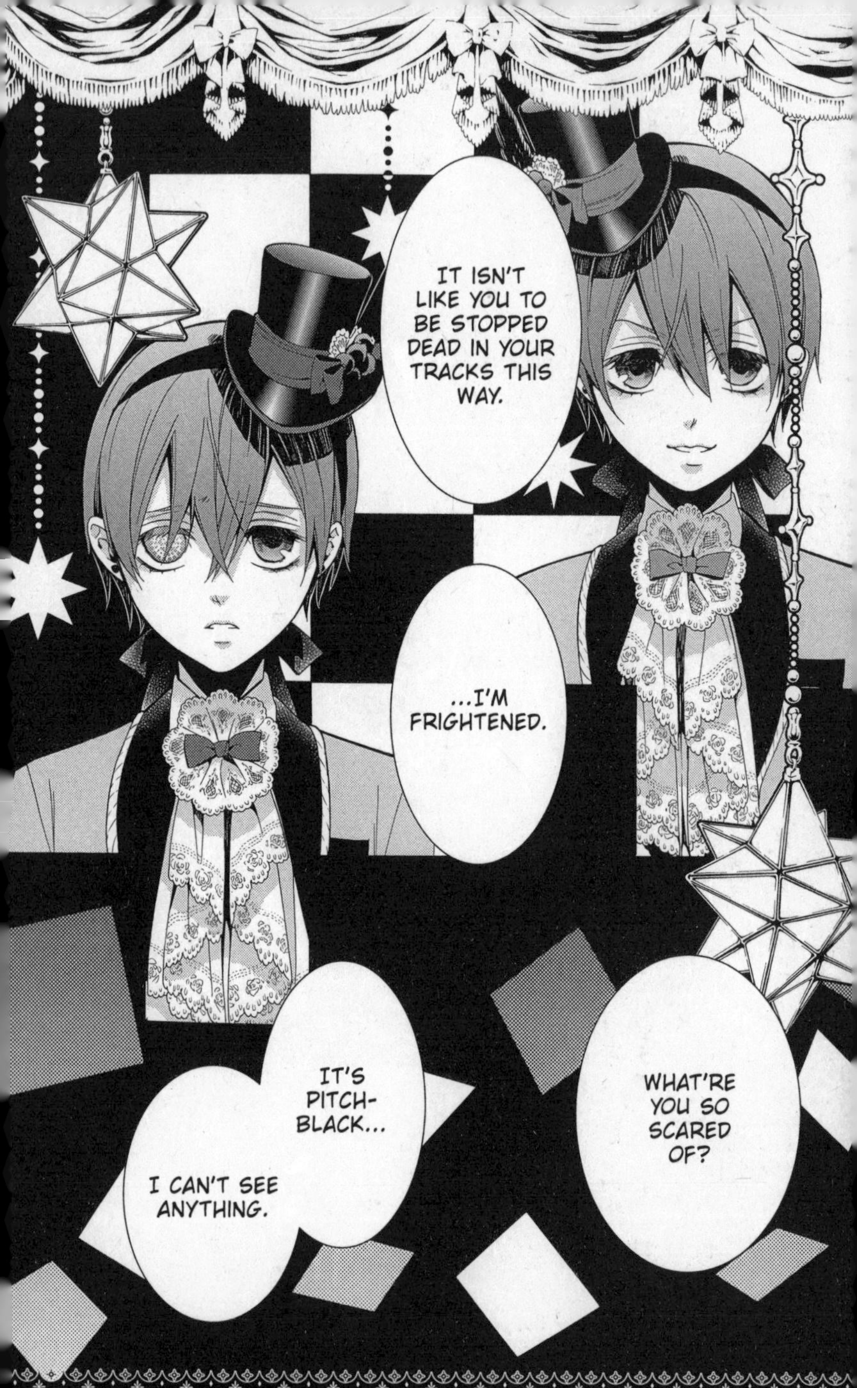

IT ISN'T LIKE YOU TO BE STOPPED DEAD IN YOUR TRACKS THIS WAY.
...I'M FRIGHTENED.
WHAT'RE YOU SO SCARED OF?
IT'S PITCH-BLACK...
I CAN'T SEE ANYTHING.

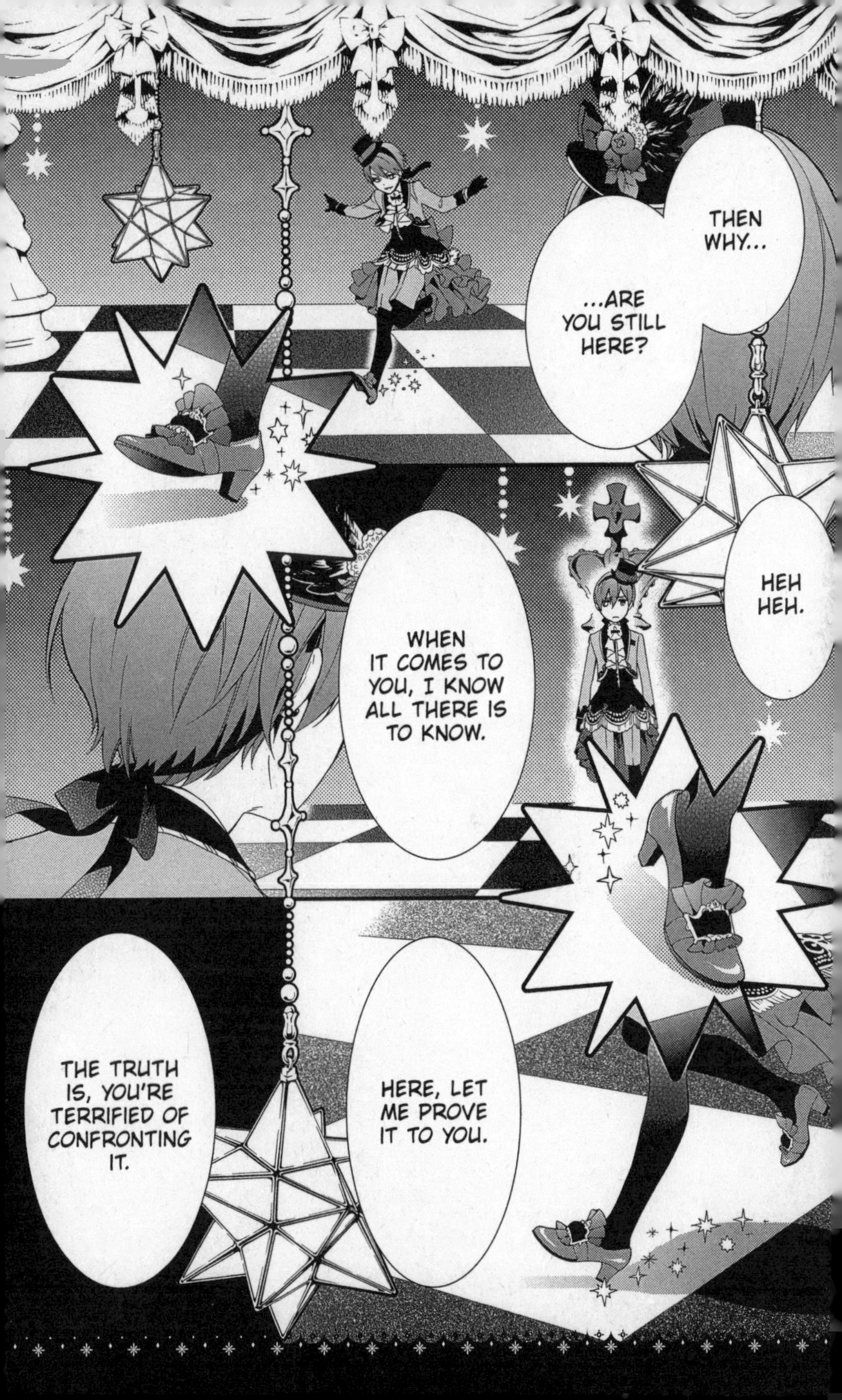
THEN WHY...
...ARE YOU STILL HERE?
HEH HEH.
WHEN IT COMES TO YOU, I KNOW ALL THERE IS TO KNOW.
HERE, LET ME PROVE IT TO YOU.
THE TRUTH IS, YOU'RE TERRIFIED OF CONFRONTING IT.

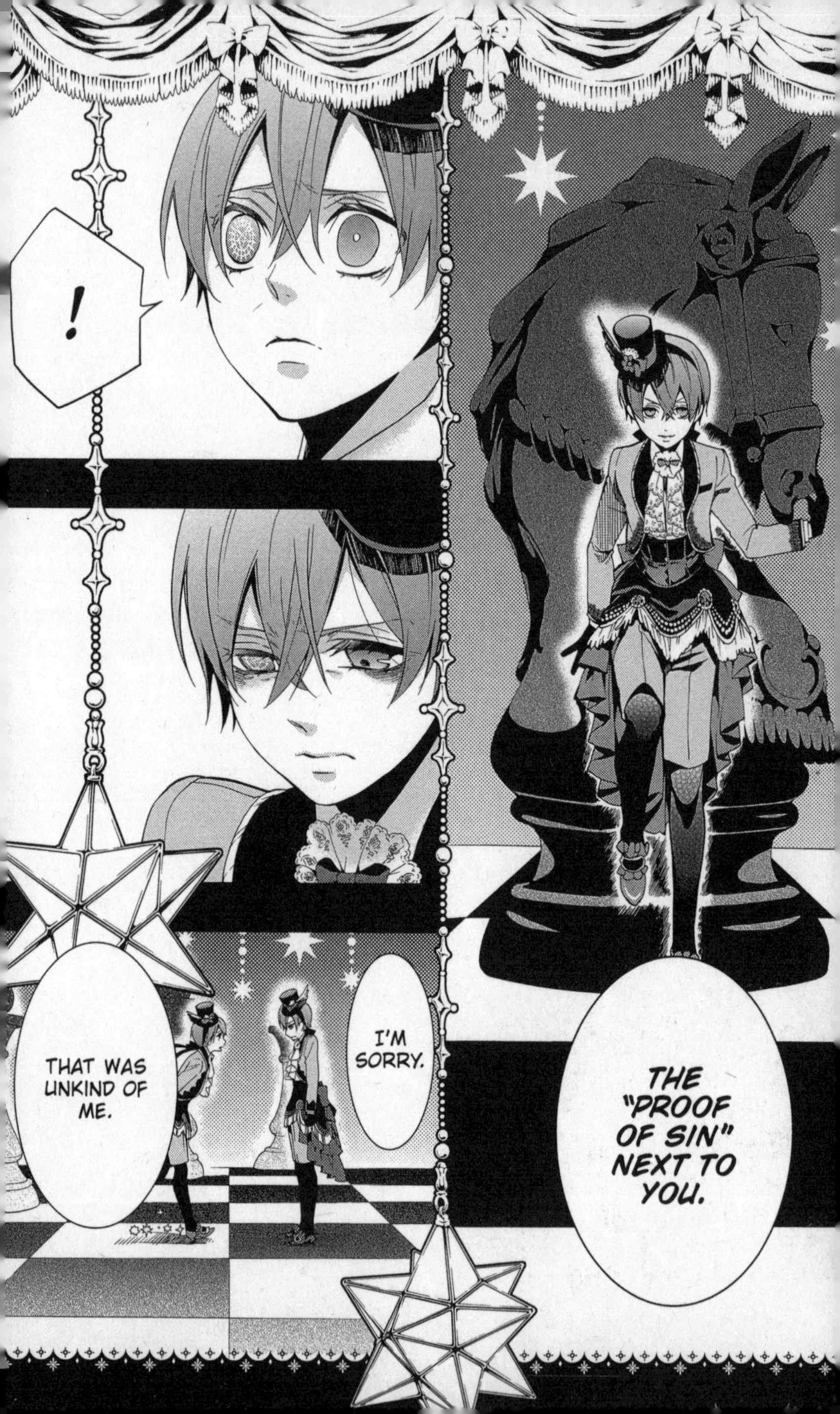
THE "PROOF OF SIN" NEXT TO YOU.
!
I'M SORRY.
THAT WAS UNKIND OF ME.

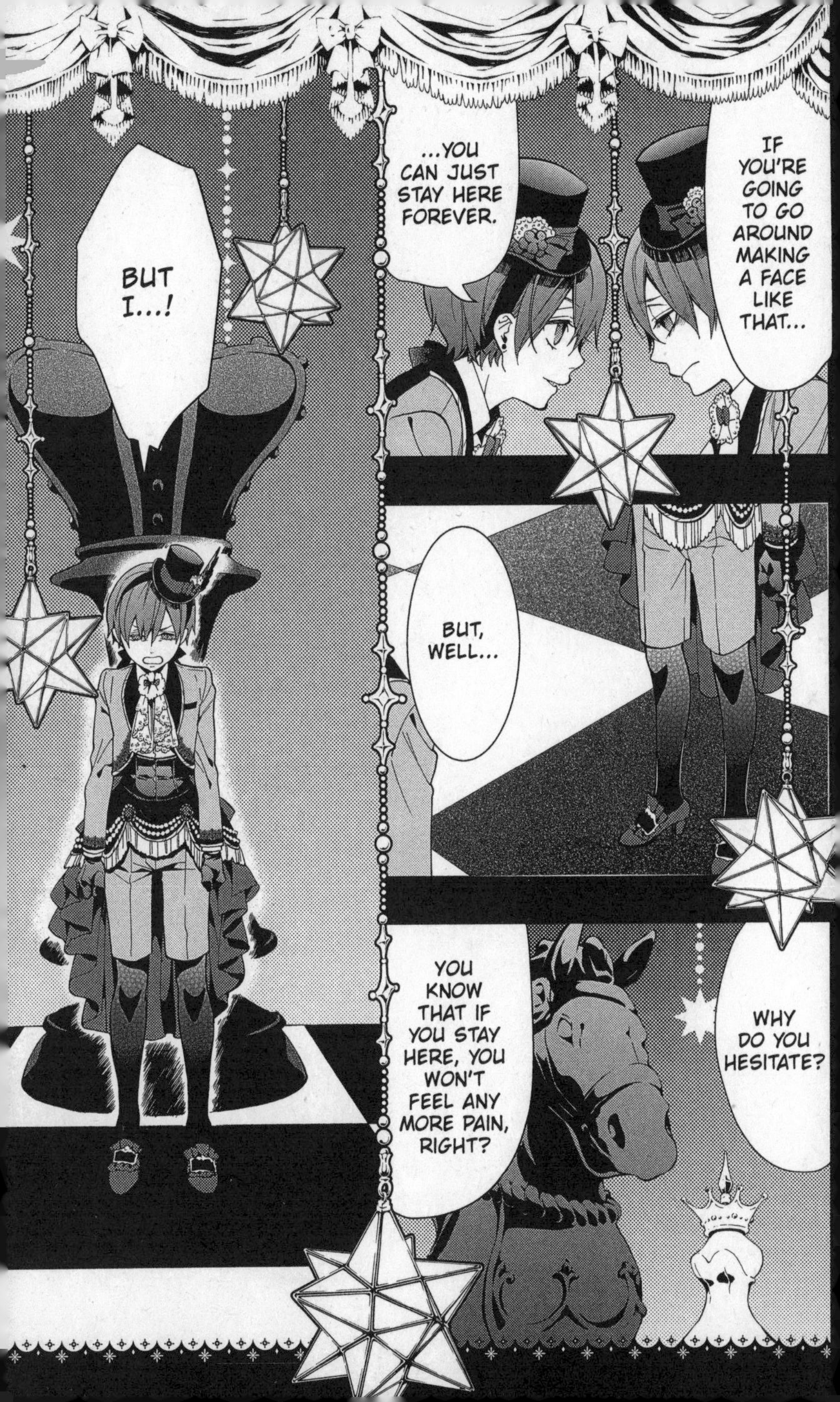
IF YOU'RE GOING TO GO AROUND MAKING A FACE LIKE THAT...
...YOU CAN JUST STAY HERE FOREVER.
BUT, WELL...
WHY DO YOU HESITATE?
YOU KNOW THAT IF YOU STAY HERE, YOU WON'T FEEL ANY MORE PAIN, RIGHT?
BUT I...!

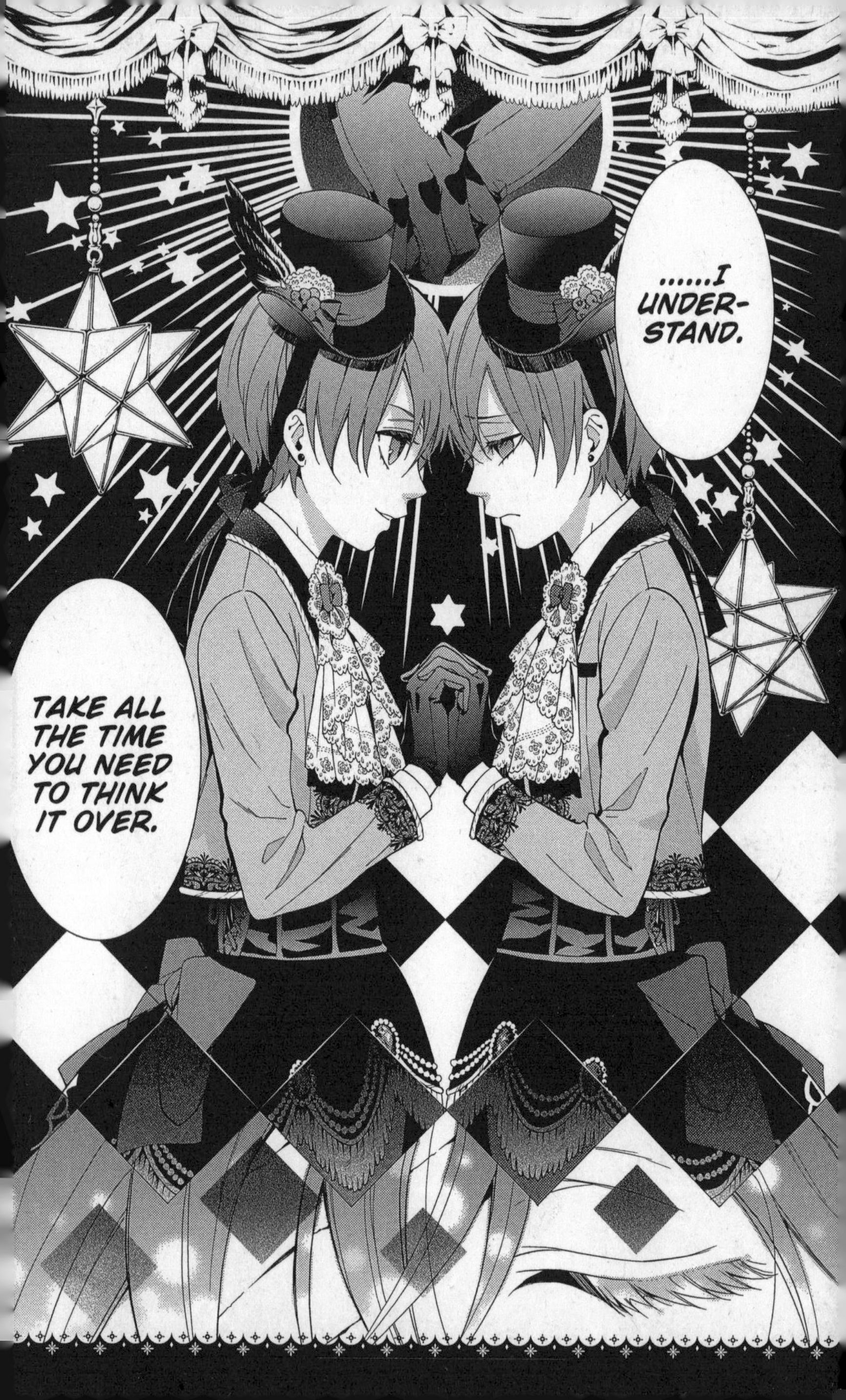
......I UNDER-STAND.
TAKE ALL THE TIME YOU NEED TO THINK IT OVER.

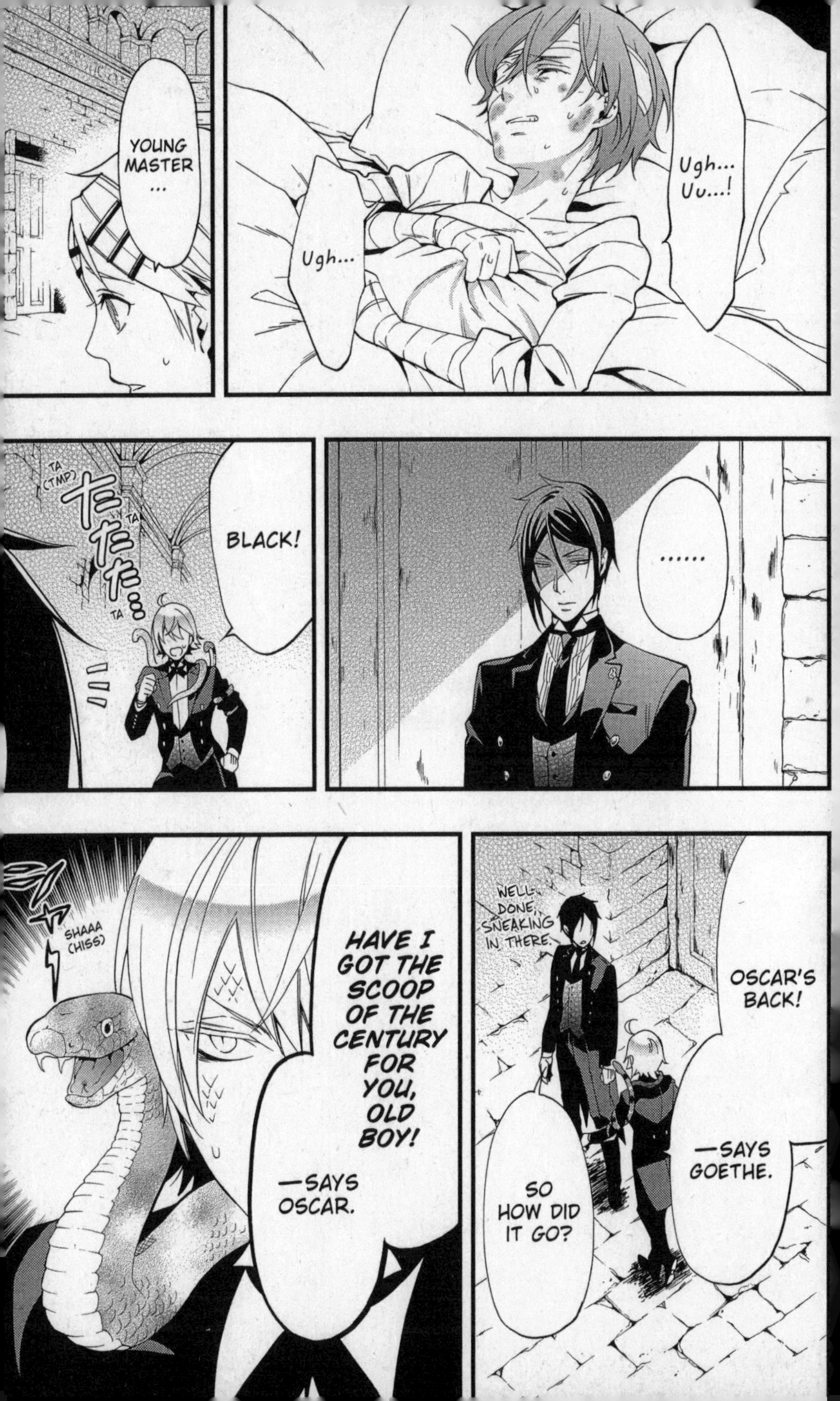
Ugh... Uu...!
Ugh...
YOUNG MASTER ...
......
BLACK!
TA (TMP)
TA
TA
OSCAR'S BACK!
—SAYS GOETHE.
WELL DONE, SNEAKING IN THERE.
SO HOW DID IT GO?
SHAAA (HISS)
HAVE I GOT THE SCOOP OF THE CENTURY FOR YOU, OLD BOY!
—SAYS OSCAR.

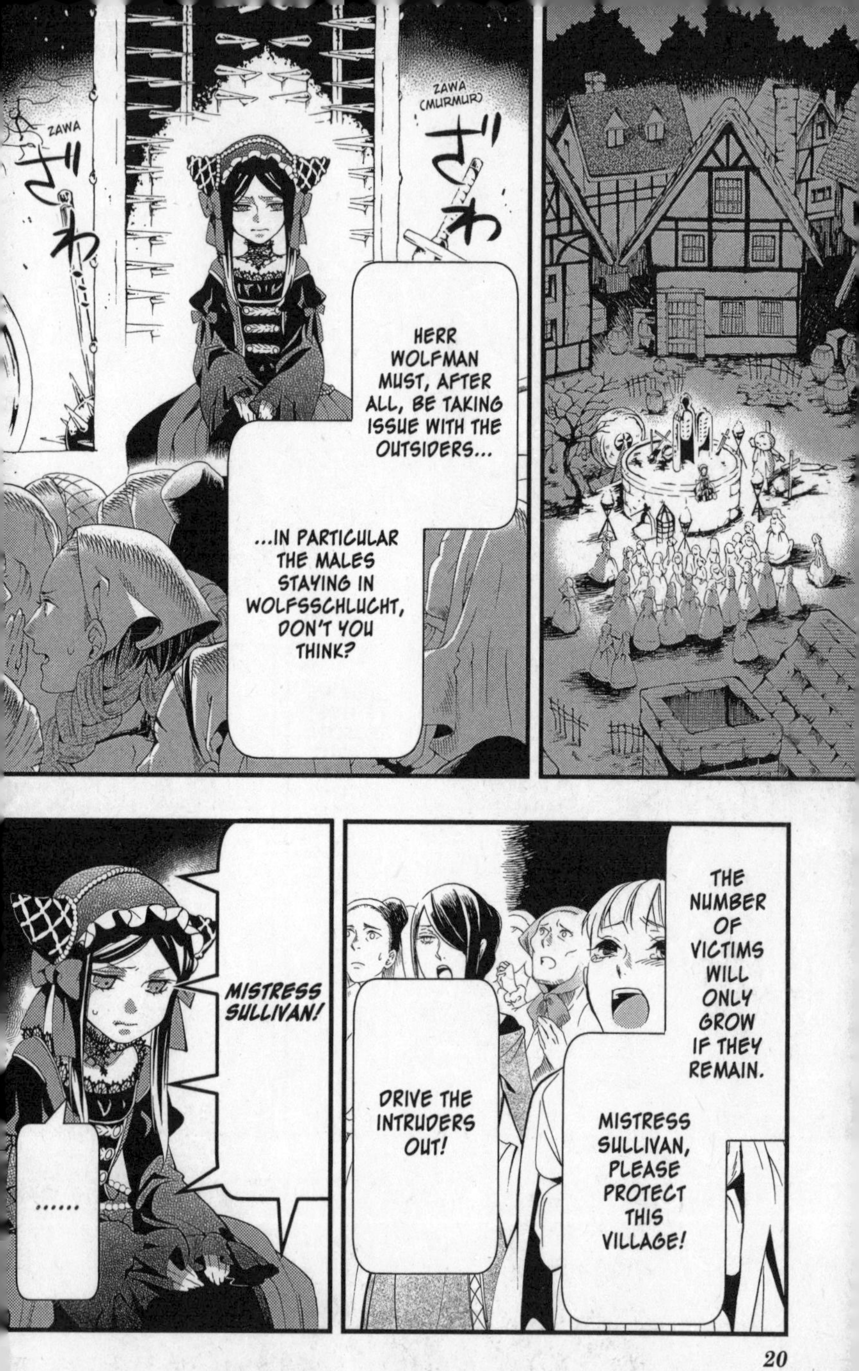
ZAWA (MURMUR)
ざわ
HERR WOLFMAN MUST, AFTER ALL, BE TAKING ISSUE WITH THE OUTSIDERS...
...IN PARTICULAR THE MALES STAYING IN WOLFSSCHLUCHT, DON'T YOU THINK?
ZAWA
ざわ
THE NUMBER OF VICTIMS WILL ONLY GROW IF THEY REMAIN.
MISTRESS SULLIVAN, PLEASE PROTECT THIS VILLAGE!
DRIVE THE INTRUDERS OUT!
MISTRESS SULLIVAN!
......

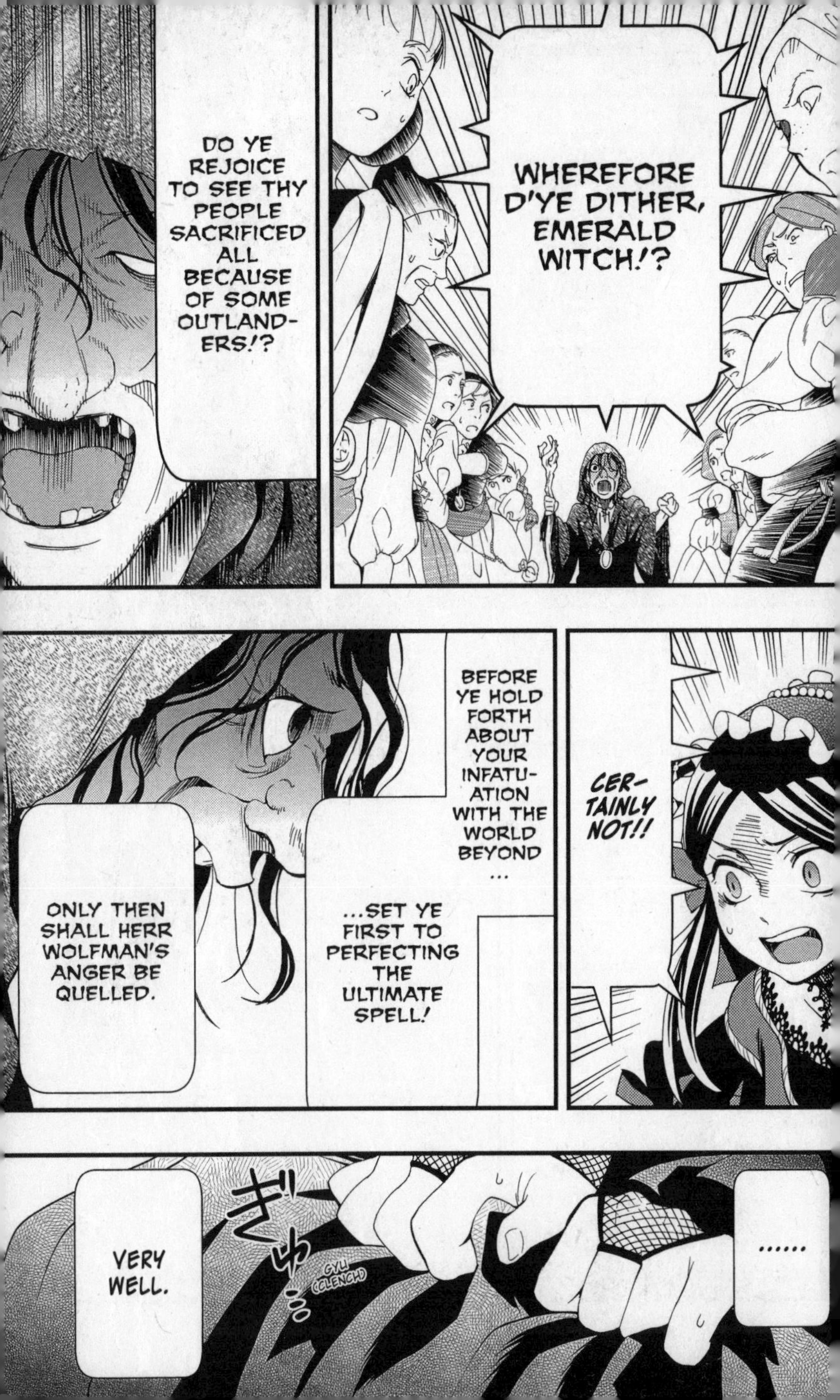
WHEREFORE D'YE DITHER, EMERALD WITCH!?
DO YE REJOICE TO SEE THY PEOPLE SACRIFICED ALL BECAUSE OF SOME OUTLAND-ERS!?
CER-TAINLY NOT!!
BEFORE YE HOLD FORTH ABOUT YOUR INFATU-ATION WITH THE WORLD BEYOND ...
...SET YE FIRST TO PERFECTING THE ULTIMATE SPELL!
ONLY THEN SHALL HERR WOLFMAN'S ANGER BE QUELLED.
......
GYU (CLENCH)
VERY WELL.

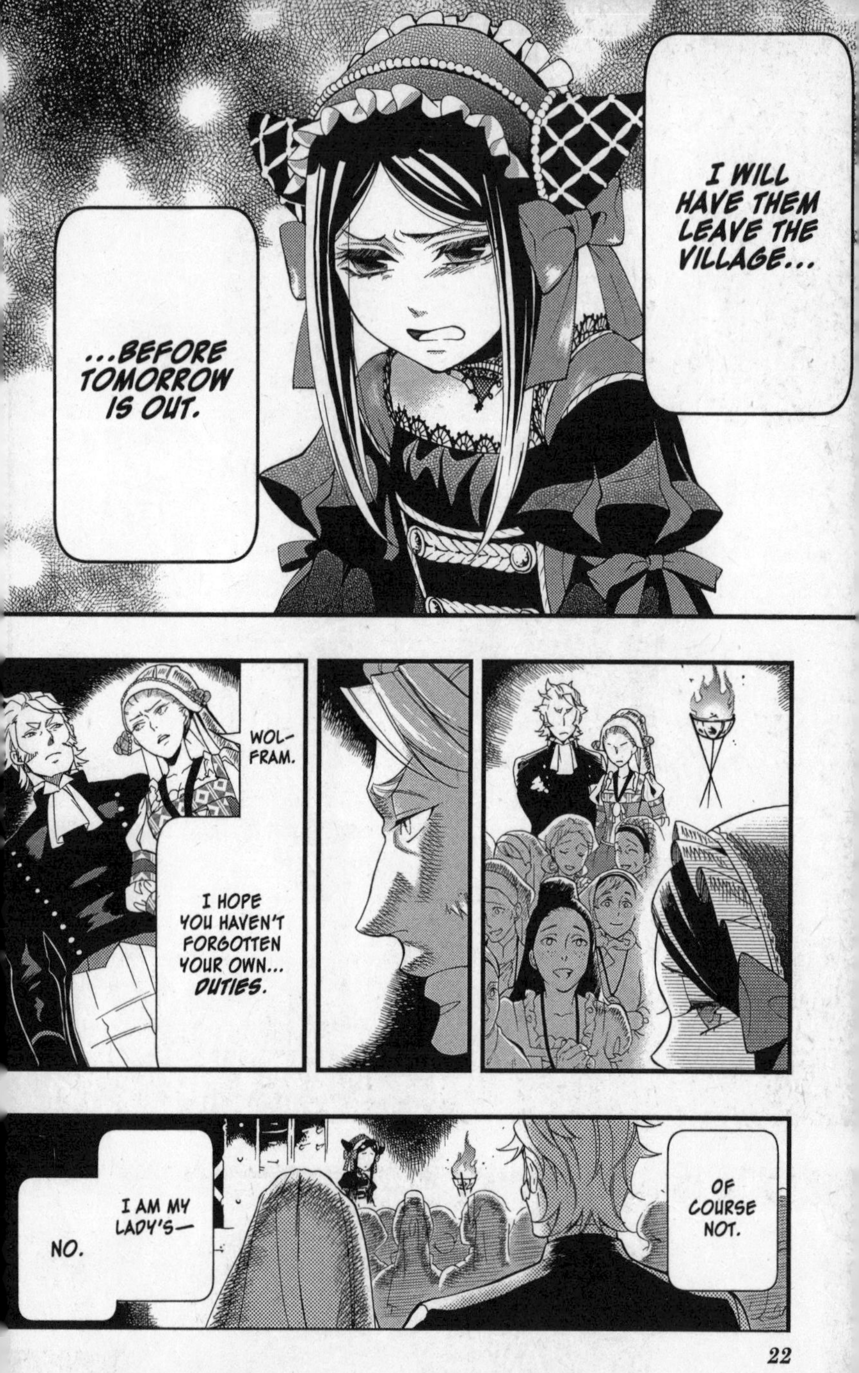
I WILL HAVE THEM LEAVE THE VILLAGE...
...BEFORE TOMORROW IS OUT.
WOL-FRAM.
I HOPE YOU HAVEN'T FORGOTTEN YOUR OWN... DUTIES.
OF COURSE NOT.
I AM MY LADY'S—
NO.

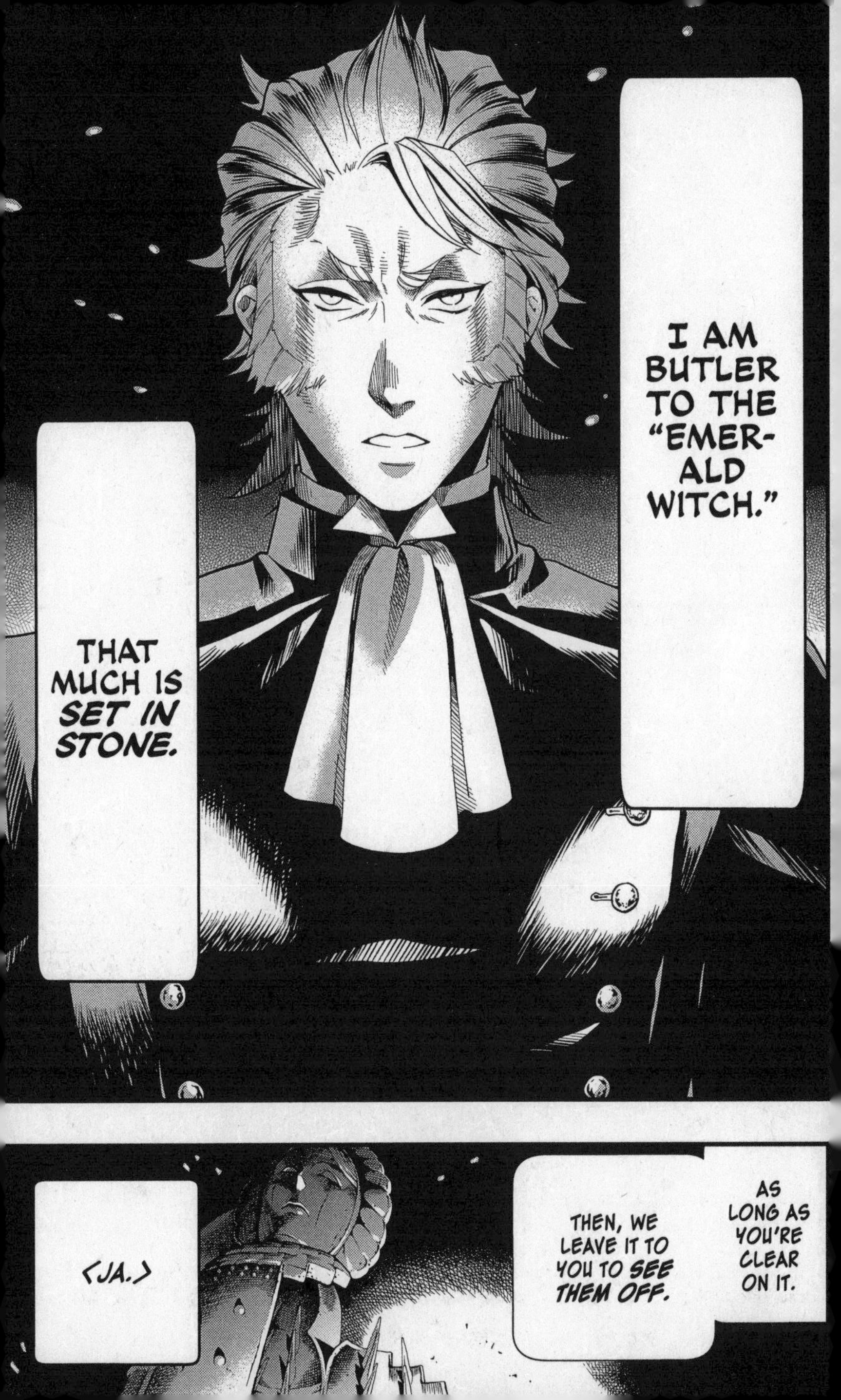
I AM BUTLER TO THE "EMERALD WITCH."
THAT MUCH IS SET IN STONE.
AS LONG AS YOU'RE CLEAR ON IT.
THEN, WE LEAVE IT TO YOU TO SEE THEM OFF.
<JA.>

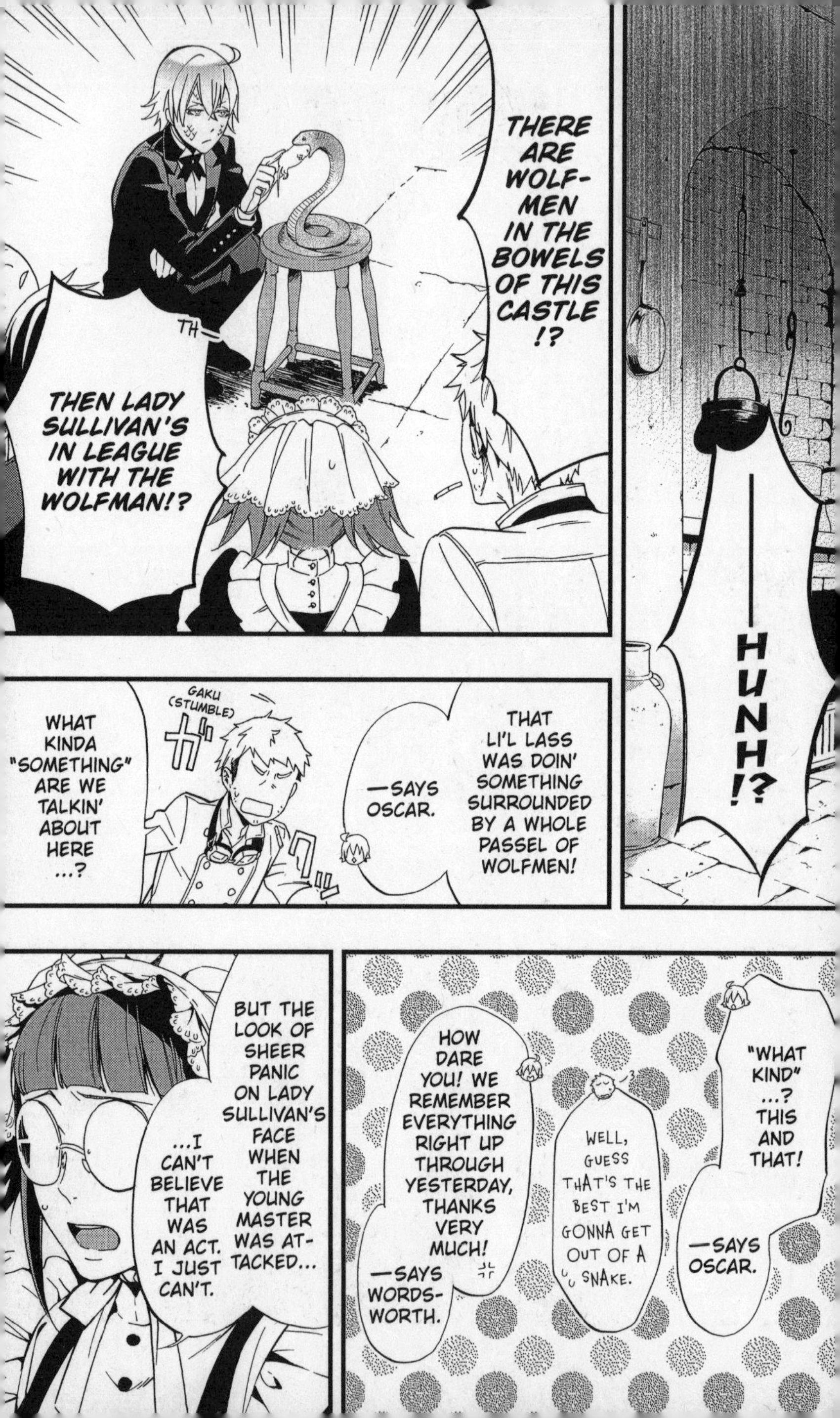
—HUNH!?
THERE ARE WOLFMEN IN THE BOWELS OF THIS CASTLE!?
TH—
THEN LADY SULLIVAN'S IN LEAGUE WITH THE WOLFMAN!?
THAT LI'L LASS WAS DOIN' SOMETHING SURROUNDED BY A WHOLE PASSEL OF WOLFMEN!
—SAYS OSCAR.
GAKU (STUMBLE)
WHAT KINDA "SOMETHING" ARE WE TALKIN' ABOUT HERE...?
"WHAT KIND"...? THIS AND THAT!
—SAYS OSCAR.
WELL, GUESS THAT'S THE BEST I'M GONNA GET OUT OF A SNAKE.
HOW DARE YOU! WE REMEMBER EVERYTHING RIGHT UP THROUGH YESTERDAY, THANKS VERY MUCH!
—SAYS WORDSWORTH.
BUT THE LOOK OF SHEER PANIC ON LADY SULLIVAN'S FACE WHEN THE YOUNG MASTER WAS ATTACKED...
...I CAN'T BELIEVE THAT WAS AN ACT. I JUST CAN'T.

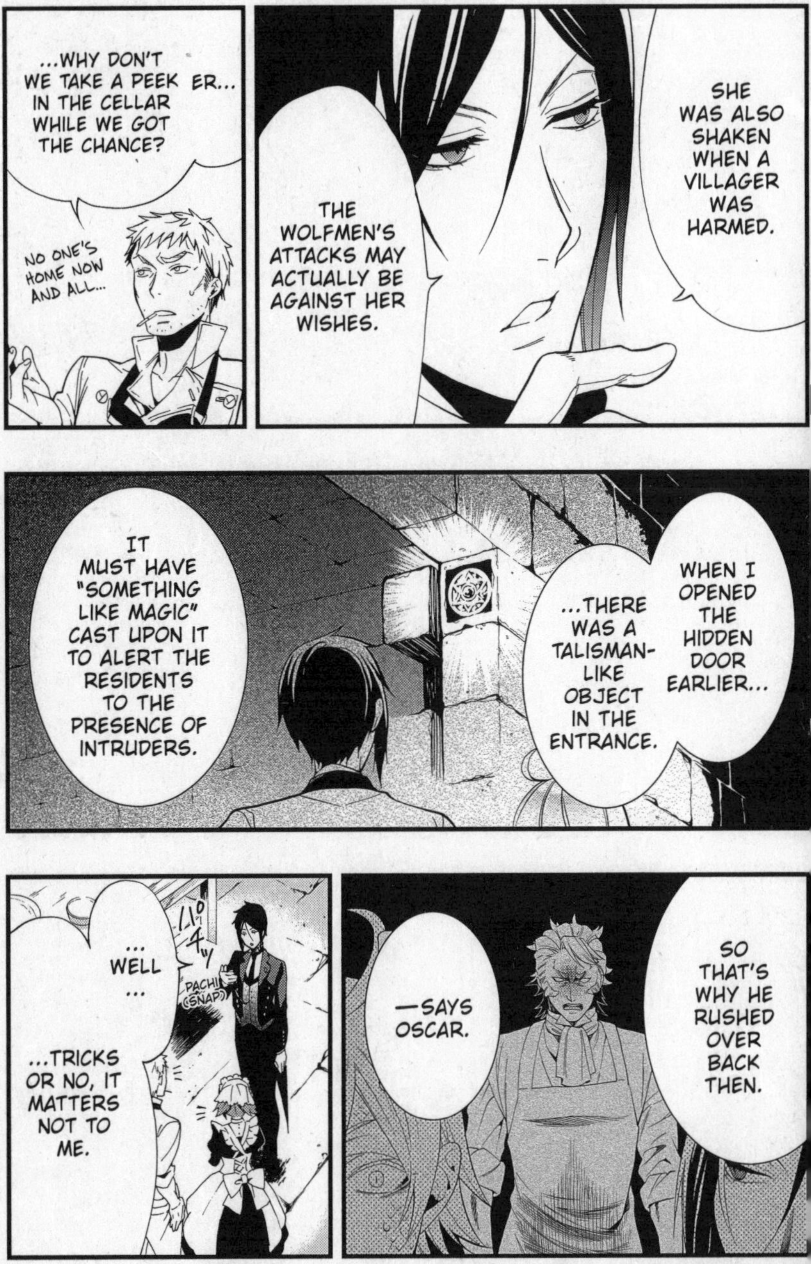

SHE WAS ALSO SHAKEN WHEN A VILLAGER WAS HARMED.
THE WOLFMEN'S ATTACKS MAY ACTUALLY BE AGAINST HER WISHES.
ER...
...WHY DON'T WE TAKE A PEEK IN THE CELLAR WHILE WE GOT THE CHANCE?
NO ONE'S HOME NOW AND ALL...
WHEN I OPENED THE HIDDEN DOOR EARLIER...
...THERE WAS A TALISMAN-LIKE OBJECT IN THE ENTRANCE.
IT MUST HAVE "SOMETHING LIKE MAGIC" CAST UPON IT TO ALERT THE RESIDENTS TO THE PRESENCE OF INTRUDERS.
SO THAT'S WHY HE RUSHED OVER BACK THEN.
—SAYS OSCAR.
... WELL ...
PACHI (SNAP)
...TRICKS OR NO, IT MATTERS NOT TO ME.

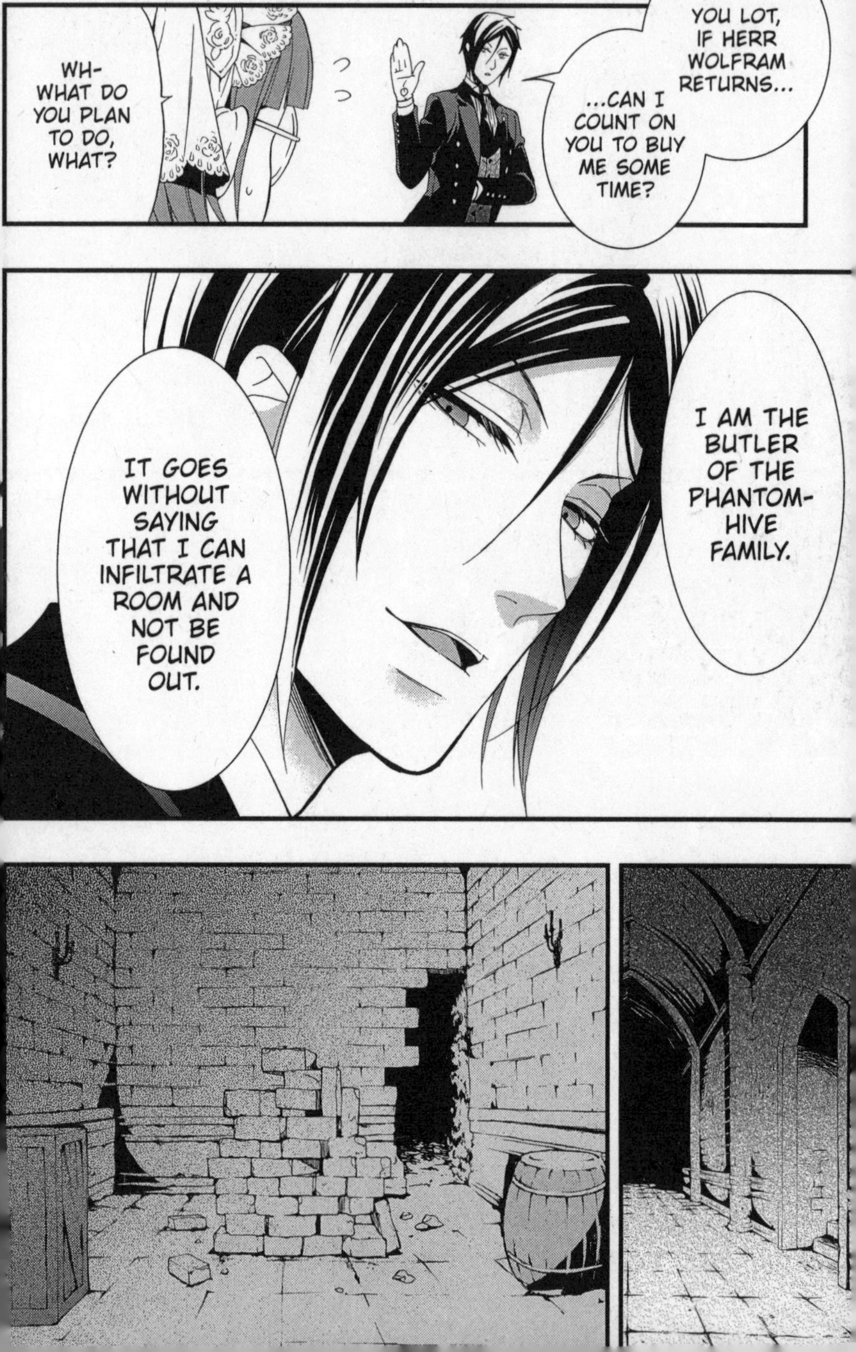
YOU LOT, IF HERR WOLFRAM RETURNS...
...CAN I COUNT ON YOU TO BUY ME SOME TIME?
WH- WHAT DO YOU PLAN TO DO, WHAT?
I AM THE BUTLER OF THE PHANTOM-HIVE FAMILY.
IT GOES WITHOUT SAYING THAT I CAN INFILTRATE A ROOM AND NOT BE FOUND OUT.

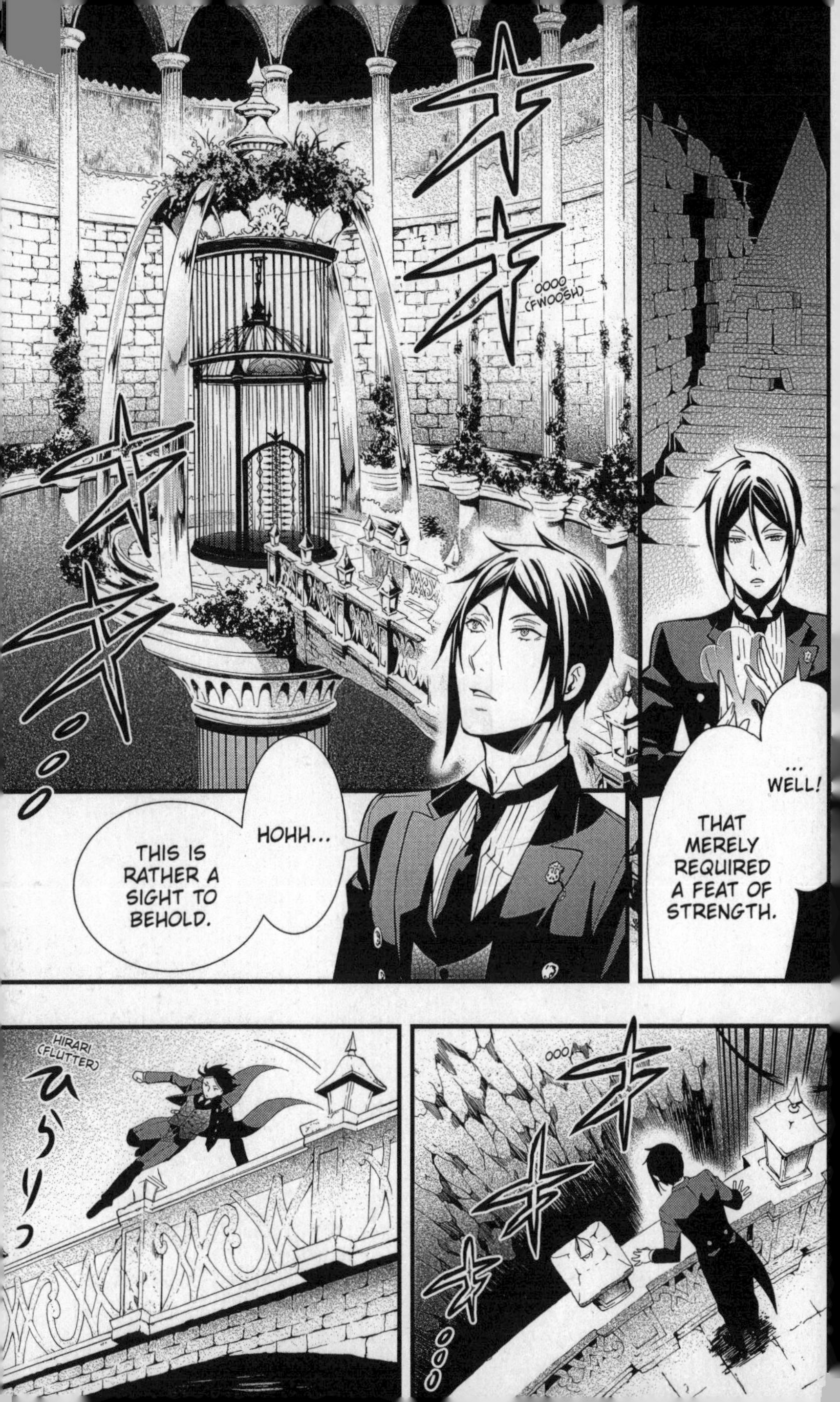
...WELL!
THAT MERELY REQUIRED A FEAT OF STRENGTH.
OOOO (FWOOSH)
HOHH...
THIS IS RATHER A SIGHT TO BEHOLD.
OOO
HIRARI (FLUTTER)
ひらりっ

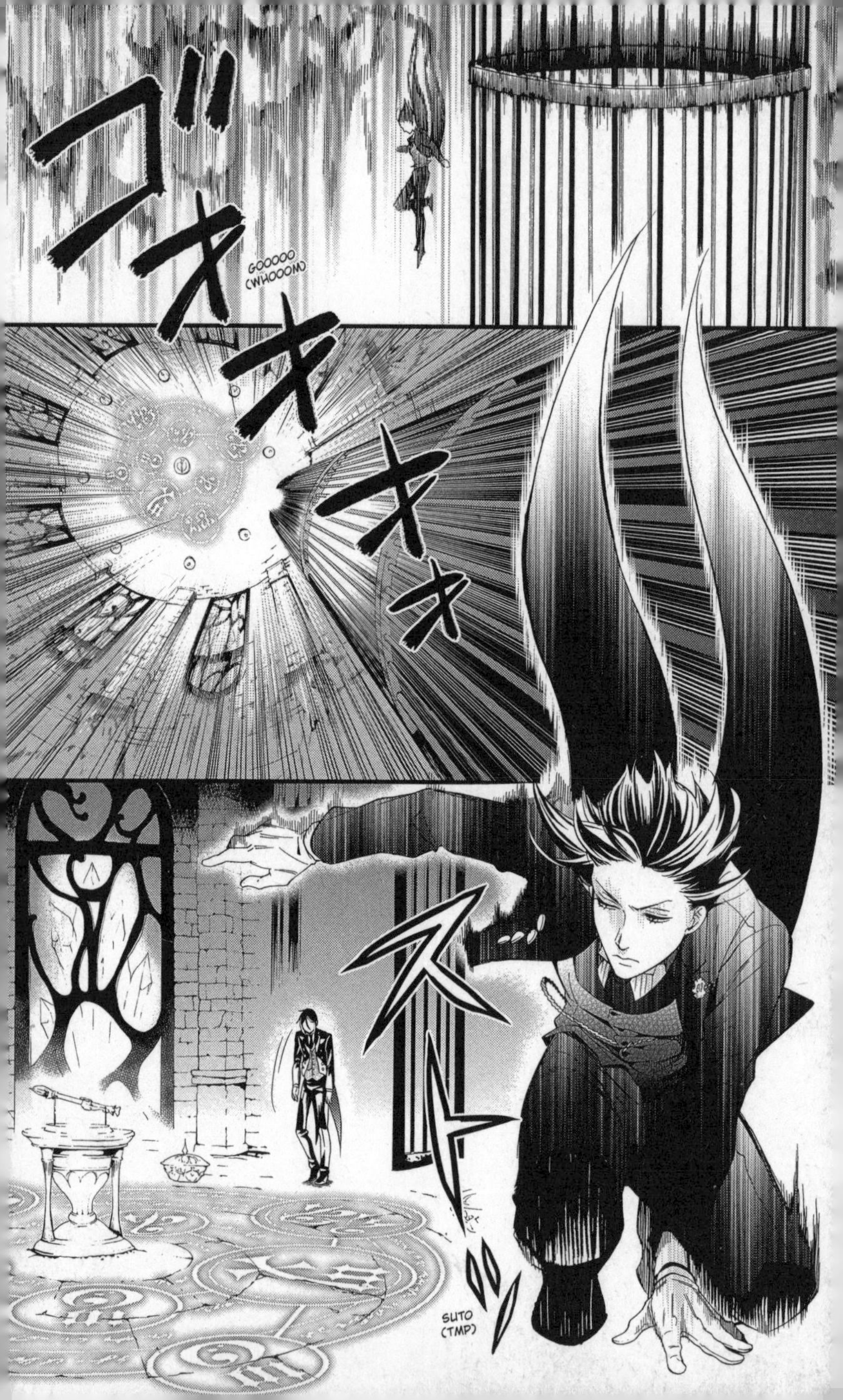
GOOOOO
(WHOOOM)
SUTO
(TMP)

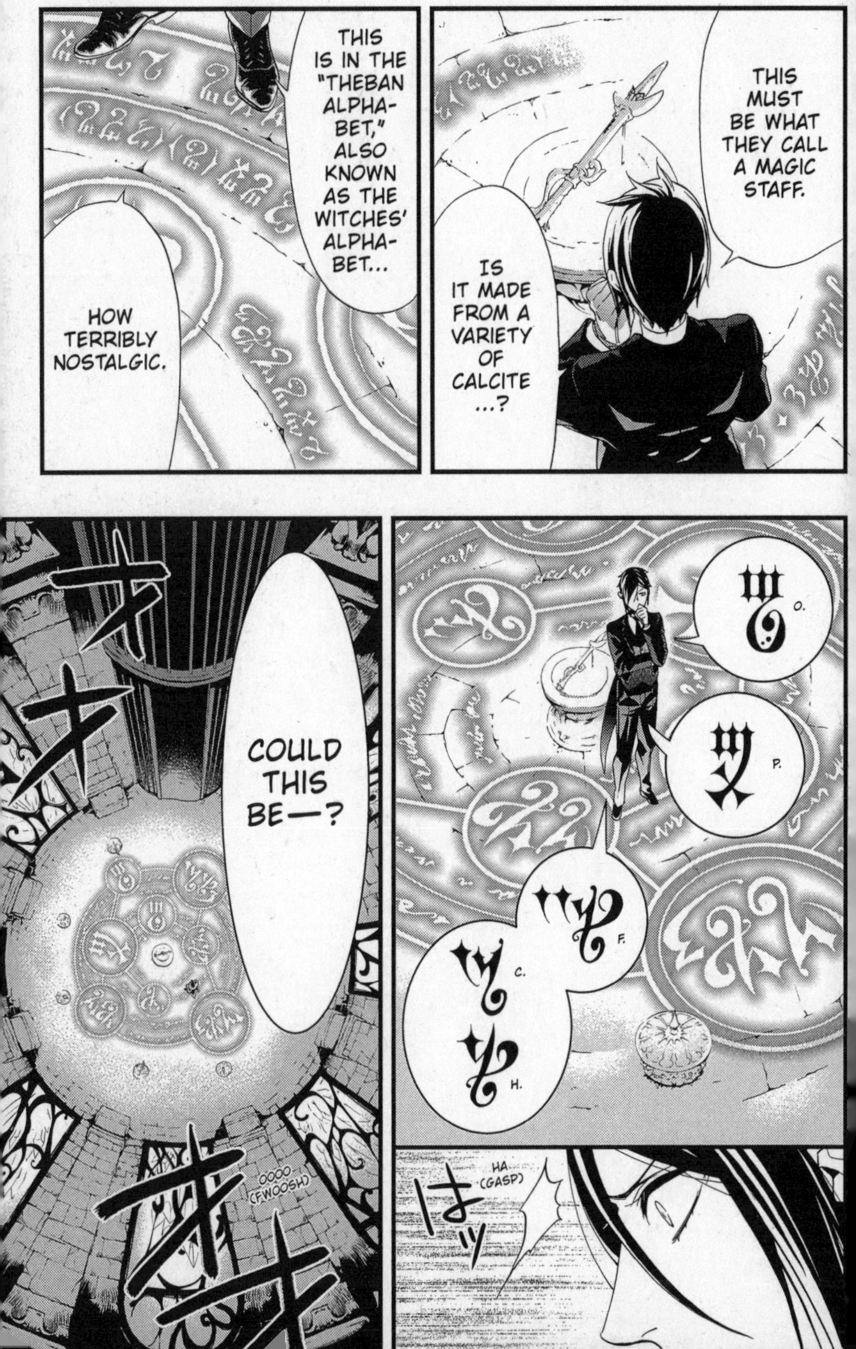
THIS MUST BE WHAT THEY CALL A MAGIC STAFF.
IS IT MADE FROM A VARIETY OF CALCITE ...?
THIS IS IN THE "THEBAN ALPHABET," ALSO KNOWN AS THE WITCHES' ALPHABET...
HOW TERRIBLY NOSTALGIC.
O.
P.
F.
C.
H.
HA (GASP)
COULD THIS BE—?
OOOO (FWOOSH)

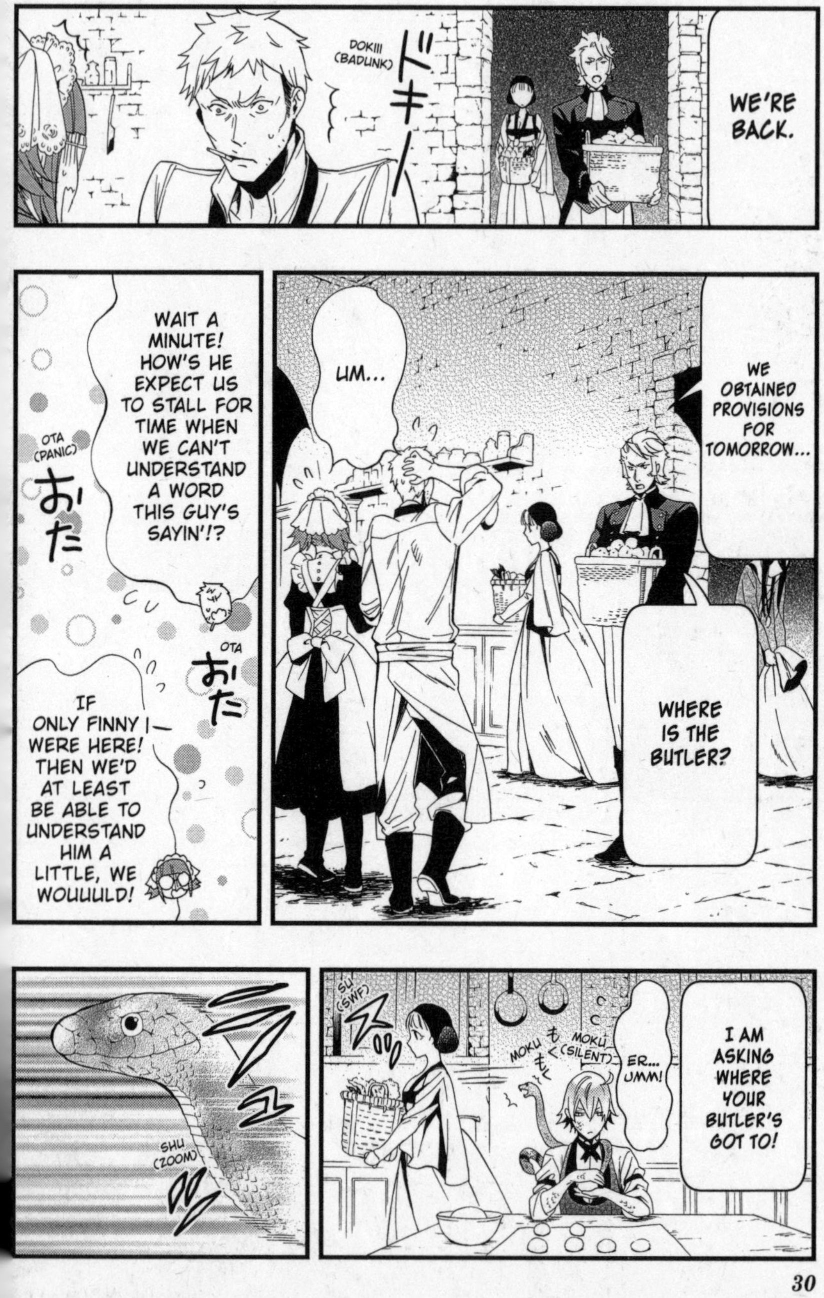
WE'RE BACK.
DOKIII (BADUNK)
ドキーッ
WE OBTAINED PROVISIONS FOR TOMORROW...
WHERE IS THE BUTLER?
UM...
WAIT A MINUTE! HOW'S HE EXPECT US TO STALL FOR TIME WHEN WE CAN'T UNDERSTAND A WORD THIS GUY'S SAYIN'!?
OTA (PANIC)
おた
OTA
おた
IF ONLY FINNY I— WERE HERE! THEN WE'D AT LEAST BE ABLE TO UNDERSTAND HIM A LITTLE, WE WOUUULD!
I AM ASKING WHERE YOUR BUTLER'S GOT TO!
ER... UMM!
MOKU MOKU (SILENT)
もくもく
SU (SWF)
SHU (ZOOM)

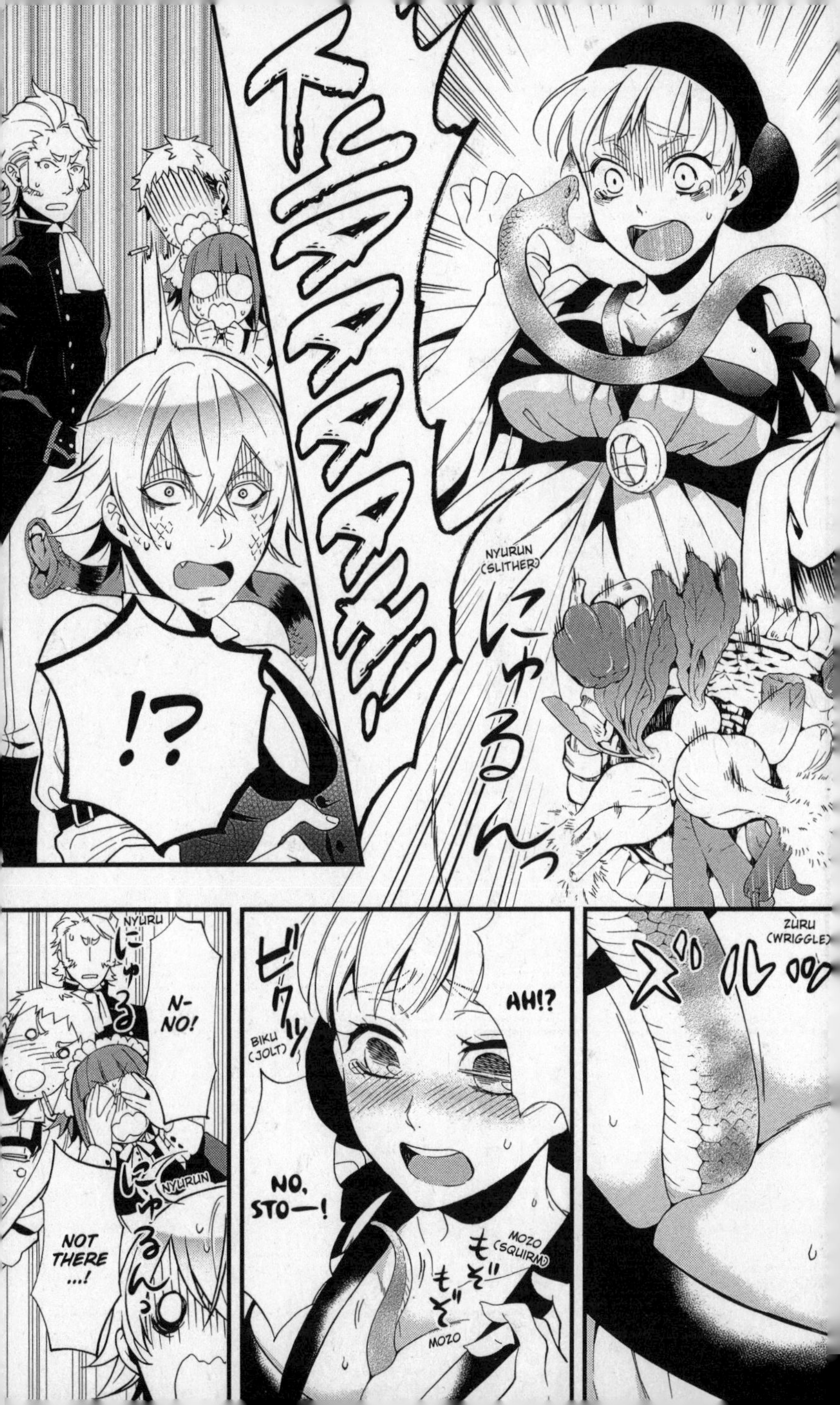
NYURUN (SLITHER)
にゅるんっ
!?
ZURU (WRIGGLE)
AH!?
BIKU (JOLT)
NO, STO—!
MOZO (SQUIRM)
もぞもぞ
MOZO
NYURU
にゅる
N- NO!
NYURUN
にゅるんっ
NOT THERE ...!

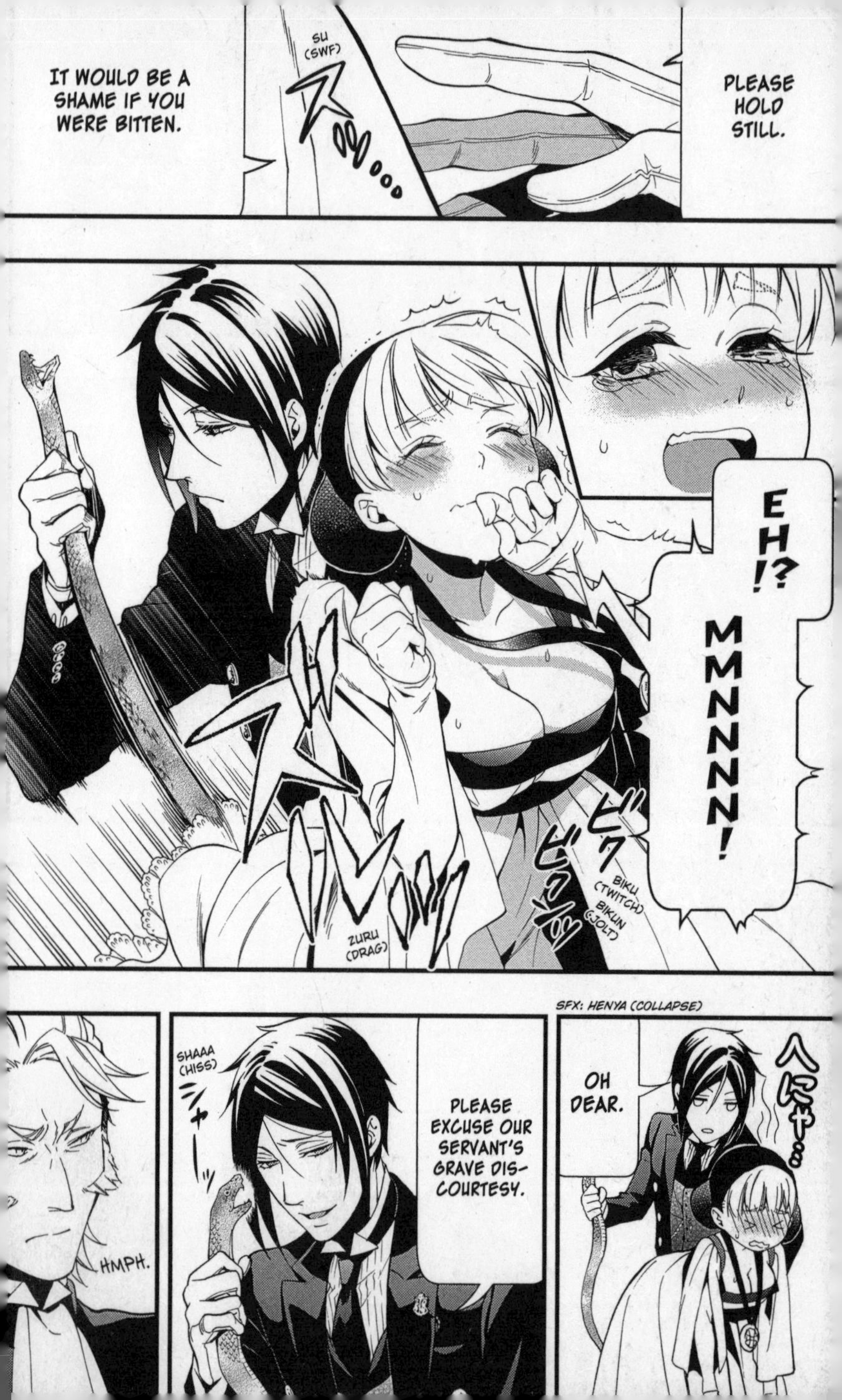

PLEASE HOLD STILL.
SU (SWF)
IT WOULD BE A SHAME IF YOU WERE BITTEN.
EH!? MMNNNN!
BIKU (TWITCH)
BIKUN (JOLT)
ZURU (DRAG)
SFX: HENYA (COLLAPSE)
OH DEAR.
PLEASE EXCUSE OUR SERVANT'S GRAVE DIS-COURTESY.
SHAAA (HISS)
HMPH.

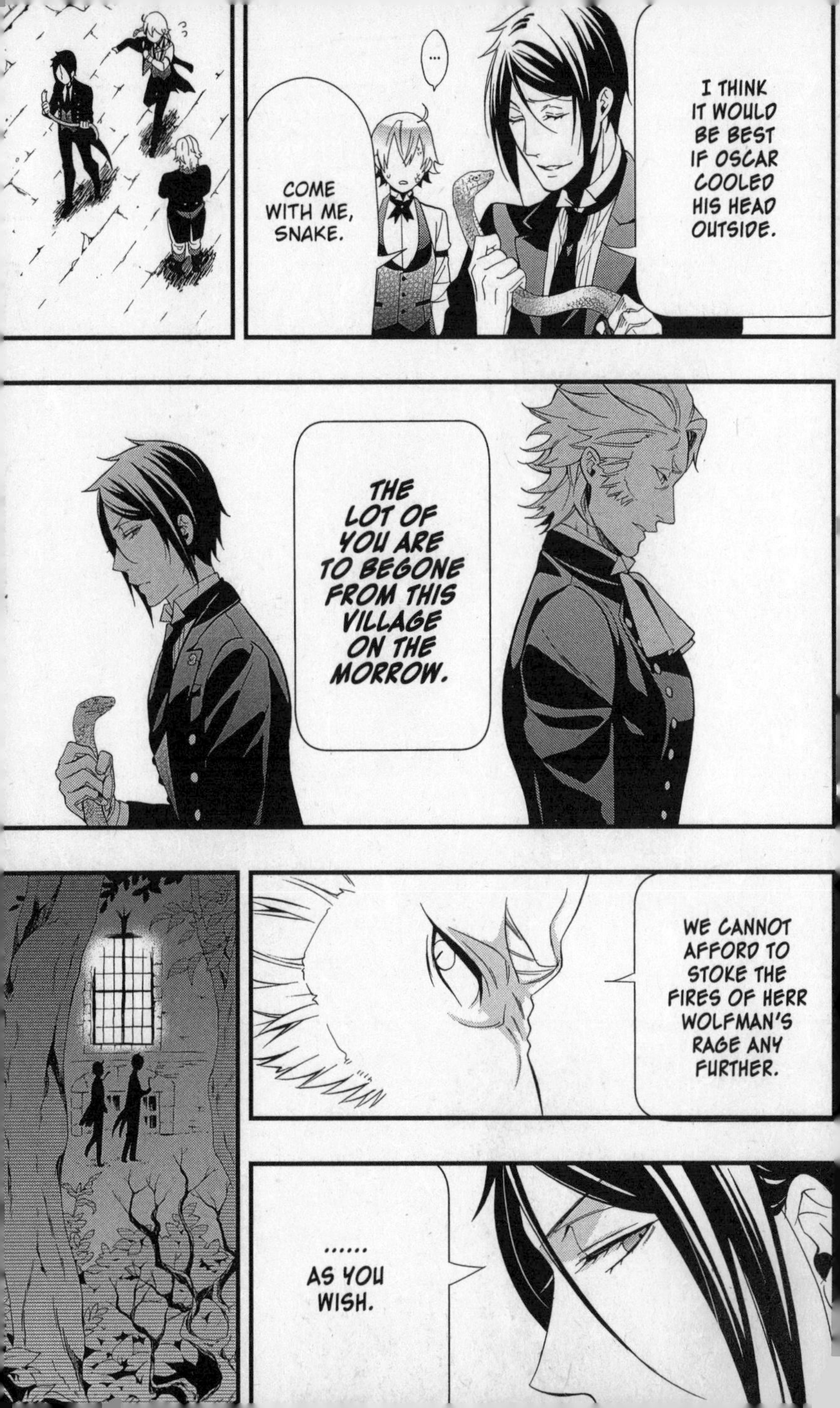
I THINK IT WOULD BE BEST IF OSCAR COOLED HIS HEAD OUTSIDE.
...
COME WITH ME, SNAKE.
THE LOT OF YOU ARE TO BEGONE FROM THIS VILLAGE ON THE MORROW.
WE CANNOT AFFORD TO STOKE THE FIRES OF HERR WOLFMAN'S RAGE ANY FURTHER.
...... AS YOU WISH.

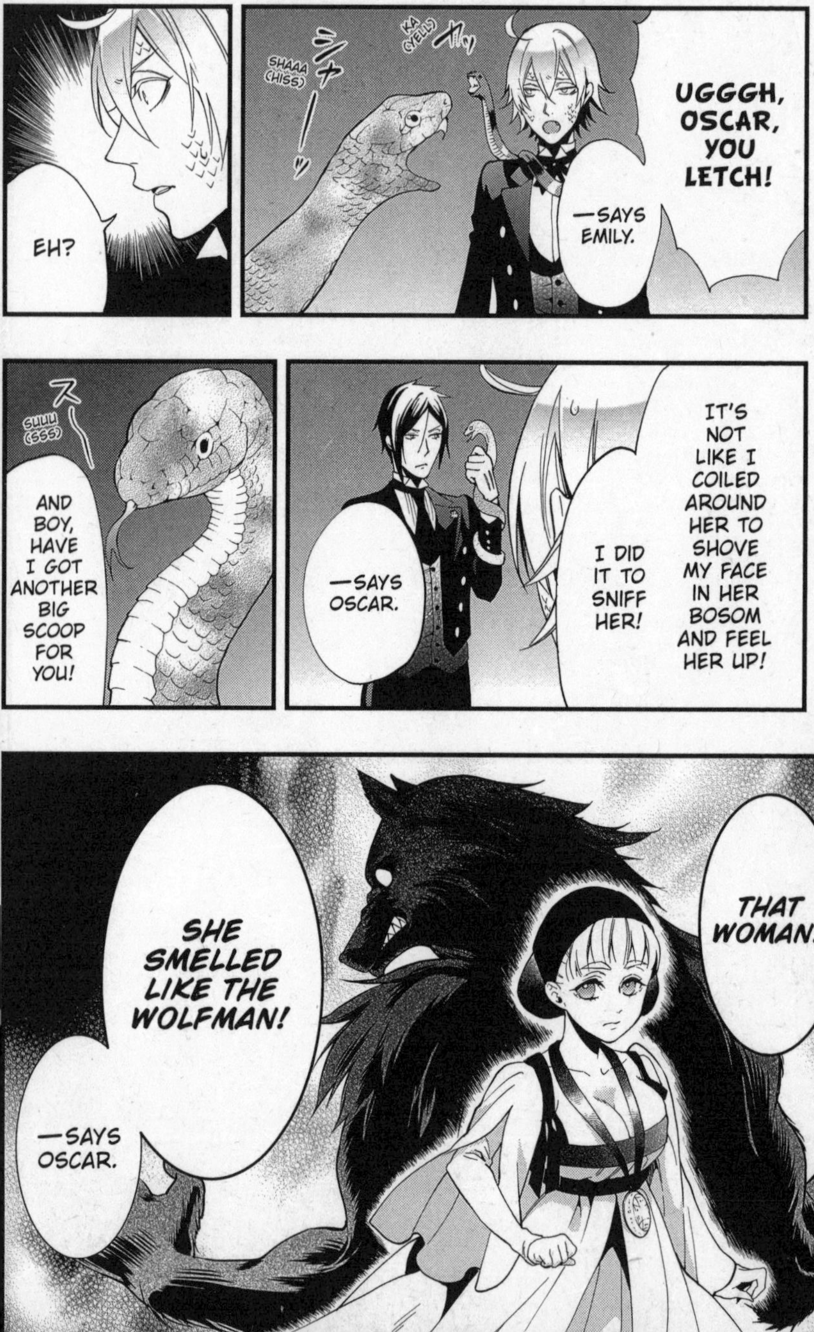
KA (YELL)
SHAAA (HISS)
UGGGH, OSCAR, YOU LETCH!
—SAYS EMILY.
EH?
IT'S NOT LIKE I COILED AROUND HER TO SHOVE MY FACE IN HER BOSOM AND FEEL HER UP!
I DID IT TO SNIFF HER!
—SAYS OSCAR.
SUUU (SSS)
AND BOY, HAVE I GOT ANOTHER BIG SCOOP FOR YOU!
THAT WOMAN!
SHE SMELLED LIKE THE WOLFMAN!
—SAYS OSCAR.

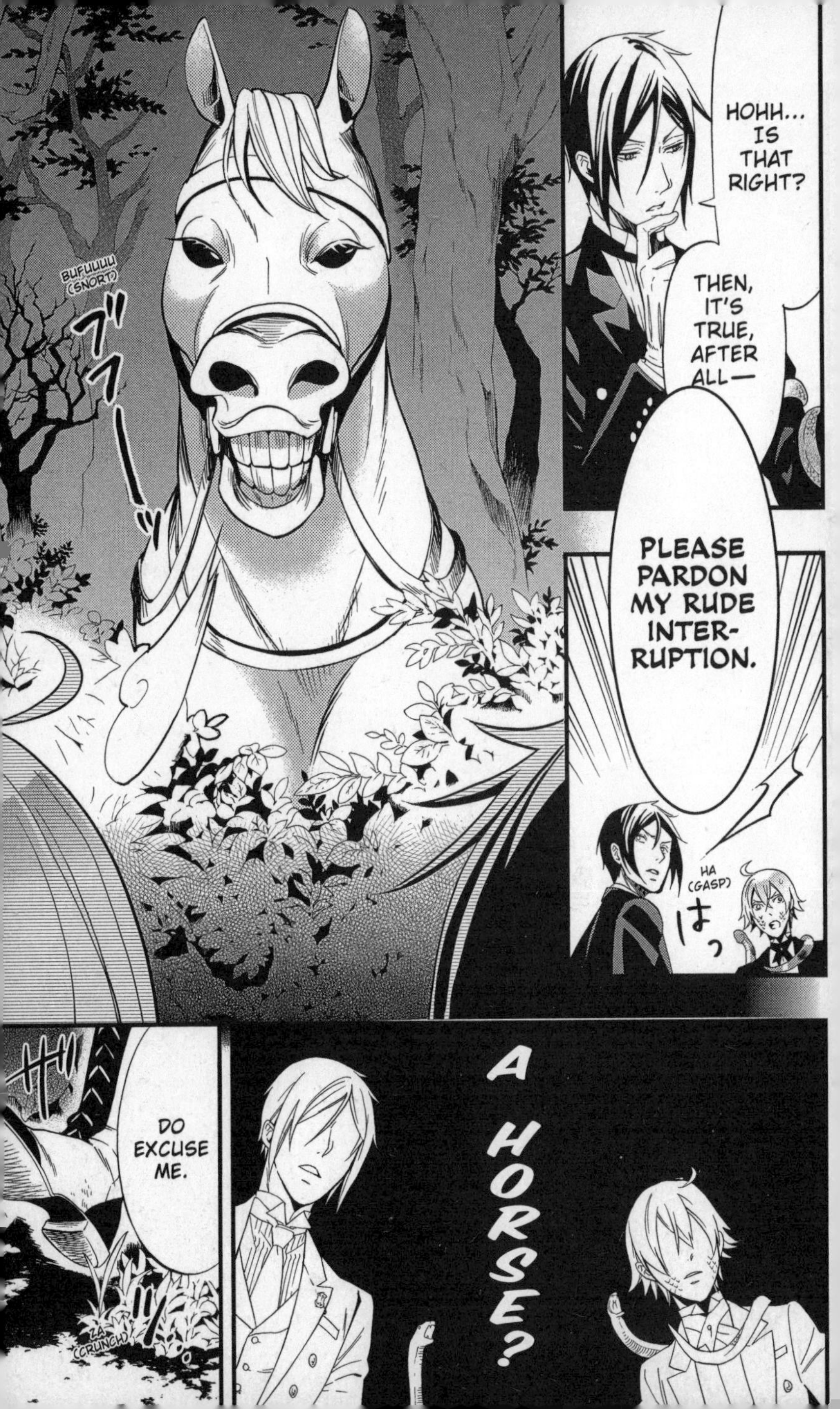
HOHH... IS THAT RIGHT?
THEN, IT'S TRUE, AFTER ALL—
PLEASE PARDON MY RUDE INTER-RUPTION.
HA (GASP)
BUFUUUU (SNORT)
A HORSE?
DO EXCUSE ME.
ZA (CRUNCH)

Black Butler

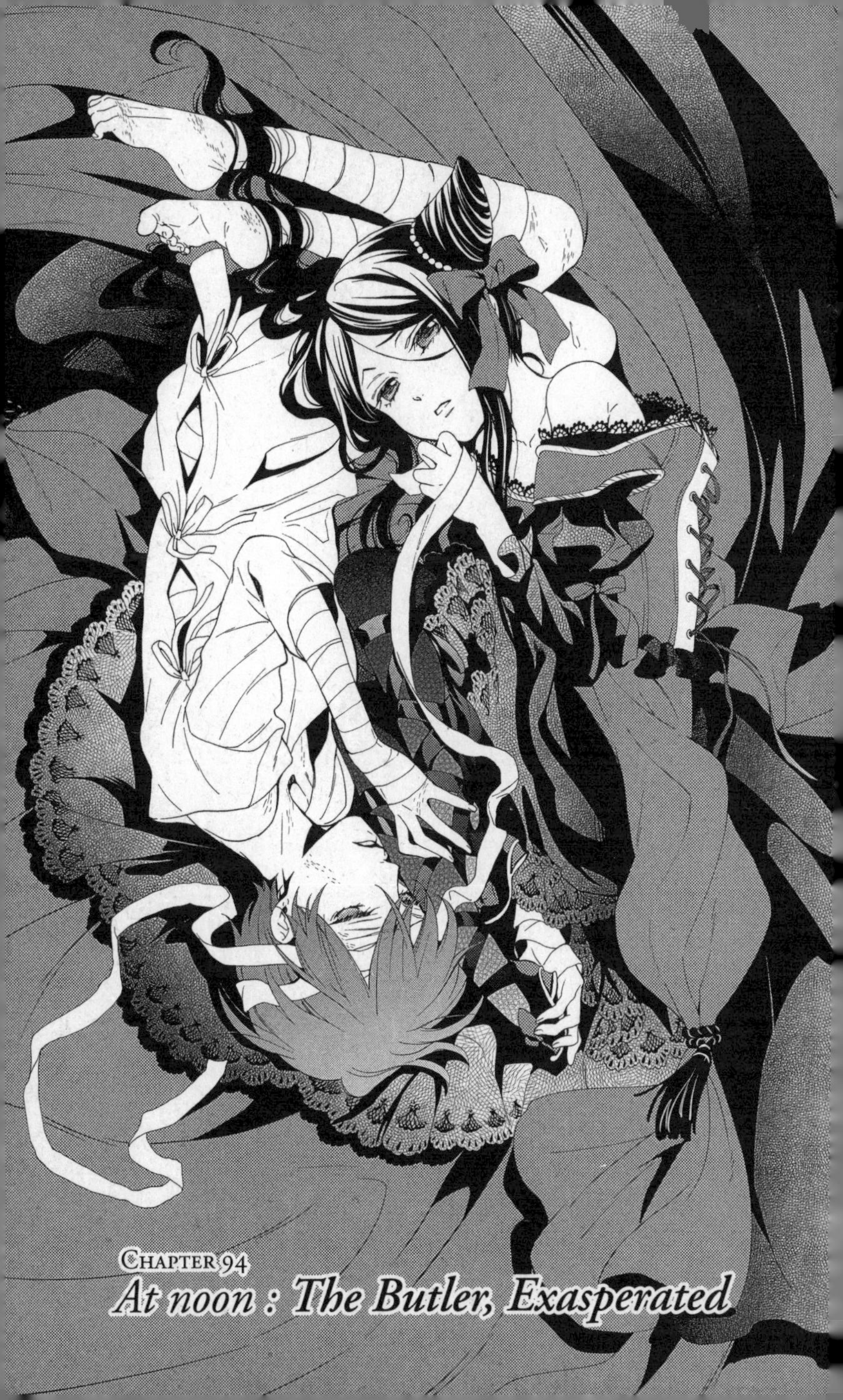

Chapter 94
At noon : The Butler, Exasperated

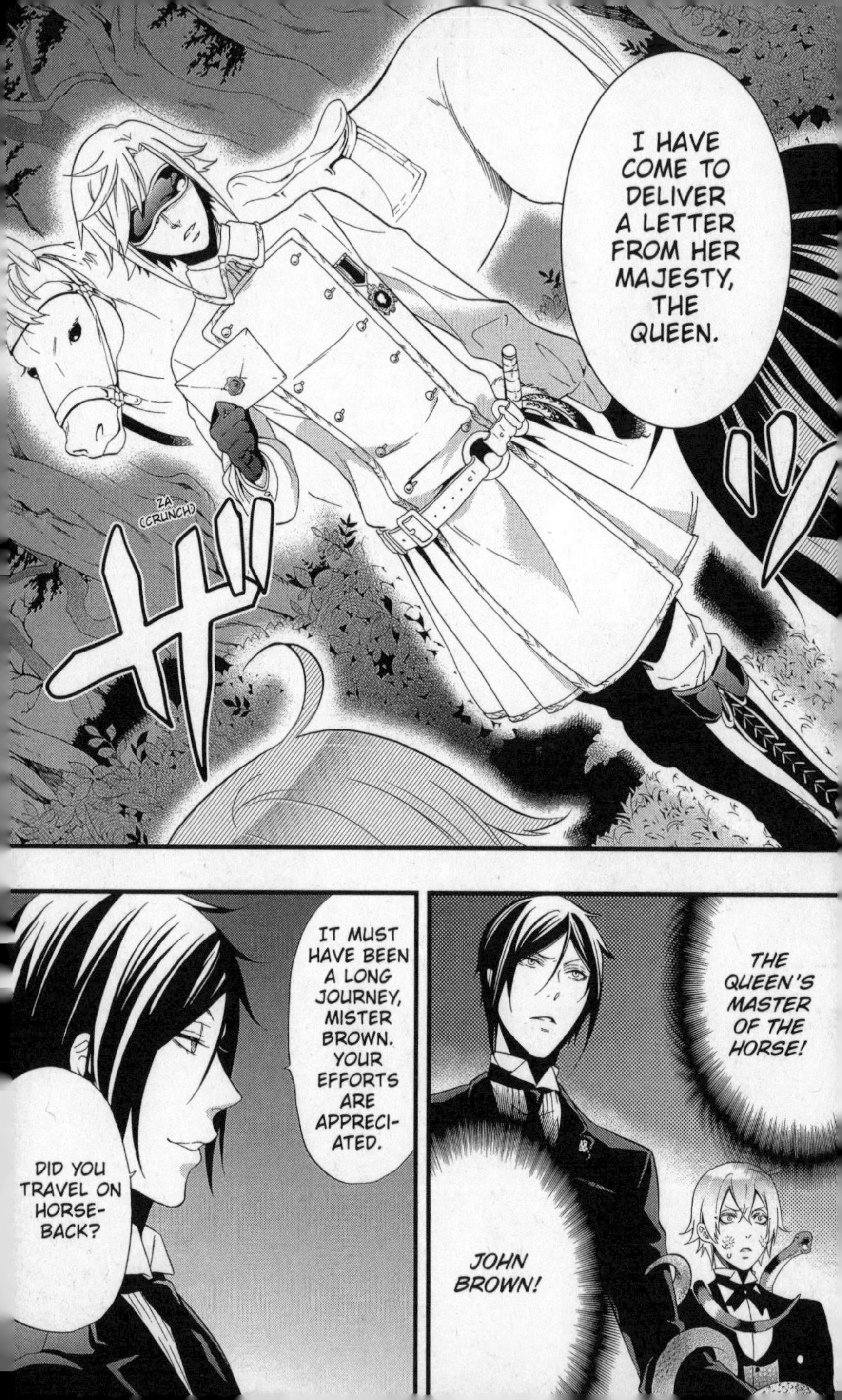

I HAVE COME TO DELIVER A LETTER FROM HER MAJESTY, THE QUEEN.
ZA (CRUNCH)
THE QUEEN'S MASTER OF THE HORSE!
JOHN BROWN!
IT MUST HAVE BEEN A LONG JOURNEY, MISTER BROWN. YOUR EFFORTS ARE APPRECI-ATED.
DID YOU TRAVEL ON HORSE-BACK?

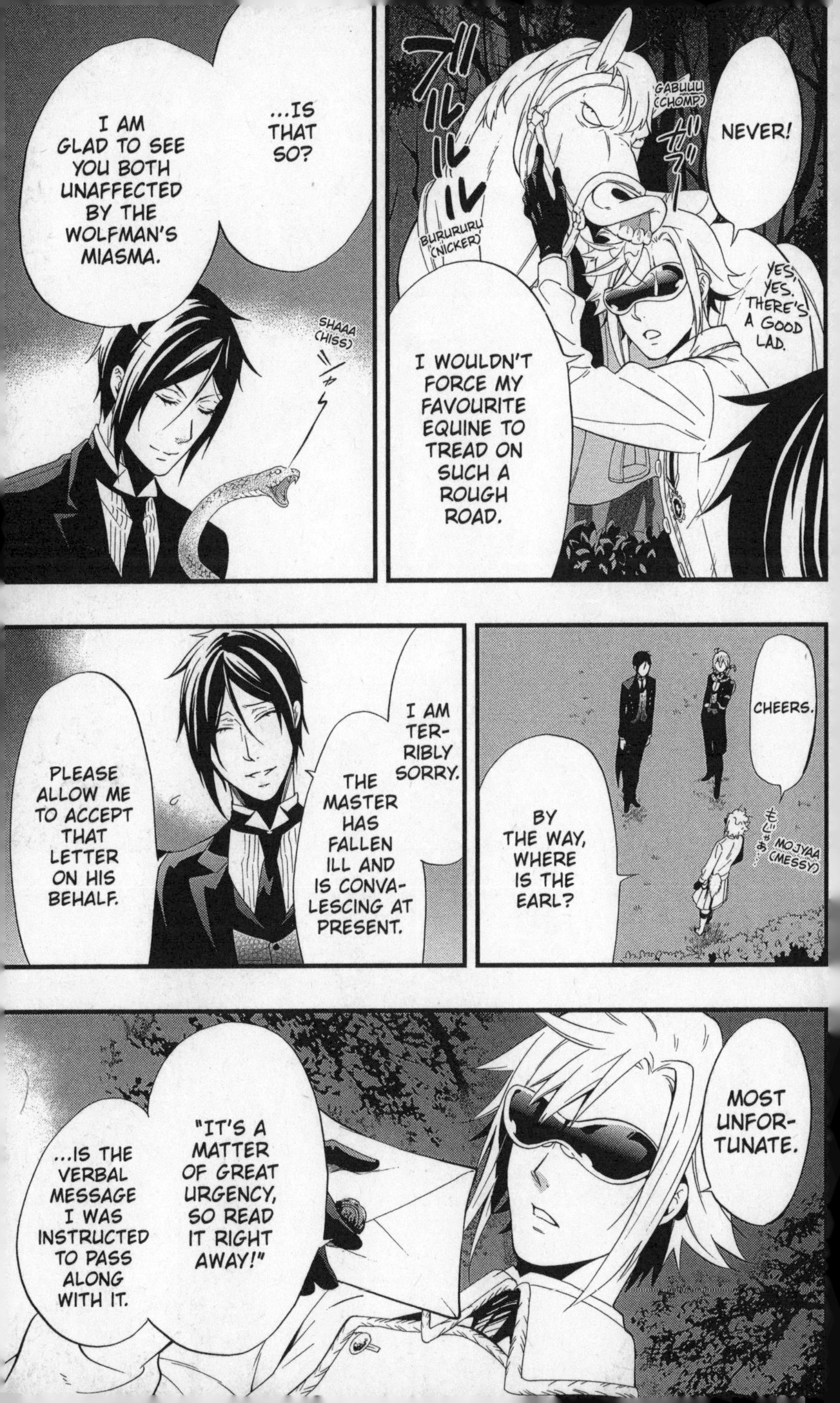
NEVER!
GABUUU (CHOMP)
YES, YES. THERE'S A GOOD LAD.
BURURURU (NICKER)
I WOULDN'T FORCE MY FAVOURITE EQUINE TO TREAD ON SUCH A ROUGH ROAD.
...IS THAT SO?
I AM GLAD TO SEE YOU BOTH UNAFFECTED BY THE WOLFMAN'S MIASMA.
SHAAA (HISS)
CHEERS.
MOJYAA (MESSY)
BY THE WAY, WHERE IS THE EARL?
I AM TERRIBLY SORRY.
THE MASTER HAS FALLEN ILL AND IS CONVALESCING AT PRESENT.
PLEASE ALLOW ME TO ACCEPT THAT LETTER ON HIS BEHALF.
MOST UNFORTUNATE.
"IT'S A MATTER OF GREAT URGENCY, SO READ IT RIGHT AWAY!"
...IS THE VERBAL MESSAGE I WAS INSTRUCTED TO PASS ALONG WITH IT.

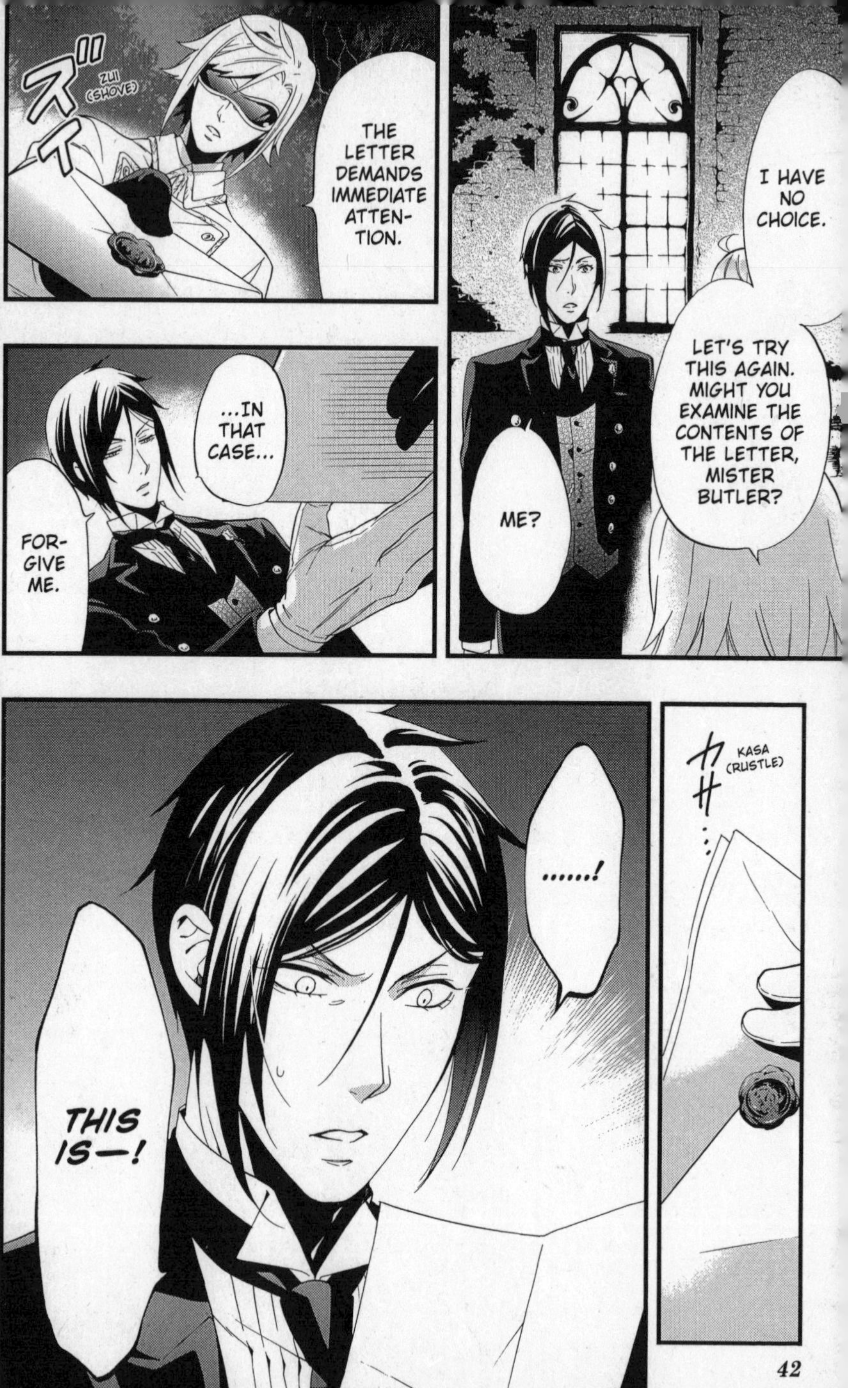
I HAVE NO CHOICE.
LET'S TRY THIS AGAIN. MIGHT YOU EXAMINE THE CONTENTS OF THE LETTER, MISTER BUTLER?
ME?
ZUI (SHOVE)
THE LETTER DEMANDS IMMEDIATE ATTEN-TION.
...IN THAT CASE...
FOR-GIVE ME.
KASA (RUSTLE)
......!
THIS IS—!

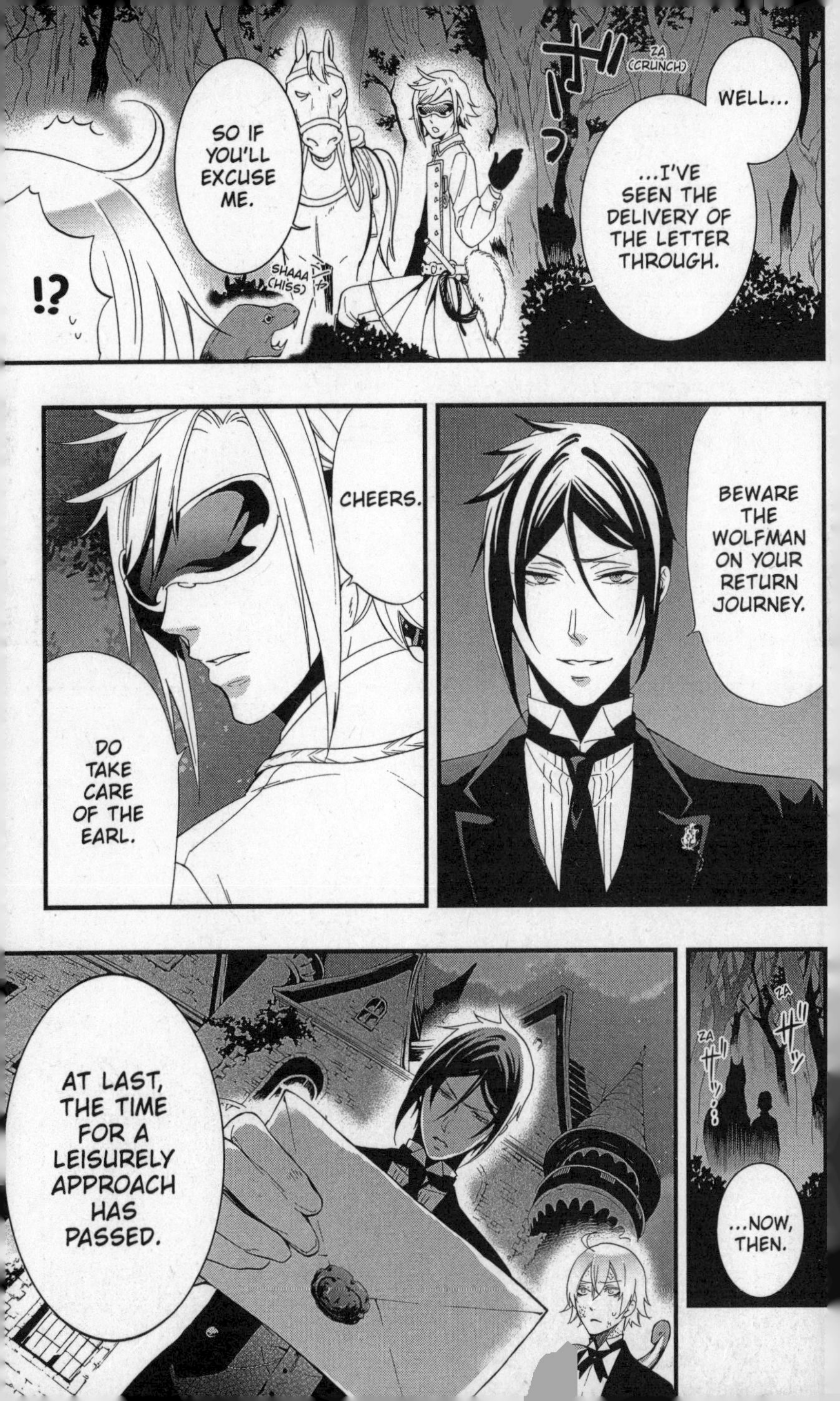
WELL...
...I'VE SEEN THE DELIVERY OF THE LETTER THROUGH.
ZA (CRUNCH)
SO IF YOU'LL EXCUSE ME.
SHAAA (HISS)
!?
BEWARE THE WOLFMAN ON YOUR RETURN JOURNEY.
CHEERS.
DO TAKE CARE OF THE EARL.
ZA
ZA
...NOW, THEN.
AT LAST, THE TIME FOR A LEISURELY APPROACH HAS PASSED.

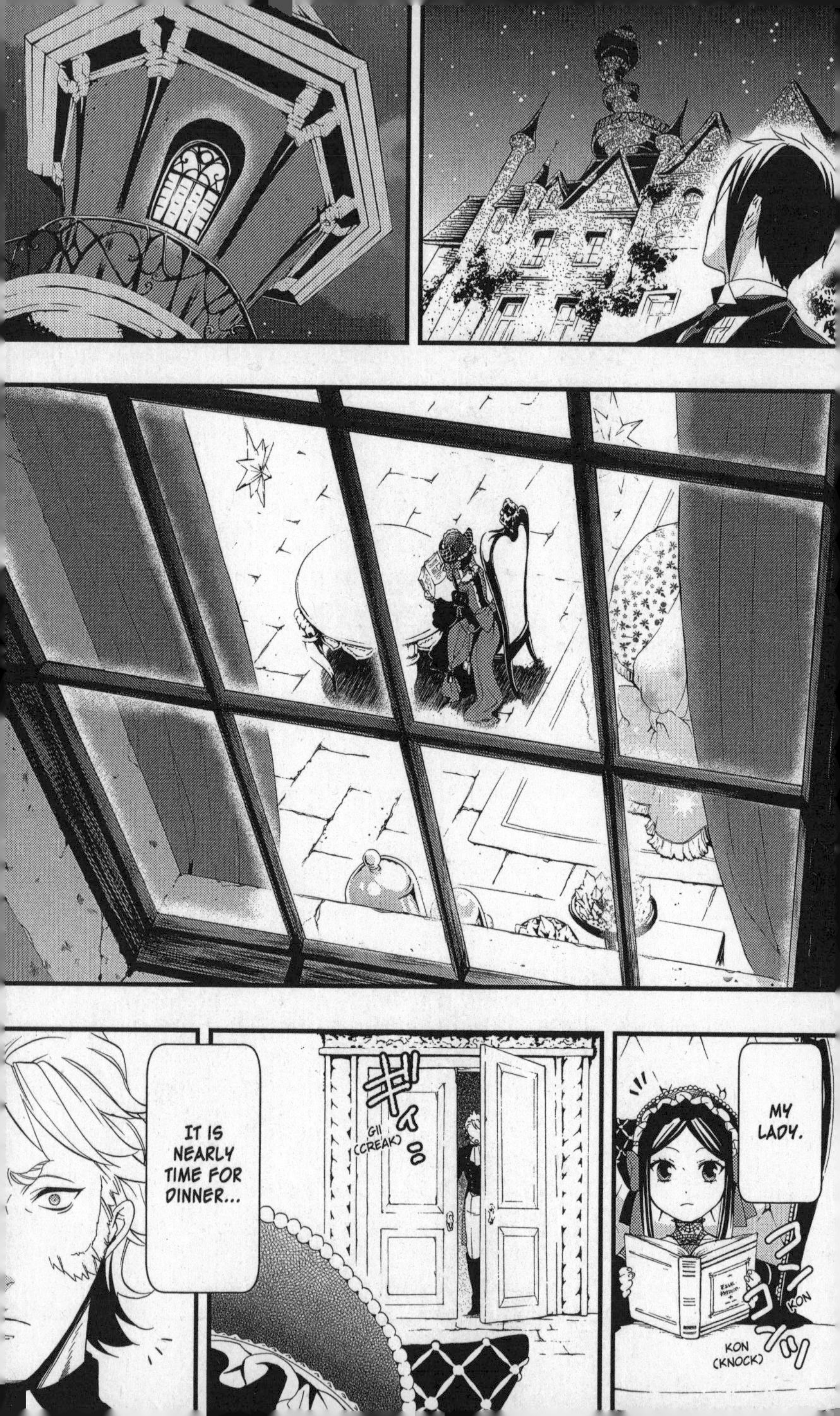
MY LADY.
KON
KON (KNOCK)
GII (CREAK)
IT IS NEARLY TIME FOR DINNER...

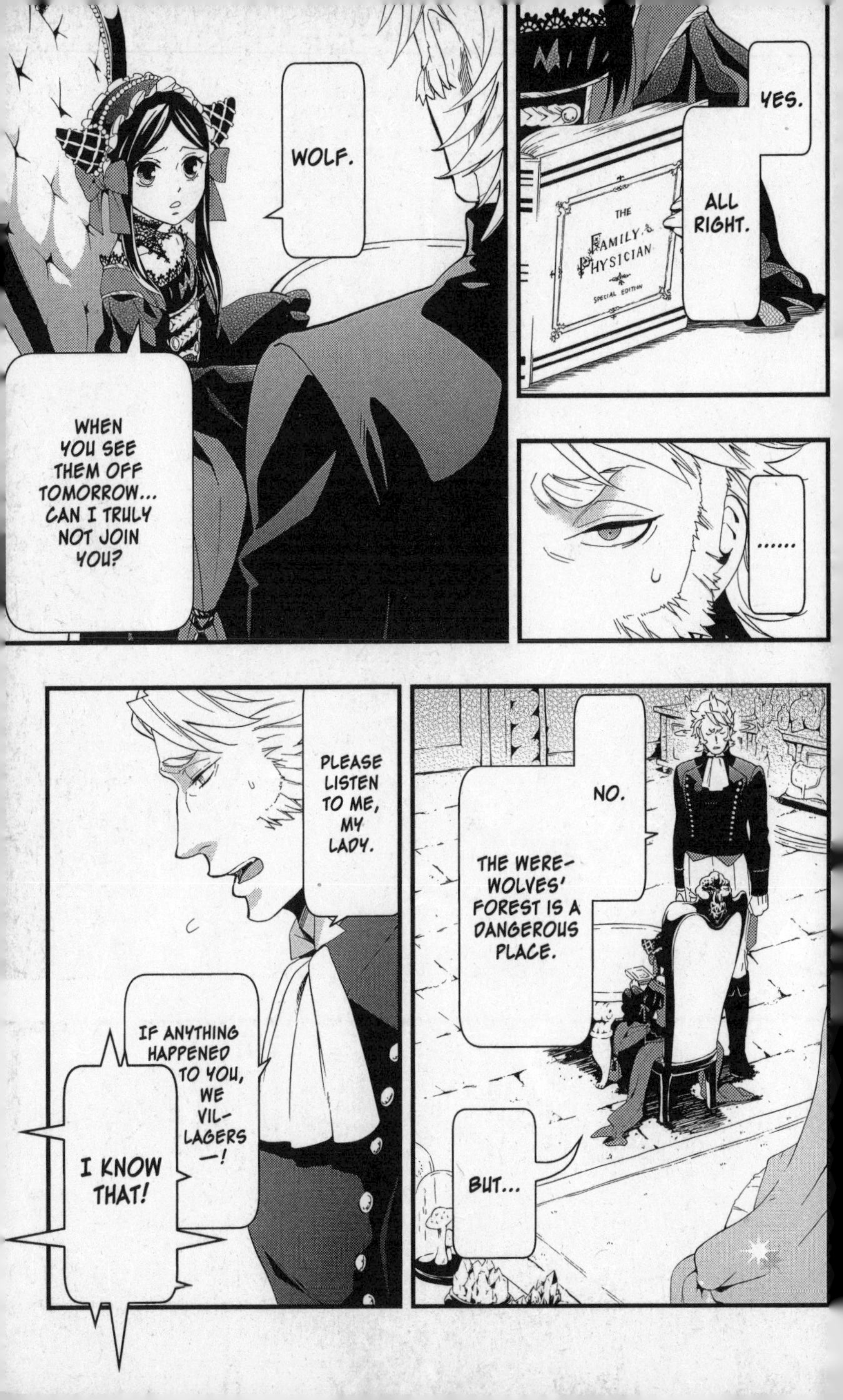
YES.
ALL RIGHT.
THE FAMILY PHYSICIAN
SPECIAL EDITION
......
WOLF.
WHEN YOU SEE THEM OFF TOMORROW... CAN I TRULY NOT JOIN YOU?
NO.
THE WERE-WOLVES' FOREST IS A DANGEROUS PLACE.
BUT...
PLEASE LISTEN TO ME, MY LADY.
IF ANYTHING HAPPENED TO YOU, WE VIL-LAGERS—!
I KNOW THAT!

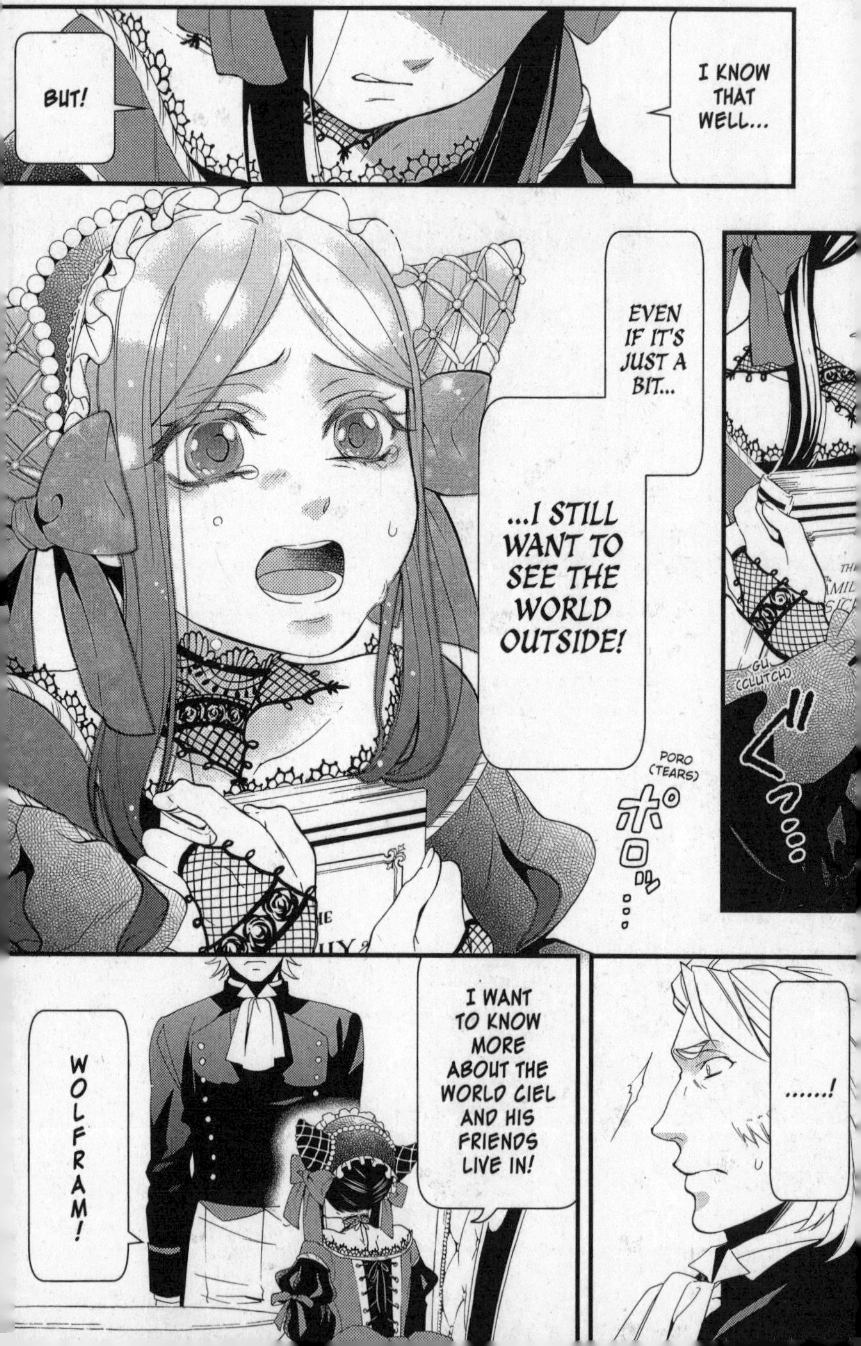
I KNOW THAT WELL...
BUT!
GU (CLUTCH)
EVEN IF IT'S JUST A BIT...
...I STILL WANT TO SEE THE WORLD OUTSIDE!
PORO (TEARS)
......!
I WANT TO KNOW MORE ABOUT THE WORLD CIEL AND HIS FRIENDS LIVE IN!
WOLFRAM!

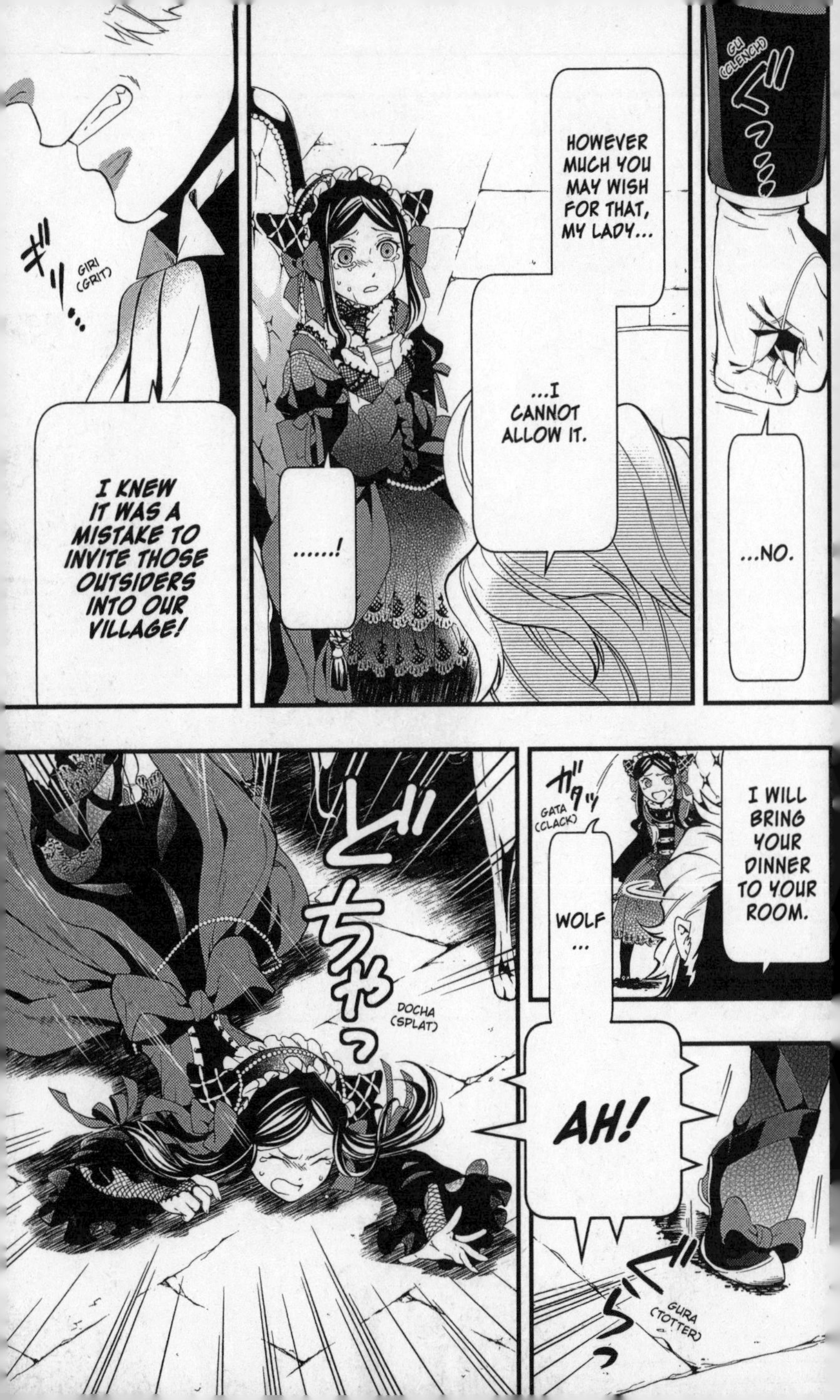
GU (CLENCH)
ぐっ
...NO.
HOWEVER MUCH YOU MAY WISH FOR THAT, MY LADY...
...I CANNOT ALLOW IT.
......!
ギリ...
GIRI (GRIT)
I KNEW IT WAS A MISTAKE TO INVITE THOSE OUTSIDERS INTO OUR VILLAGE!
I WILL BRING YOUR DINNER TO YOUR ROOM.
ガタッ
GATA (CLACK)
WOLF ...
AH!
ぐら
GURA (TOTTER)
どちゃっ
DOCHA (SPLAT)

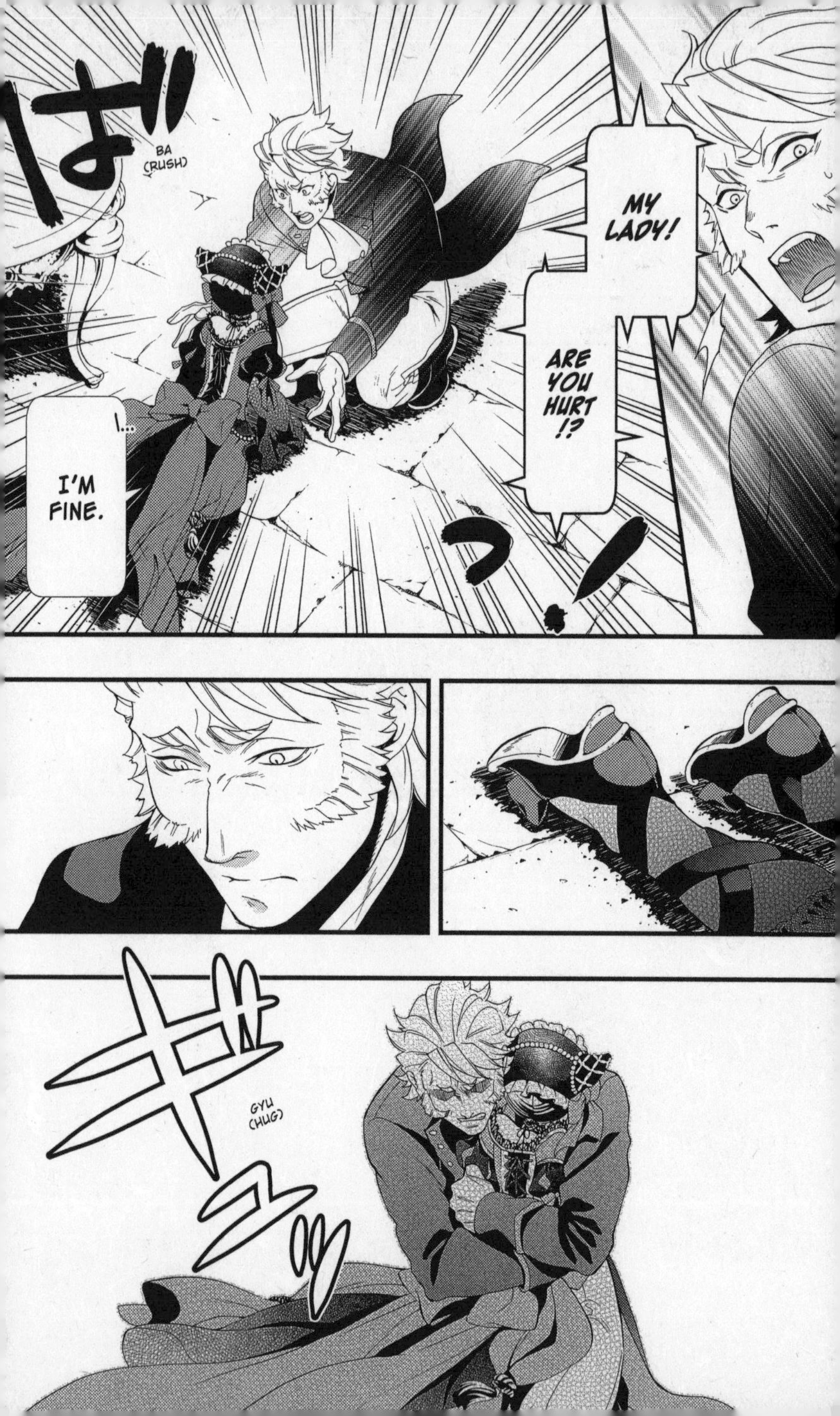
MY LADY!
ARE YOU HURT!?
BA (RUSH)
I... I'M FINE.
GYU (HUG)

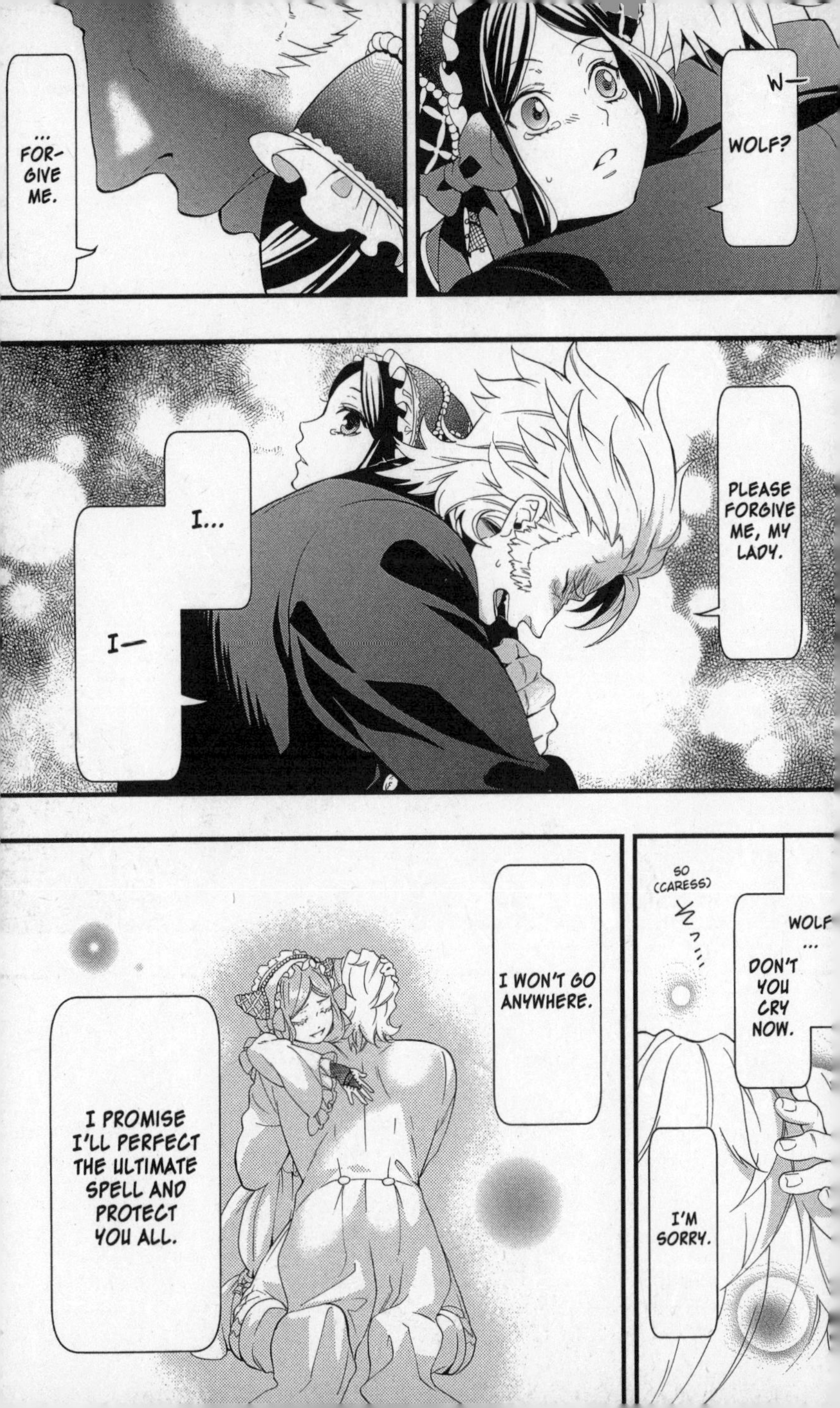
W—
WOLF?
...FOR-GIVE ME.
PLEASE FORGIVE ME, MY LADY.
I...
I—
SO (CARESS)
WOLF... DON'T YOU CRY NOW.
I'M SORRY.
I WON'T GO ANYWHERE.
I PROMISE I'LL PERFECT THE ULTIMATE SPELL AND PROTECT YOU ALL.

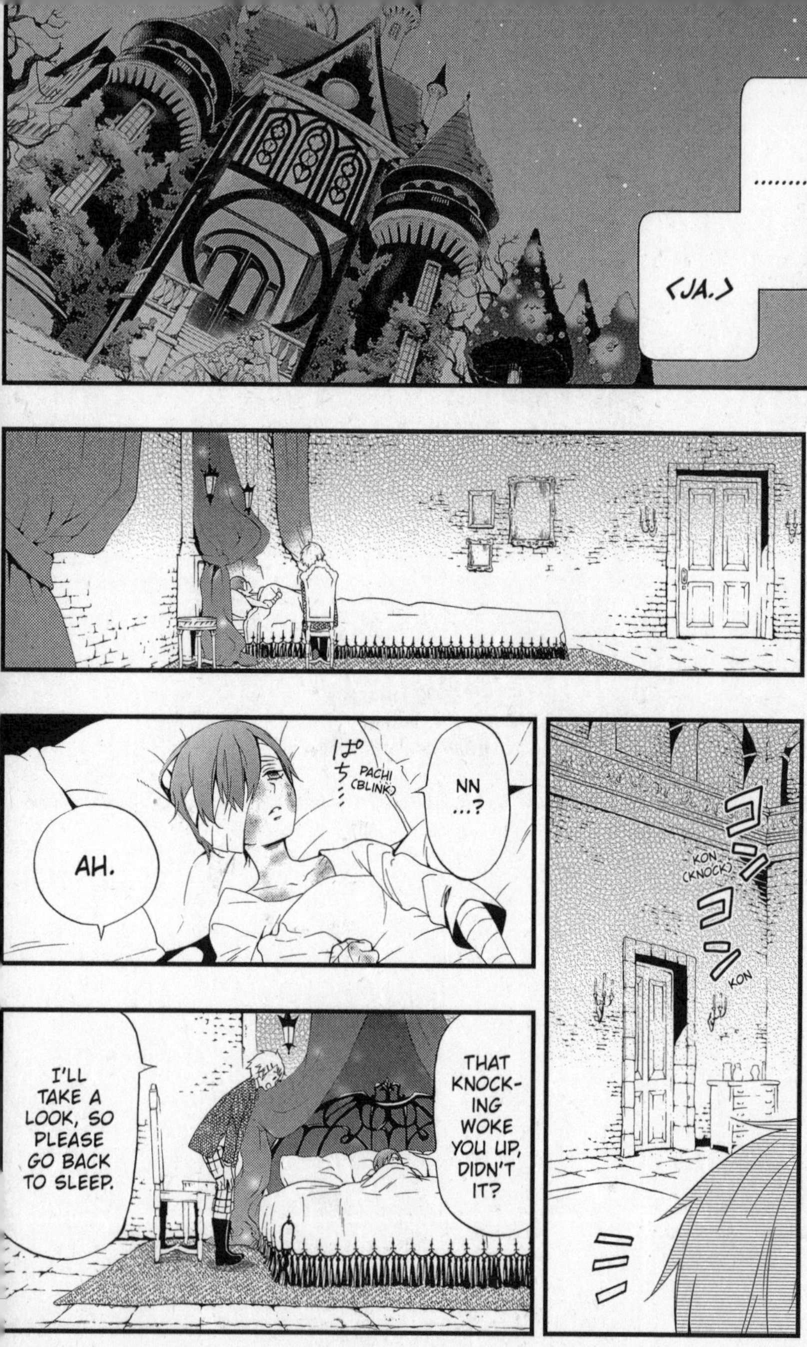

....
<JA.>
コンコンコン
KON (KNOCK) KON
ぱち
PACHI (BLINK)
NN ...?
AH.
THAT KNOCKING WOKE YOU UP, DIDN'T IT?
I'LL TAKE A LOOK, SO PLEASE GO BACK TO SLEEP.

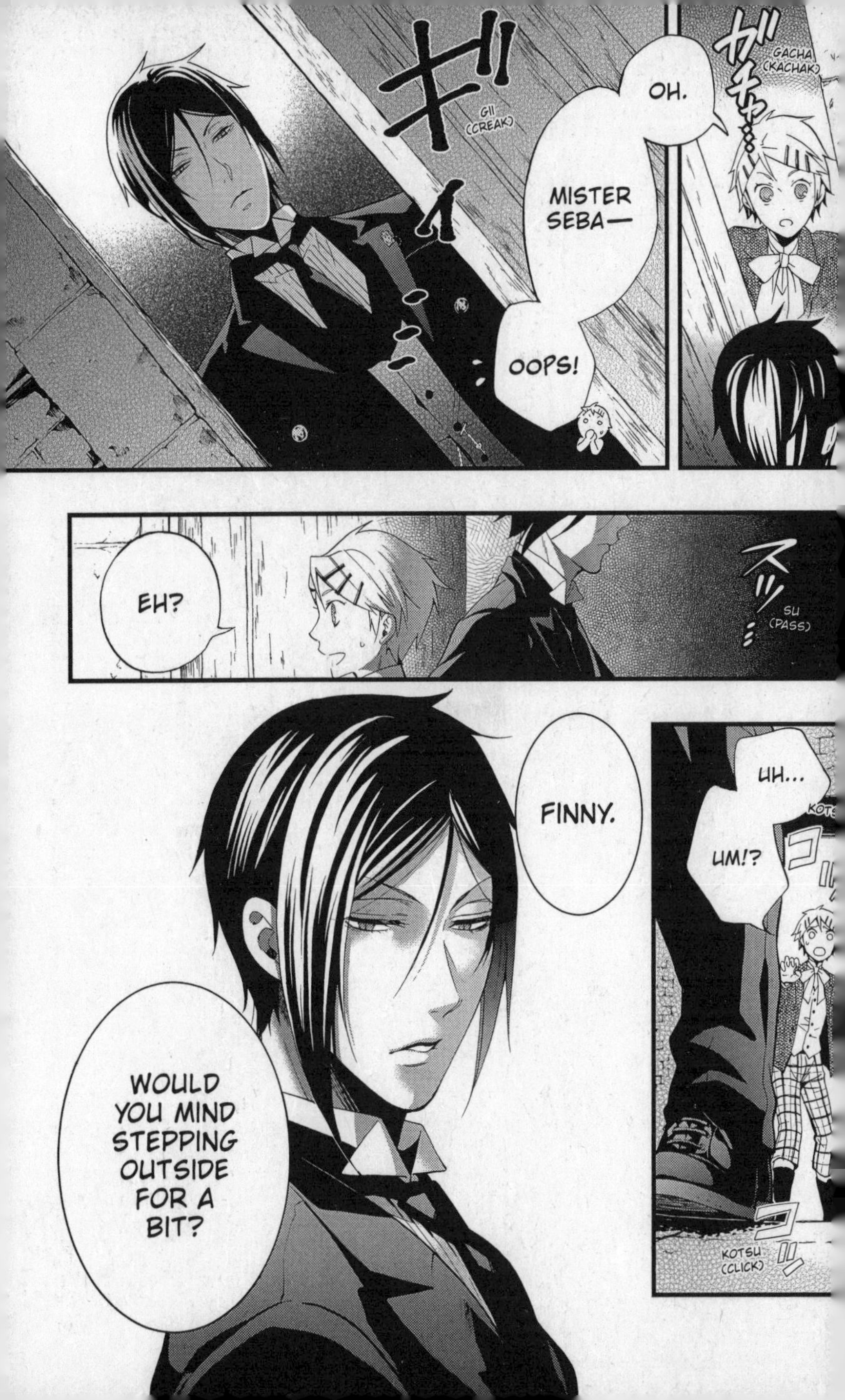
ガチャ
GACHA (KACHAK)
OH.
MISTER SEBA—
OOPS!
ギィ
GII (CREAK)
スッ
SU (PASS)
EH?
UH...
UM!?
コツ
KOTSU (CLICK)
コツ
FINNY.
WOULD YOU MIND STEPPING OUTSIDE FOR A BIT?

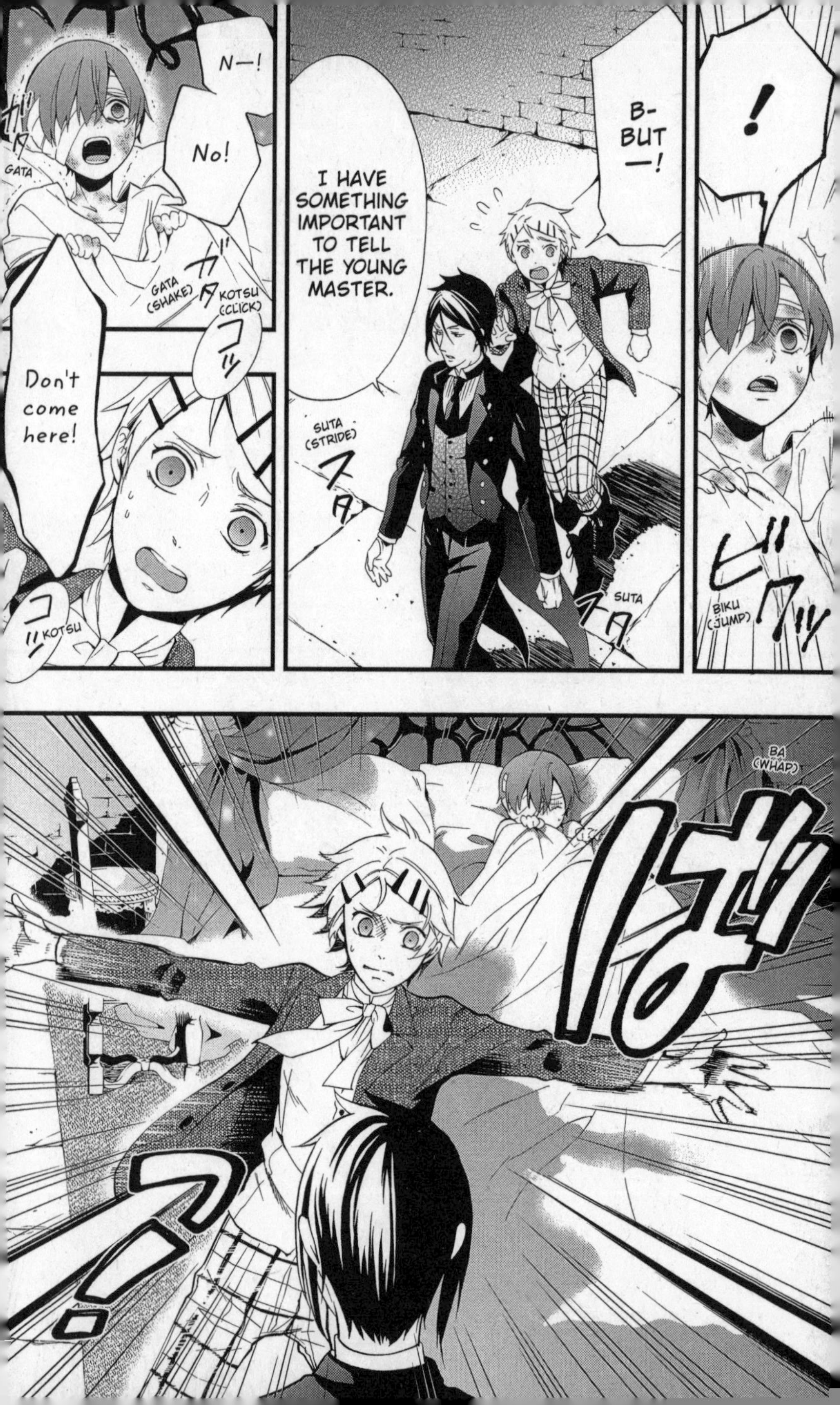
!
BIKU (JUMP)
B-BUT—!
I HAVE SOMETHING IMPORTANT TO TELL THE YOUNG MASTER.
SUTA (STRIDE)
SUTA
N—!
No!
GATA
GATA (SHAKE)
KOTSU (CLICK)
Don't come here!
KOTSU
BA (WHAP)

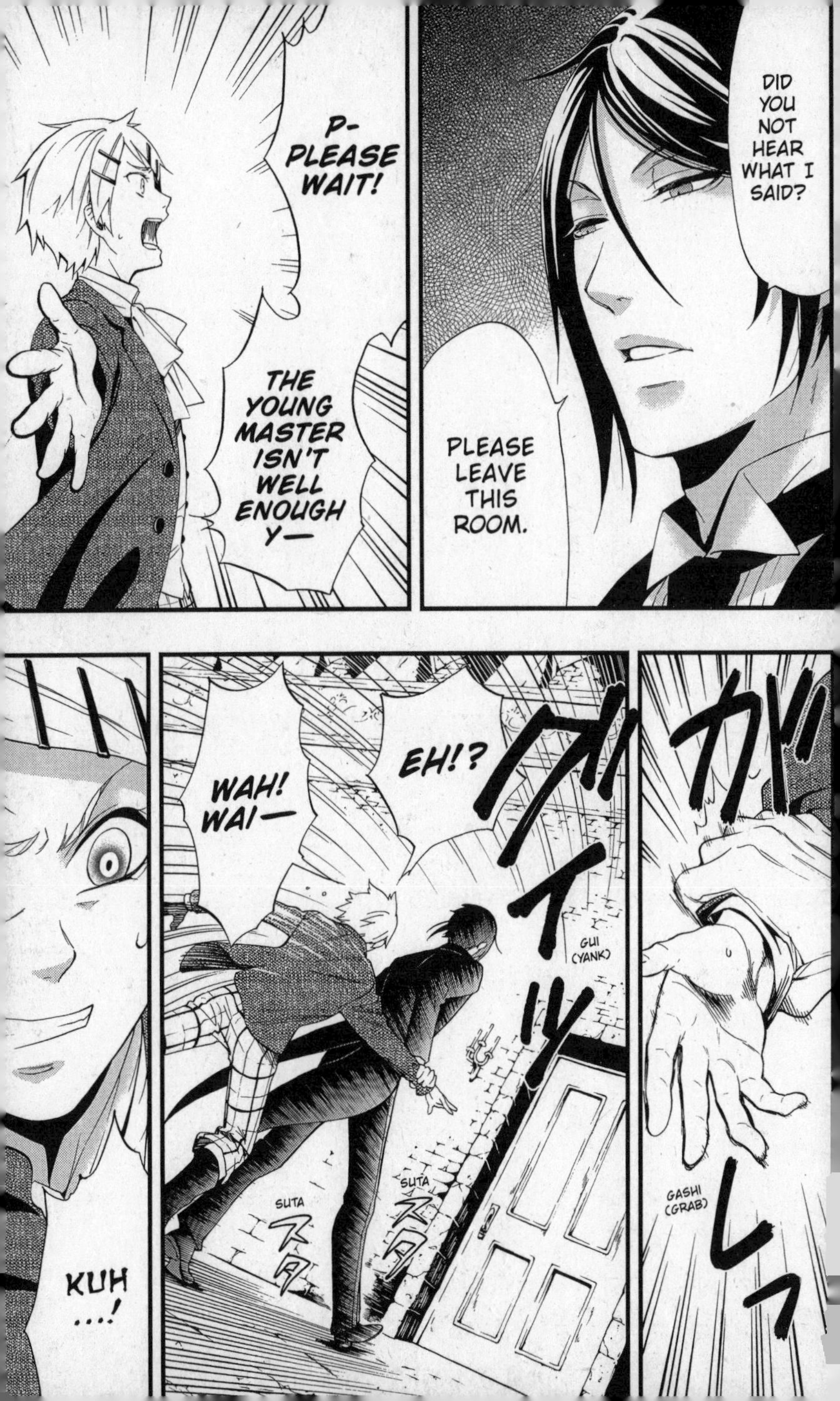
DID YOU NOT HEAR WHAT I SAID?
PLEASE LEAVE THIS ROOM.
P-PLEASE WAIT!
THE YOUNG MASTER ISN'T WELL ENOUGH Y—
ガシッ
GASHI (GRAB)
グイッ
GUI (YANK)
EH!?
WAH! WAI—
スタ
SUTA
スタ
SUTA
KUH ...!

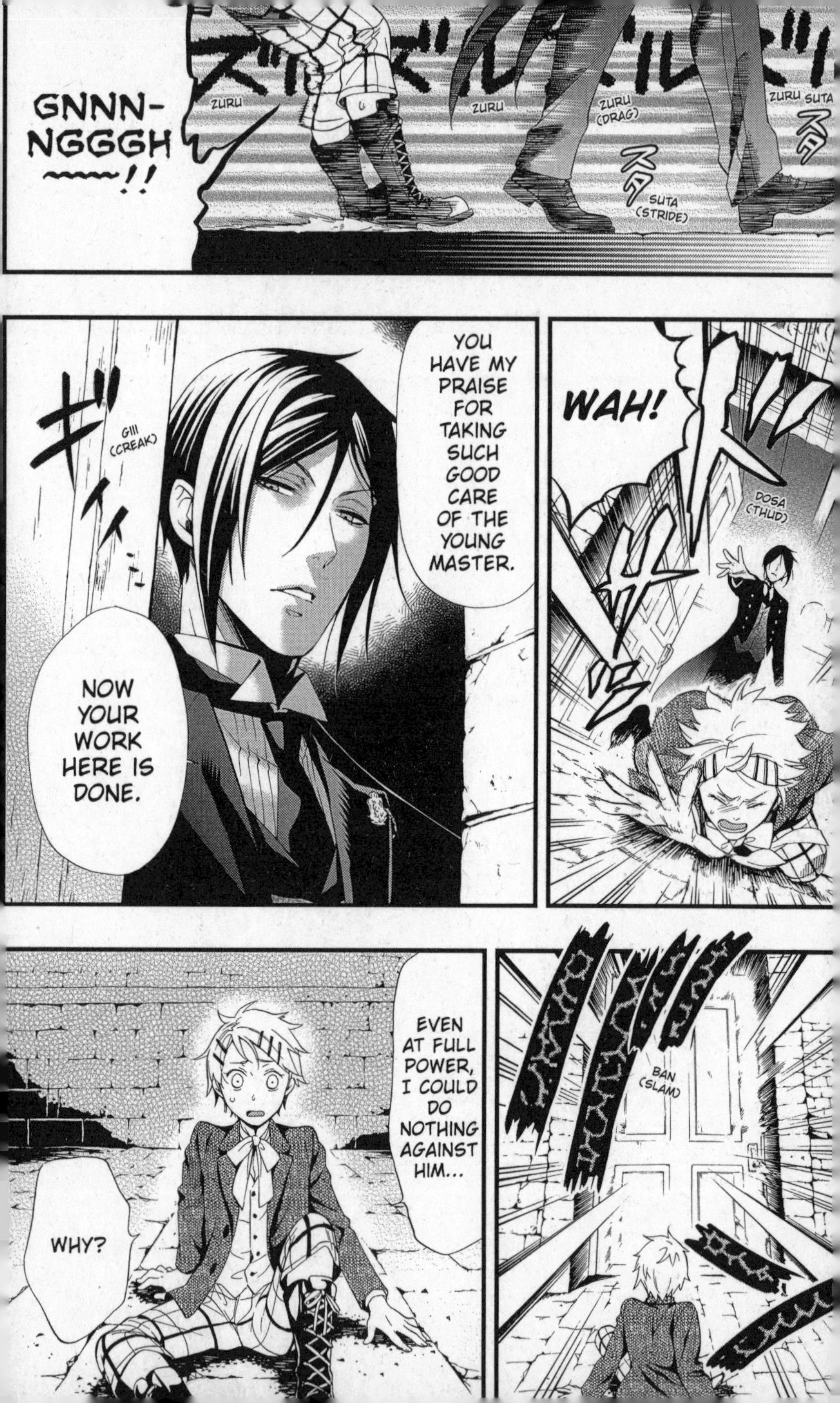
ZURU
SUTA
SUTA (STRIDE)
ZURU (DRAG)
ZURU
ZURU
GNNN-NGGGH~~~!!
WAH!
DOSA (THUD)
YOU HAVE MY PRAISE FOR TAKING SUCH GOOD CARE OF THE YOUNG MASTER.
GIII (CREAK)
NOW YOUR WORK HERE IS DONE.
BAN (SLAM)
EVEN AT FULL POWER, I COULD DO NOTHING AGAINST HIM...
WHY?

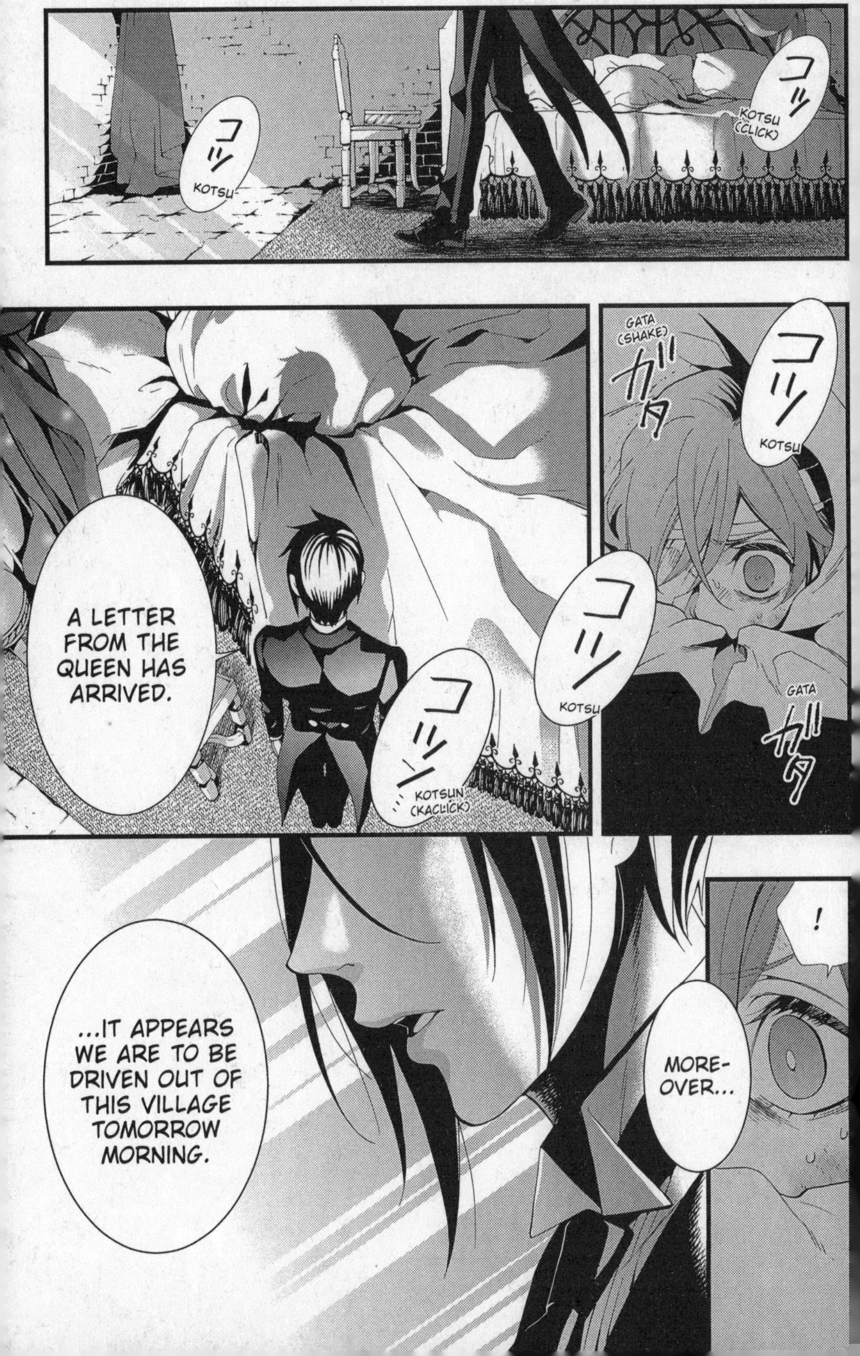
コッ
KOTSU (CLICK)
コッ
KOTSU
ガタ
GATA (SHAKE)
コッ
KOTSU
ガタ
GATA
コッ
KOTSU
コツン
KOTSUN (KACLICK)
A LETTER FROM THE QUEEN HAS ARRIVED.
!
MORE-OVER...
...IT APPEARS WE ARE TO BE DRIVEN OUT OF THIS VILLAGE TOMORROW MORNING.

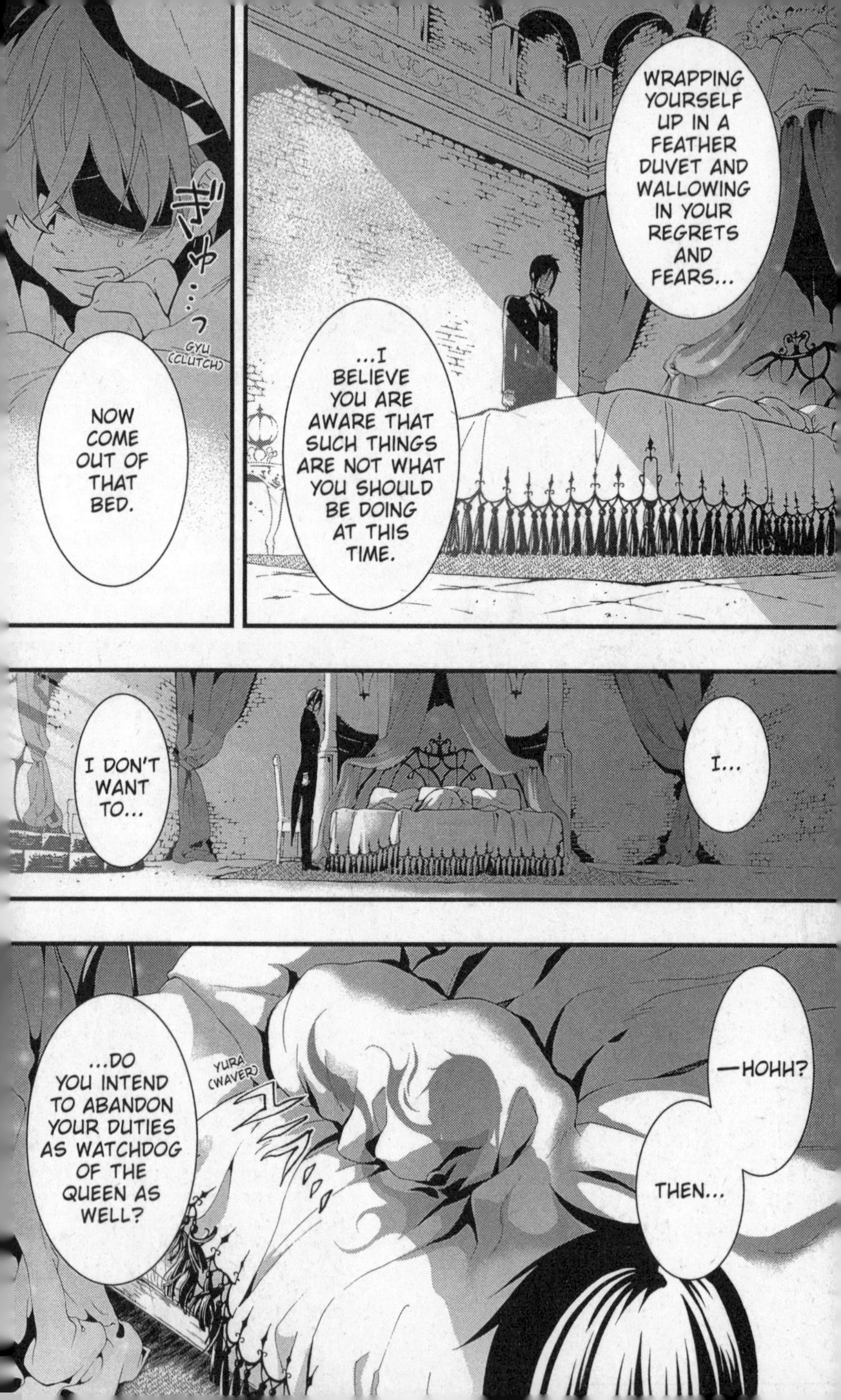
WRAPPING YOURSELF UP IN A FEATHER DUVET AND WALLOWING IN YOUR REGRETS AND FEARS...
...I BELIEVE YOU ARE AWARE THAT SUCH THINGS ARE NOT WHAT YOU SHOULD BE DOING AT THIS TIME.
ギュ…っ
GYU (CLUTCH)
NOW COME OUT OF THAT BED.
I...
I DON'T WANT TO...
—HOHH?
THEN...
YURA (WAVER)
...DO YOU INTEND TO ABANDON YOUR DUTIES AS WATCHDOG OF THE QUEEN AS WELL?

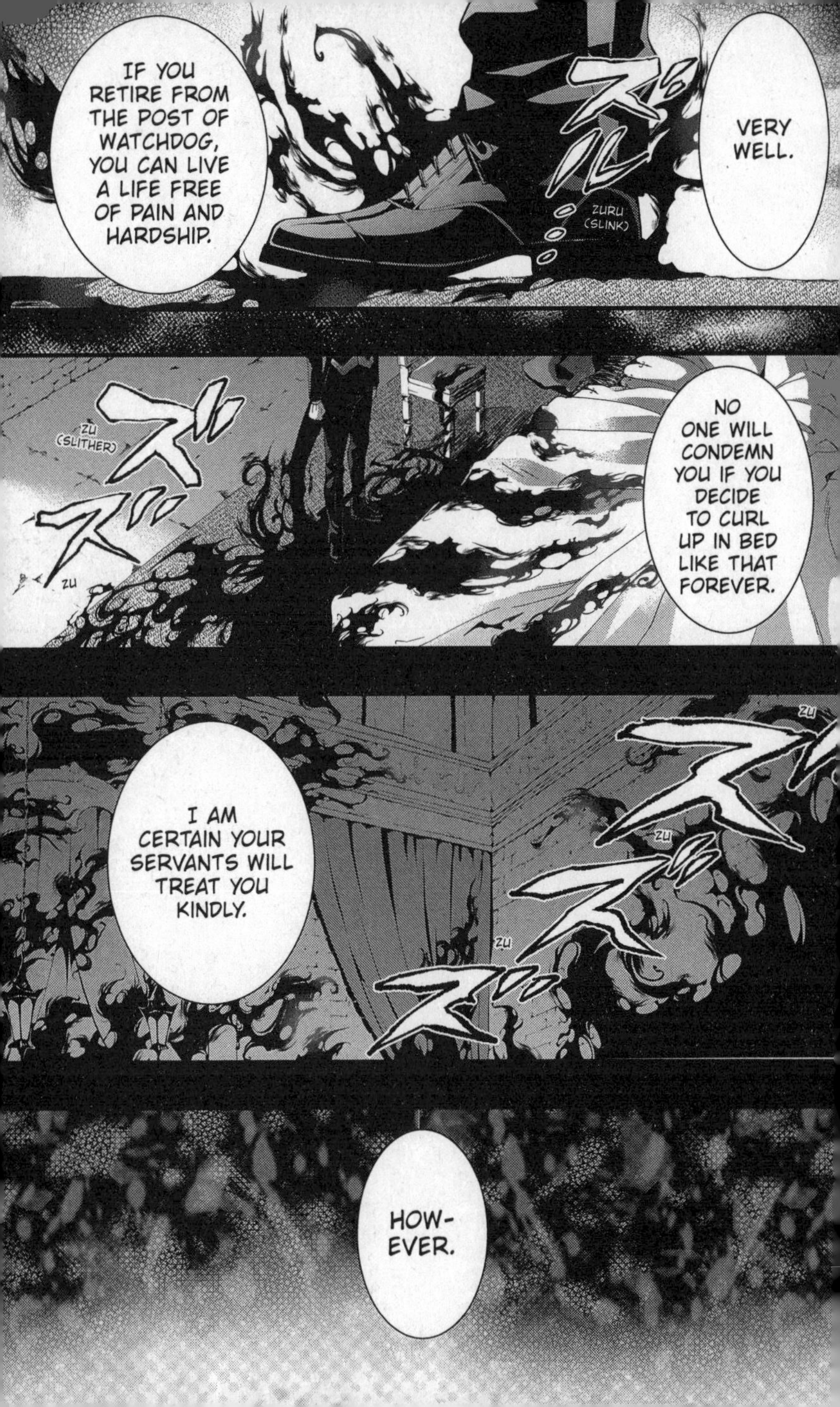
VERY WELL.
ZURU (SLINK)
IF YOU RETIRE FROM THE POST OF WATCHDOG, YOU CAN LIVE A LIFE FREE OF PAIN AND HARDSHIP.
NO ONE WILL CONDEMN YOU IF YOU DECIDE TO CURL UP IN BED LIKE THAT FOREVER.
ZU (SLITHER)
ZU
ZU
ZU
ZU
I AM CERTAIN YOUR SERVANTS WILL TREAT YOU KINDLY.
HOW-EVER.

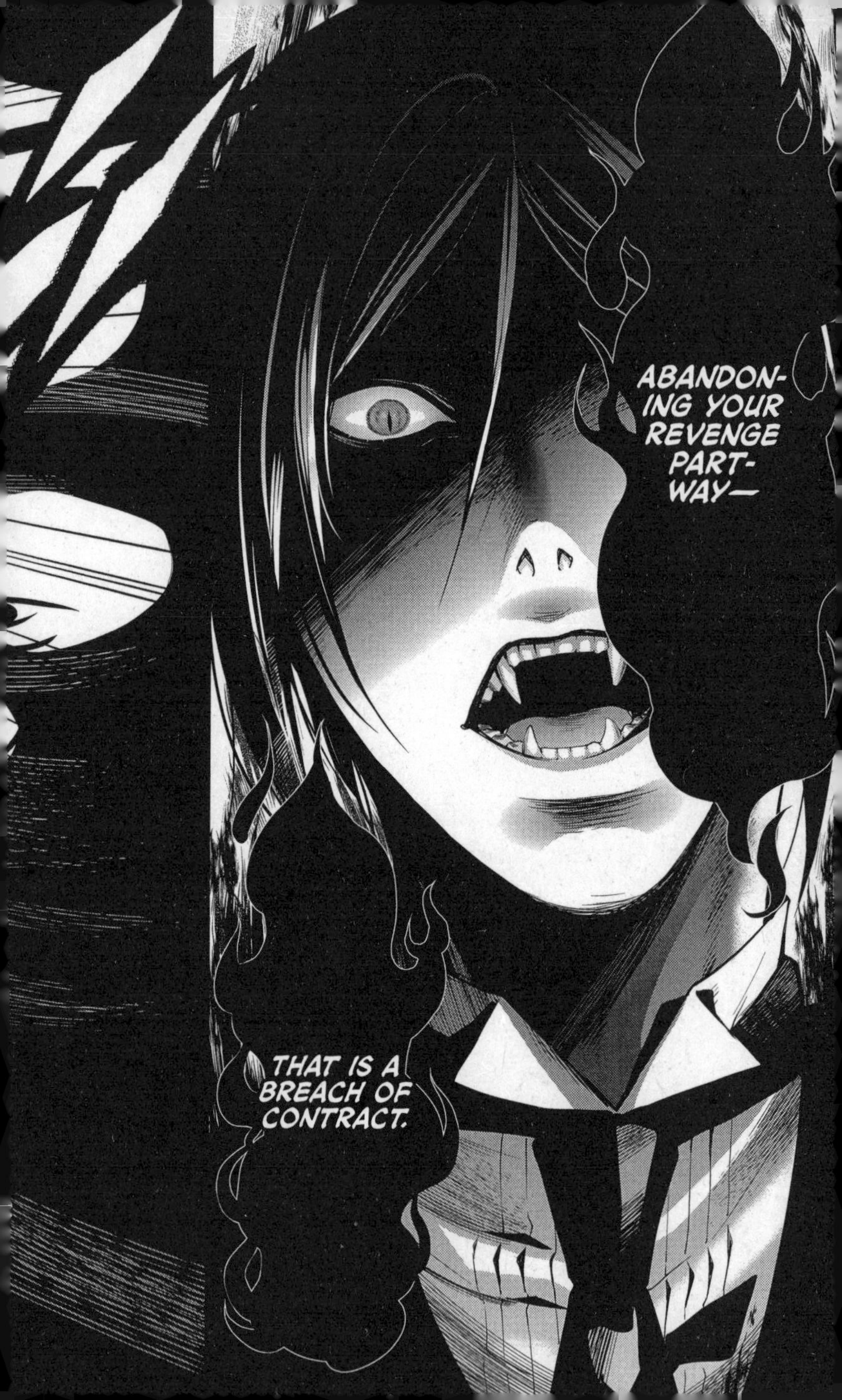
ABANDONING YOUR REVENGE PARTWAY—
THAT IS A BREACH OF CONTRACT.

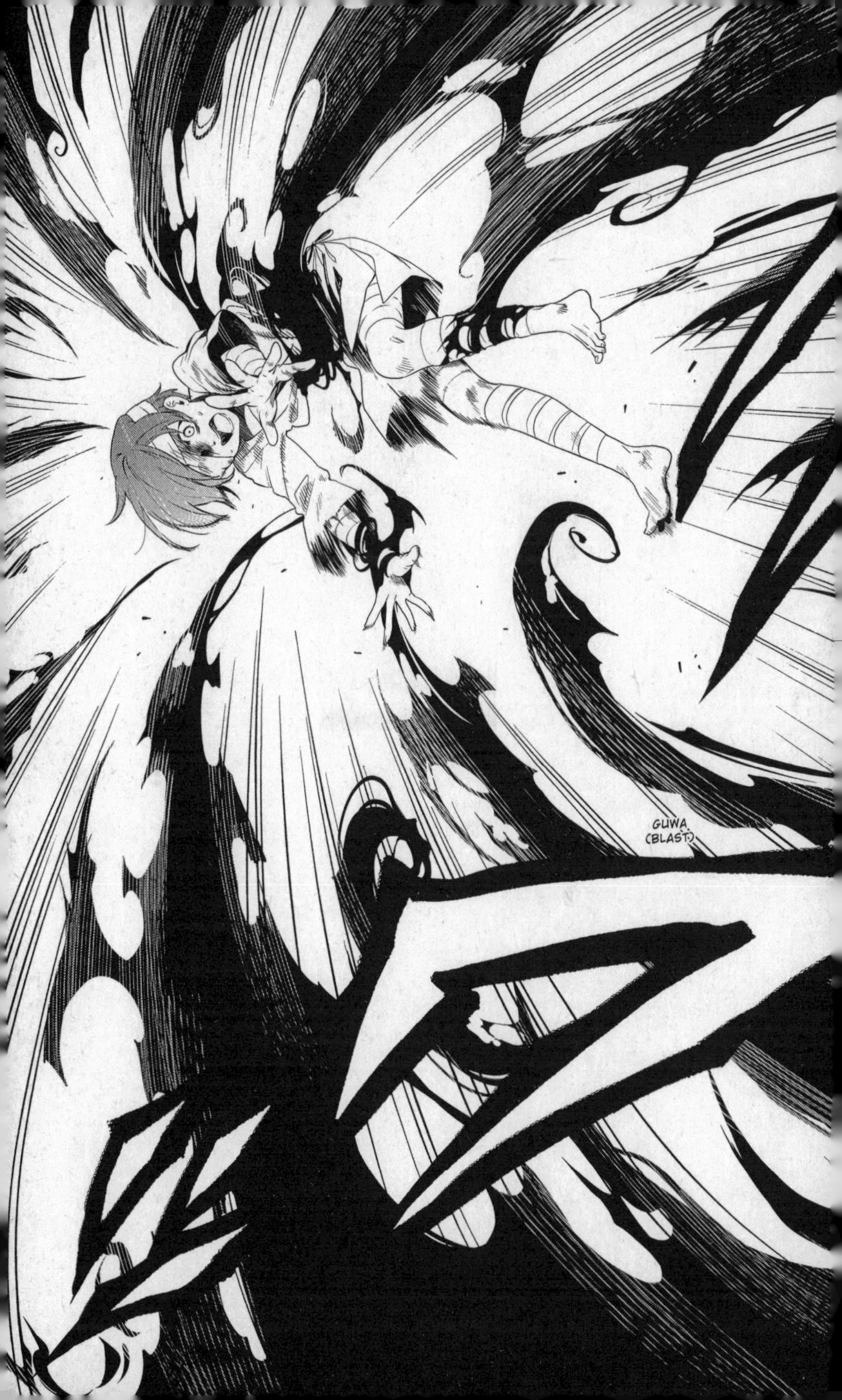
GUWA
(BLAST)

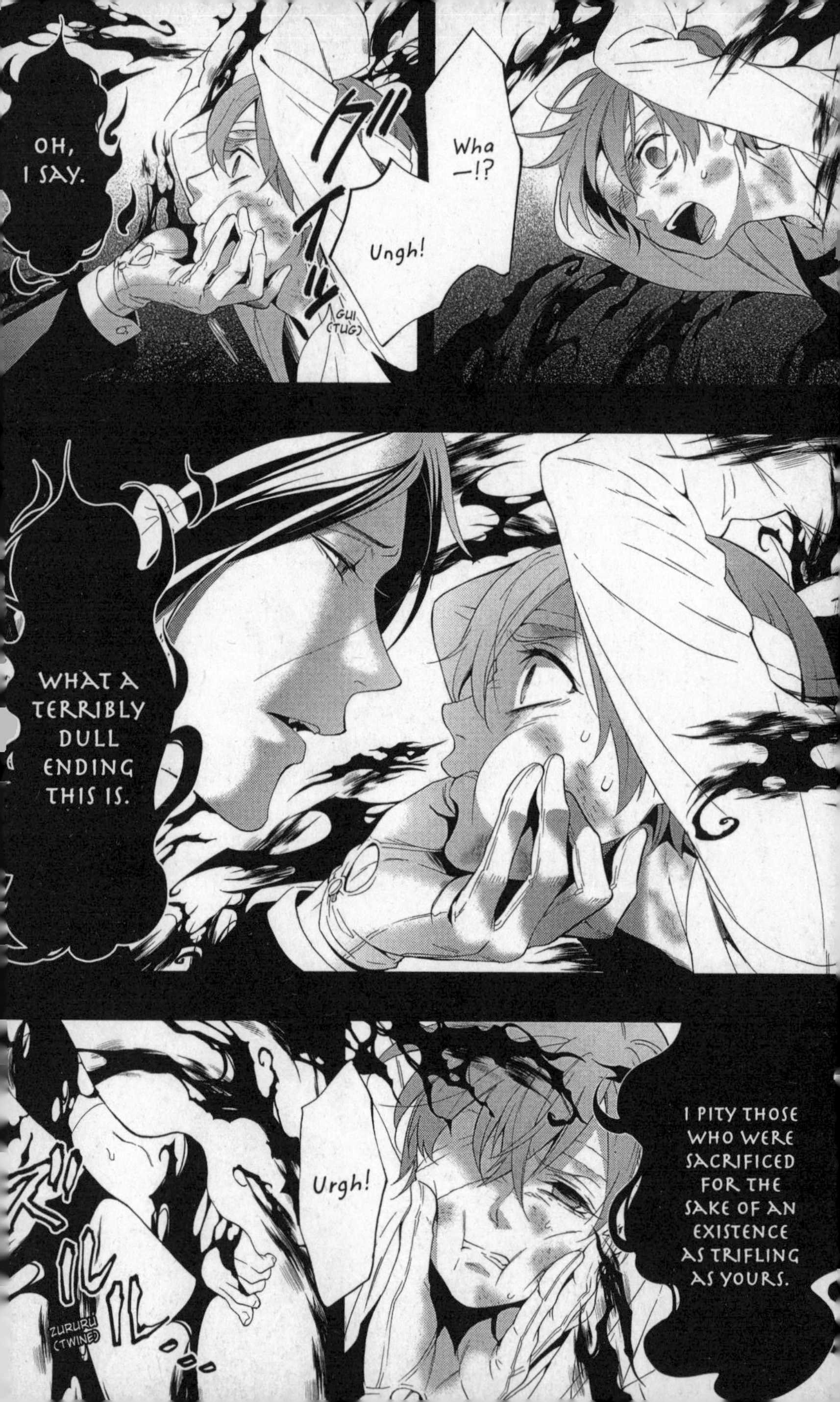
Wha—!?
Ungh!
OH, I SAY.
GUI (TUG)
WHAT A TERRIBLY DULL ENDING THIS IS.
I PITY THOSE WHO WERE SACRIFICED FOR THE SAKE OF AN EXISTENCE AS TRIFLING AS YOURS.
Urgh!
ZURURU (TWINE)

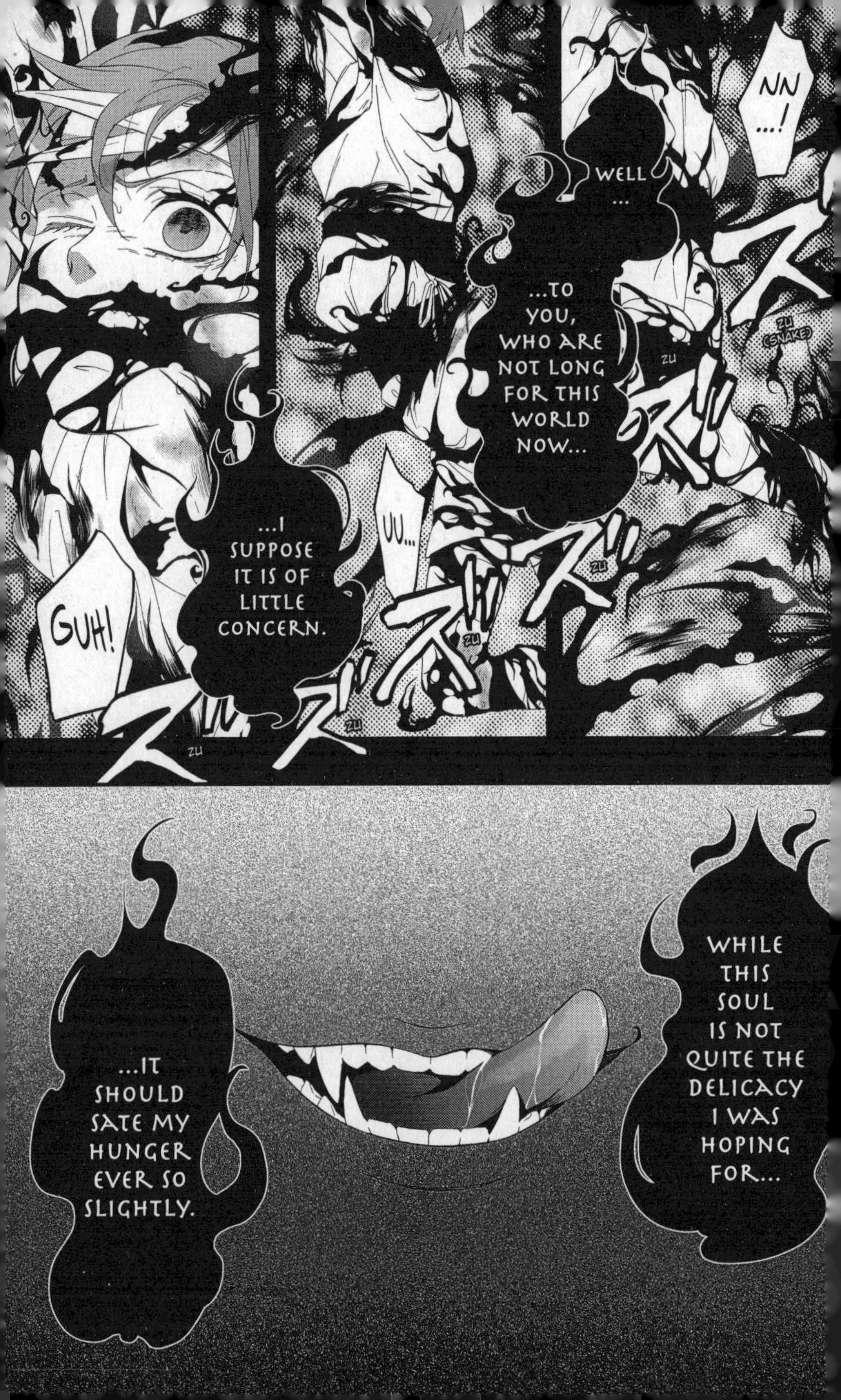
NN ...!
WELL ...
...TO YOU, WHO ARE NOT LONG FOR THIS WORLD NOW...
ZU (SNAKE)
ZU
UU...
ZU
ZU
...I SUPPOSE IT IS OF LITTLE CONCERN.
GUH!
ZU
ZU
WHILE THIS SOUL IS NOT QUITE THE DELICACY I WAS HOPING FOR...
...IT SHOULD SATE MY HUNGER EVER SO SLIGHTLY.

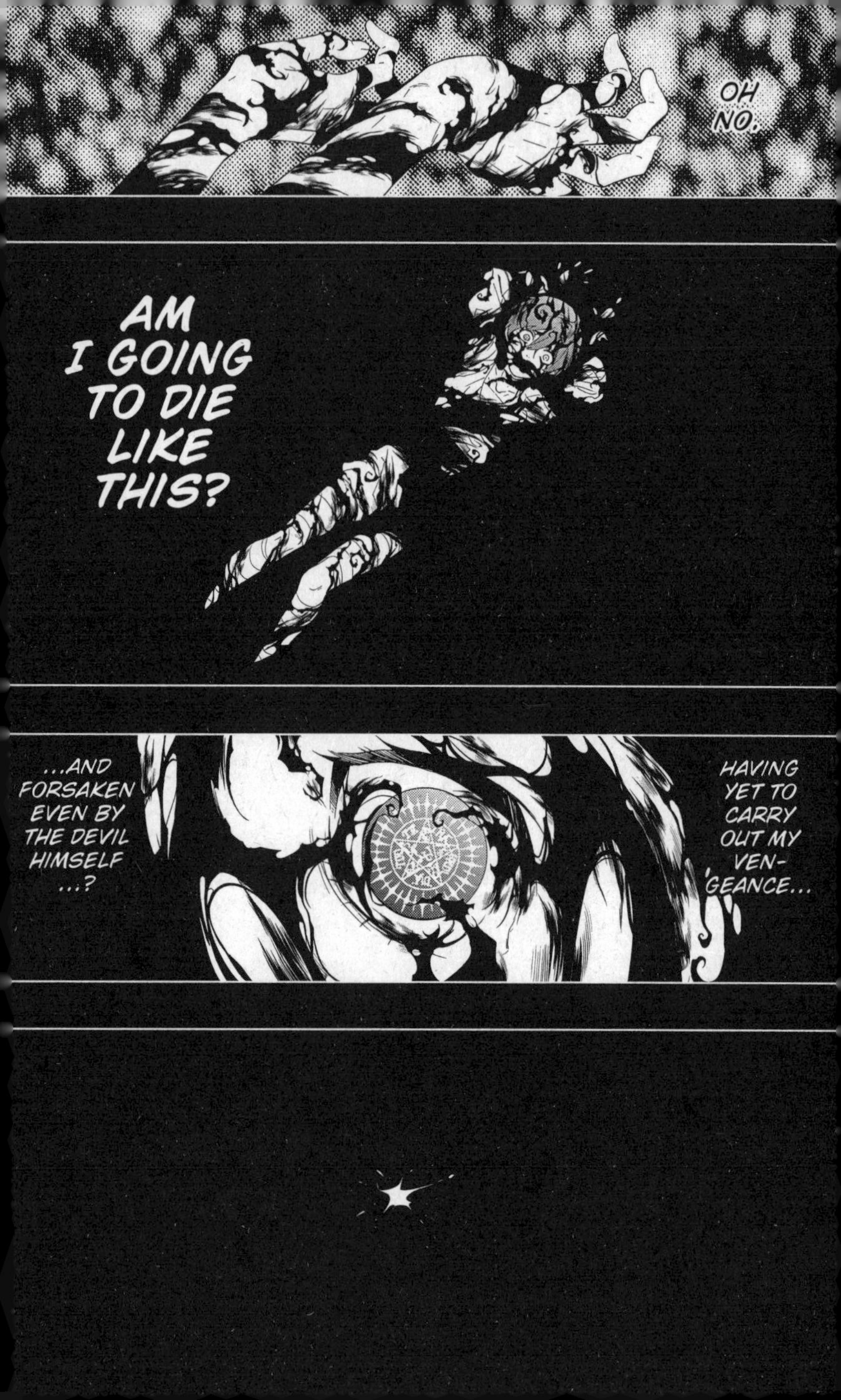
OH NO.
AM I GOING TO DIE LIKE THIS?
HAVING YET TO CARRY OUT MY VEN-GEANCE...
...AND FORSAKEN EVEN BY THE DEVIL HIMSELF ...?

Black Butler

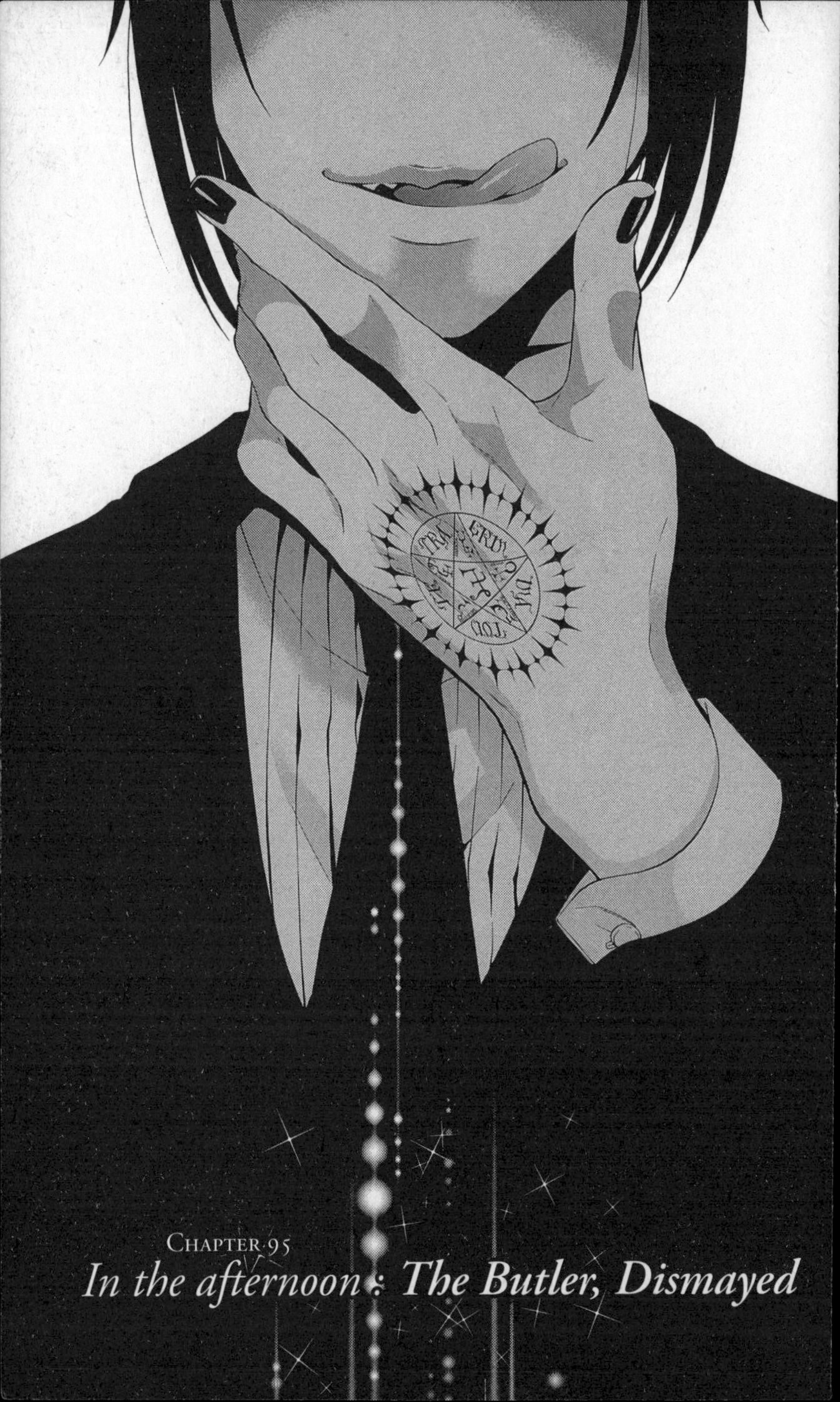
CHAPTER 95
In the afternoon: The Butler, Dismayed

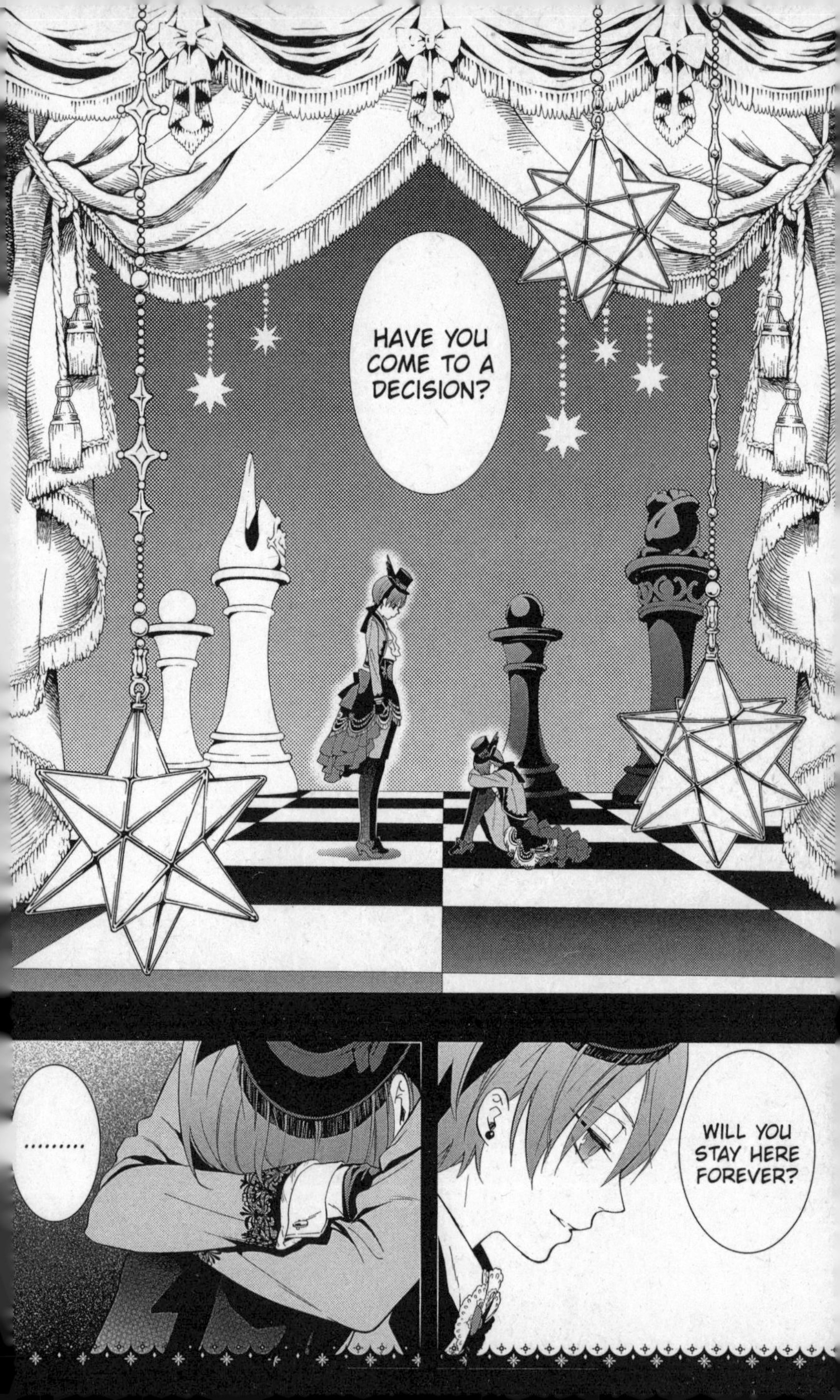
HAVE YOU COME TO A DECISION?
WILL YOU STAY HERE FOREVER?
....

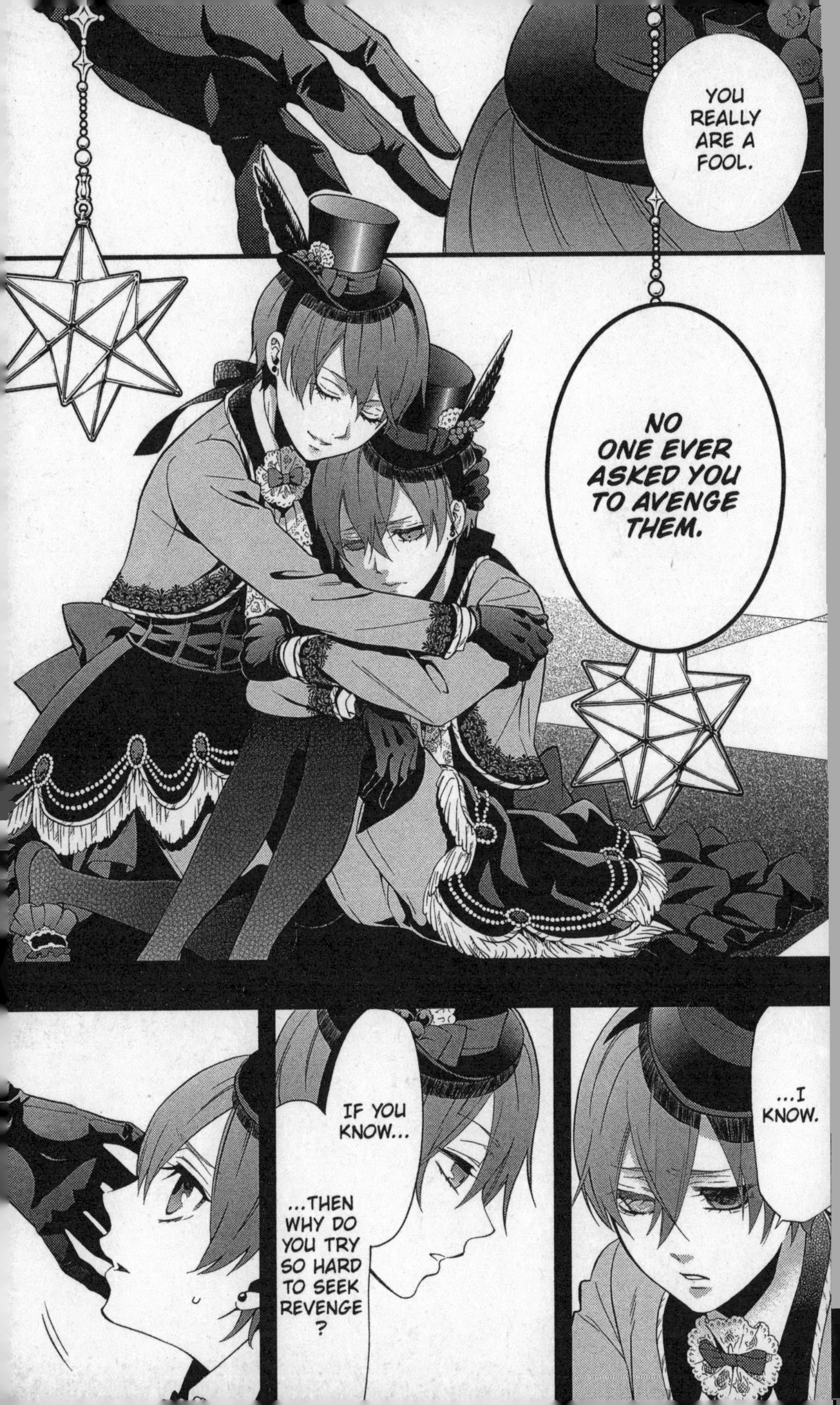
YOU REALLY ARE A FOOL.
NO ONE EVER ASKED YOU TO AVENGE THEM.
...I KNOW.
IF YOU KNOW...
...THEN WHY DO YOU TRY SO HARD TO SEEK REVENGE?

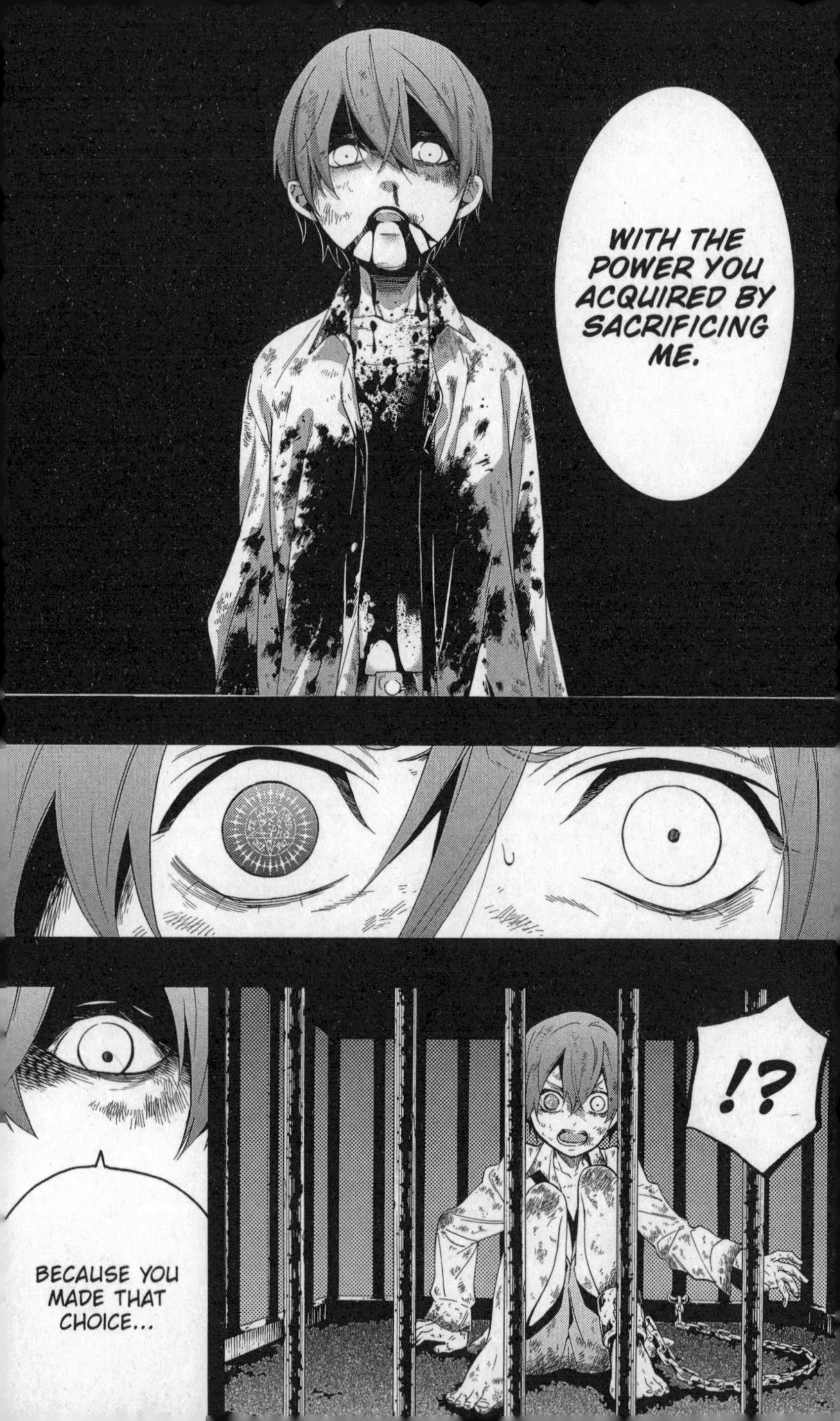
WITH THE POWER YOU ACQUIRED BY SACRIFICING ME.
!?
BECAUSE YOU MADE THAT CHOICE...

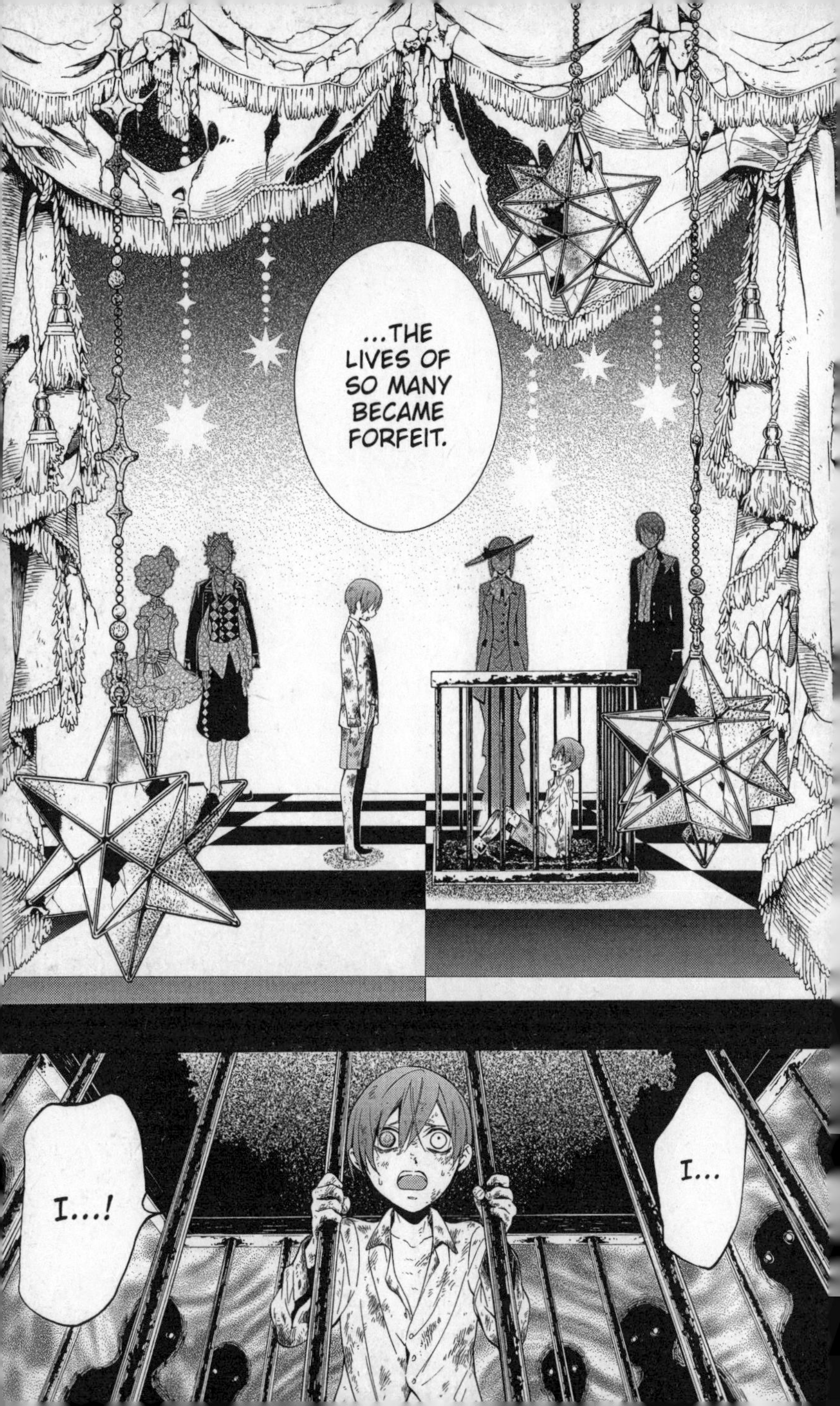
...THE LIVES OF SO MANY BECAME FORFEIT.
I...
I...!

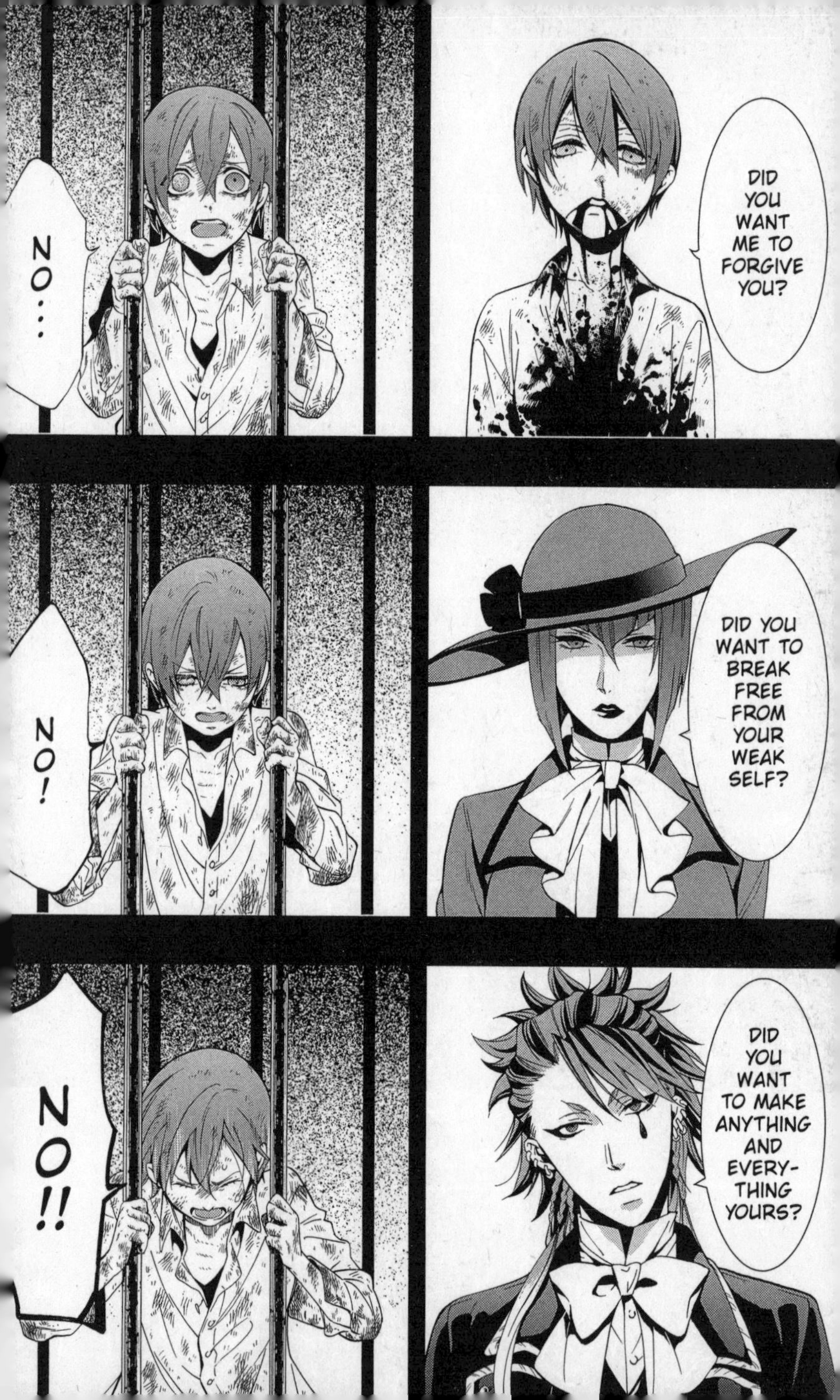
DID YOU WANT ME TO FORGIVE YOU?
NO...
DID YOU WANT TO BREAK FREE FROM YOUR WEAK SELF?
NO!
DID YOU WANT TO MAKE ANYTHING AND EVERY-THING YOURS?
NO!!

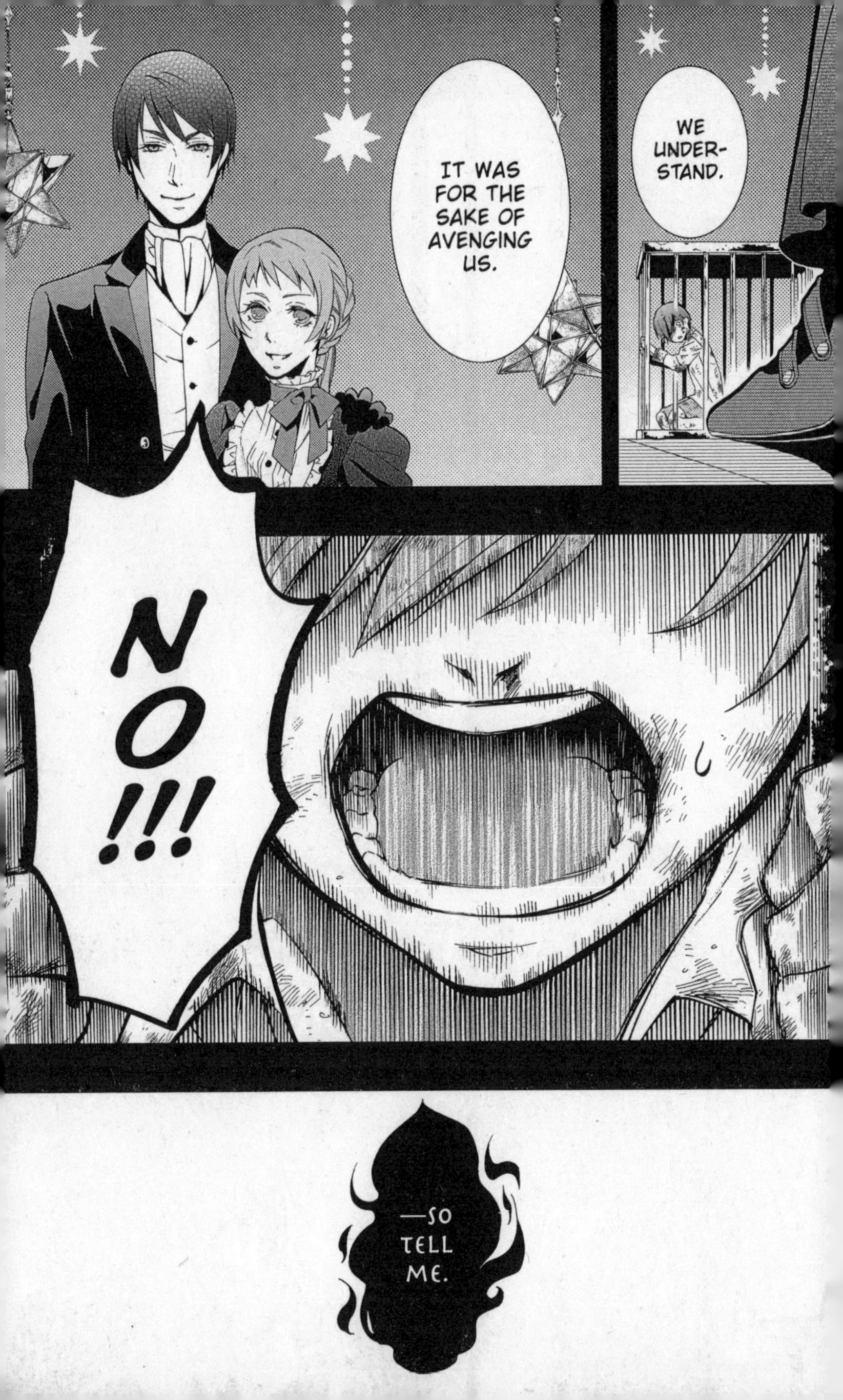
WE UNDER-STAND.
IT WAS FOR THE SAKE OF AVENGING US.
NO!!!
—SO TELL ME.

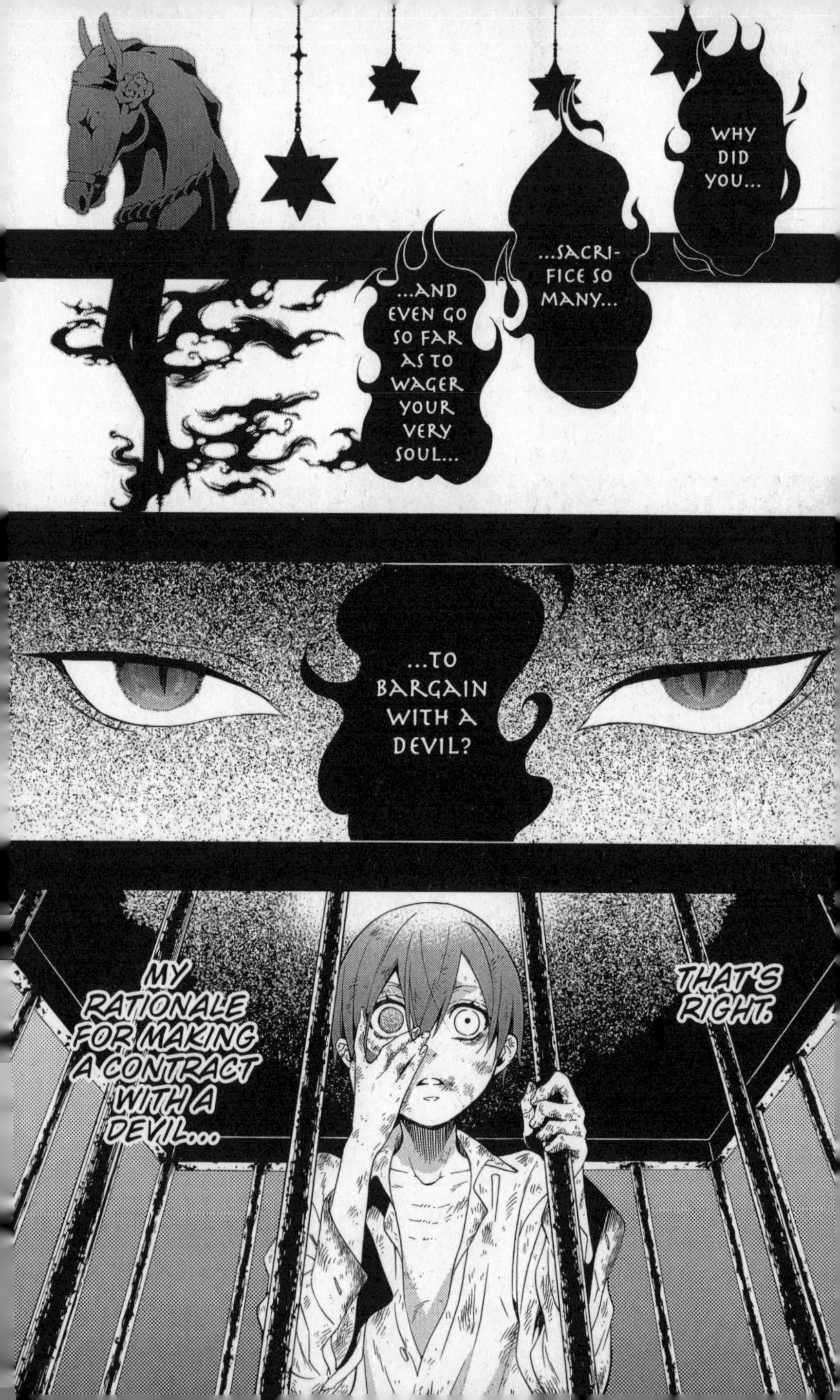
WHY DID YOU...
...SACRIFICE SO MANY...
...AND EVEN GO SO FAR AS TO WAGER YOUR VERY SOUL...
...TO BARGAIN WITH A DEVIL?
THAT'S RIGHT.
MY RATIONALE FOR MAKING A CONTRACT WITH A DEVIL...

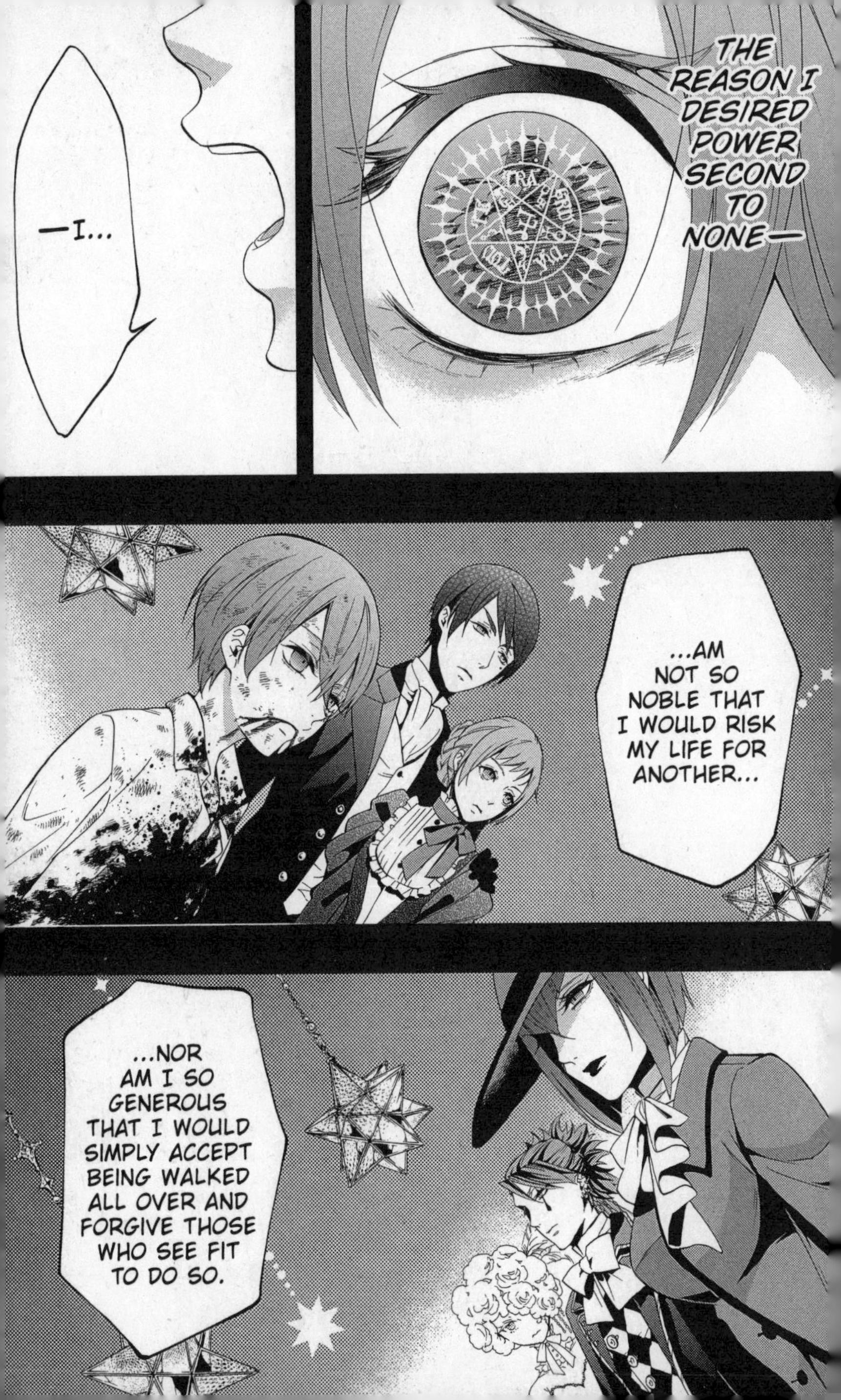
THE REASON I DESIRED POWER SECOND TO NONE—
—I...
...AM NOT SO NOBLE THAT I WOULD RISK MY LIFE FOR ANOTHER...
...NOR AM I SO GENEROUS THAT I WOULD SIMPLY ACCEPT BEING WALKED ALL OVER AND FORGIVE THOSE WHO SEE FIT TO DO SO.

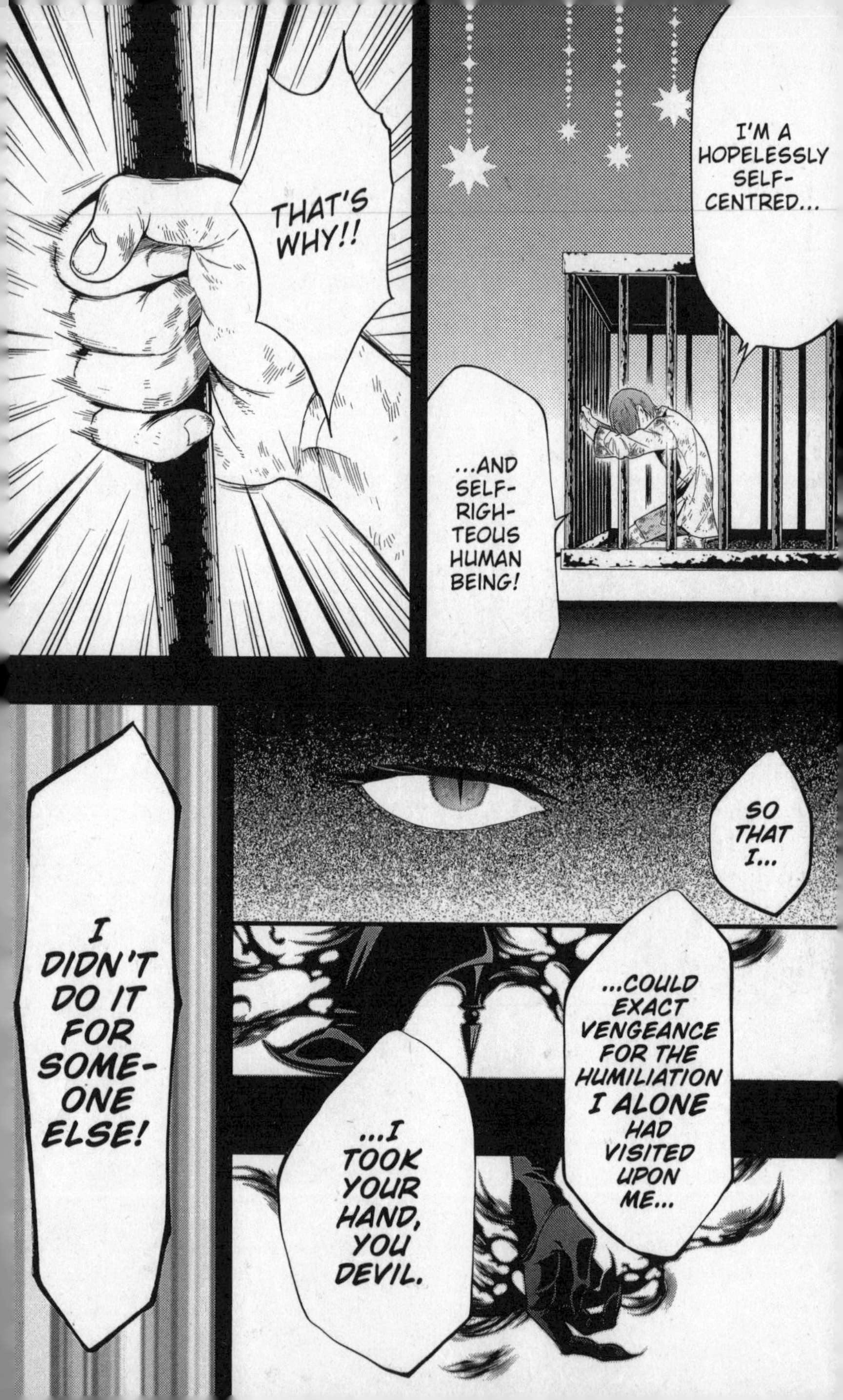
I'M A HOPELESSLY SELF-CENTRED...
...AND SELF-RIGHTEOUS HUMAN BEING!
THAT'S WHY!!
SO THAT I...
...COULD EXACT VENGEANCE FOR THE HUMILIATION I ALONE HAD VISITED UPON ME...
...I TOOK YOUR HAND, YOU DEVIL.
I DIDN'T DO IT FOR SOMEONE ELSE!

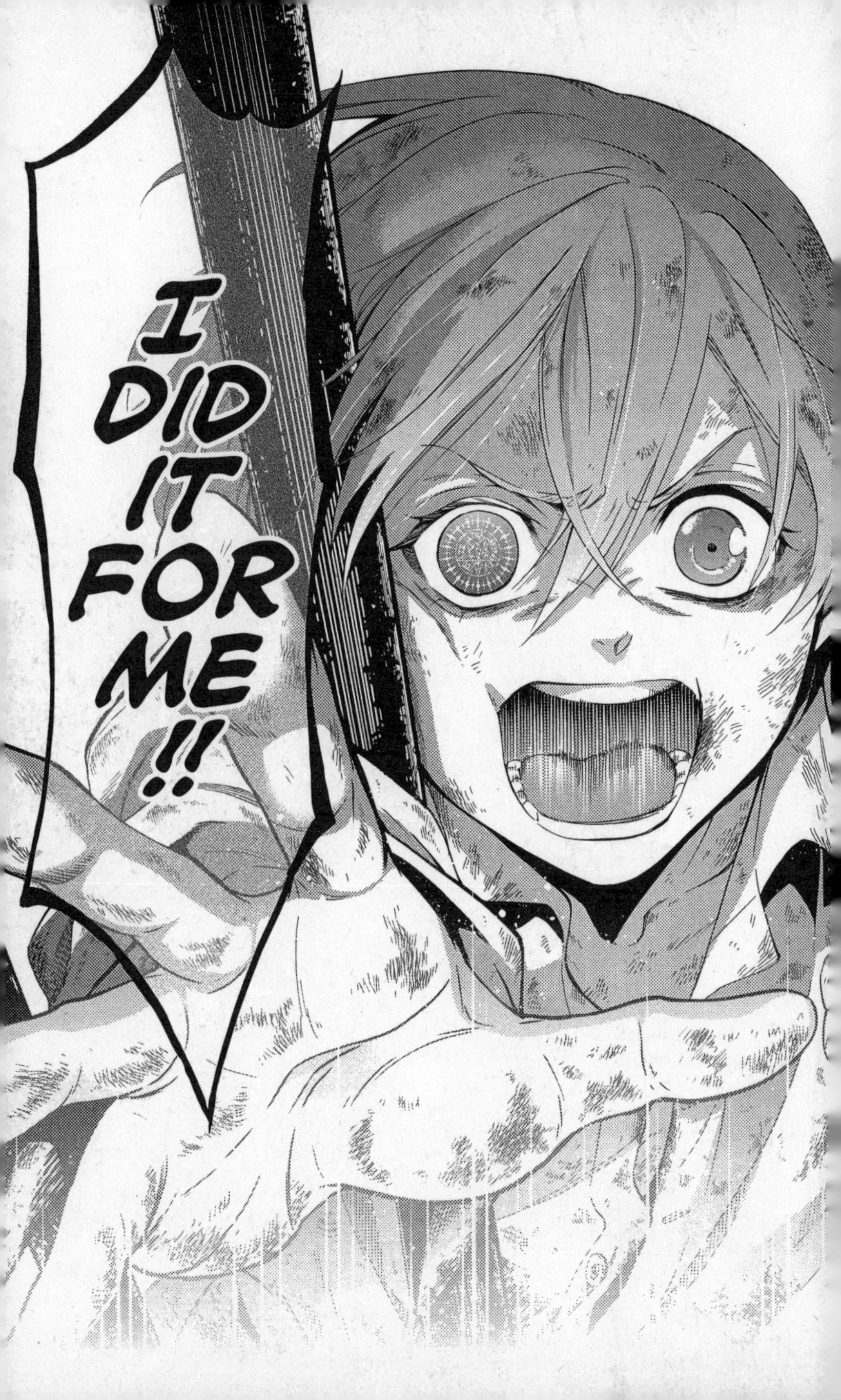
I DID IT FOR ME!!

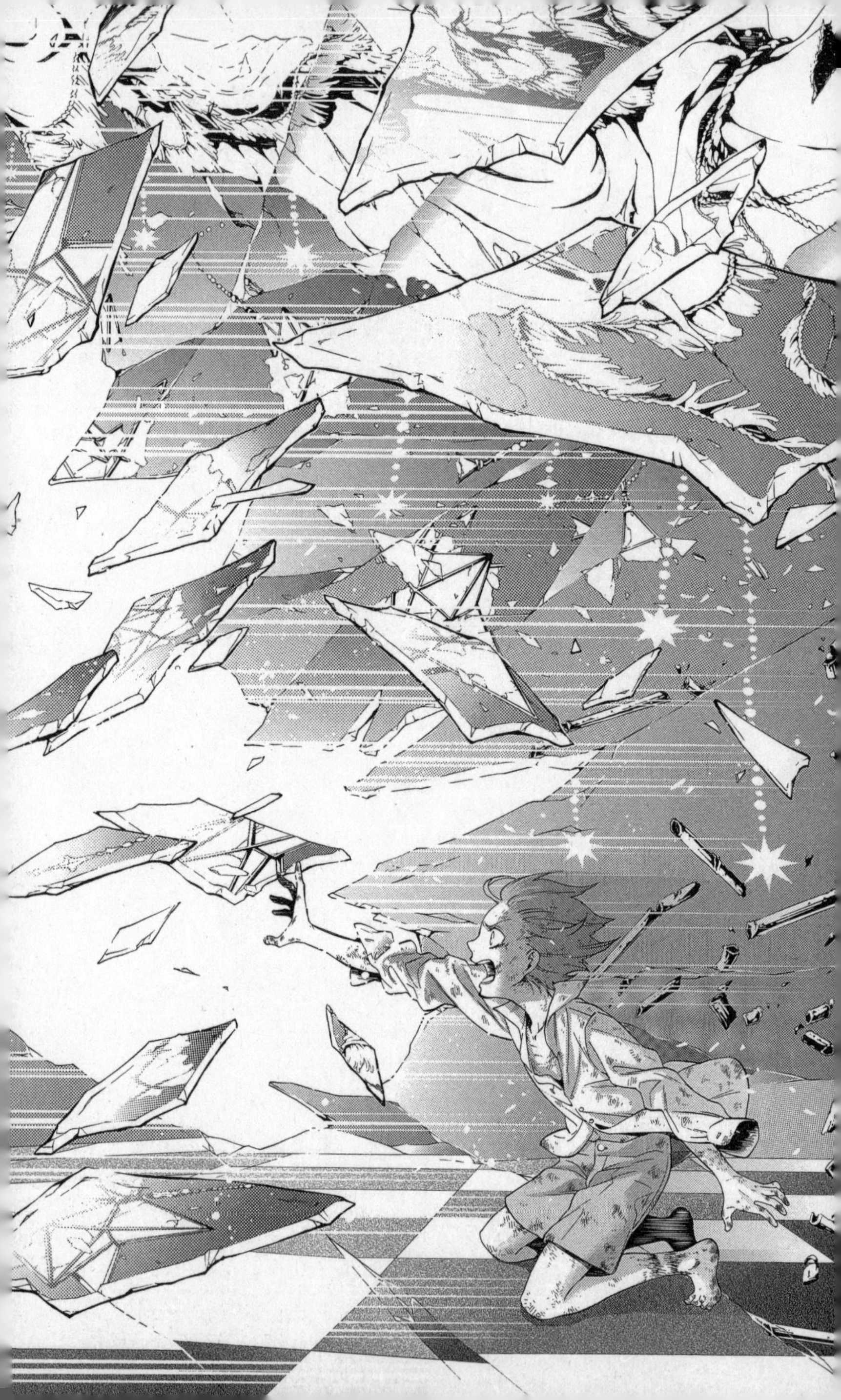

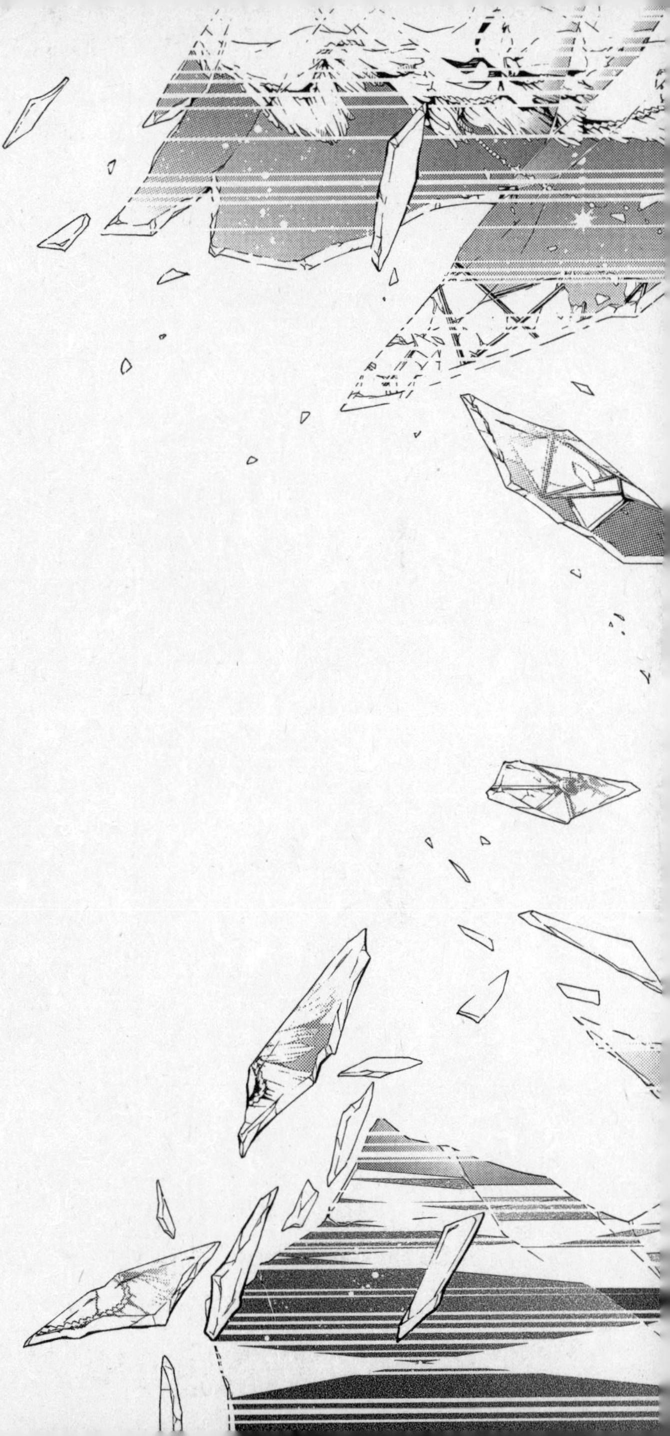

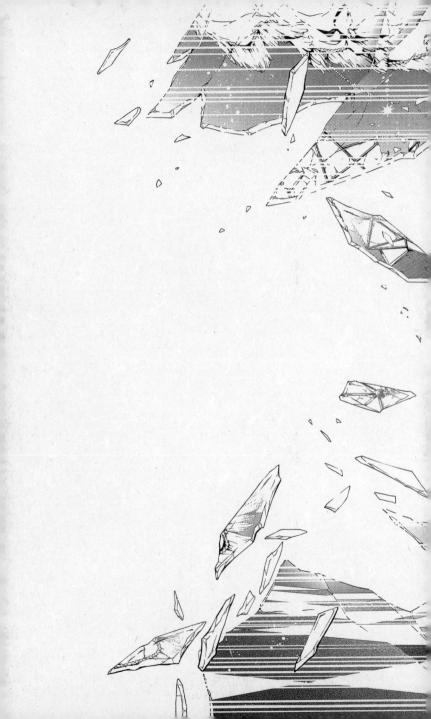

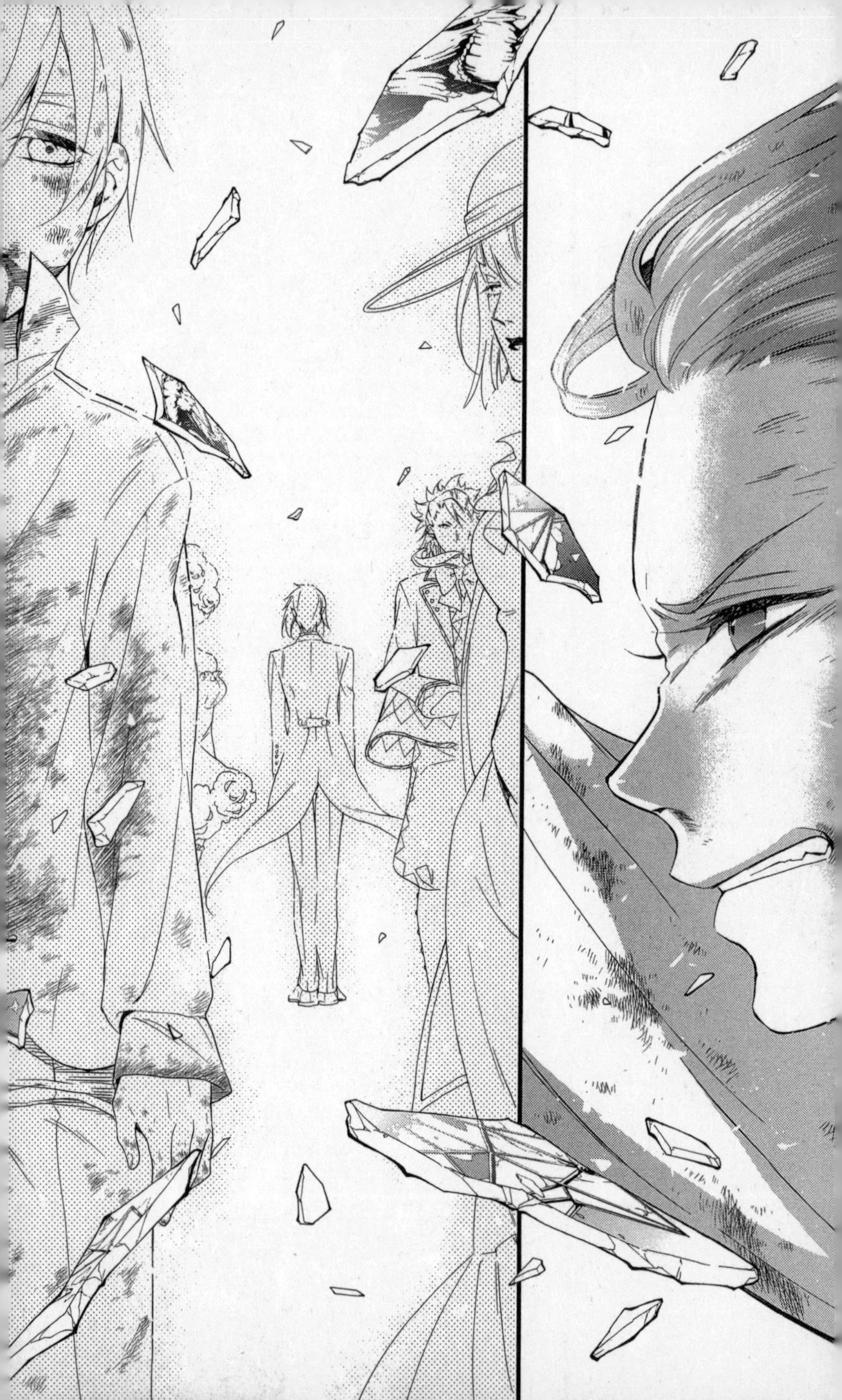

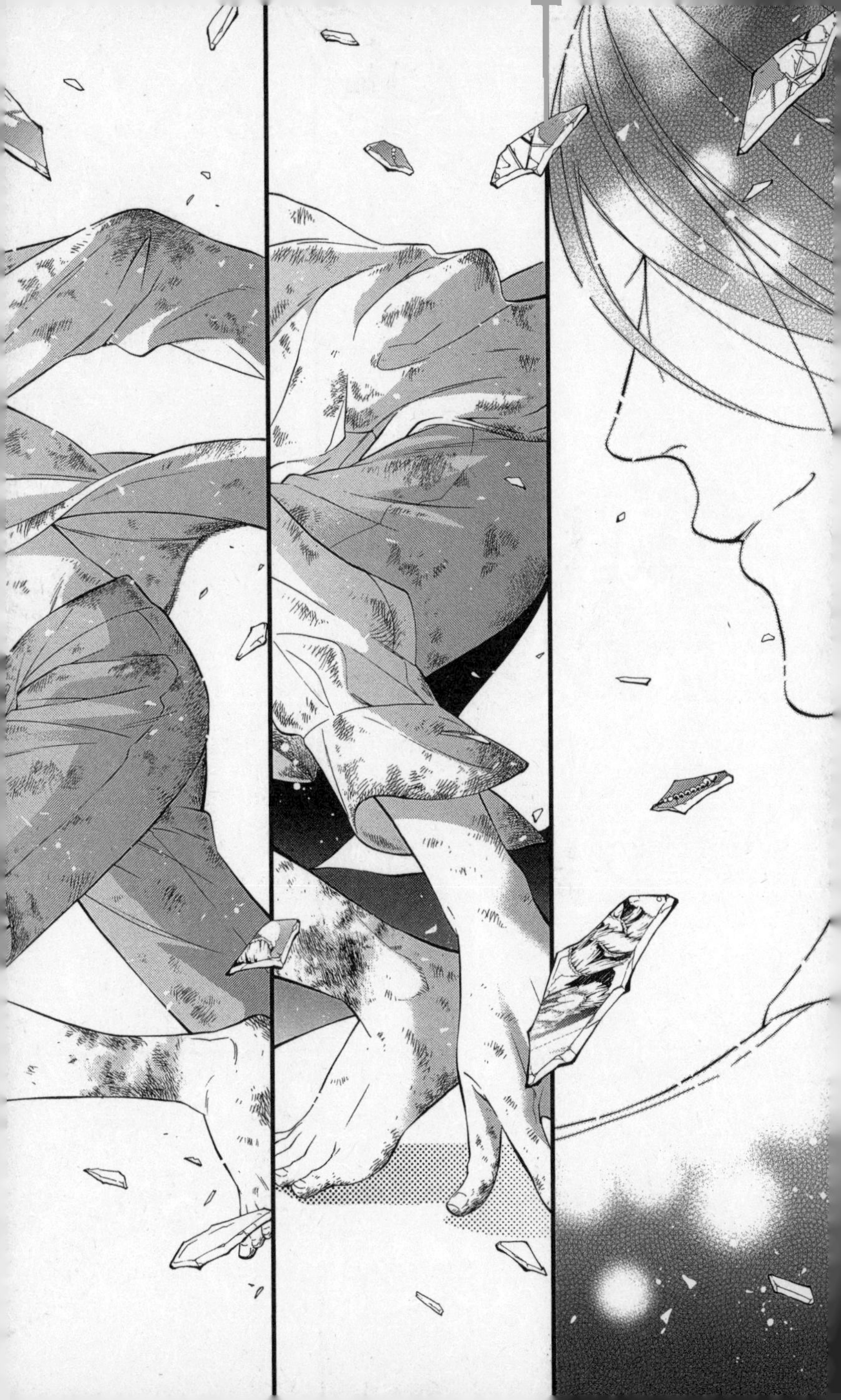

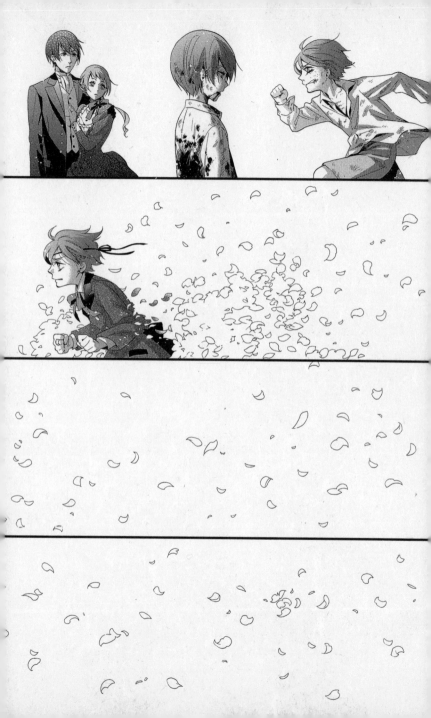

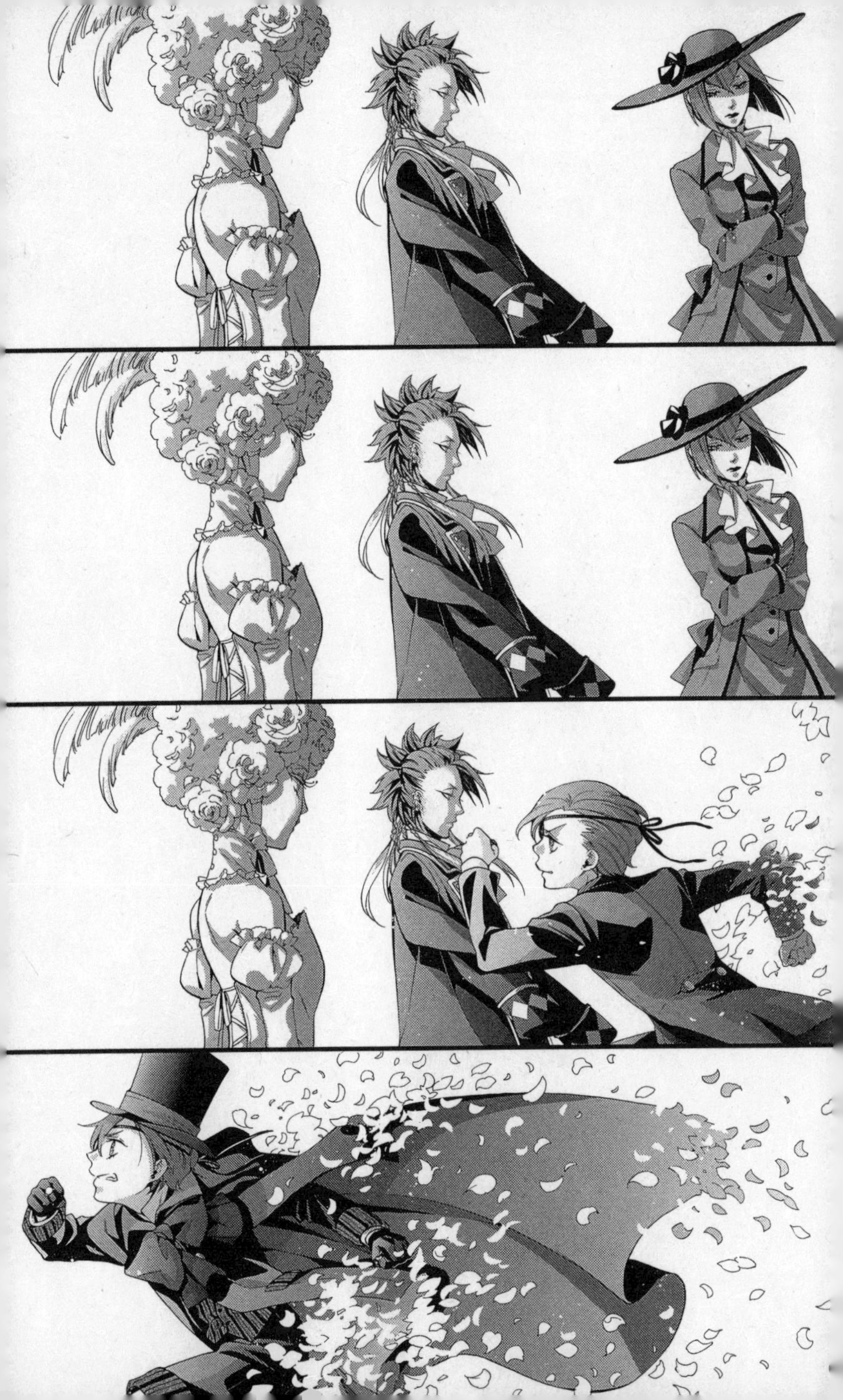

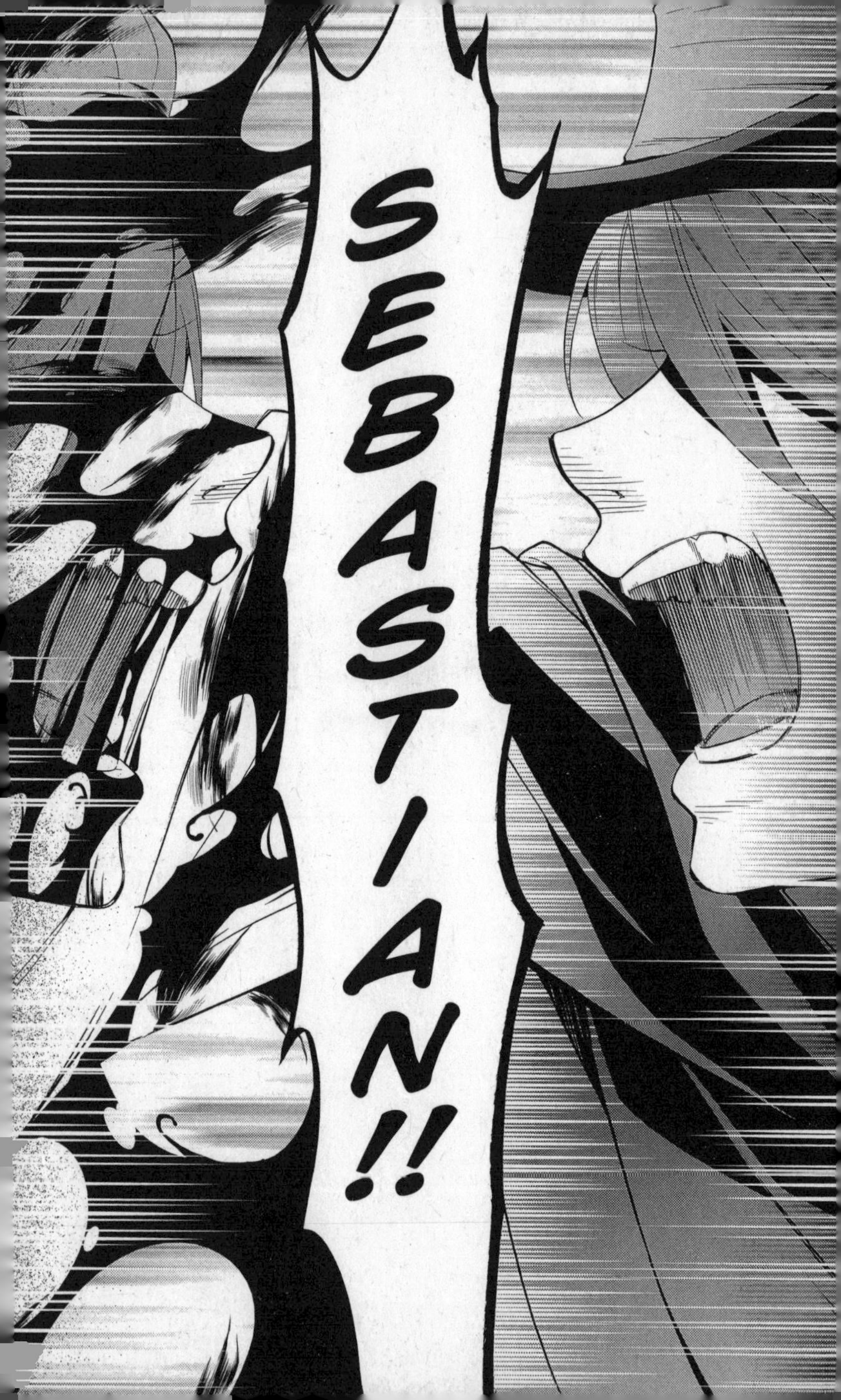
SEBASTIAN!!

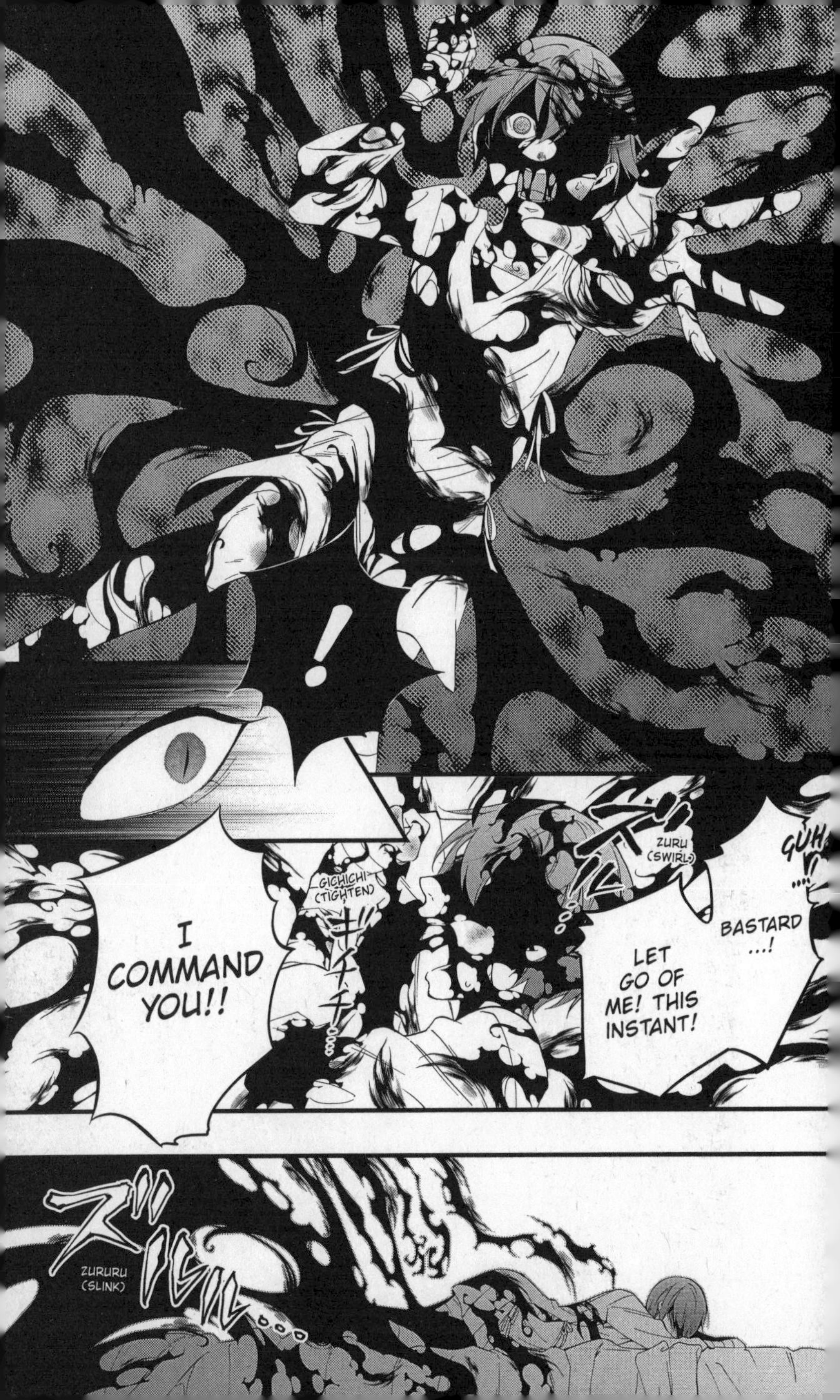
!
GUH ....!!
BASTARD ...!
ZURU (SWIRL)
LET GO OF ME! THIS INSTANT!
GICHICHI (TIGHTEN)
I COMMAND YOU!!
ZURURU (SLINK)

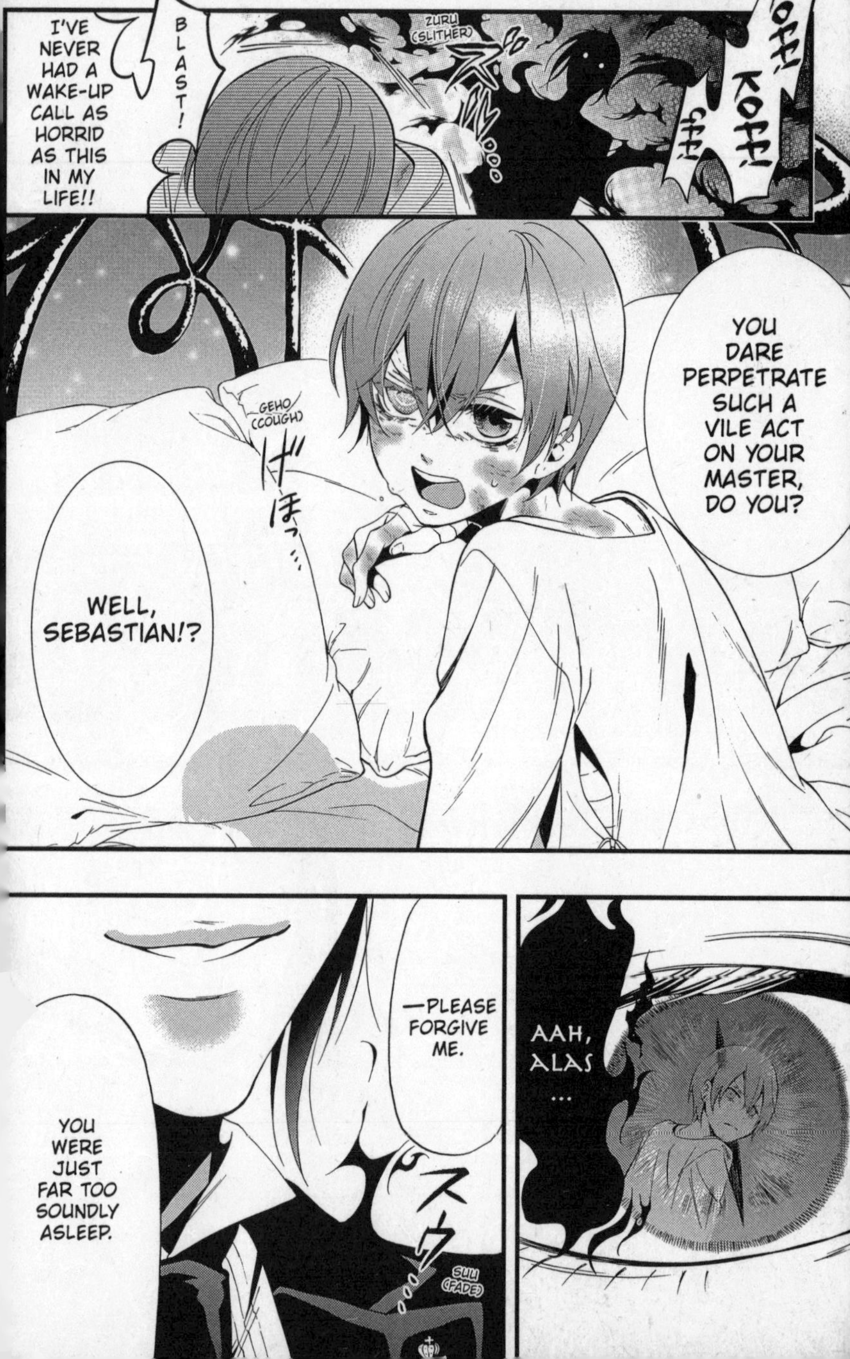
ZURU (SLITHER)
BLAST!
I'VE NEVER HAD A WAKE-UP CALL AS HORRID AS THIS IN MY LIFE!!
YOU DARE PERPETRATE SUCH A VILE ACT ON YOUR MASTER, DO YOU?
GEHO (COUGH)
WELL, SEBASTIAN!?
AAH, ALAS ...
—PLEASE FORGIVE ME.
SUU (FADE)
YOU WERE JUST FAR TOO SOUNDLY ASLEEP.

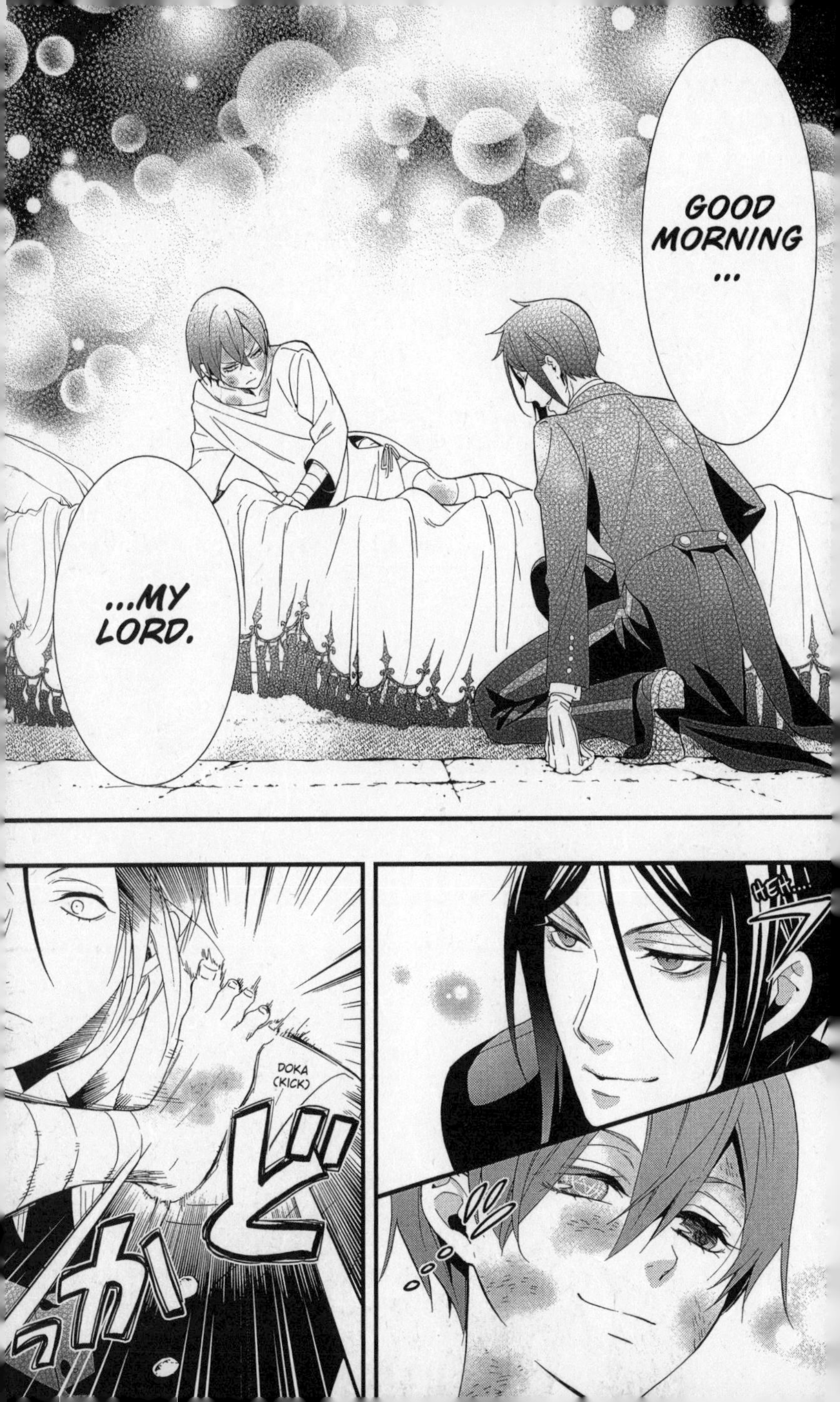
GOOD MORNING ...
...MY LORD.
HEH...
DOKA (KICK)

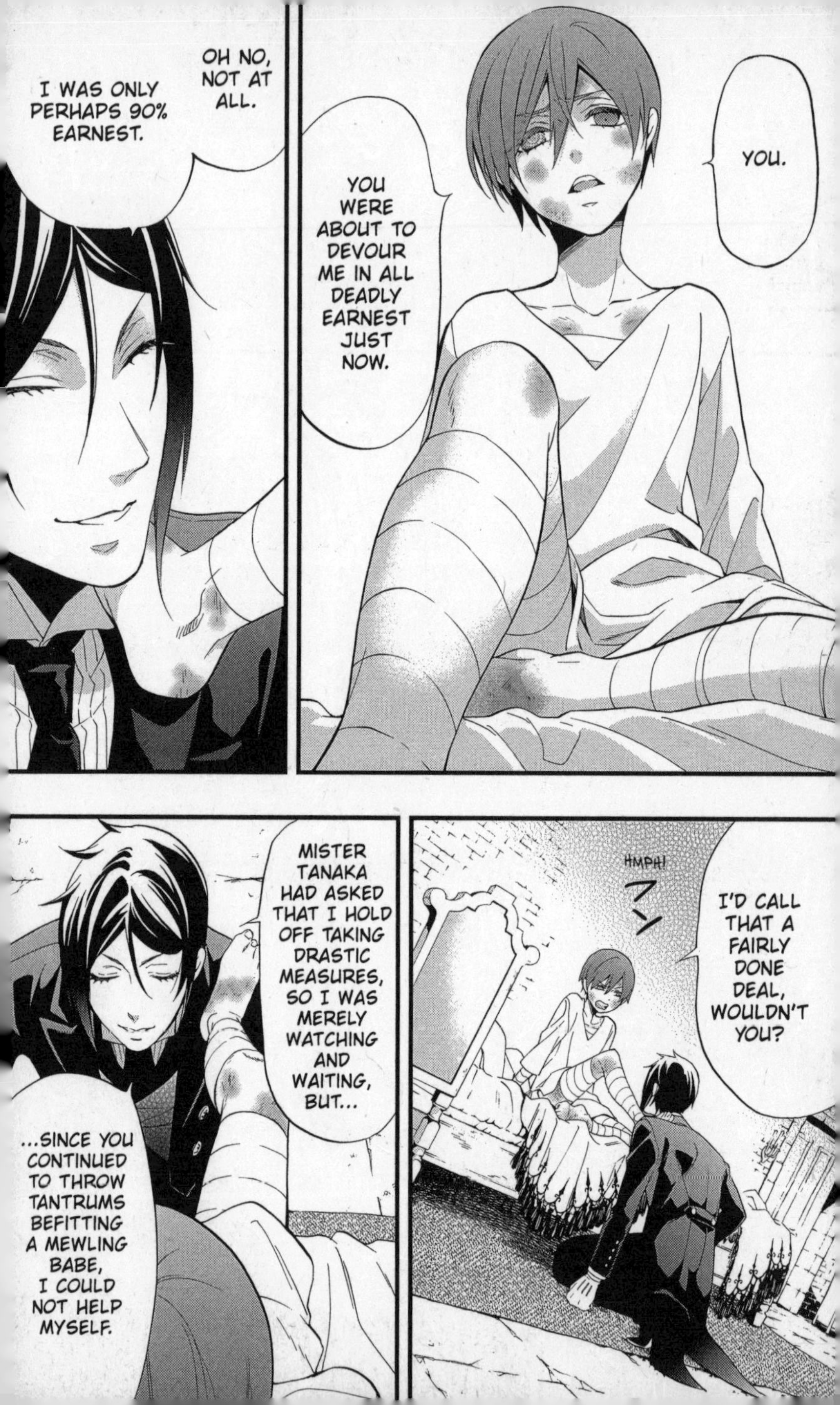
YOU.
YOU WERE ABOUT TO DEVOUR ME IN ALL DEADLY EARNEST JUST NOW.
OH NO, NOT AT ALL.
I WAS ONLY PERHAPS 90% EARNEST.
HMPH!
I'D CALL THAT A FAIRLY DONE DEAL, WOULDN'T YOU?
MISTER TANAKA HAD ASKED THAT I HOLD OFF TAKING DRASTIC MEASURES, SO I WAS MERELY WATCHING AND WAITING, BUT...
...SINCE YOU CONTINUED TO THROW TANTRUMS BEFITTING A MEWLING BABE, I COULD NOT HELP MYSELF.

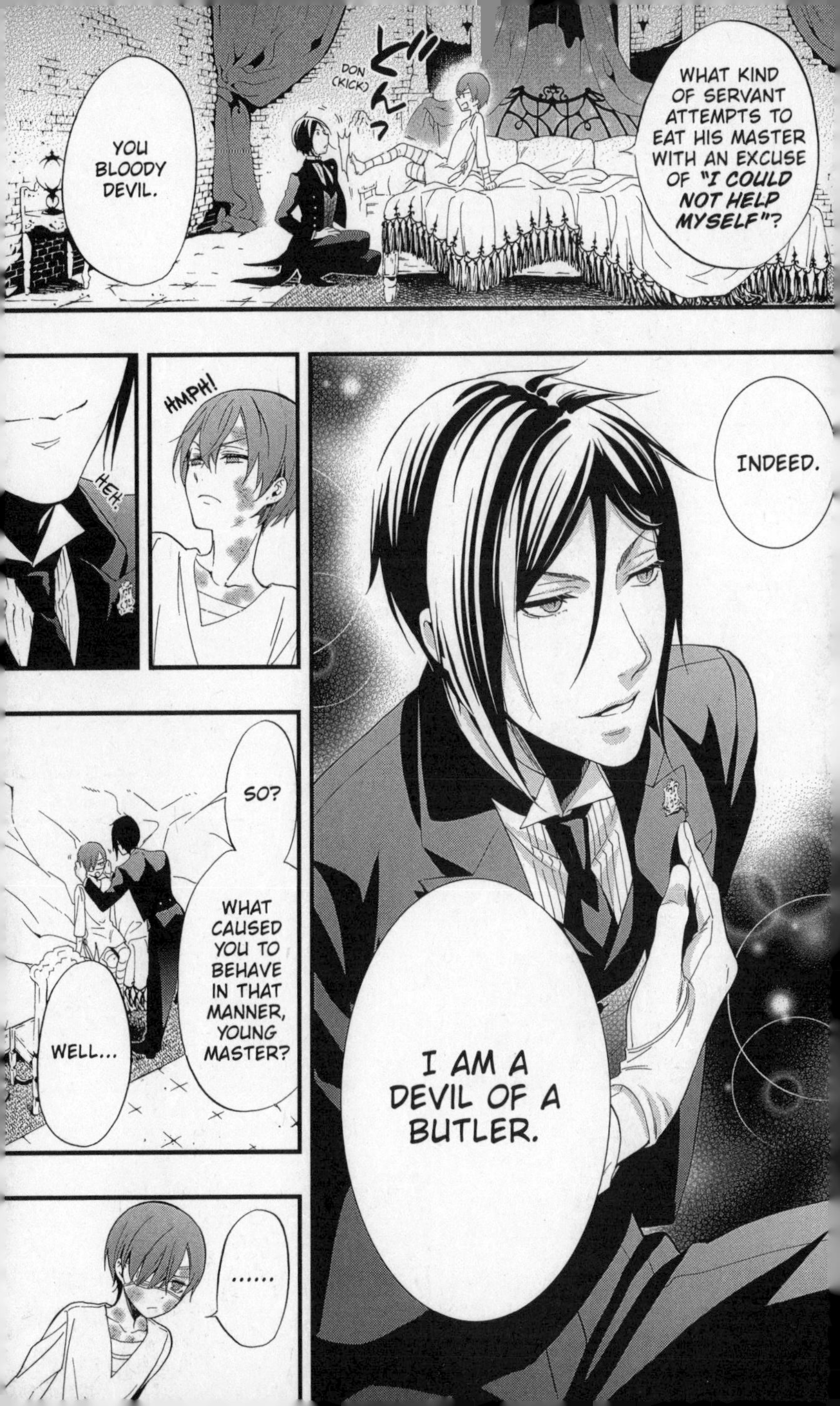

WHAT KIND OF SERVANT ATTEMPTS TO EAT HIS MASTER WITH AN EXCUSE OF *"I COULD NOT HELP MYSELF"*?
どんっ
DON (KICK)
YOU BLOODY DEVIL.
INDEED.
I AM A DEVIL OF A BUTLER.
HMPH!
HEH.
SO?
WHAT CAUSED YOU TO BEHAVE IN THAT MANNER, YOUNG MASTER?
WELL...
....

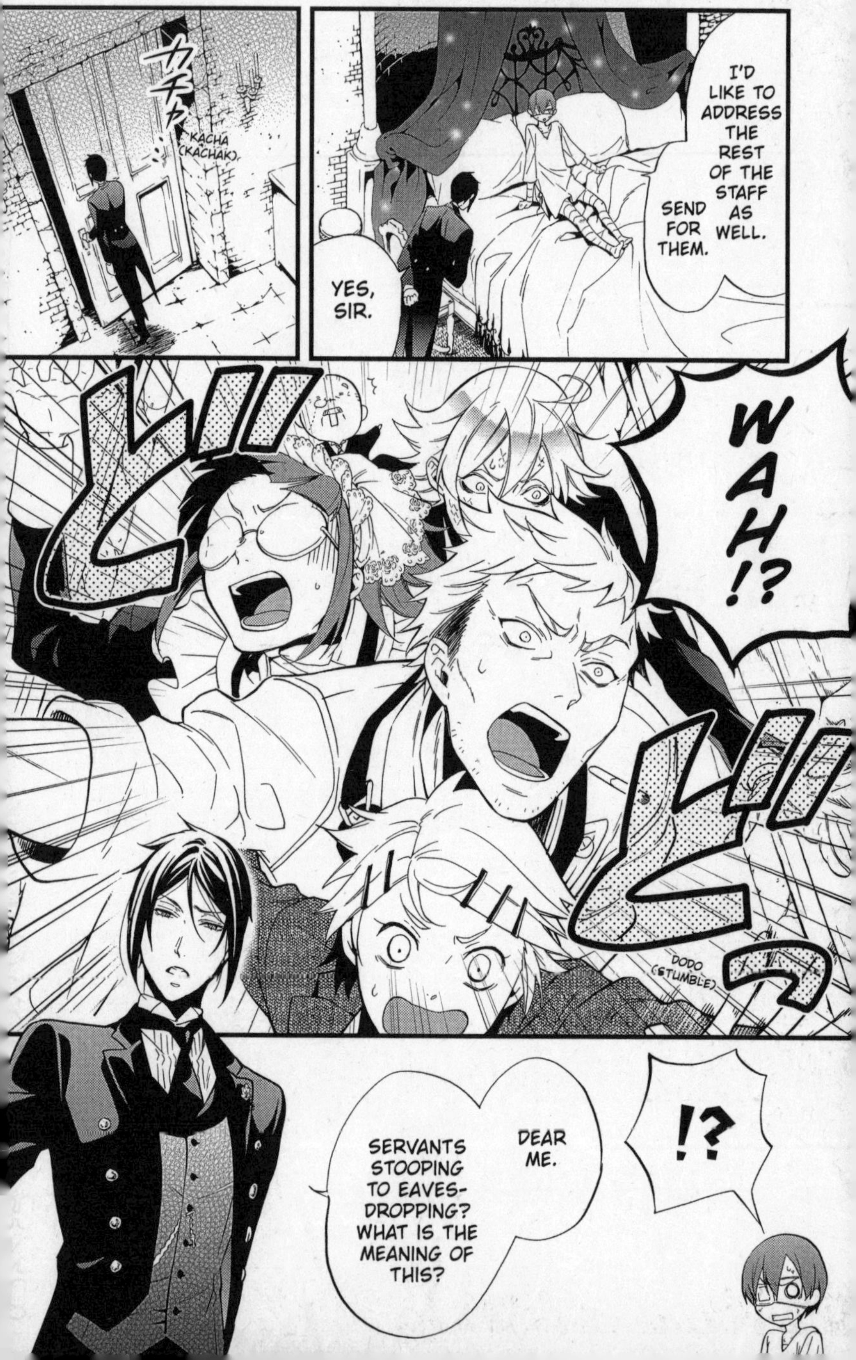

I'D LIKE TO ADDRESS THE REST OF THE STAFF AS WELL.
SEND FOR THEM.
YES, SIR.
カチャ
KACHA (KACHAK)
WAH!?
DODO (STUMBLE)
!?
DEAR ME.
SERVANTS STOOPING TO EAVES-DROPPING? WHAT IS THE MEANING OF THIS?

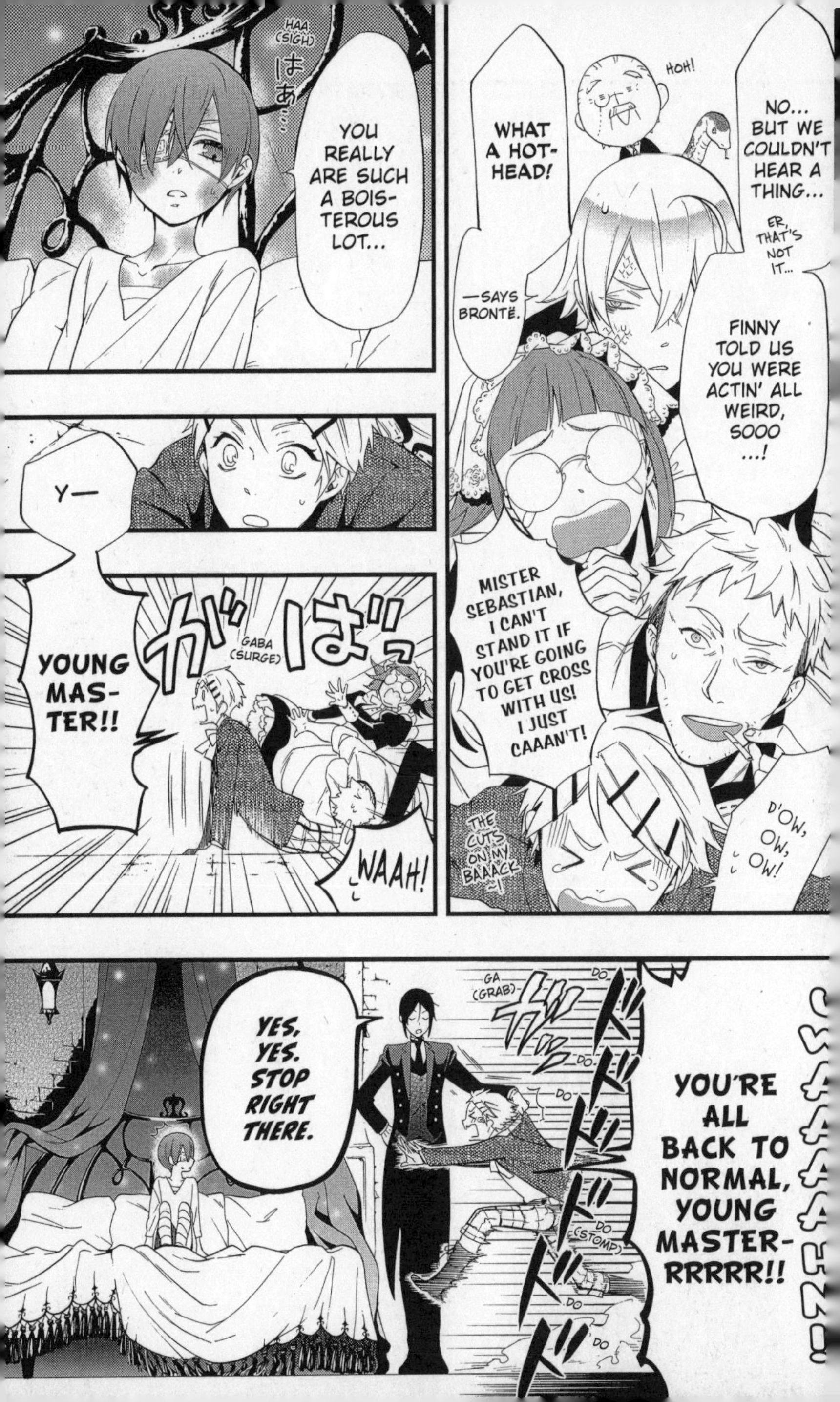
NO... BUT WE COULDN'T HEAR A THING...
ER, THAT'S NOT IT...
HOH!
WHAT A HOT-HEAD!
—SAYS BRONTË.
FINNY TOLD US YOU WERE ACTIN' ALL WEIRD, SOOO ...!
MISTER SEBASTIAN, I CAN'T STAND IT IF YOU'RE GOING TO GET CROSS WITH US! I JUST CAAAN'T!
D'OW, OW, OW!
THE CUTS ON MY BAAACK~!
HAA (SIGH)
はぁ…
YOU REALLY ARE SUCH A BOISTEROUS LOT...
Y—
GABA (SURGE)
YOUNG MASTER!!
WAAH!
YOU'RE ALL BACK TO NORMAL, YOUNG MASTER-RRRRR!!
DO DO DO (STOMP) DO DO
GA (GRAB)
YES, YES. STOP RIGHT THERE.

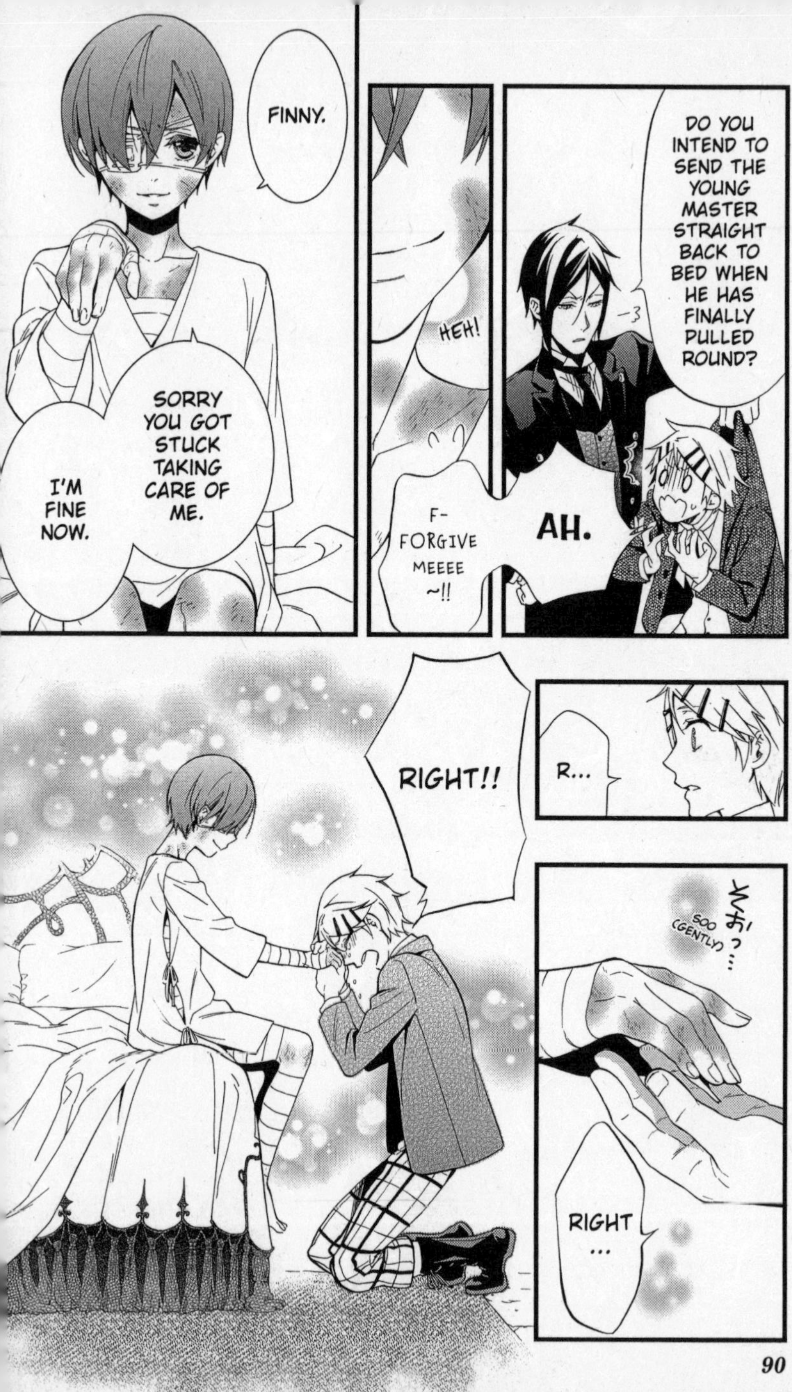
DO YOU INTEND TO SEND THE YOUNG MASTER STRAIGHT BACK TO BED WHEN HE HAS FINALLY PULLED ROUND?
AH.
F-FORGIVE MEEEE ~!!
HEH!
FINNY.
SORRY YOU GOT STUCK TAKING CARE OF ME.
I'M FINE NOW.
R...
とぉ？…
SOO (GENTLY)
RIGHT ...
RIGHT!!

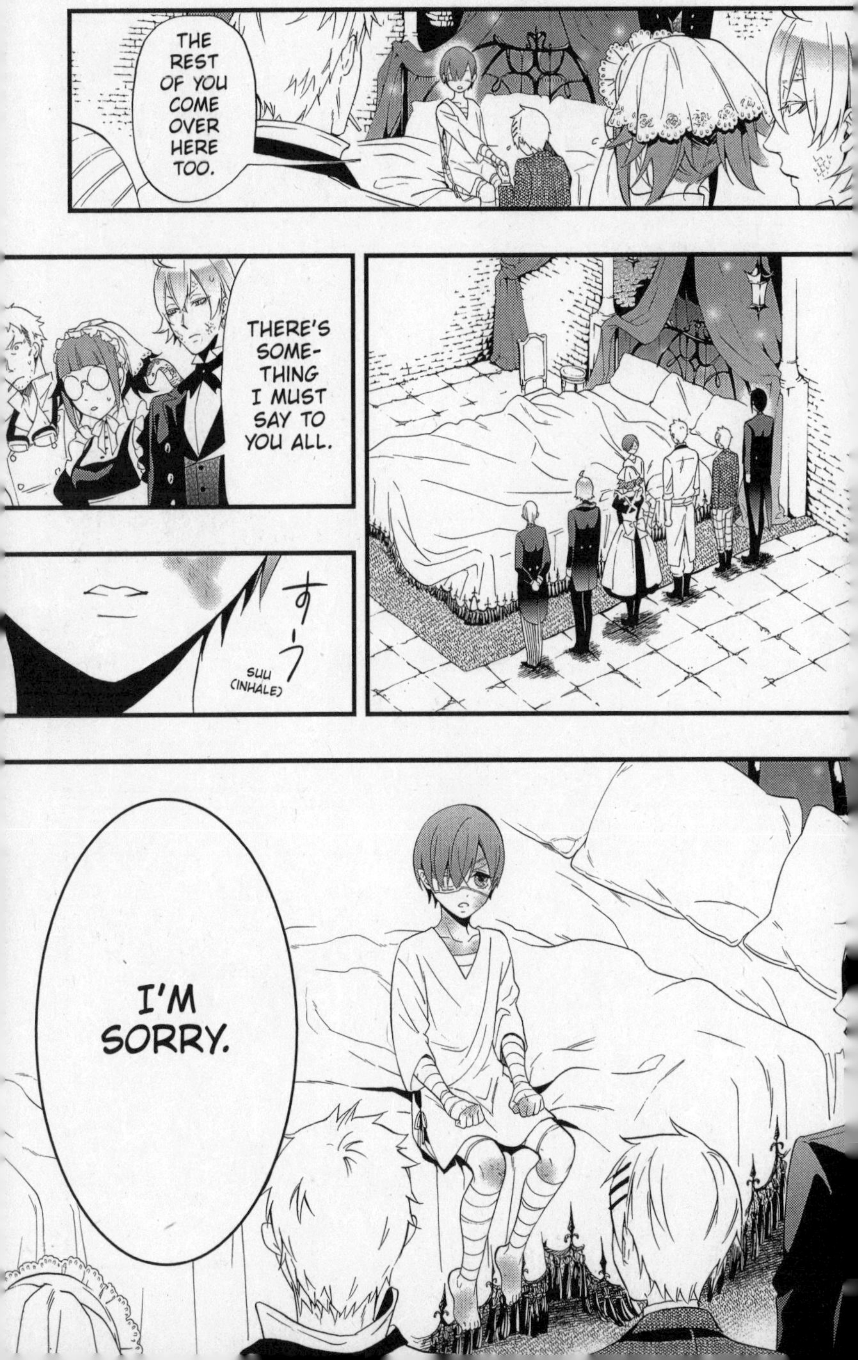
THE REST OF YOU COME OVER HERE TOO.
THERE'S SOME-THING I MUST SAY TO YOU ALL.
すぅ
SUU (INHALE)
I'M SORRY.

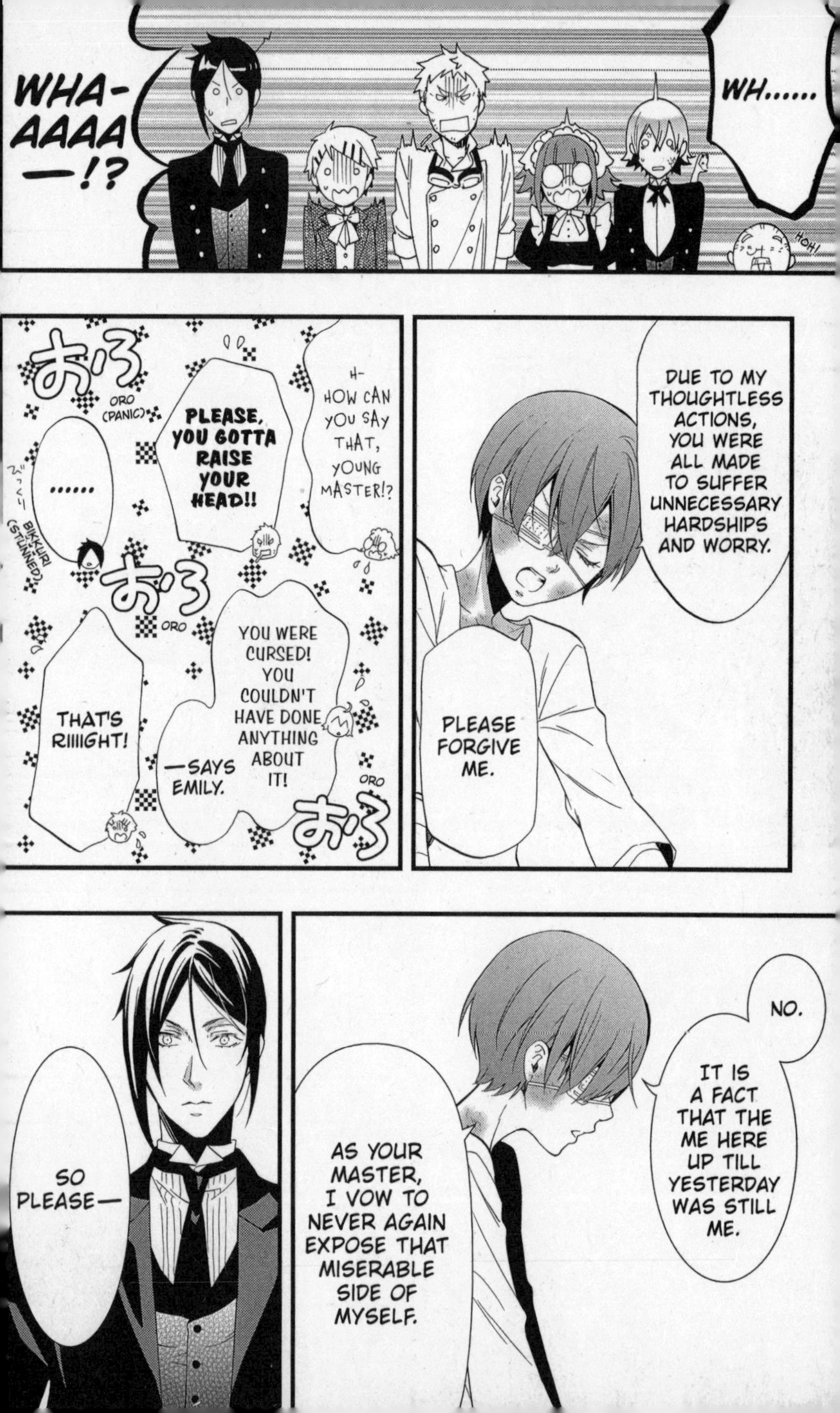
WH......
WHA-AAAA—!?
HOH!
DUE TO MY THOUGHTLESS ACTIONS, YOU WERE ALL MADE TO SUFFER UNNECESSARY HARDSHIPS AND WORRY.
PLEASE FORGIVE ME.
H-HOW CAN YOU SAY THAT, YOUNG MASTER!?
PLEASE, YOU GOTTA RAISE YOUR HEAD!!
おろ
ORO (PANIC)
びっくり
BIKKURI (STUNNED)
......
おろ
ORO
YOU WERE CURSED! YOU COULDN'T HAVE DONE ANYTHING ABOUT IT!
—SAYS EMILY.
THAT'S RIIIIGHT!
おろ
ORO
NO.
IT IS A FACT THAT THE ME HERE UP TILL YESTERDAY WAS STILL ME.
AS YOUR MASTER, I VOW TO NEVER AGAIN EXPOSE THAT MISERABLE SIDE OF MYSELF.
SO PLEASE—

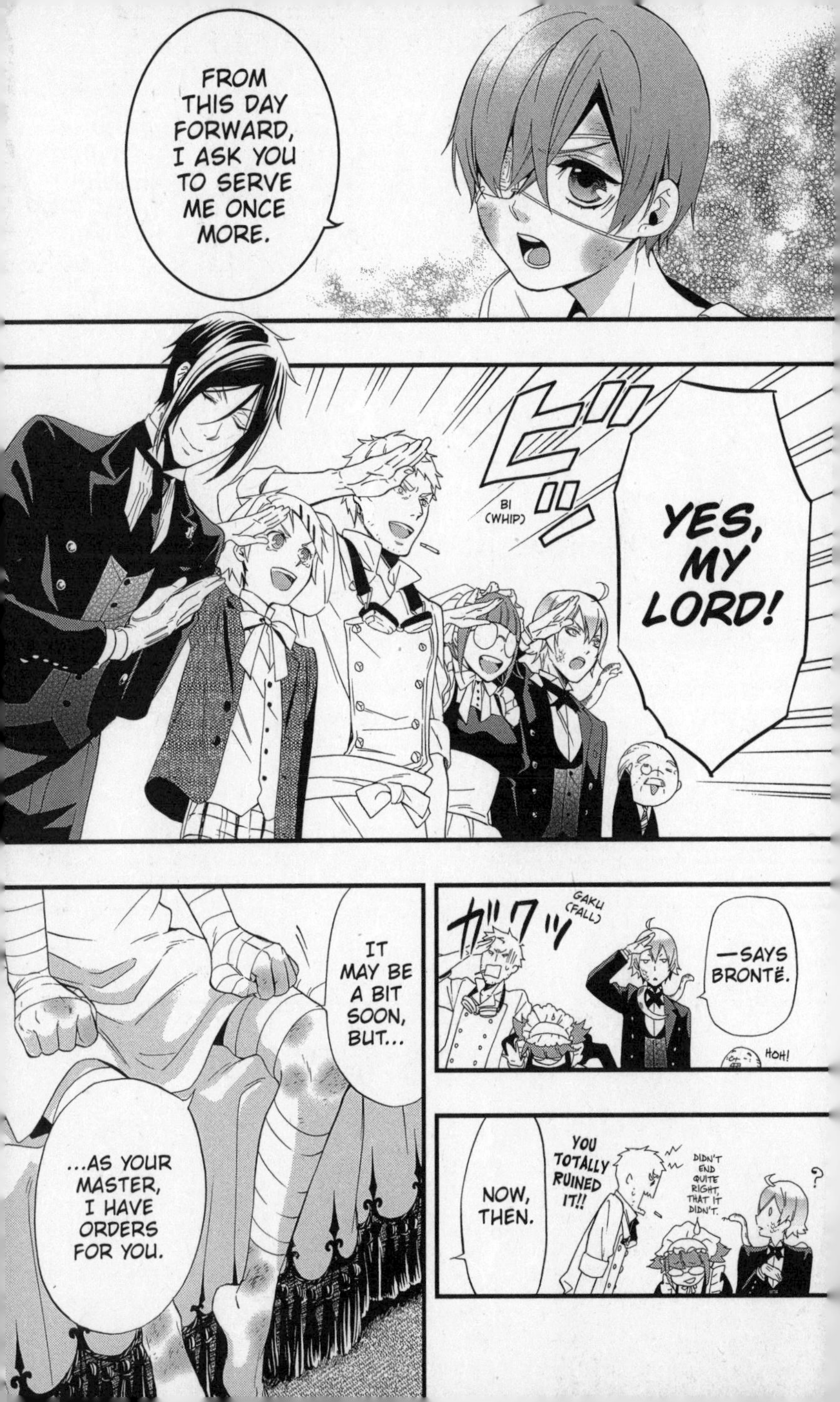
FROM THIS DAY FORWARD, I ASK YOU TO SERVE ME ONCE MORE.
YES, MY LORD!
BI (WHIP)
—SAYS BRONTË.
HOH!
GAKU (FALL)
DIDN'T END QUITE RIGHT, THAT IT DIDN'T.
YOU TOTALLY RUINED IT!!
NOW, THEN.
IT MAY BE A BIT SOON, BUT...
...AS YOUR MASTER, I HAVE ORDERS FOR YOU.

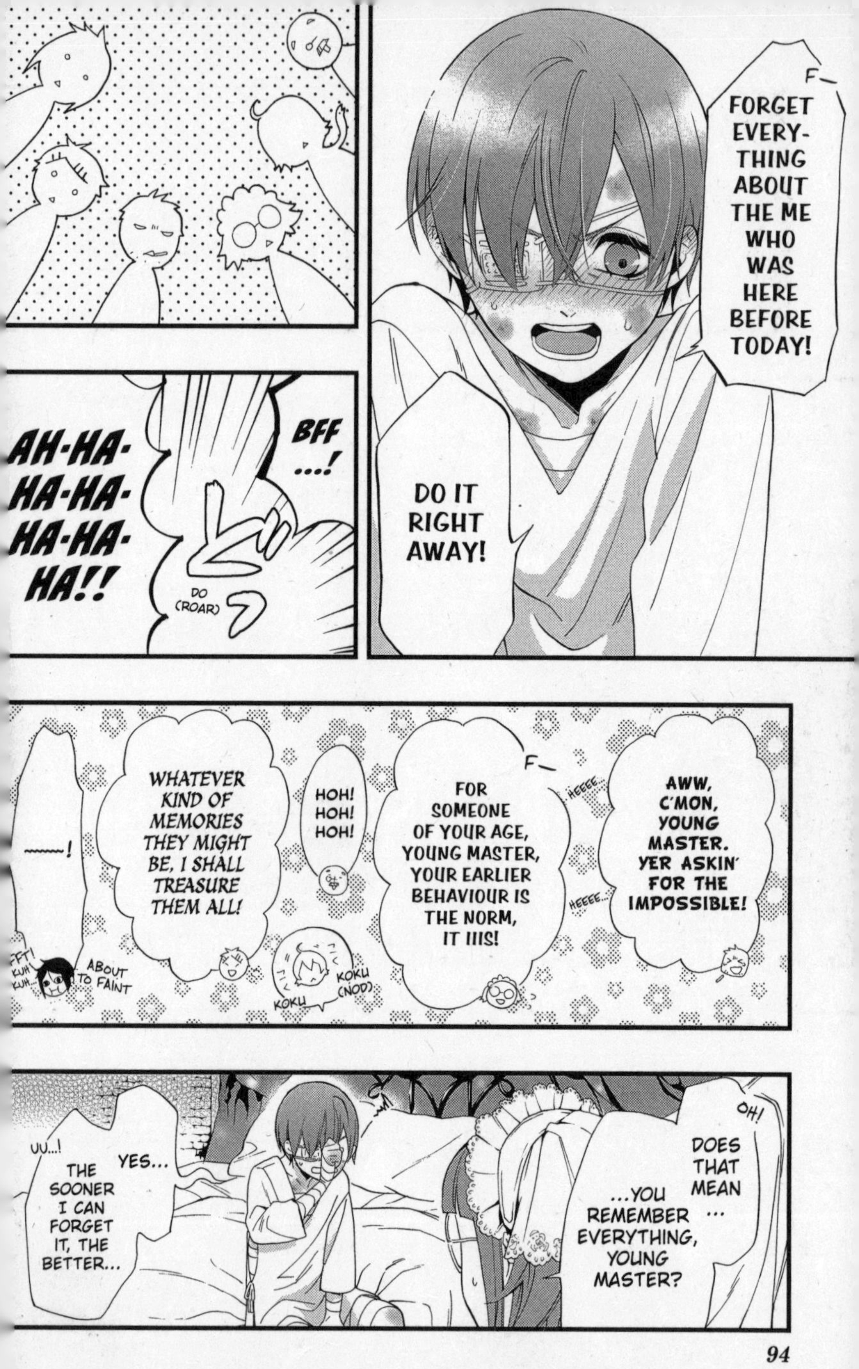
F—
FORGET EVERY-THING ABOUT THE ME WHO WAS HERE BEFORE TODAY!
DO IT RIGHT AWAY!
BFF ...!
AH-HA-HA-HA-HA-HA-HA!!
DO (ROAR)
AWW, C'MON, YOUNG MASTER. YER ASKIN' FOR THE IMPOSSIBLE!
HEEEE...
HEEEE...
F—
FOR SOMEONE OF YOUR AGE, YOUNG MASTER, YOUR EARLIER BEHAVIOUR IS THE NORM, IT IIIS!
HOH! HOH! HOH!
KOKU KOKU (NOD)
WHATEVER KIND OF MEMORIES THEY MIGHT BE, I SHALL TREASURE THEM ALL!
~~~~!
ABOUT TO FAINT
FFT! KUH KUH...
OH!
DOES THAT MEAN ...
...YOU REMEMBER EVERYTHING, YOUNG MASTER?
YES...
UU...!
THE SOONER I CAN FORGET IT, THE BETTER...
~~~~

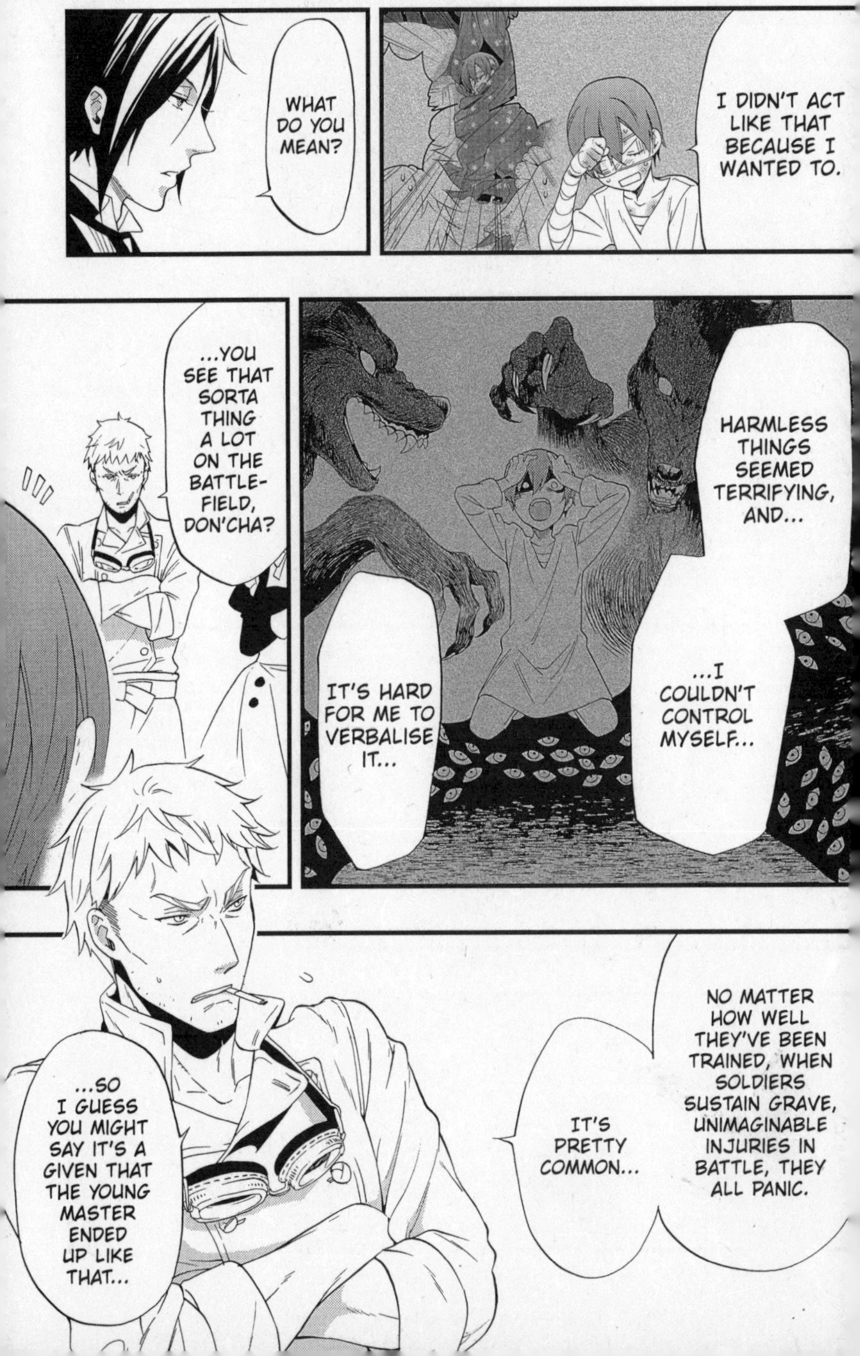
I DIDN'T ACT LIKE THAT BECAUSE I WANTED TO.
WHAT DO YOU MEAN?
HARMLESS THINGS SEEMED TERRIFYING, AND...
...I COULDN'T CONTROL MYSELF...
IT'S HARD FOR ME TO VERBALISE IT...
...YOU SEE THAT SORTA THING A LOT ON THE BATTLE-FIELD, DON'CHA?
NO MATTER HOW WELL THEY'VE BEEN TRAINED, WHEN SOLDIERS SUSTAIN GRAVE, UNIMAGINABLE INJURIES IN BATTLE, THEY ALL PANIC.
IT'S PRETTY COMMON...
...SO I GUESS YOU MIGHT SAY IT'S A GIVEN THAT THE YOUNG MASTER ENDED UP LIKE THAT...

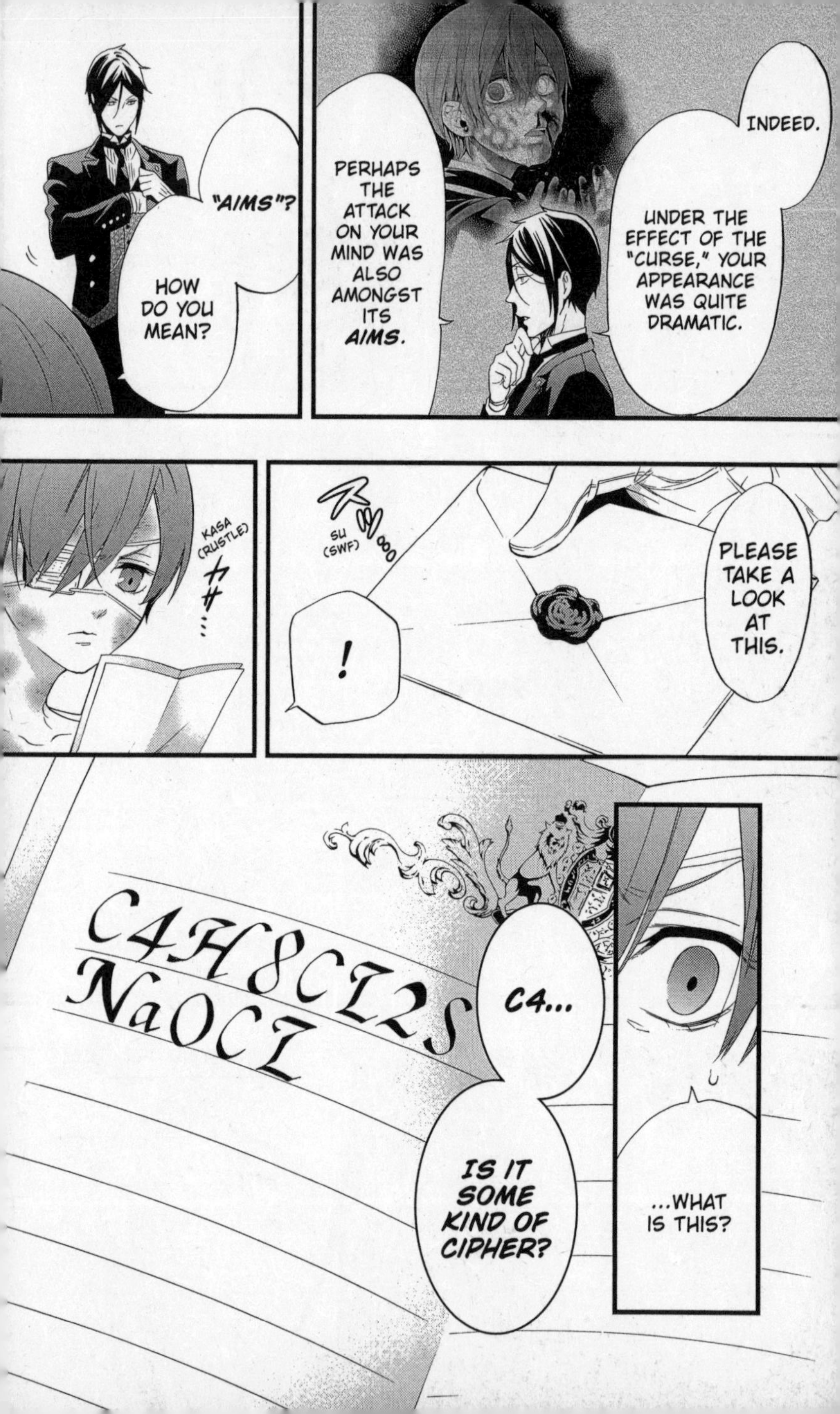
INDEED.
UNDER THE EFFECT OF THE "CURSE," YOUR APPEARANCE WAS QUITE DRAMATIC.
PERHAPS THE ATTACK ON YOUR MIND WAS ALSO AMONGST ITS AIMS.
"AIMS"?
HOW DO YOU MEAN?
SU (SWF)
PLEASE TAKE A LOOK AT THIS.
!
KASA (RUSTLE)
...WHAT IS THIS?
C4H8CL2S
NaOCL
C4...
IS IT SOME KIND OF CIPHER?

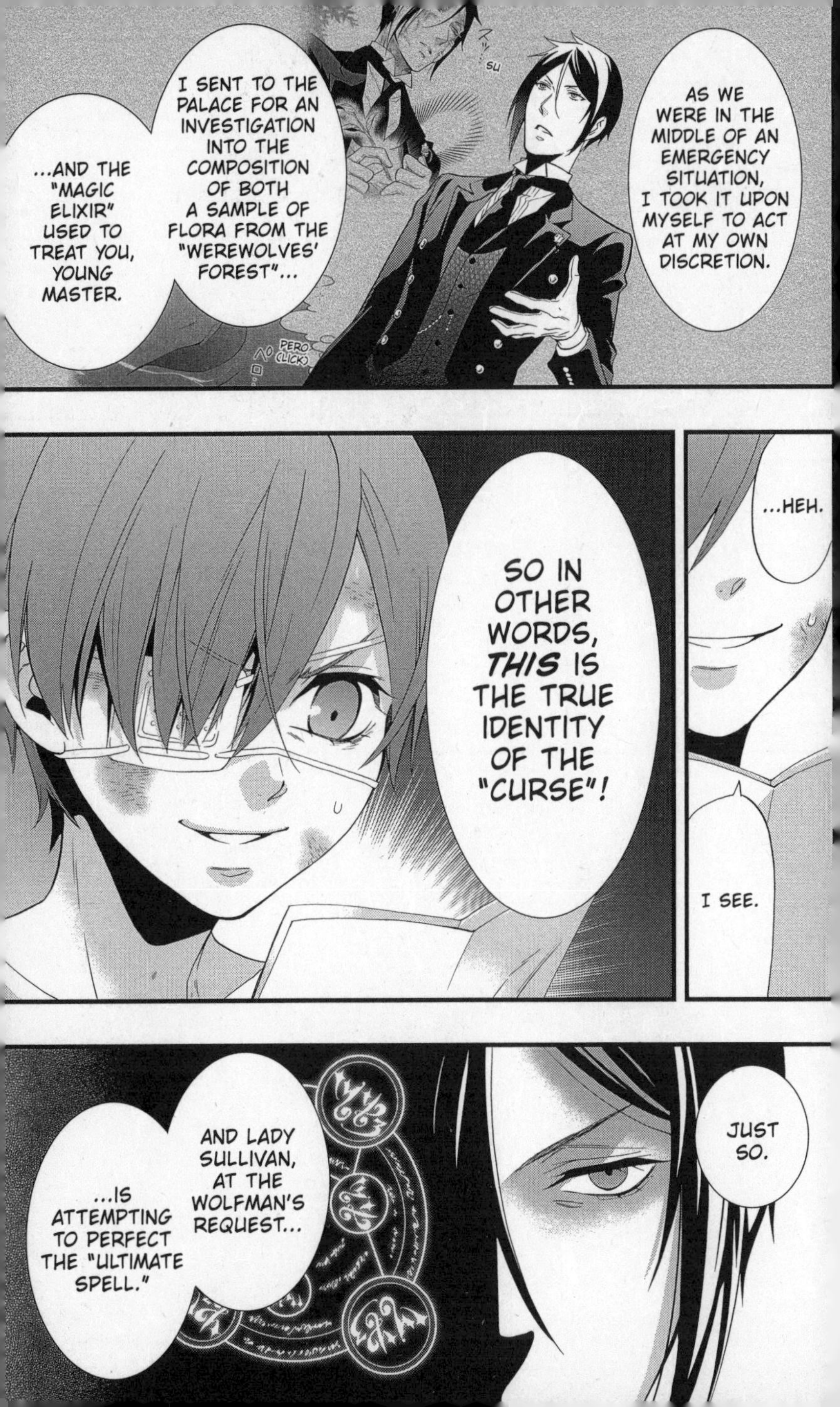
SU
AS WE WERE IN THE MIDDLE OF AN EMERGENCY SITUATION, I TOOK IT UPON MYSELF TO ACT AT MY OWN DISCRETION.
I SENT TO THE PALACE FOR AN INVESTIGATION INTO THE COMPOSITION OF BOTH A SAMPLE OF FLORA FROM THE "WEREWOLVES' FOREST"...
...AND THE "MAGIC ELIXIR" USED TO TREAT YOU, YOUNG MASTER.
PERO (LICK)
...HEH.
I SEE.
SO IN OTHER WORDS, ***THIS*** IS THE TRUE IDENTITY OF THE "CURSE"!
JUST SO.
AND LADY SULLIVAN, AT THE WOLFMAN'S REQUEST...
...IS ATTEMPTING TO PERFECT THE "ULTIMATE SPELL."

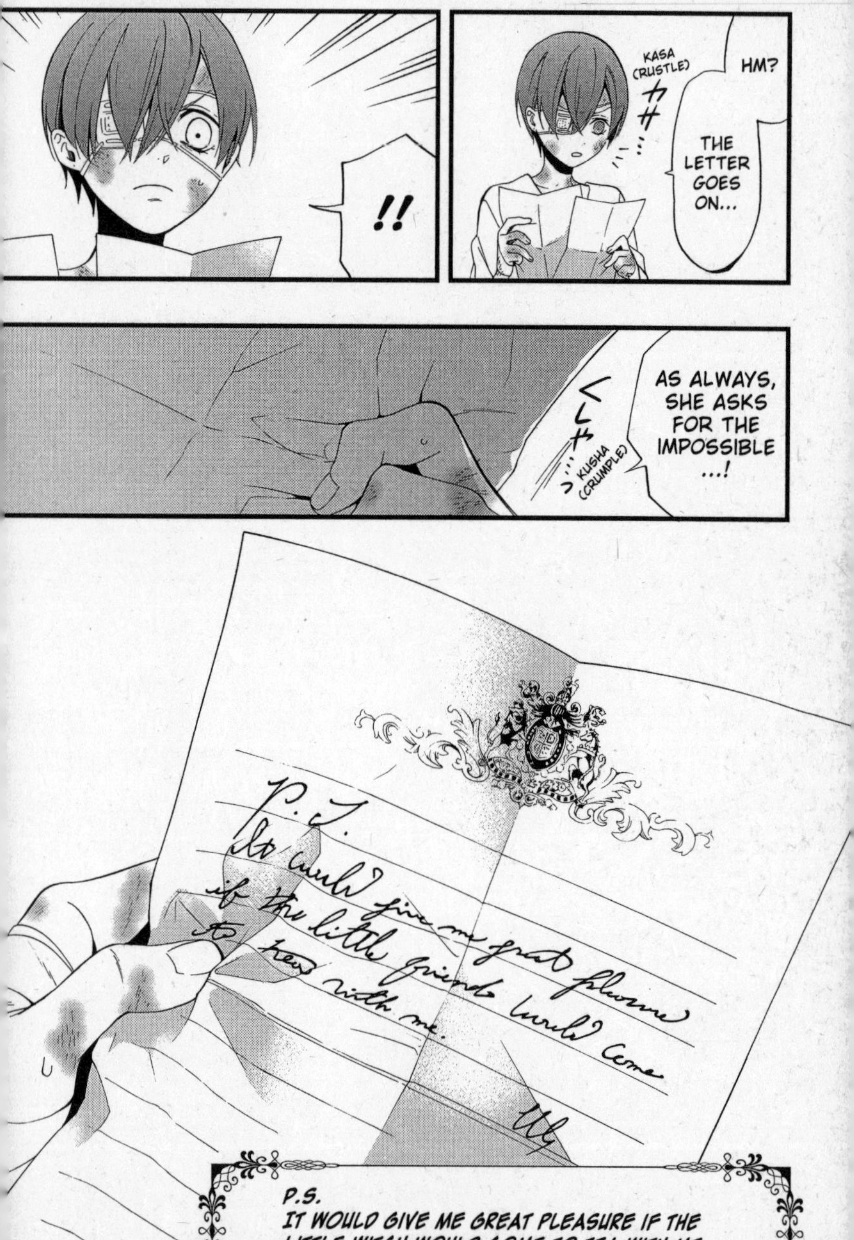
HM?
THE LETTER GOES ON...
KASA (RUSTLE)
!!
AS ALWAYS, SHE ASKS FOR THE IMPOSSIBLE ...!
KUSHA (CRUMPLE)
P.S.
IT WOULD GIVE ME GREAT PLEASURE IF THE LITTLE WITCH WOULD COME TO TEA WITH ME.
—VICTORIA

Black Butler

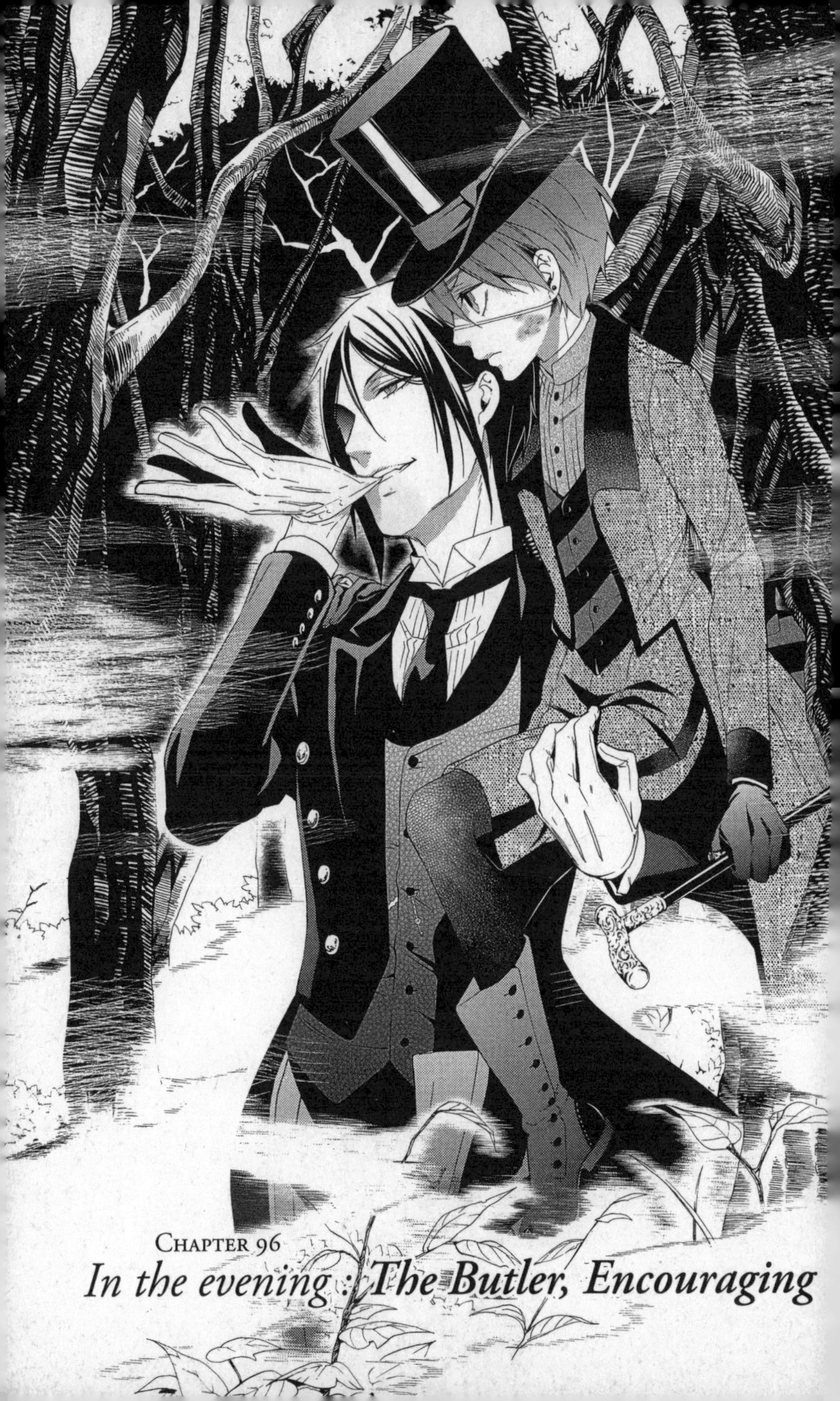

CHAPTER 96
In the evening : The Butler, Encouraging

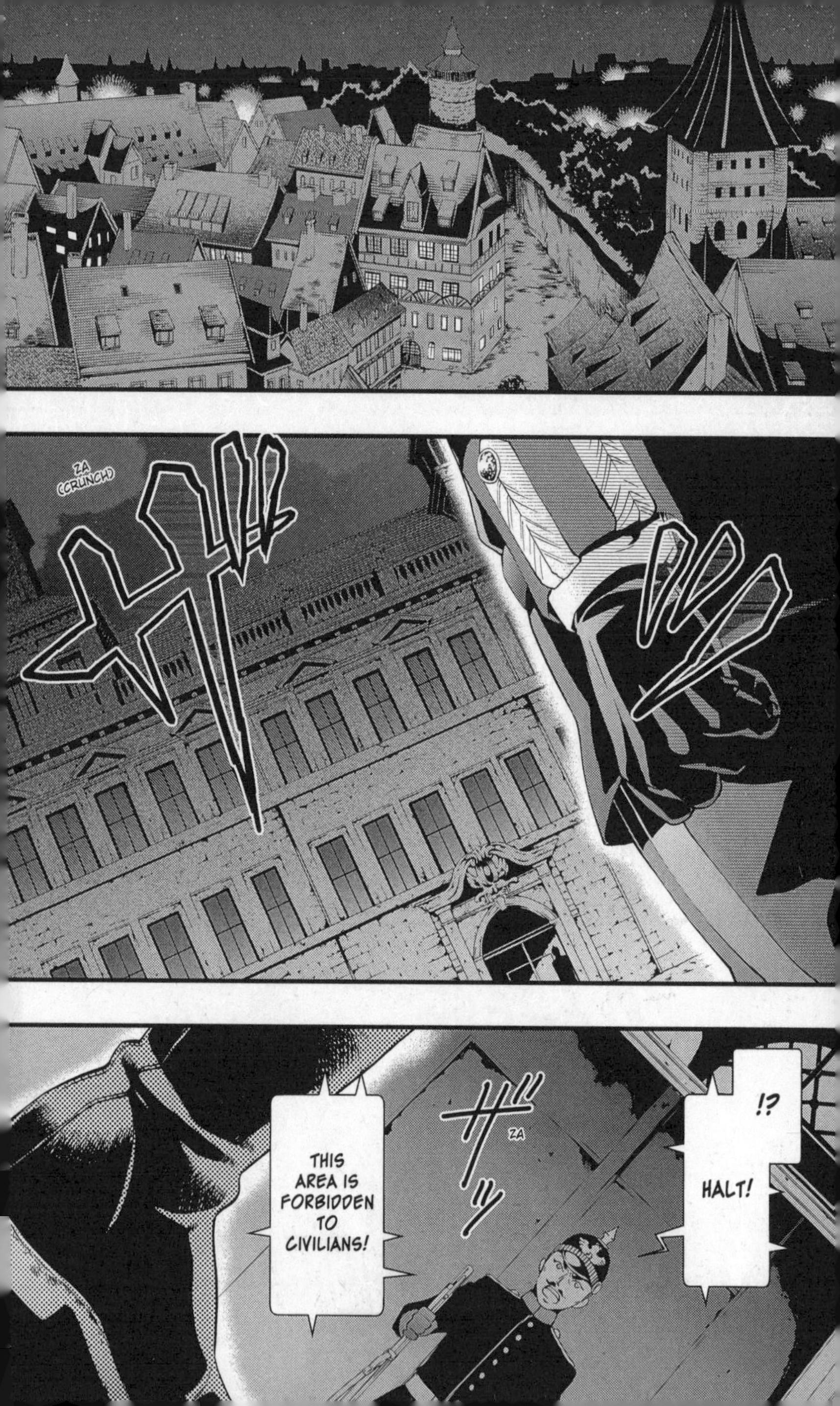
ZA (CRUNCH)
!? HALT!
ZA
THIS AREA IS FORBIDDEN TO CIVILIANS!

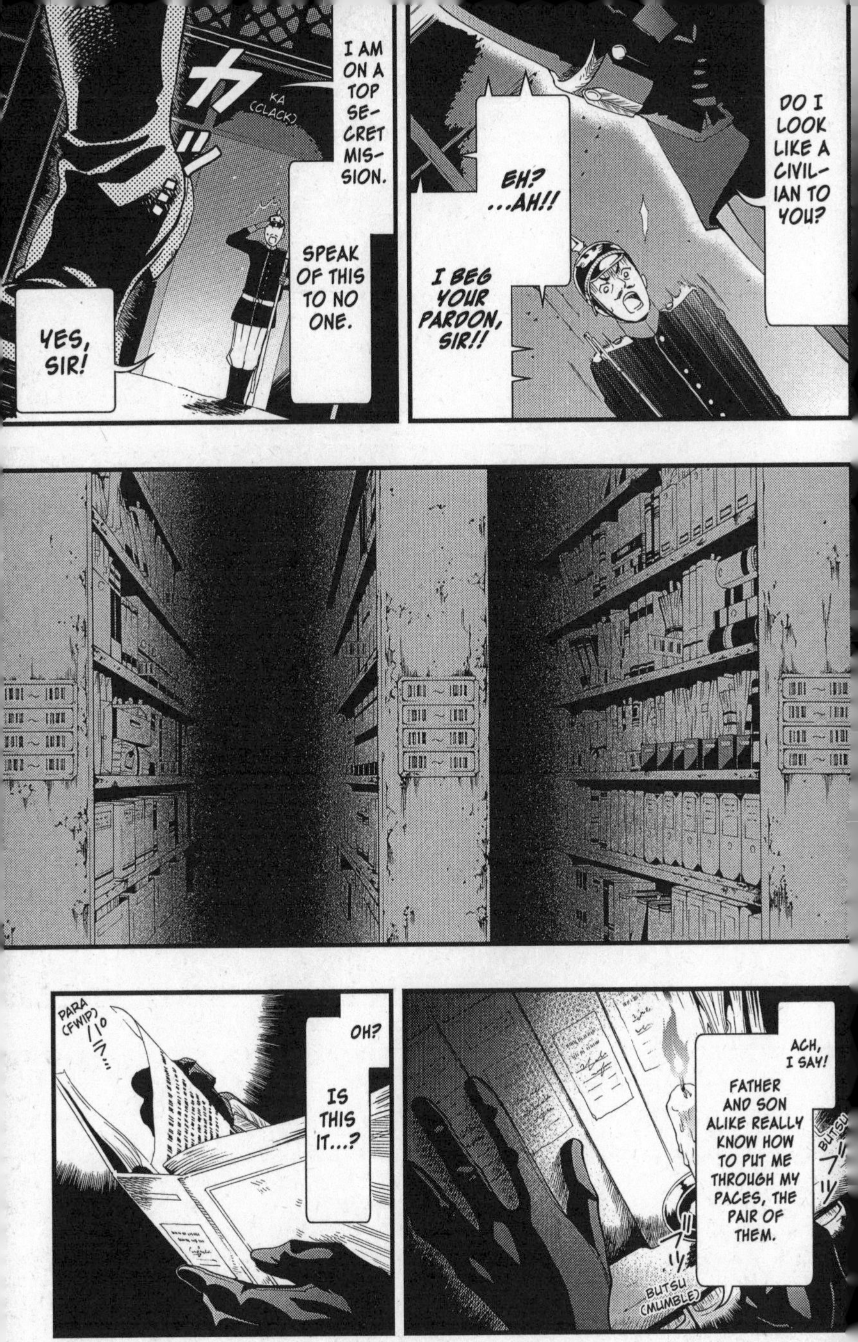
DO I LOOK LIKE A CIVILIAN TO YOU?
EH? ...AH!!
I BEG YOUR PARDON, SIR!!
I AM ON A TOP SECRET MISSION.
SPEAK OF THIS TO NO ONE.
KA (CLACK)
YES, SIR!
ACH, I SAY!
FATHER AND SON ALIKE REALLY KNOW HOW TO PUT ME THROUGH MY PACES, THE PAIR OF THEM.
BUTSU
BUTSU (MUMBLE)
PARA (FWIP)
OH?
IS THIS IT...?

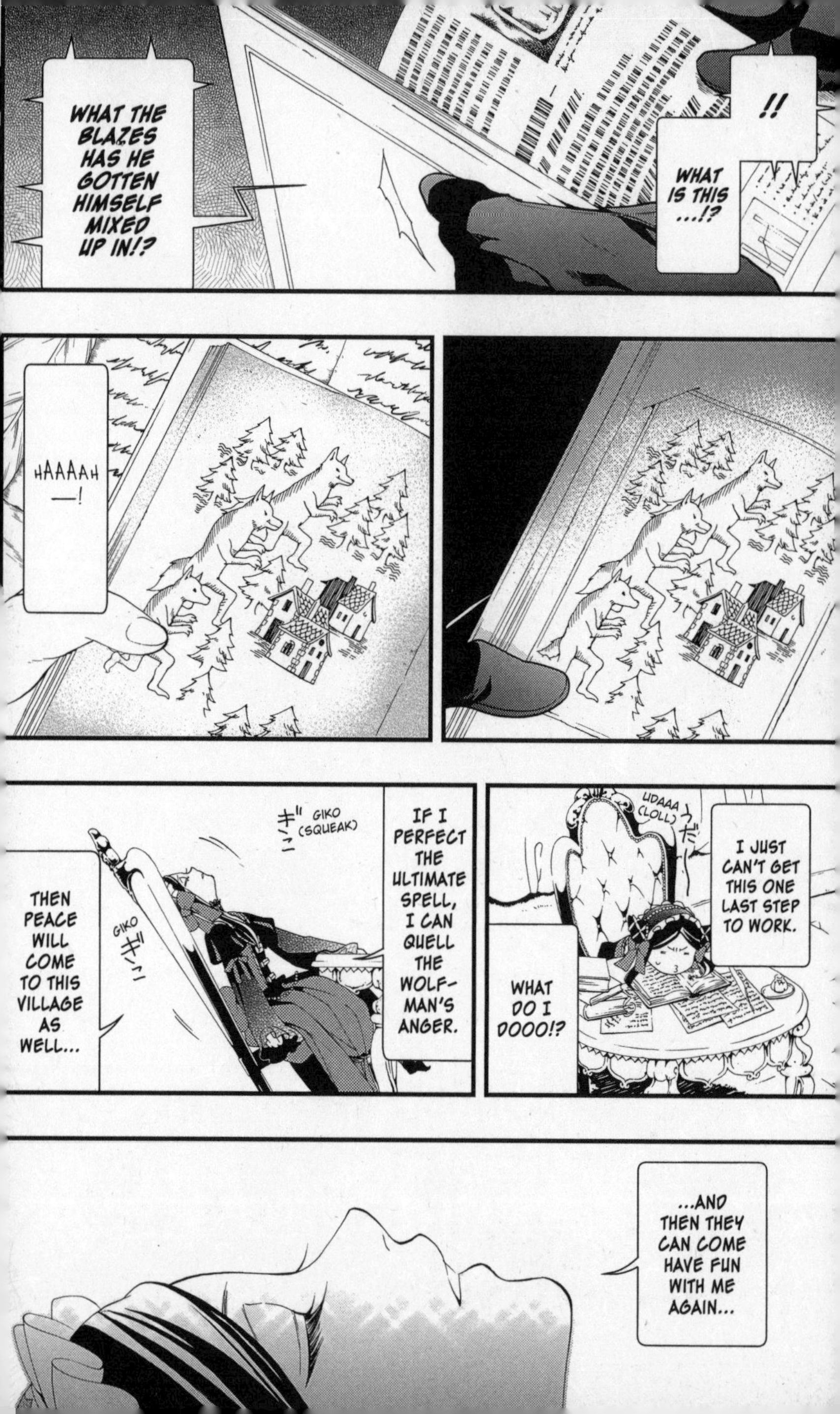
!!
WHAT IS THIS ...!?
WHAT THE BLAZES HAS HE GOTTEN HIMSELF MIXED UP IN!?
HAAAAH —!
UDAAA (LOLL)
I JUST CAN'T GET THIS ONE LAST STEP TO WORK.
WHAT DO I DOOO!?
IF I PERFECT THE ULTIMATE SPELL, I CAN QUELL THE WOLF-MAN'S ANGER.
GIKO (SQUEAK)
GIKO
THEN PEACE WILL COME TO THIS VILLAGE AS WELL...
...AND THEN THEY CAN COME HAVE FUN WITH ME AGAIN...

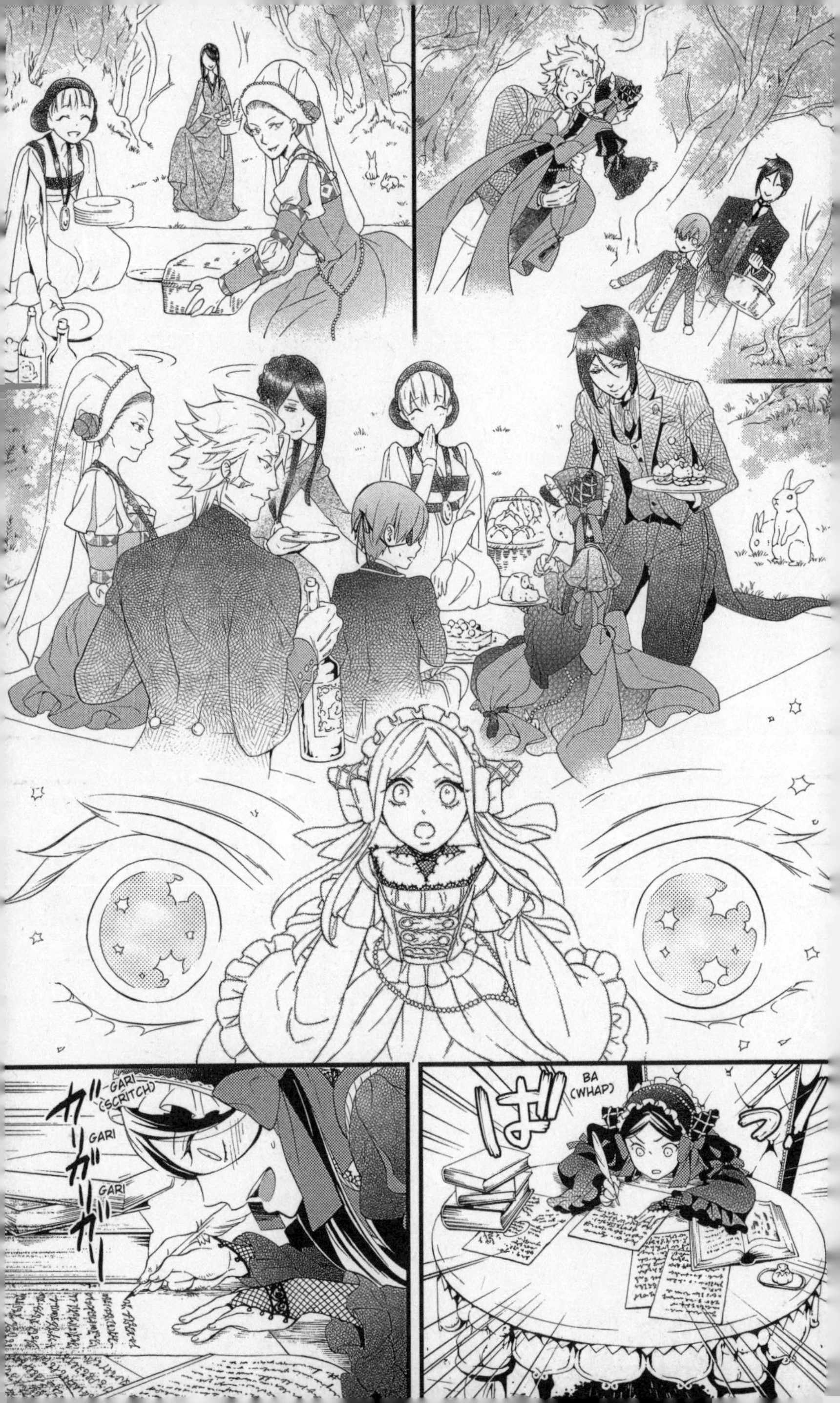

BA (WHAP)
GARI (SCRITCH)
GARI
GARI

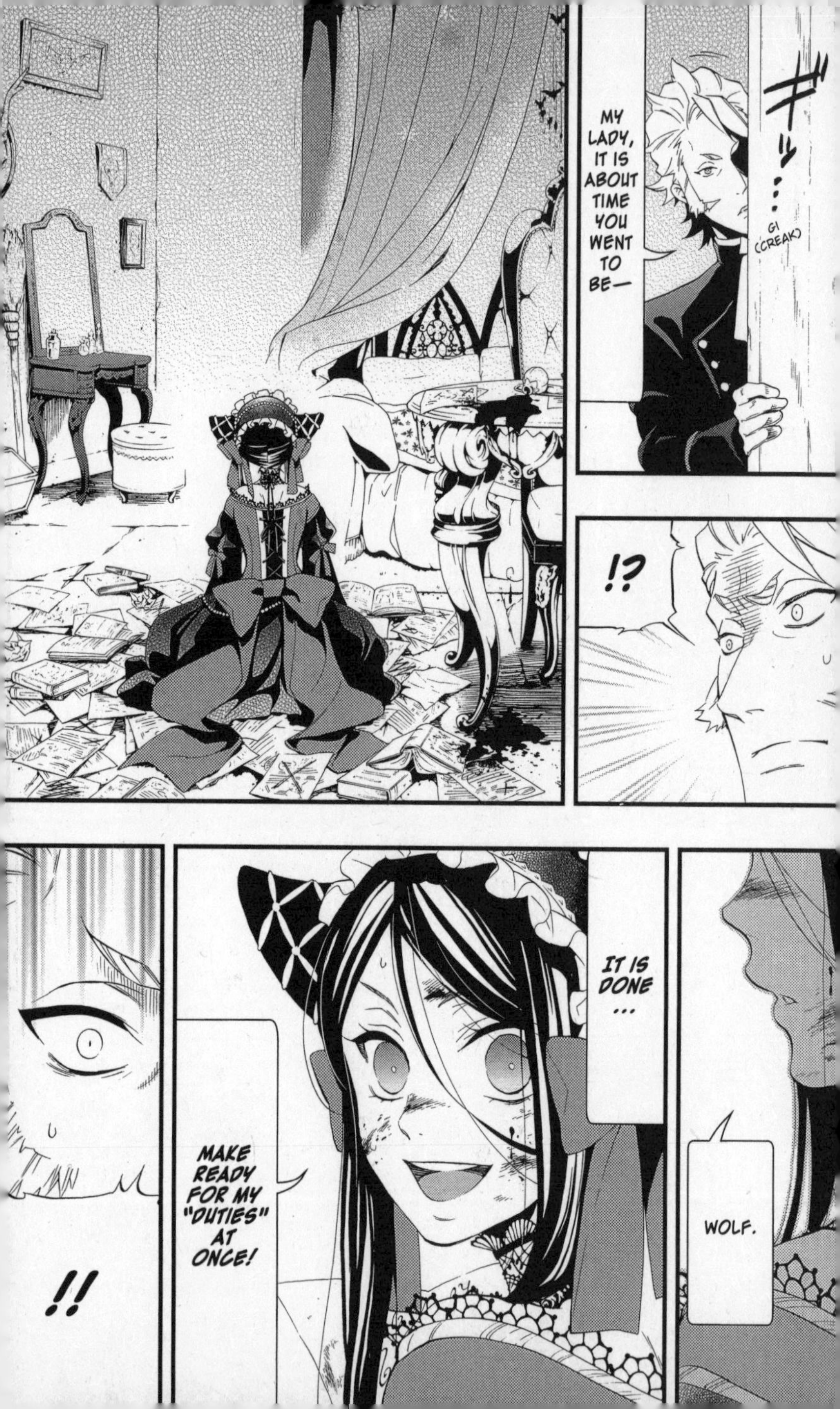
ギッ…
GI (CREAK)
MY LADY, IT IS ABOUT TIME YOU WENT TO BE—
!?
WOLF.
IT IS DONE ...
MAKE READY FOR MY "DUTIES" AT ONCE!
!!

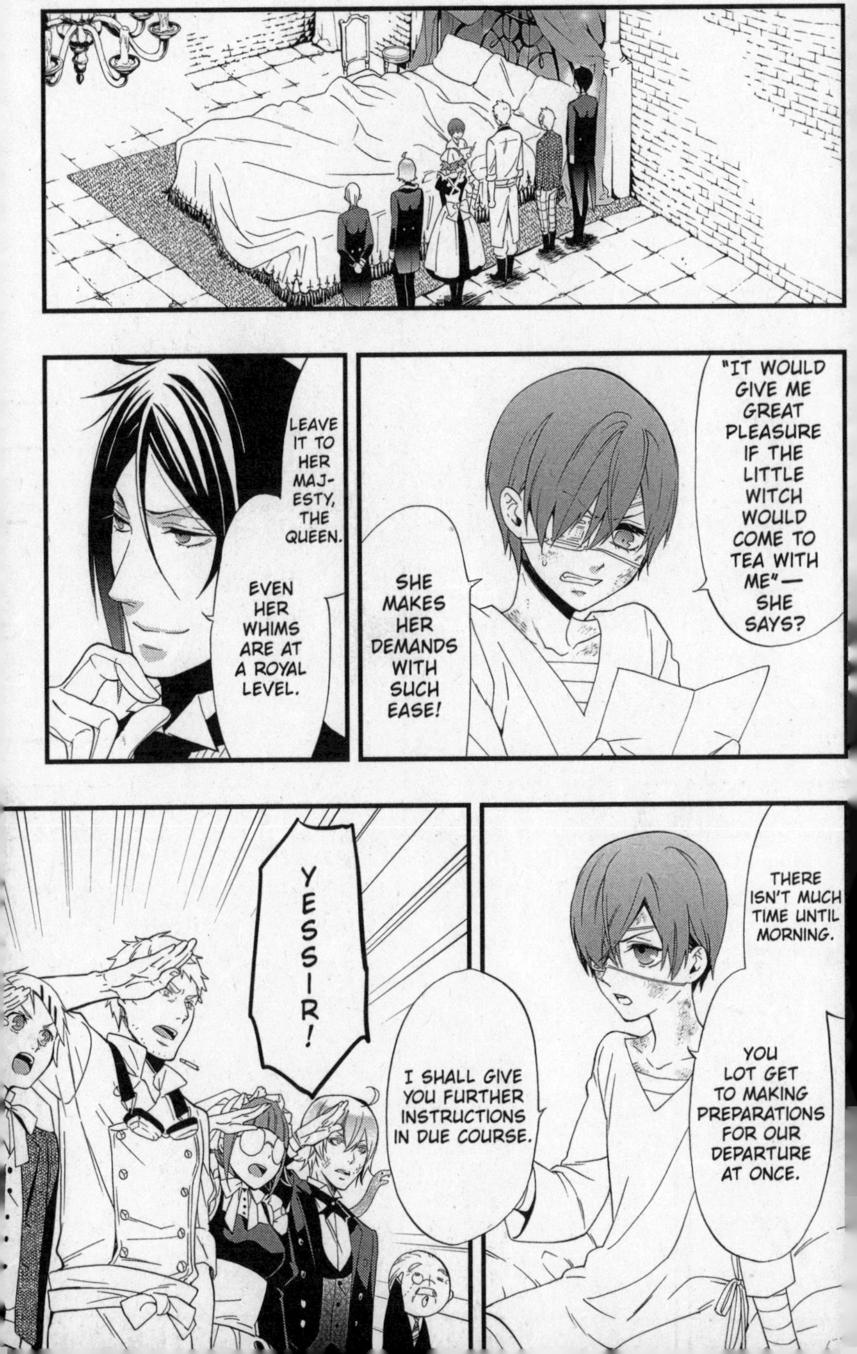
"IT WOULD GIVE ME GREAT PLEASURE IF THE LITTLE WITCH WOULD COME TO TEA WITH ME"—SHE SAYS?
SHE MAKES HER DEMANDS WITH SUCH EASE!
LEAVE IT TO HER MAJESTY, THE QUEEN.
EVEN HER WHIMS ARE AT A ROYAL LEVEL.
THERE ISN'T MUCH TIME UNTIL MORNING.
YOU LOT GET TO MAKING PREPARATIONS FOR OUR DEPARTURE AT ONCE.
I SHALL GIVE YOU FURTHER INSTRUCTIONS IN DUE COURSE.
YESSIR!

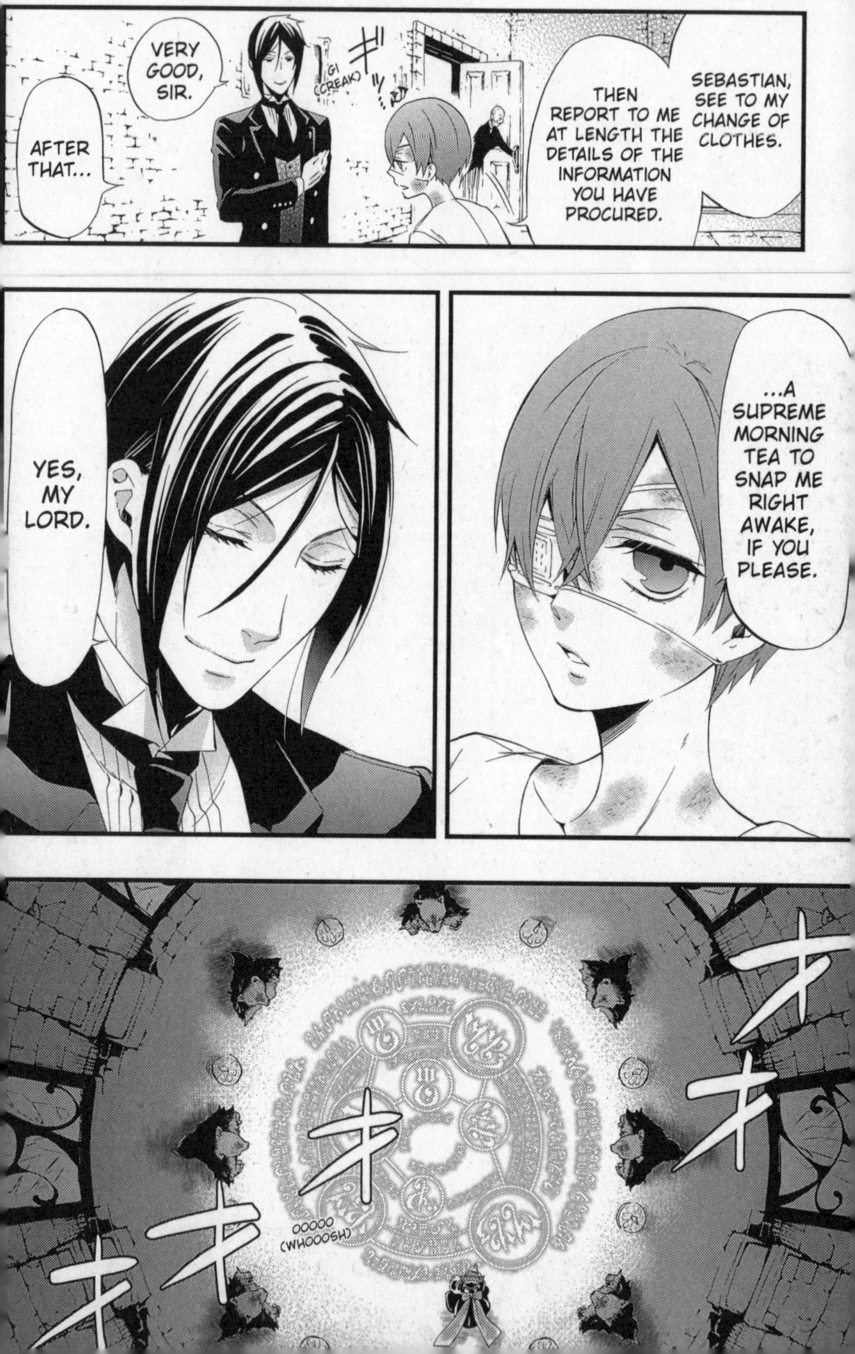
SEBASTIAN, SEE TO MY CHANGE OF CLOTHES.
THEN REPORT TO ME AT LENGTH THE DETAILS OF THE INFORMATION YOU HAVE PROCURED.
GI (CREAK)
VERY GOOD, SIR.
AFTER THAT...
...A SUPREME MORNING TEA TO SNAP ME RIGHT AWAKE, IF YOU PLEASE.
YES, MY LORD.
OOOOO (WHOOOSH)

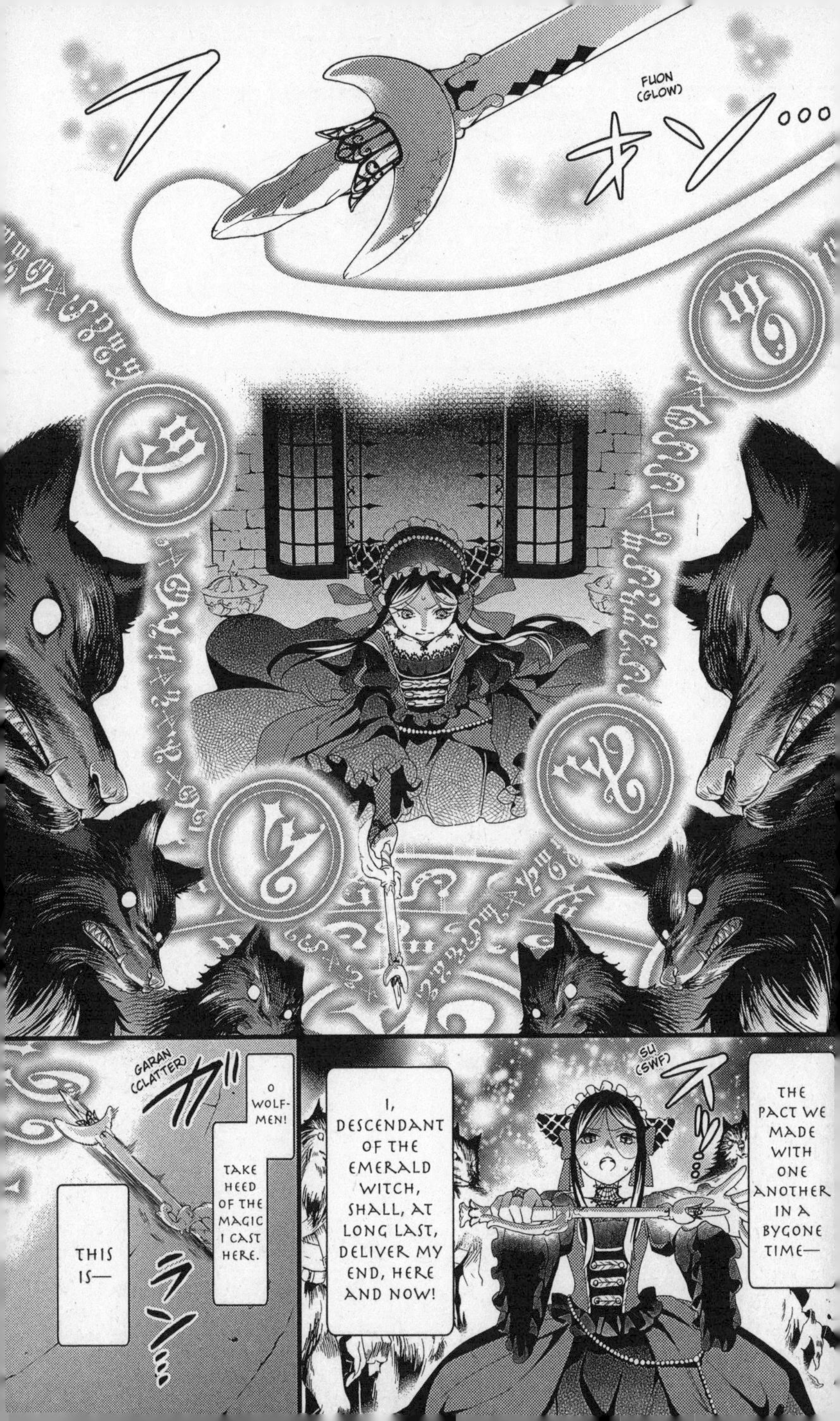
FUON (GLOW)
SU (SWF)
THE PACT WE MADE WITH ONE ANOTHER IN A BYGONE TIME—
I, DESCENDANT OF THE EMERALD WITCH, SHALL, AT LONG LAST, DELIVER MY END, HERE AND NOW!
GARAN (CLATTER)
O WOLF-MEN!
TAKE HEED OF THE MAGIC I CAST HERE.
THIS IS—

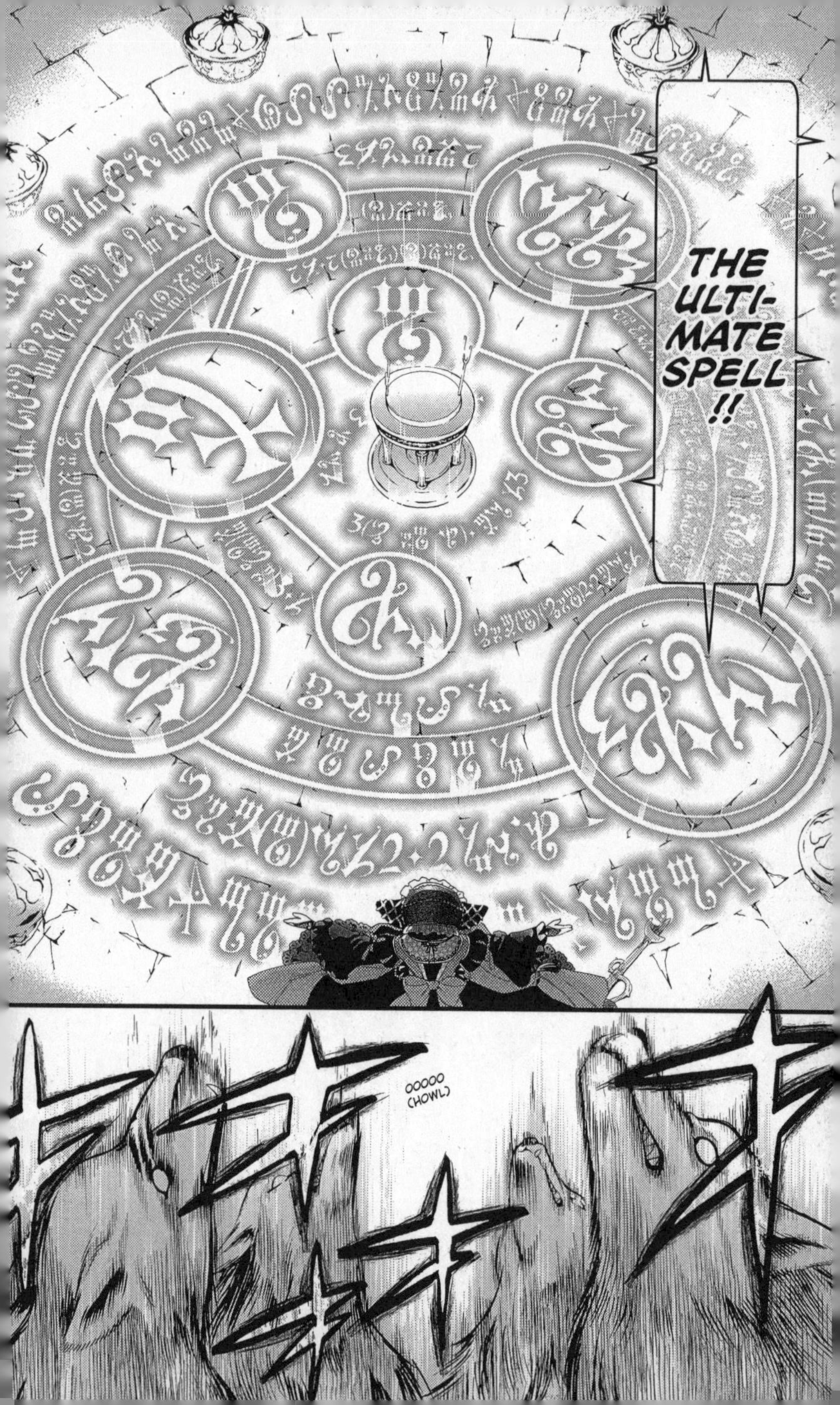
THE ULTIMATE SPELL!!
OOOOO (HOWL)

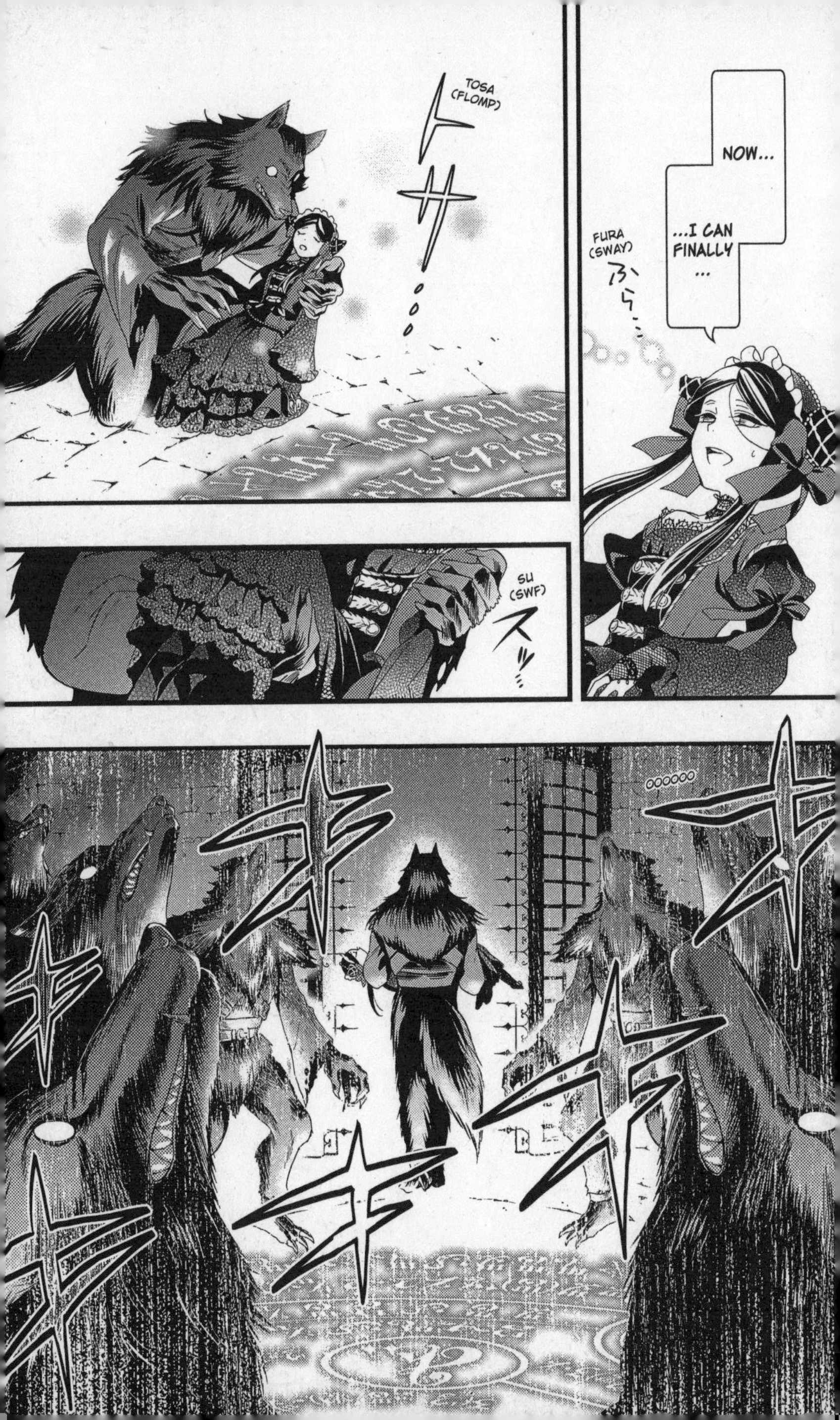
NOW...
...I CAN FINALLY ...
FURA (SWAY)
ふら…
TOSA (FLOMP)
トサ…
SU (SWF)
スッ…
oooooo

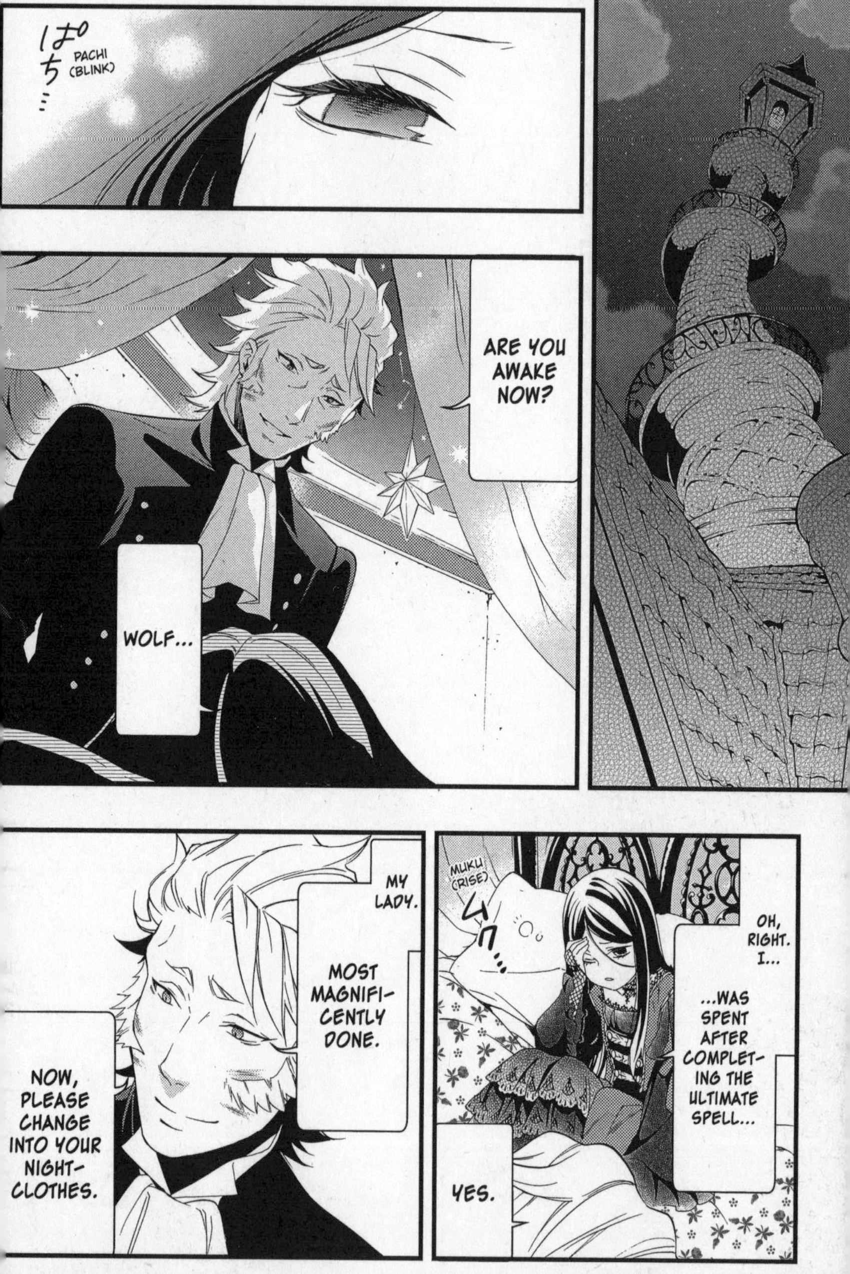

ぱち
PACHI (BLINK)
ARE YOU AWAKE NOW?
WOLF...
OH, RIGHT. I...
MUKU (RISE)
...WAS SPENT AFTER COMPLETING THE ULTIMATE SPELL...
YES.
MY LADY.
MOST MAGNIFICENTLY DONE.
NOW, PLEASE CHANGE INTO YOUR NIGHTCLOTHES.

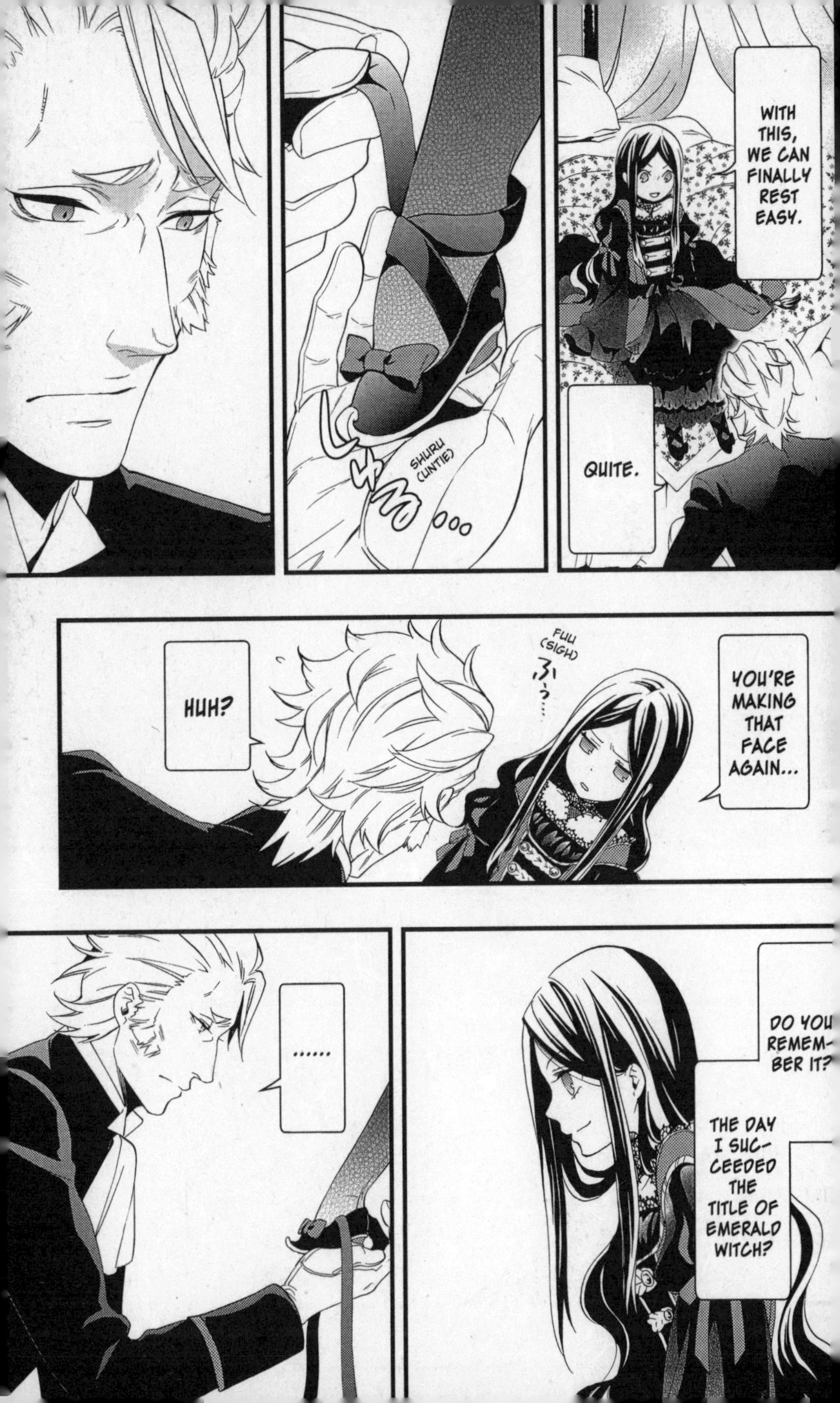
WITH THIS, WE CAN FINALLY REST EASY.
QUITE.
SHURU (UNTIE)
ooo
YOU'RE MAKING THAT FACE AGAIN...
FUU (SIGH)
HUH?
DO YOU REMEMBER IT?
THE DAY I SUCCEEDED THE TITLE OF EMERALD WITCH?
......

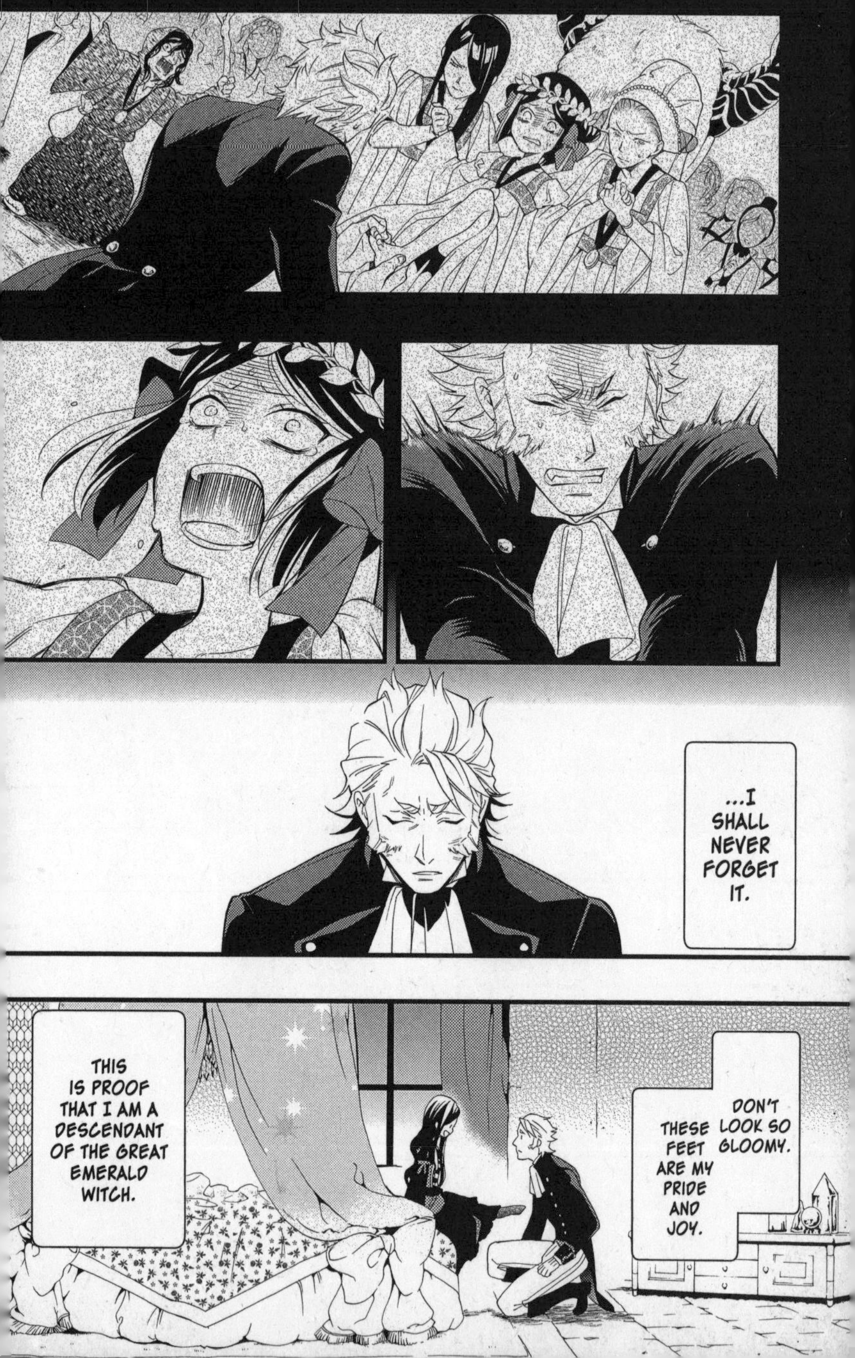
...I SHALL NEVER FORGET IT.
DON'T LOOK SO GLOOMY.
THESE FEET ARE MY PRIDE AND JOY.
THIS IS PROOF THAT I AM A DESCENDANT OF THE GREAT EMERALD WITCH.

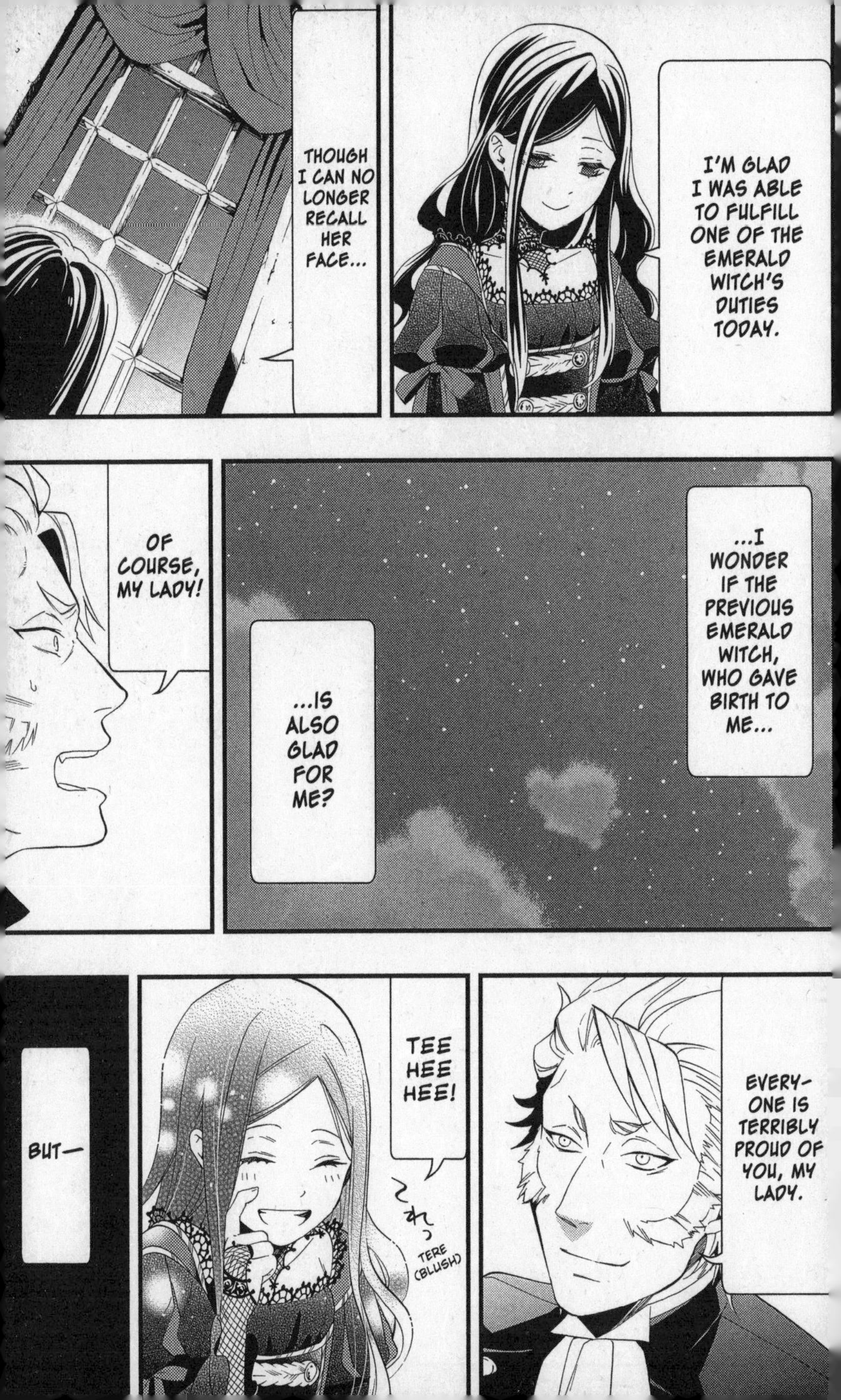
I'M GLAD I WAS ABLE TO FULFILL ONE OF THE EMERALD WITCH'S DUTIES TODAY.
THOUGH I CAN NO LONGER RECALL HER FACE...
...I WONDER IF THE PREVIOUS EMERALD WITCH, WHO GAVE BIRTH TO ME...
...IS ALSO GLAD FOR ME?
OF COURSE, MY LADY!
EVERYONE IS TERRIBLY PROUD OF YOU, MY LADY.
TEE HEE HEE!
てれっ
TERE (BLUSH)
BUT—

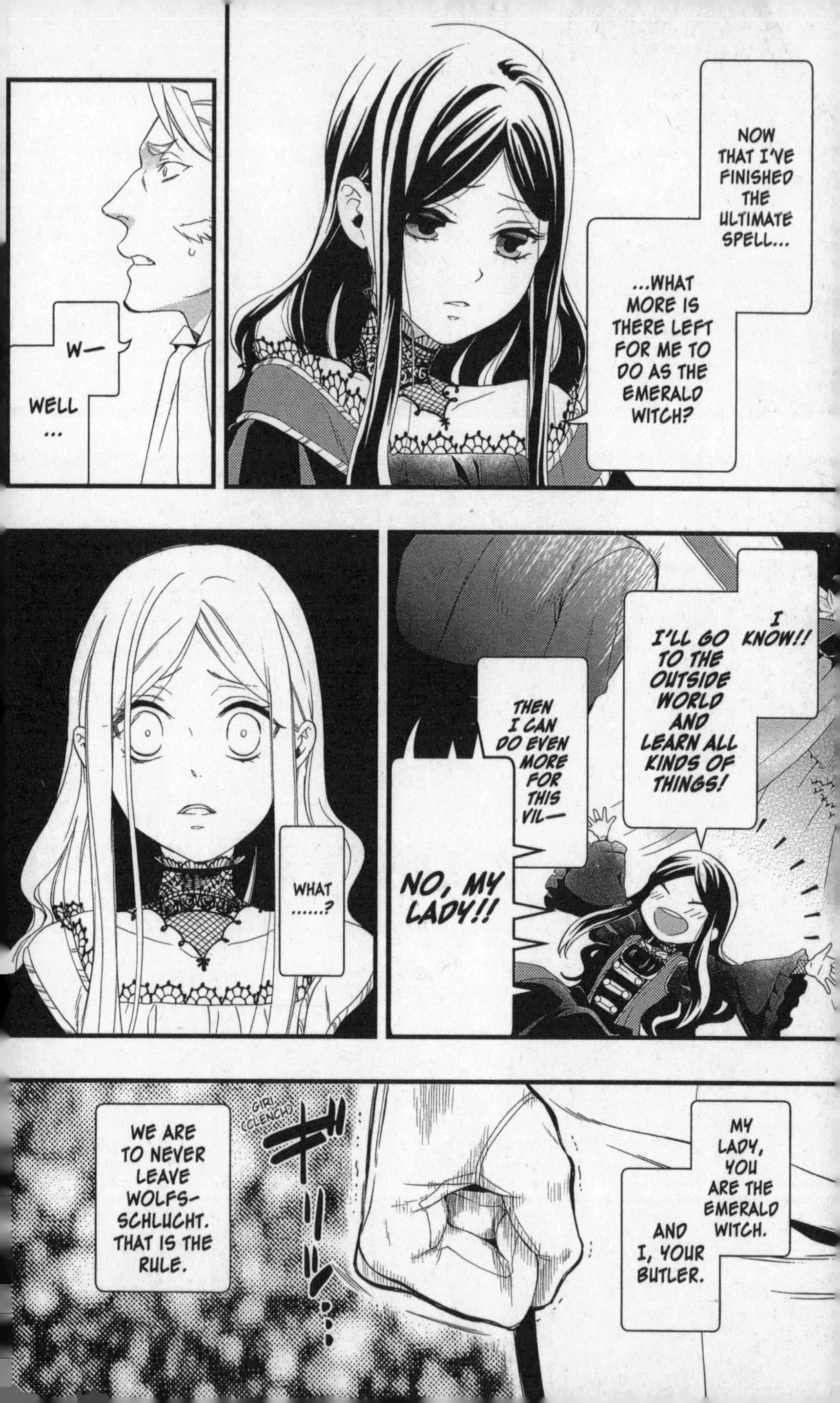
NOW THAT I'VE FINISHED THE ULTIMATE SPELL...
...WHAT MORE IS THERE LEFT FOR ME TO DO AS THE EMERALD WITCH?
W— WELL ...
I KNOW!!
I'LL GO TO THE OUTSIDE WORLD AND LEARN ALL KINDS OF THINGS!
THEN I CAN DO EVEN MORE FOR THIS VIL—
NO, MY LADY!!
WHAT ......?
MY LADY, YOU ARE THE EMERALD WITCH.
AND I, YOUR BUTLER.
GIRI (CLENCH)
WE ARE TO NEVER LEAVE WOLFS-SCHLUCHT. THAT IS THE RULE.

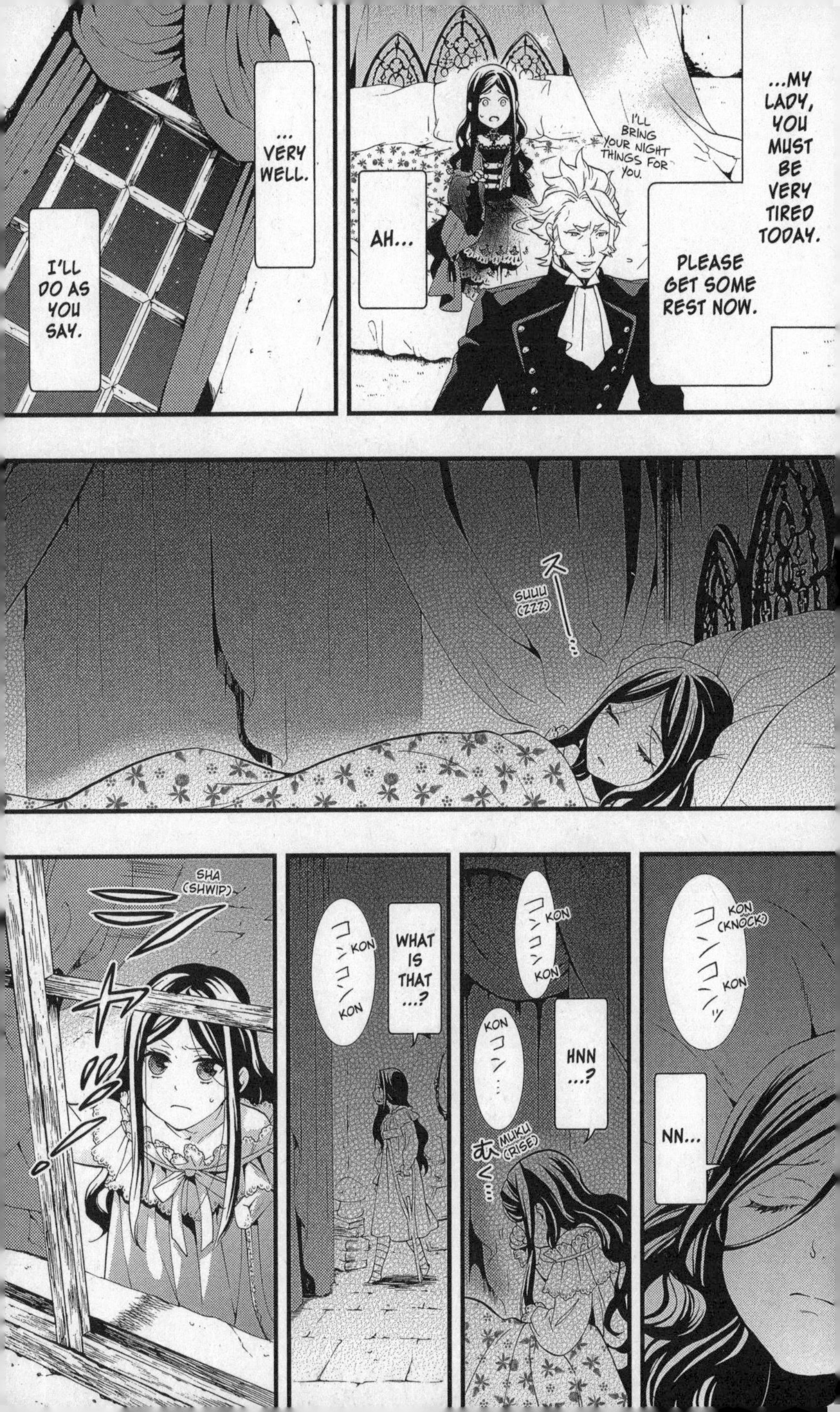
...MY LADY, YOU MUST BE VERY TIRED TODAY.
PLEASE GET SOME REST NOW.
I'LL BRING YOUR NIGHT THINGS FOR YOU.
AH...
... VERY WELL.
I'LL DO AS YOU SAY.
SUUU (ZZZ)
KON (KNOCK)
KON
NN...
KON
KON
HNN ...?
KON
MUKU (RISE)
WHAT IS THAT ...?
KON
KON
SHA (SHWIP)

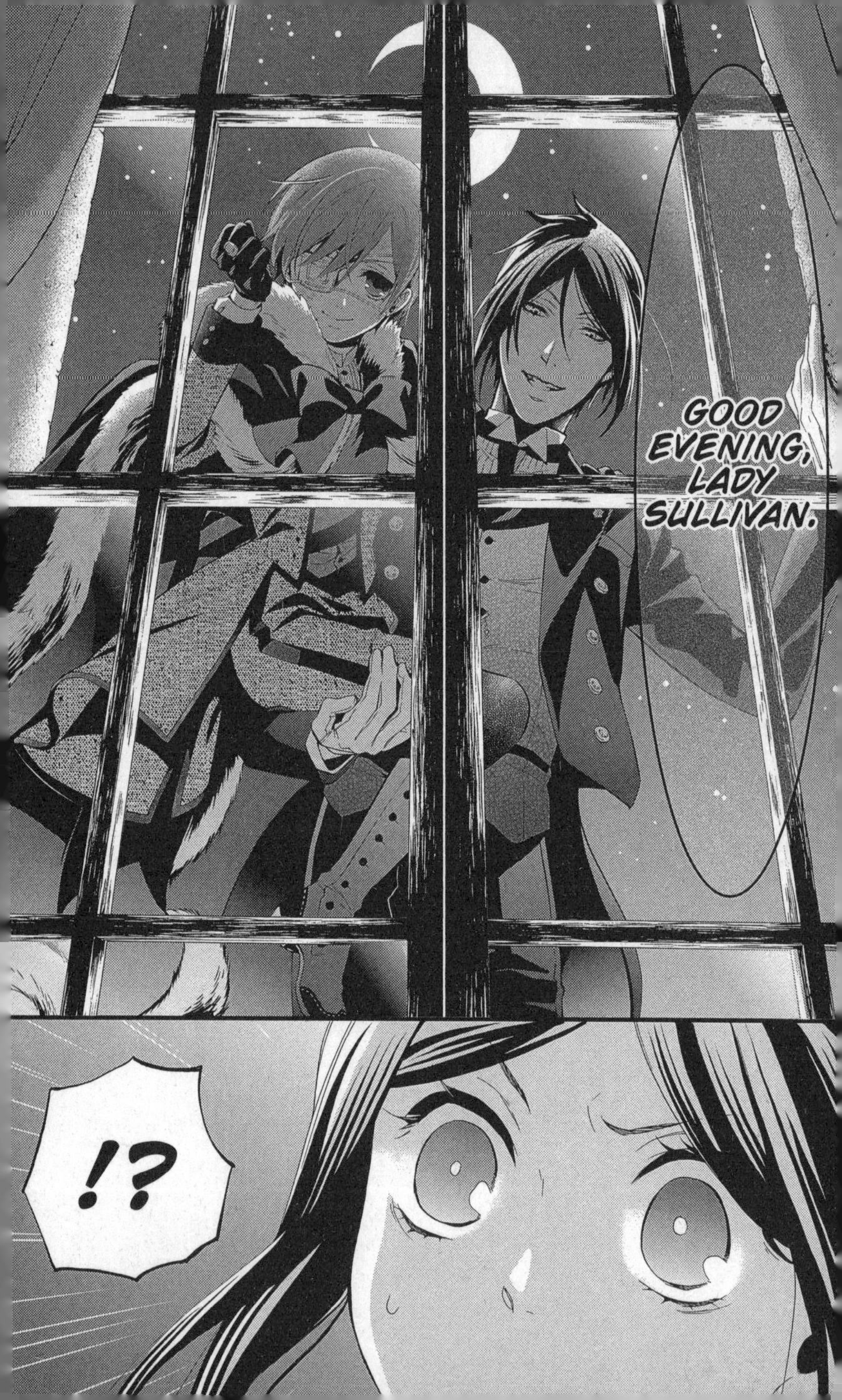
GOOD EVENING, LADY SULLIVAN.
!?

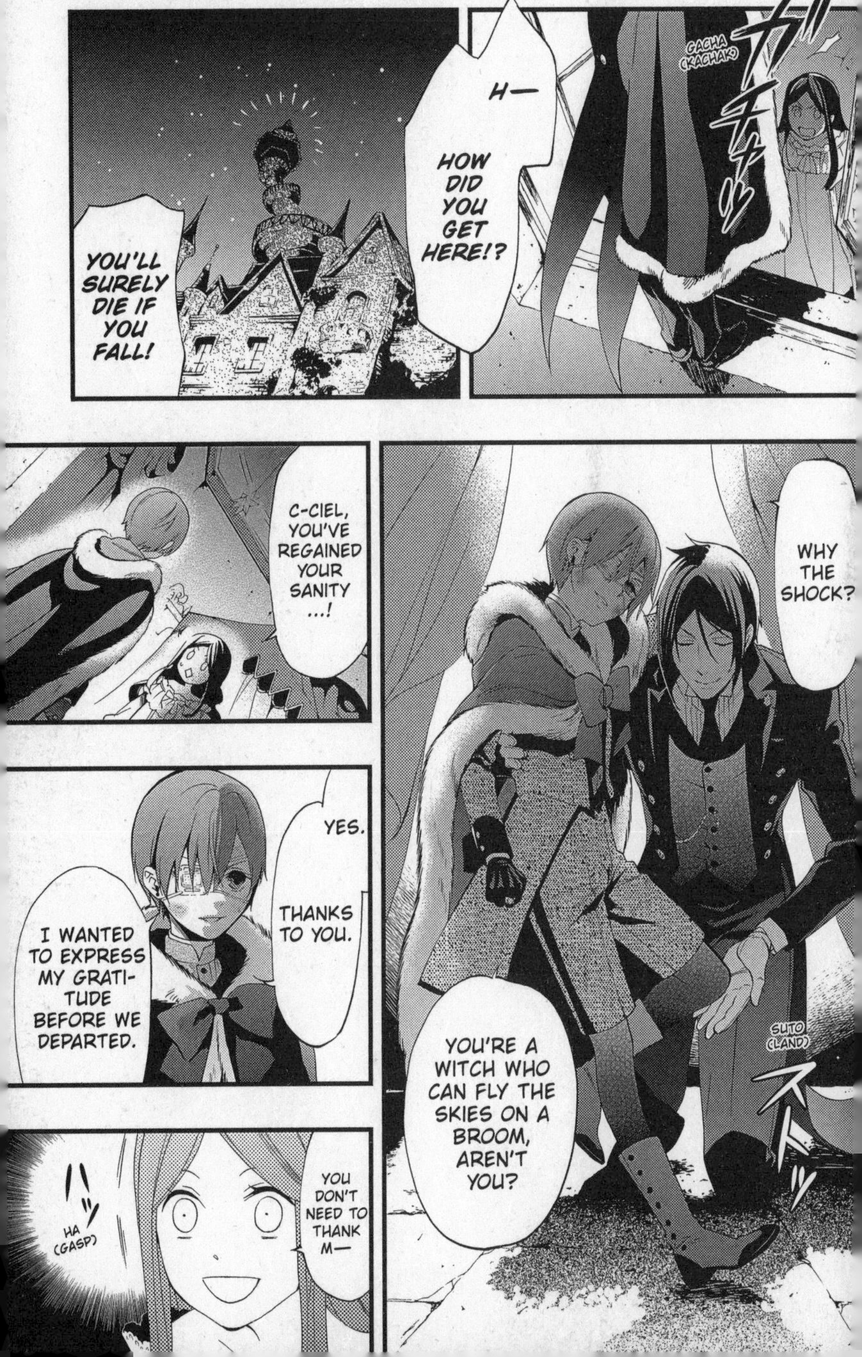
GACHA (KACHAK)
H—
HOW DID YOU GET HERE!?
YOU'LL SURELY DIE IF YOU FALL!
WHY THE SHOCK?
SUTO (LAND)
YOU'RE A WITCH WHO CAN FLY THE SKIES ON A BROOM, AREN'T YOU?
C-CIEL, YOU'VE REGAINED YOUR SANITY ...!
YES.
THANKS TO YOU.
I WANTED TO EXPRESS MY GRATI-TUDE BEFORE WE DEPARTED.
HA (GASP)
YOU DON'T NEED TO THANK M—

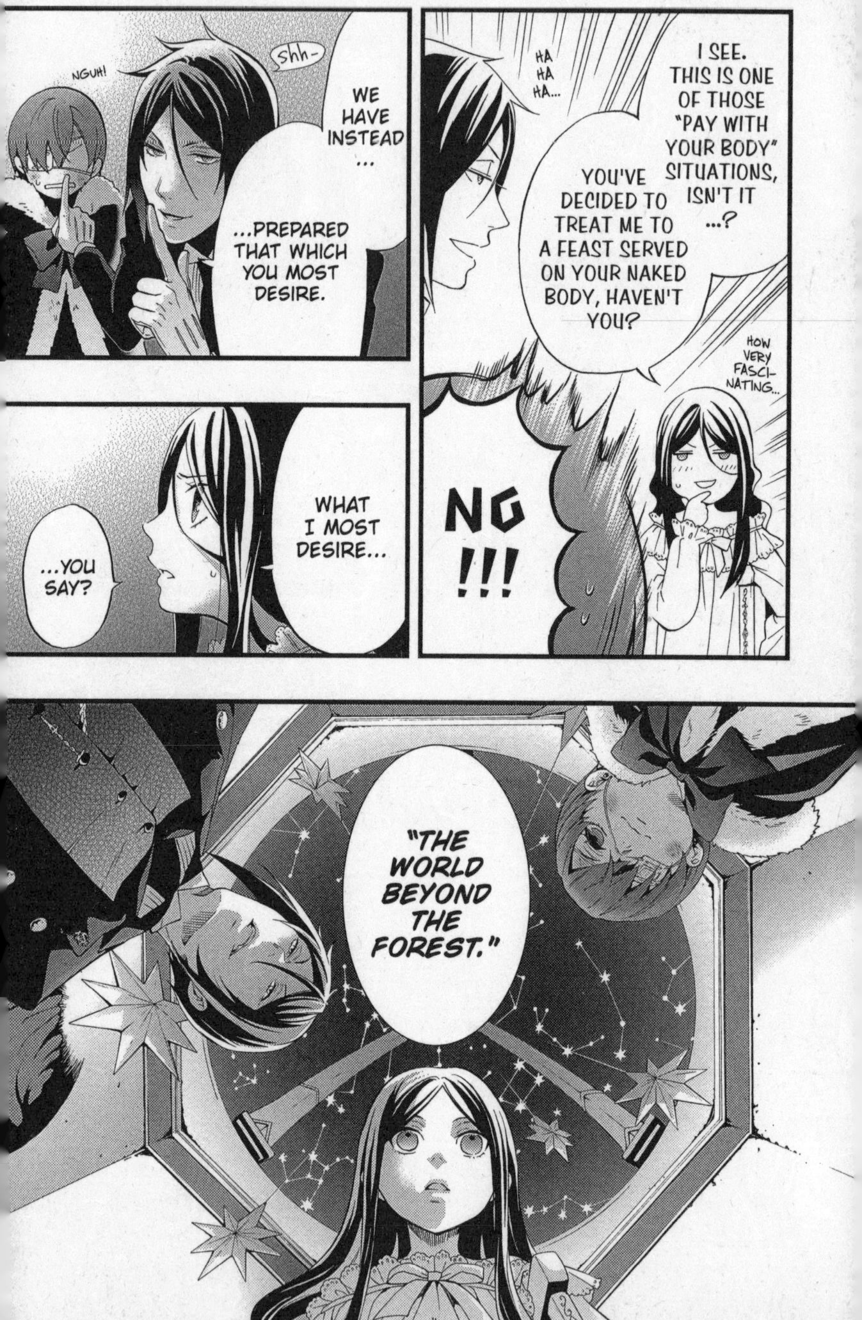
I SEE. THIS IS ONE OF THOSE "PAY WITH YOUR BODY" SITUATIONS, ISN'T IT ...?
HA HA HA...
YOU'VE DECIDED TO TREAT ME TO A FEAST SERVED ON YOUR NAKED BODY, HAVEN'T YOU?
HOW VERY FASCINATING...
NG !!!
WE HAVE INSTEAD ...
Shh-
NGUH!
...PREPARED THAT WHICH YOU MOST DESIRE.
WHAT I MOST DESIRE...
...YOU SAY?
"THE WORLD BEYOND THE FOREST."

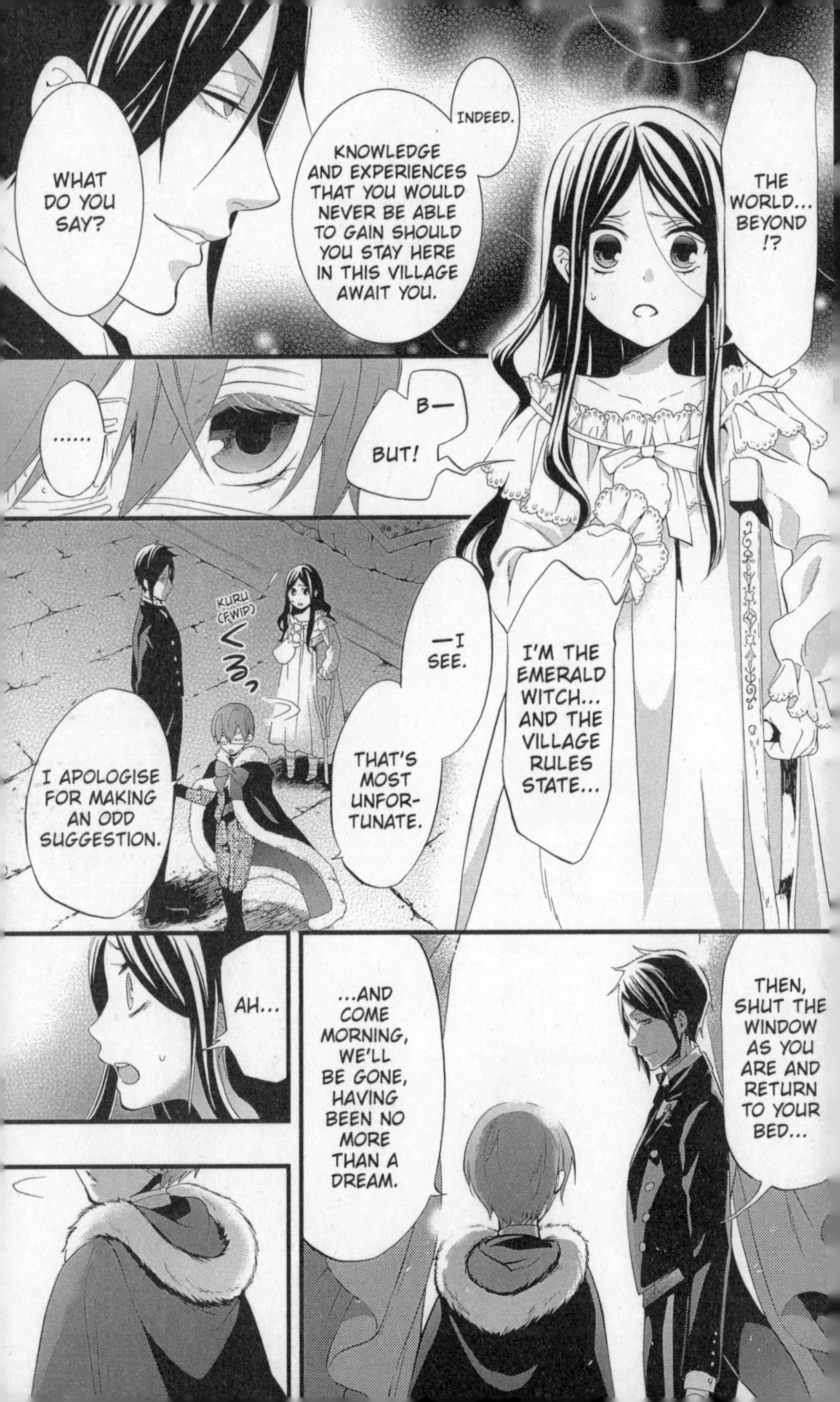

THE WORLD... BEYOND !?
INDEED.
KNOWLEDGE AND EXPERIENCES THAT YOU WOULD NEVER BE ABLE TO GAIN SHOULD YOU STAY HERE IN THIS VILLAGE AWAIT YOU.
WHAT DO YOU SAY?
......
B— BUT!
I'M THE EMERALD WITCH... AND THE VILLAGE RULES STATE...
—I SEE.
THAT'S MOST UNFORTUNATE.
KURU (FWIP)
I APOLOGISE FOR MAKING AN ODD SUGGESTION.
THEN, SHUT THE WINDOW AS YOU ARE AND RETURN TO YOUR BED...
...AND COME MORNING, WE'LL BE GONE, HAVING BEEN NO MORE THAN A DREAM.
AH...

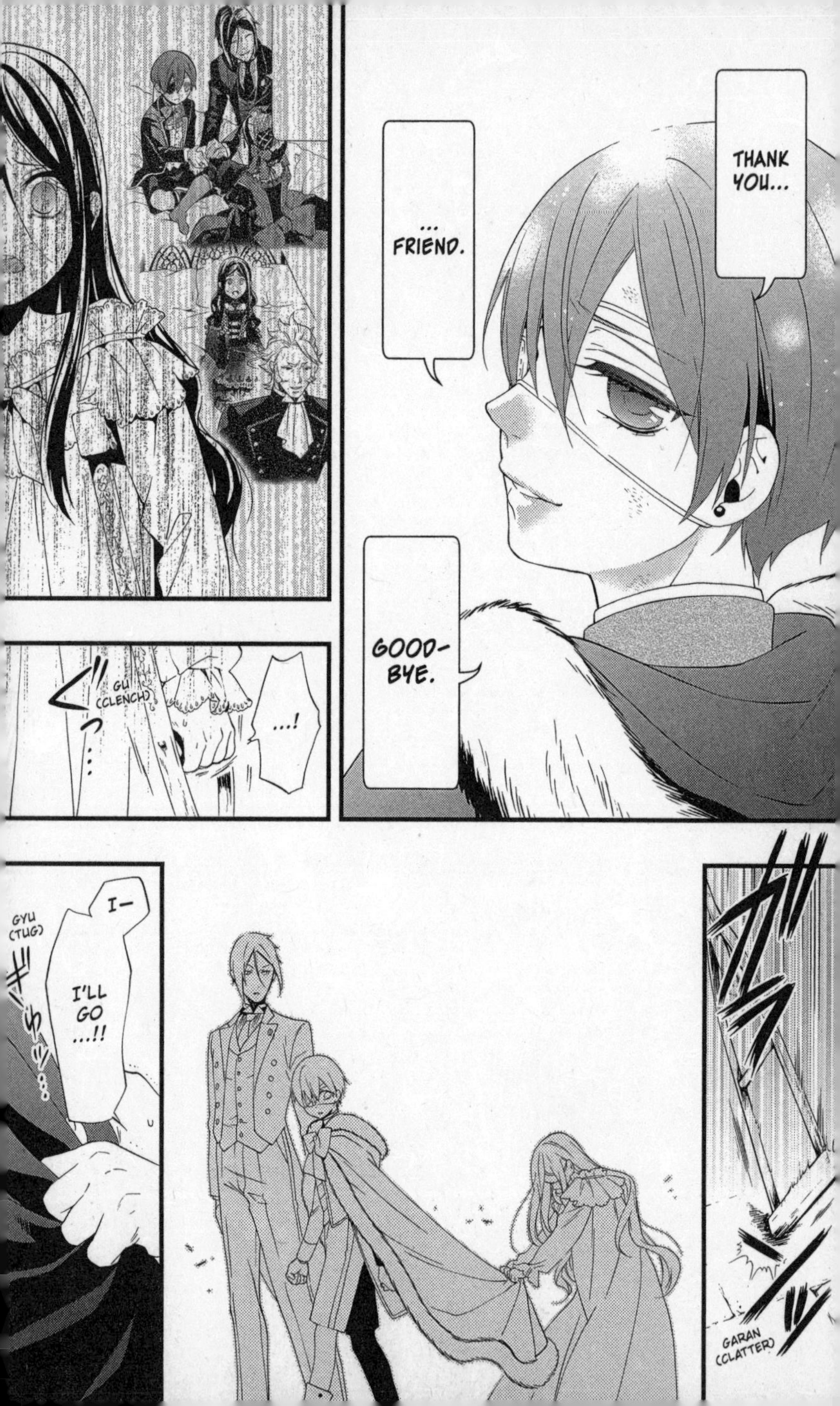

THANK YOU...
...FRIEND.
GOOD-BYE.
...!
GU (CLENCH)
GARAN (CLATTER)
I—
I'LL GO ...!!
GYU (TUG)

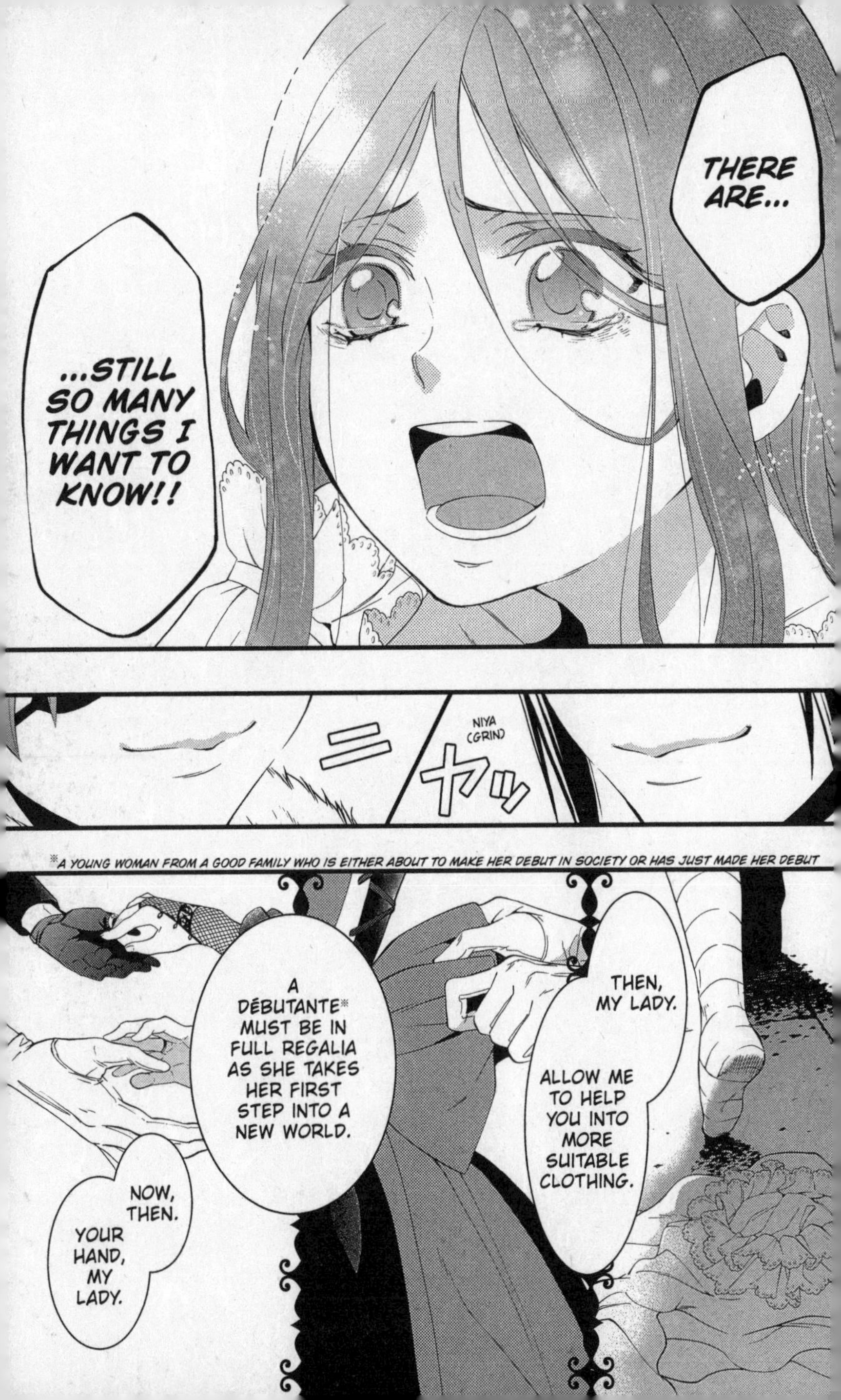
THERE ARE...
...STILL SO MANY THINGS I WANT TO KNOW!!
NIYA (GRIN)
ニヤッ
THEN, MY LADY.
ALLOW ME TO HELP YOU INTO MORE SUITABLE CLOTHING.
A DÉBUTANTE※ MUST BE IN FULL REGALIA AS SHE TAKES HER FIRST STEP INTO A NEW WORLD.
NOW, THEN.
YOUR HAND, MY LADY.

※A YOUNG WOMAN FROM A GOOD FAMILY WHO IS EITHER ABOUT TO MAKE HER DEBUT IN SOCIETY OR HAS JUST MADE HER DEBUT

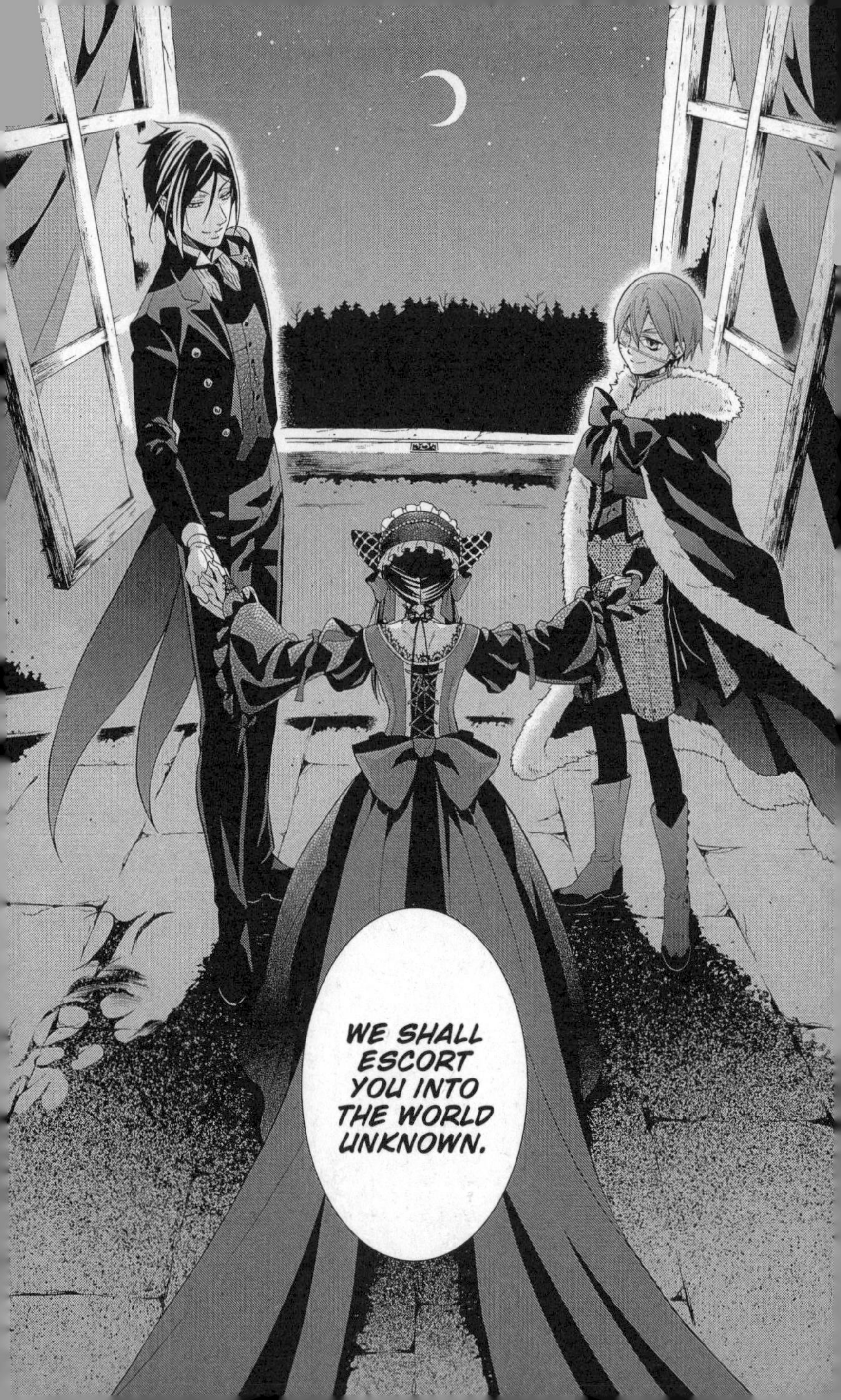
WE SHALL ESCORT YOU INTO THE WORLD UNKNOWN.

Black Butler

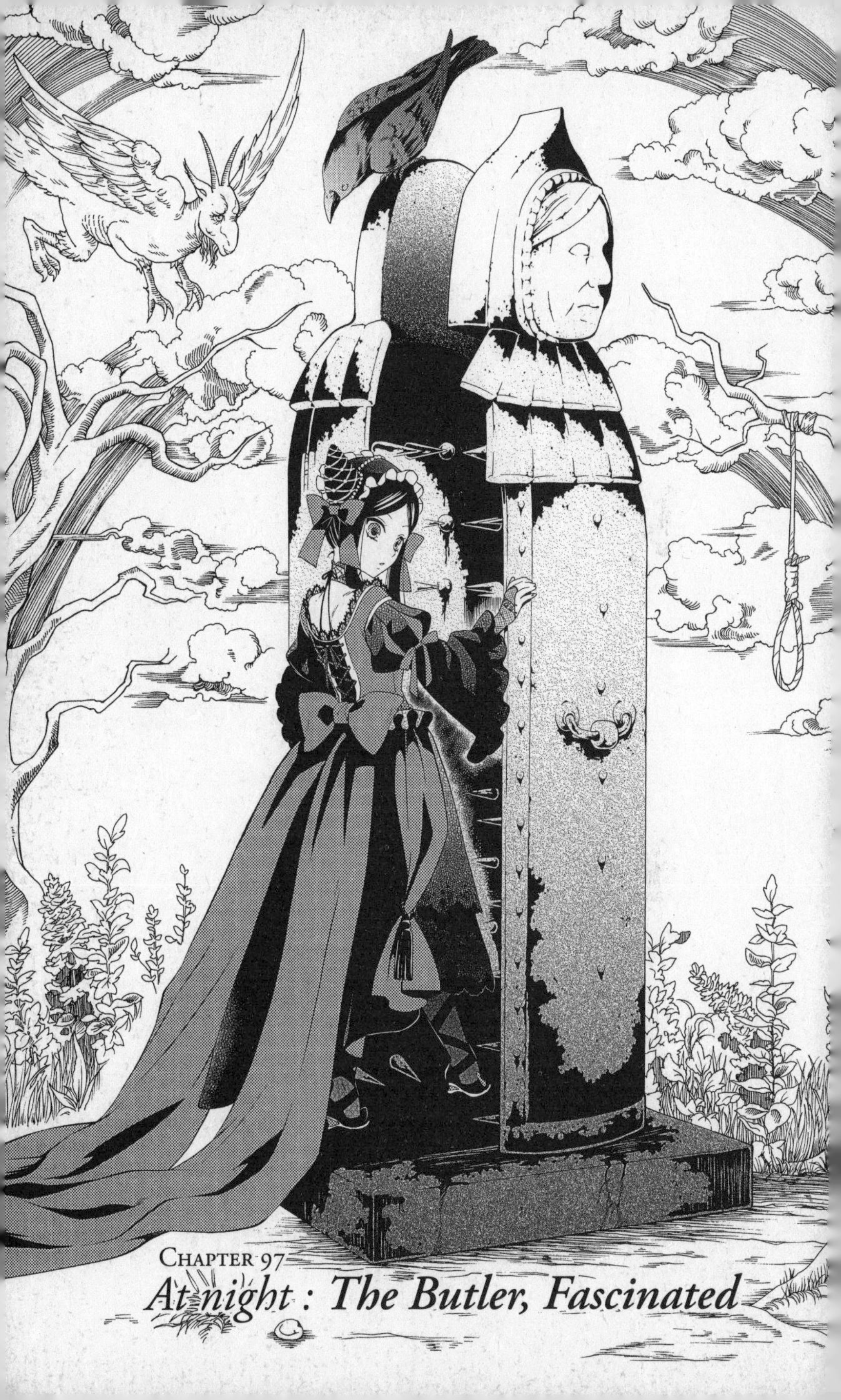

CHAPTER 97

At night : The Butler, Fascinated

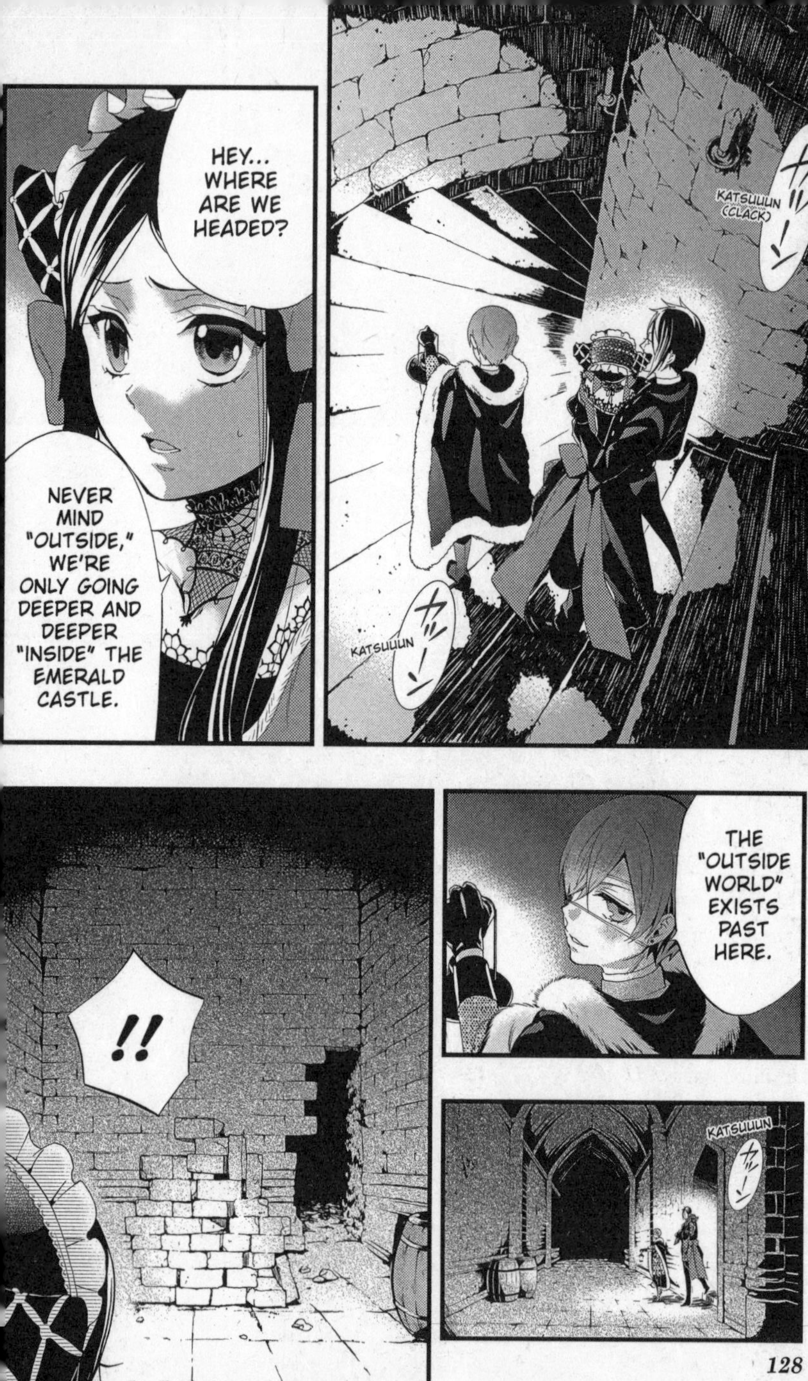
KATSUUUN (CLACK)
KATSUUUN
HEY... WHERE ARE WE HEADED?
NEVER MIND "OUTSIDE," WE'RE ONLY GOING DEEPER AND DEEPER "INSIDE" THE EMERALD CASTLE.
THE "OUTSIDE WORLD" EXISTS PAST HERE.
KATSUUUN
!!

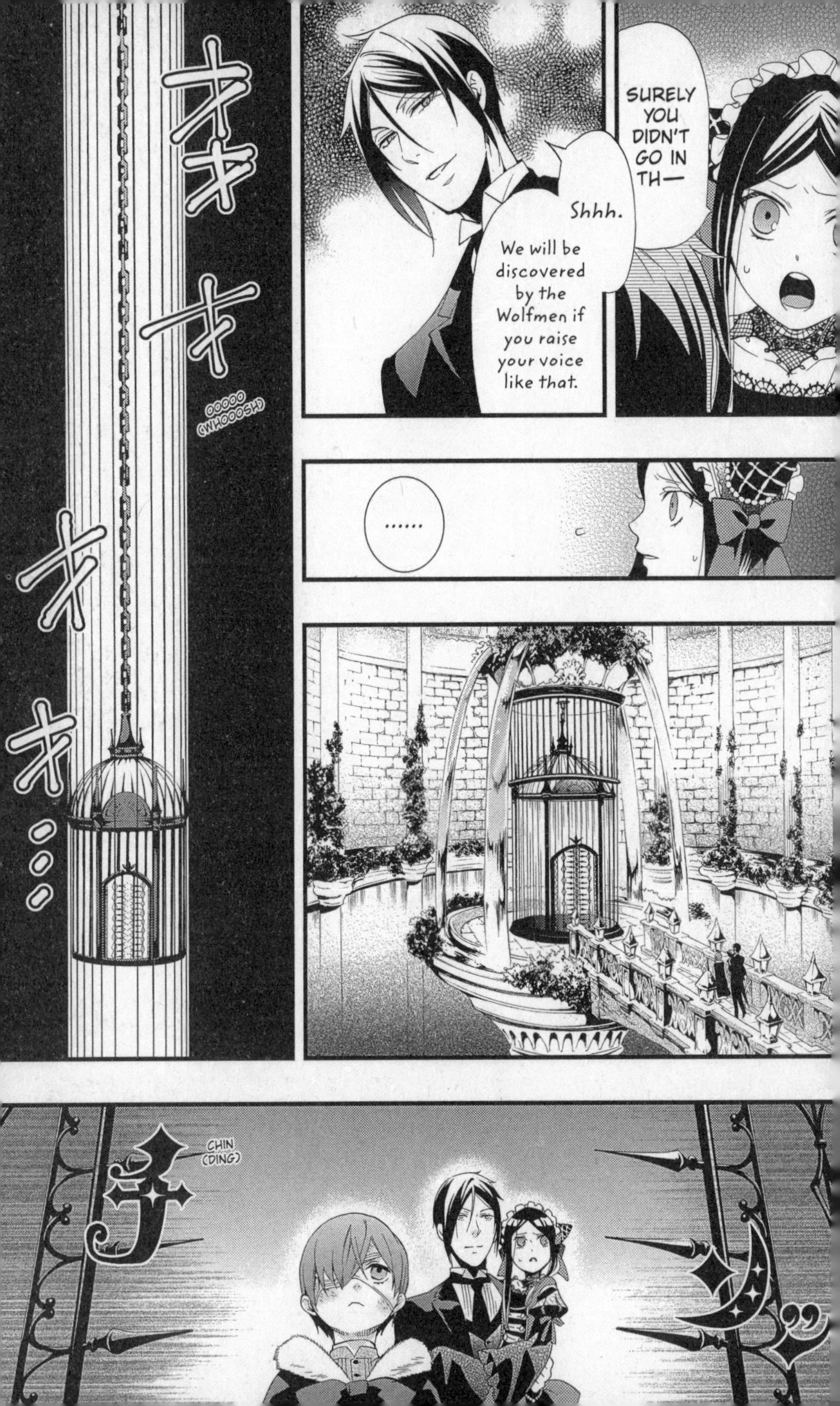
SURELY YOU DIDN'T GO IN TH—
Shhh.
We will be discovered by the Wolfmen if you raise your voice like that.
......
オォォォ…
OOOOO (WHOOOSH)
CHIN (DING)

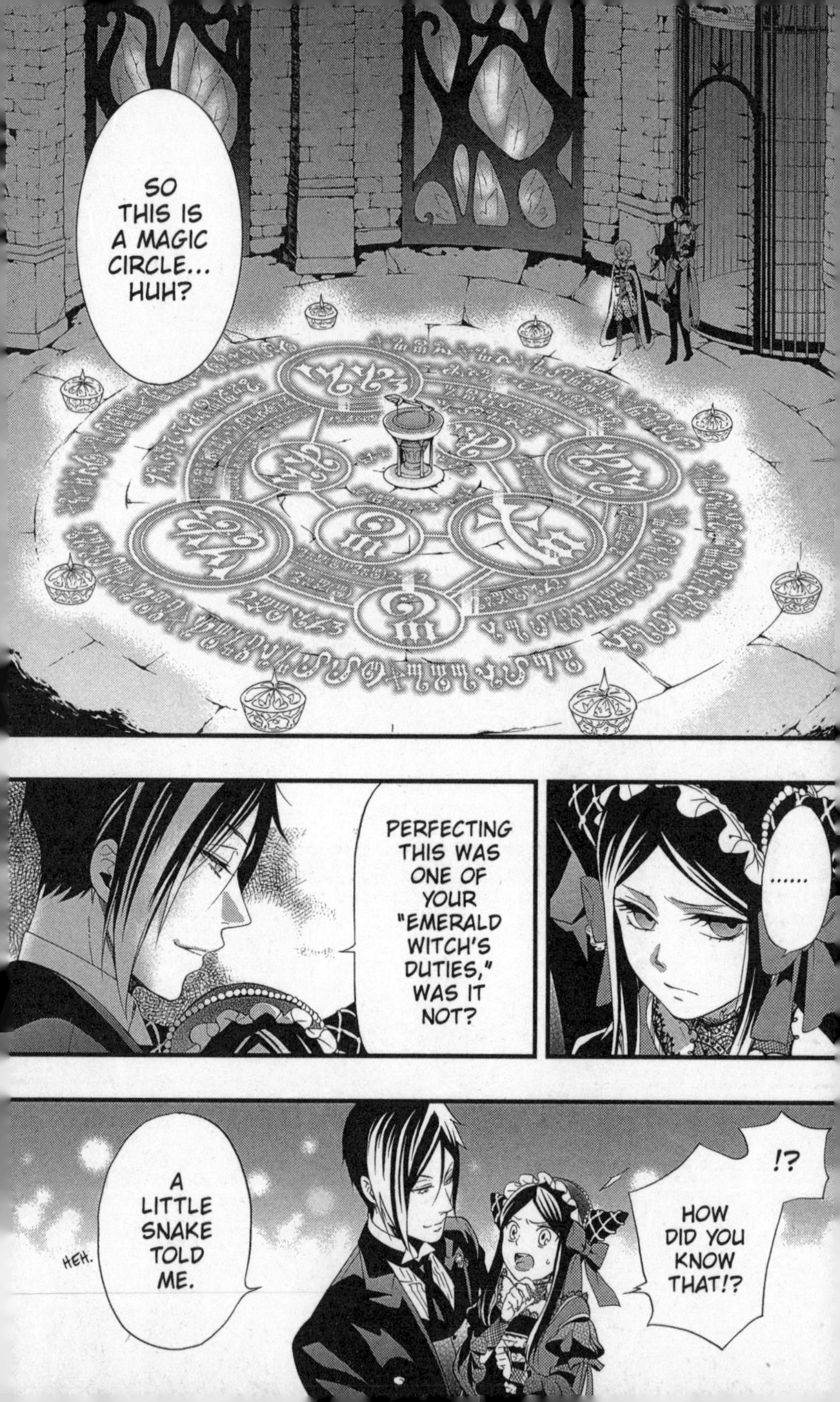
SO THIS IS A MAGIC CIRCLE... HUH?
......
PERFECTING THIS WAS ONE OF YOUR "EMERALD WITCH'S DUTIES," WAS IT NOT?
!?
HOW DID YOU KNOW THAT!?
A LITTLE SNAKE TOLD ME.
HEH.

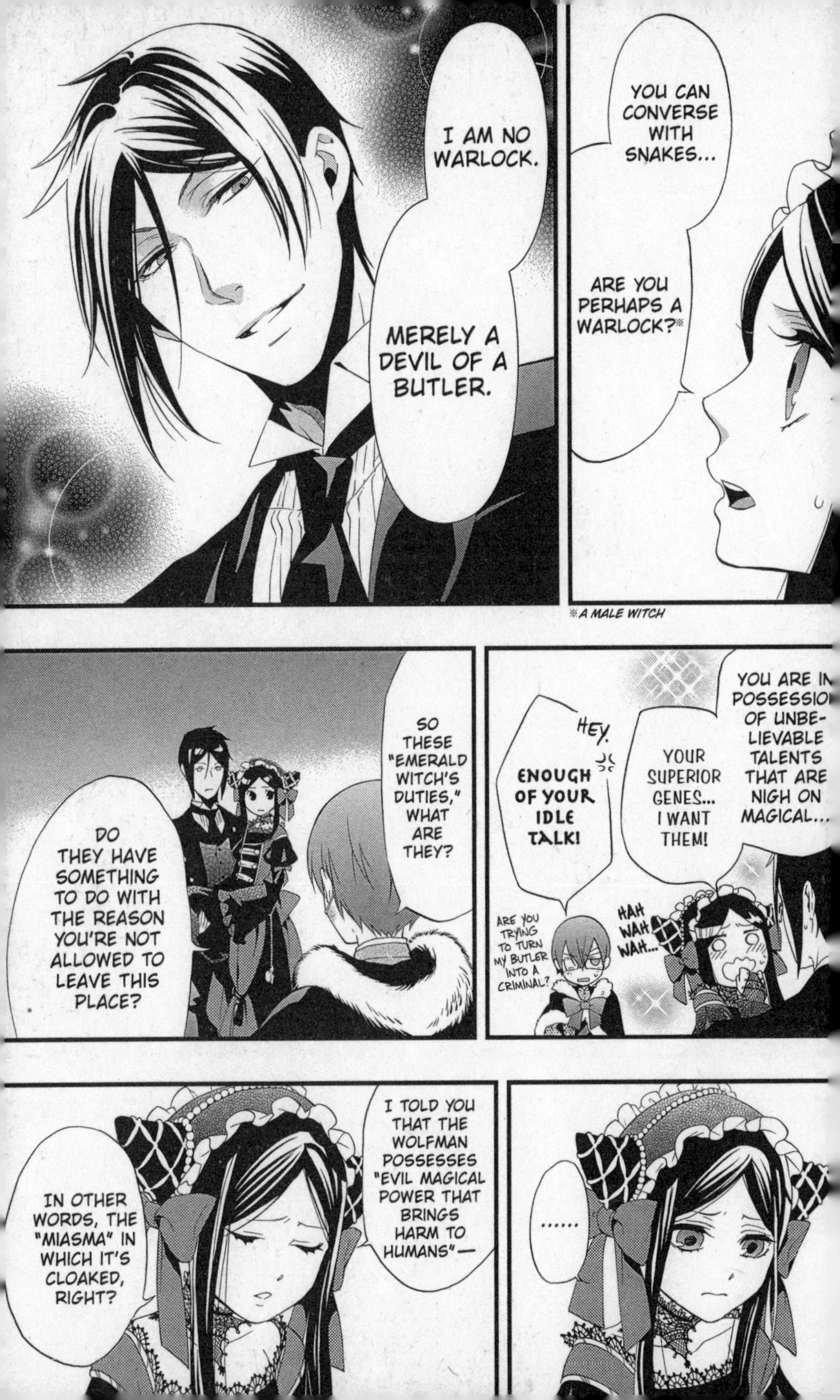
YOU CAN CONVERSE WITH SNAKES...
ARE YOU PERHAPS A WARLOCK?※
I AM NO WARLOCK.
MERELY A DEVIL OF A BUTLER.
※A MALE WITCH
YOU ARE IN POSSESSIO OF UNBE-LIEVABLE TALENTS THAT ARE NIGH ON MAGICAL...
YOUR SUPERIOR GENES... I WANT THEM!
HEY.
ENOUGH OF YOUR IDLE TALK!
ARE YOU TRYING TO TURN MY BUTLER INTO A CRIMINAL?
HAH WAH WAH...
SO THESE "EMERALD WITCH'S DUTIES," WHAT ARE THEY?
DO THEY HAVE SOMETHING TO DO WITH THE REASON YOU'RE NOT ALLOWED TO LEAVE THIS PLACE?
......
I TOLD YOU THAT THE WOLFMAN POSSESSES "EVIL MAGICAL POWER THAT BRINGS HARM TO HUMANS"—
IN OTHER WORDS, THE "MIASMA" IN WHICH IT'S CLOAKED, RIGHT?

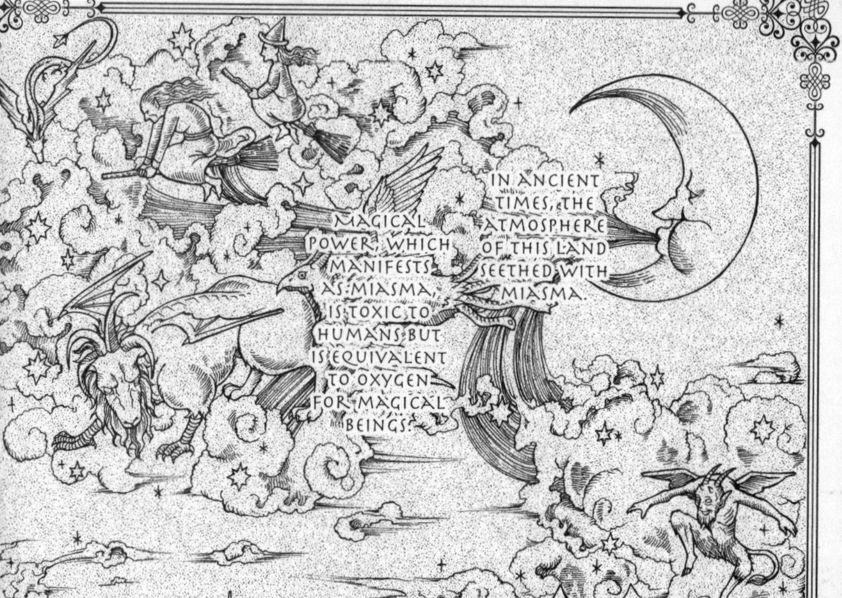
IN ANCIENT TIMES, THE ATMOSPHERE OF THIS LAND SEETHED WITH MIASMA.
MAGICAL POWER, WHICH MANIFESTS AS MIASMA, IS TOXIC TO HUMANS BUT IS EQUIVALENT TO OXYGEN FOR MAGICAL BEINGS.
HOWEVER, AS THE PRICE OF HUMAN PROSPERITY, IT WAS LOST.
IT IS SAID THAT IS WHY WE WITCHES LOST OUR POWERS AS WELL.
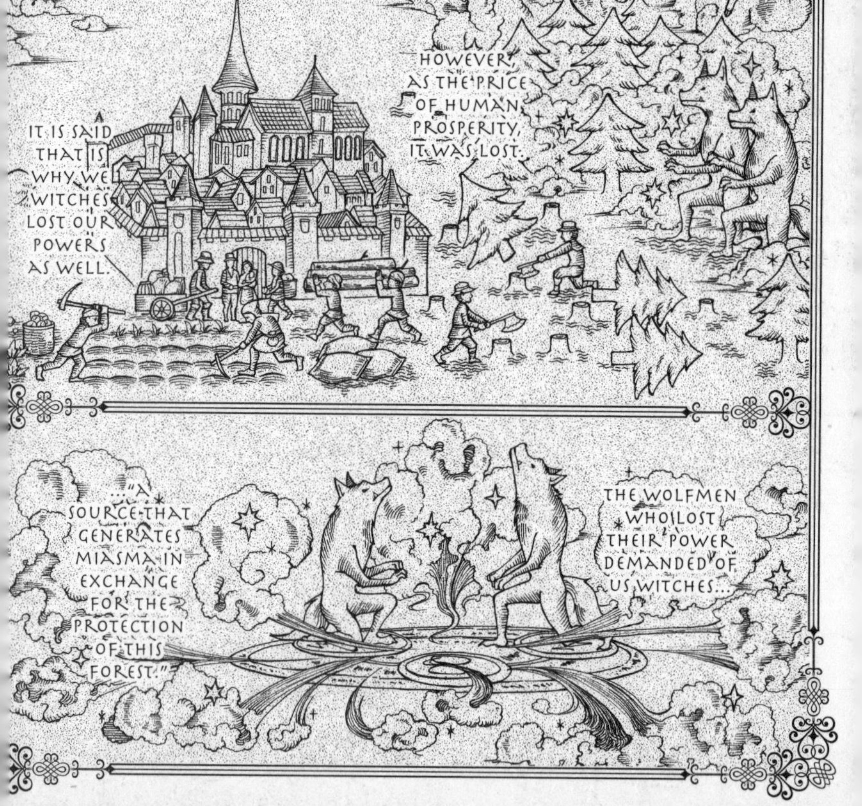
THE WOLFMEN WHO LOST THEIR POWER DEMANDED OF US WITCHES...
..."A SOURCE THAT GENERATES MIASMA IN EXCHANGE FOR THE PROTECTION OF THIS FOREST."

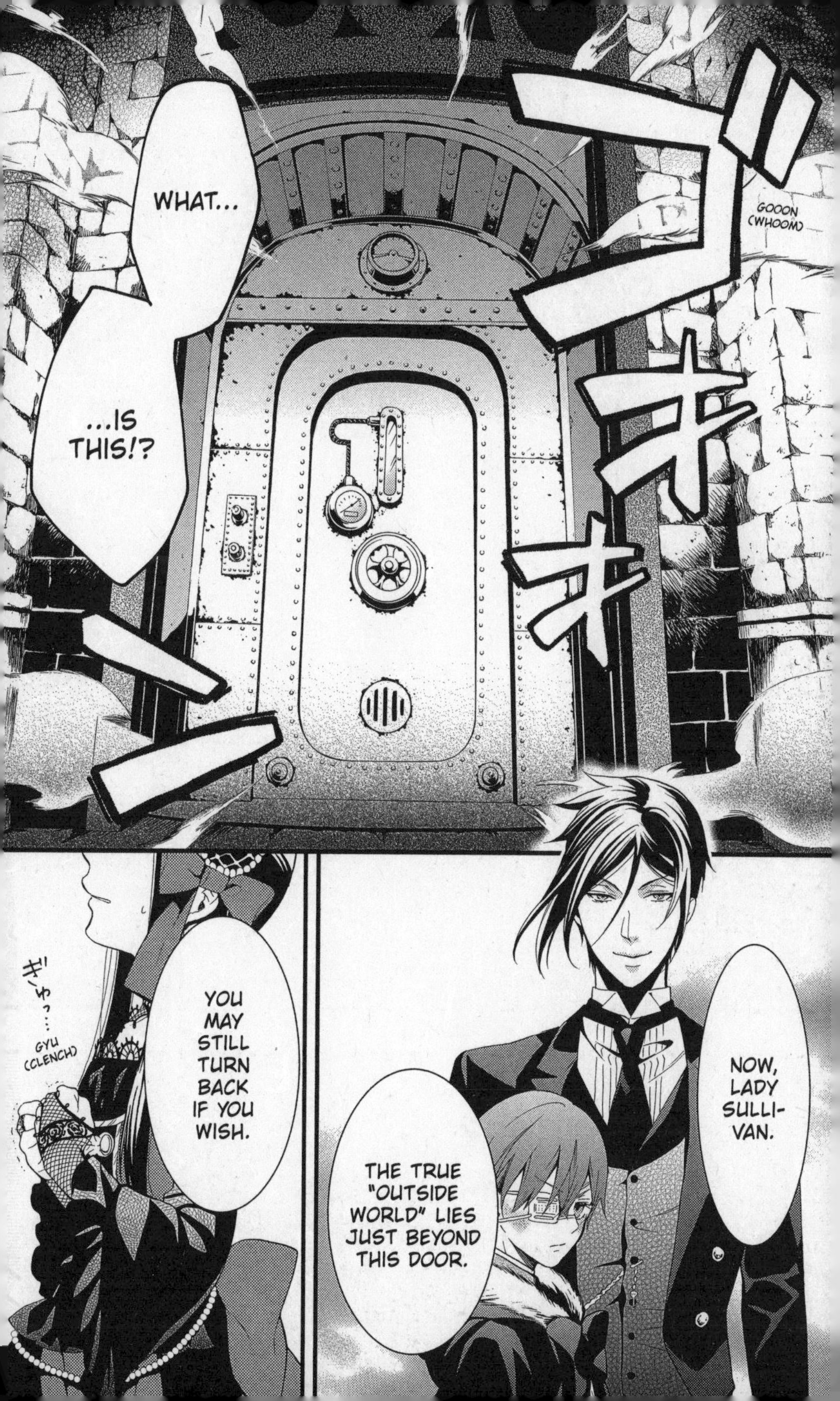
GOOON (WHOOM)
WHAT...
...IS THIS!?
NOW, LADY SULLIVAN.
THE TRUE "OUTSIDE WORLD" LIES JUST BEYOND THIS DOOR.
YOU MAY STILL TURN BACK IF YOU WISH.
ぎゅっ…
GYU (CLENCH)

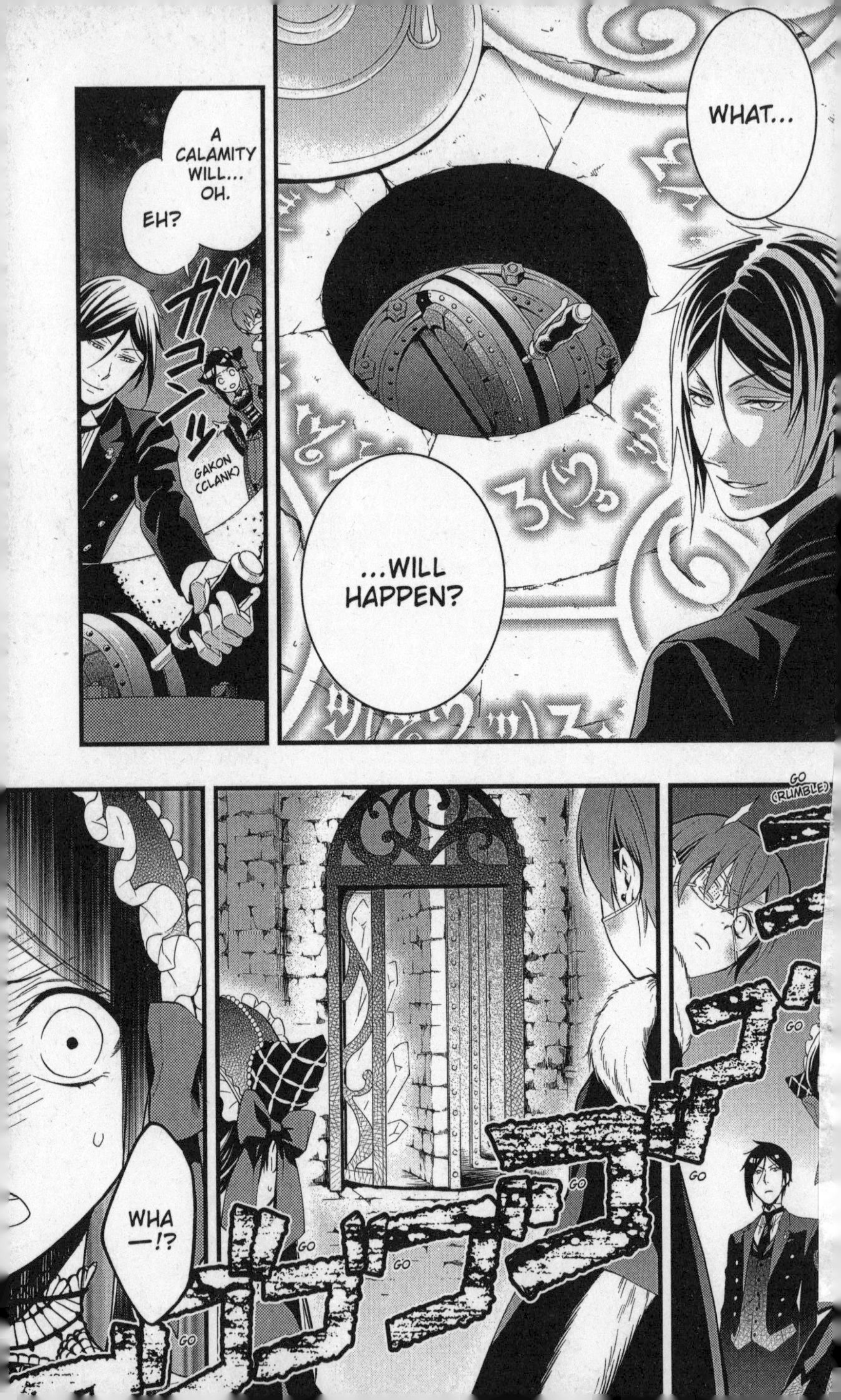
WHAT...
...WILL HAPPEN?
A CALAMITY WILL... OH.
EH?
GAKON (CLANK)
GO (RUMBLE)
GO
GO
GO
GO
GO
WHA—!?
GO

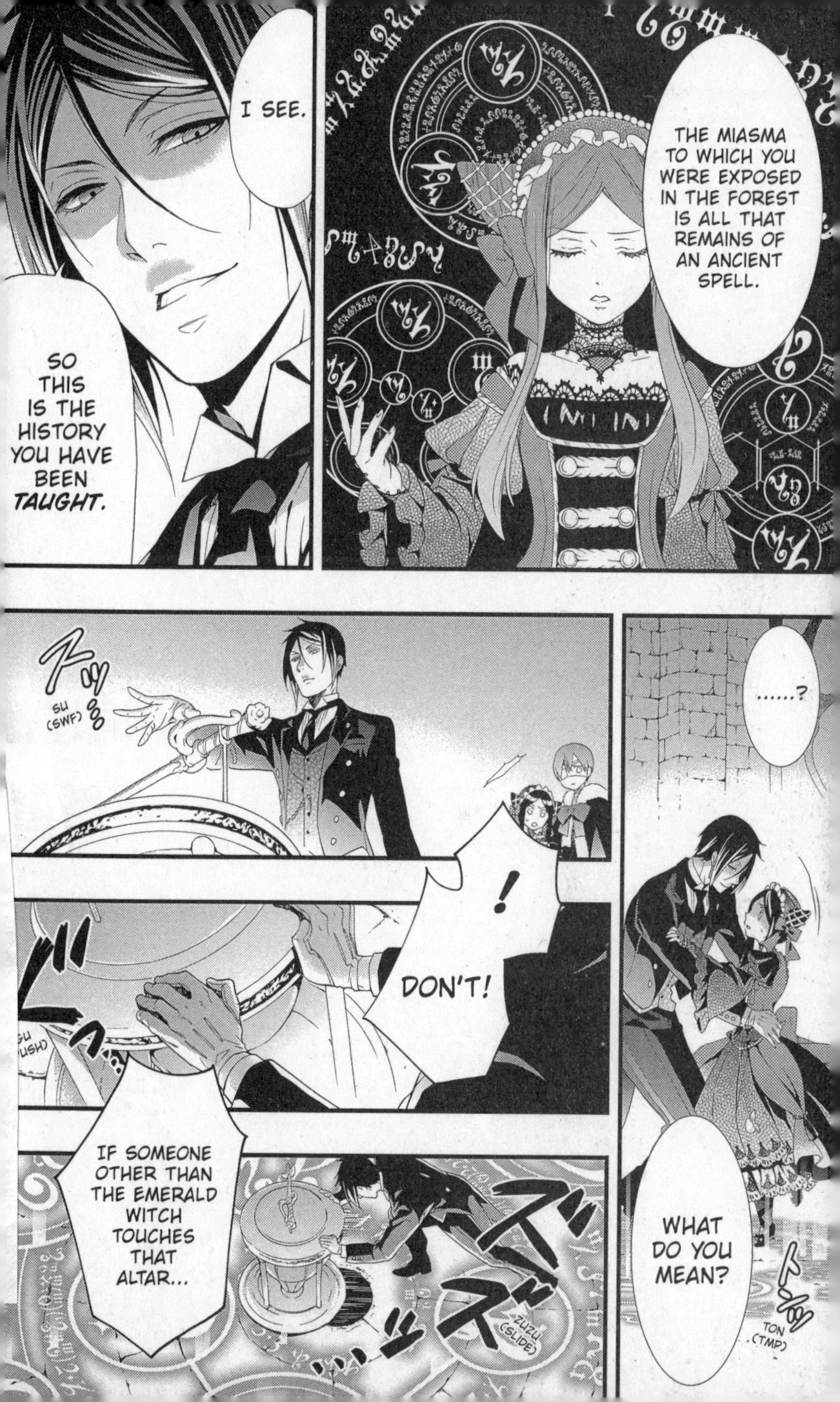

THE MIASMA TO WHICH YOU WERE EXPOSED IN THE FOREST IS ALL THAT REMAINS OF AN ANCIENT SPELL.
I SEE.
SO THIS IS THE HISTORY YOU HAVE BEEN *TAUGHT*.
......?
WHAT DO YOU MEAN?
TON (TMP)
SU (SWF)
!
DON'T!
GU
IF SOMEONE OTHER THAN THE EMERALD WITCH TOUCHES THAT ALTAR...
ZUZU (SLIDE)

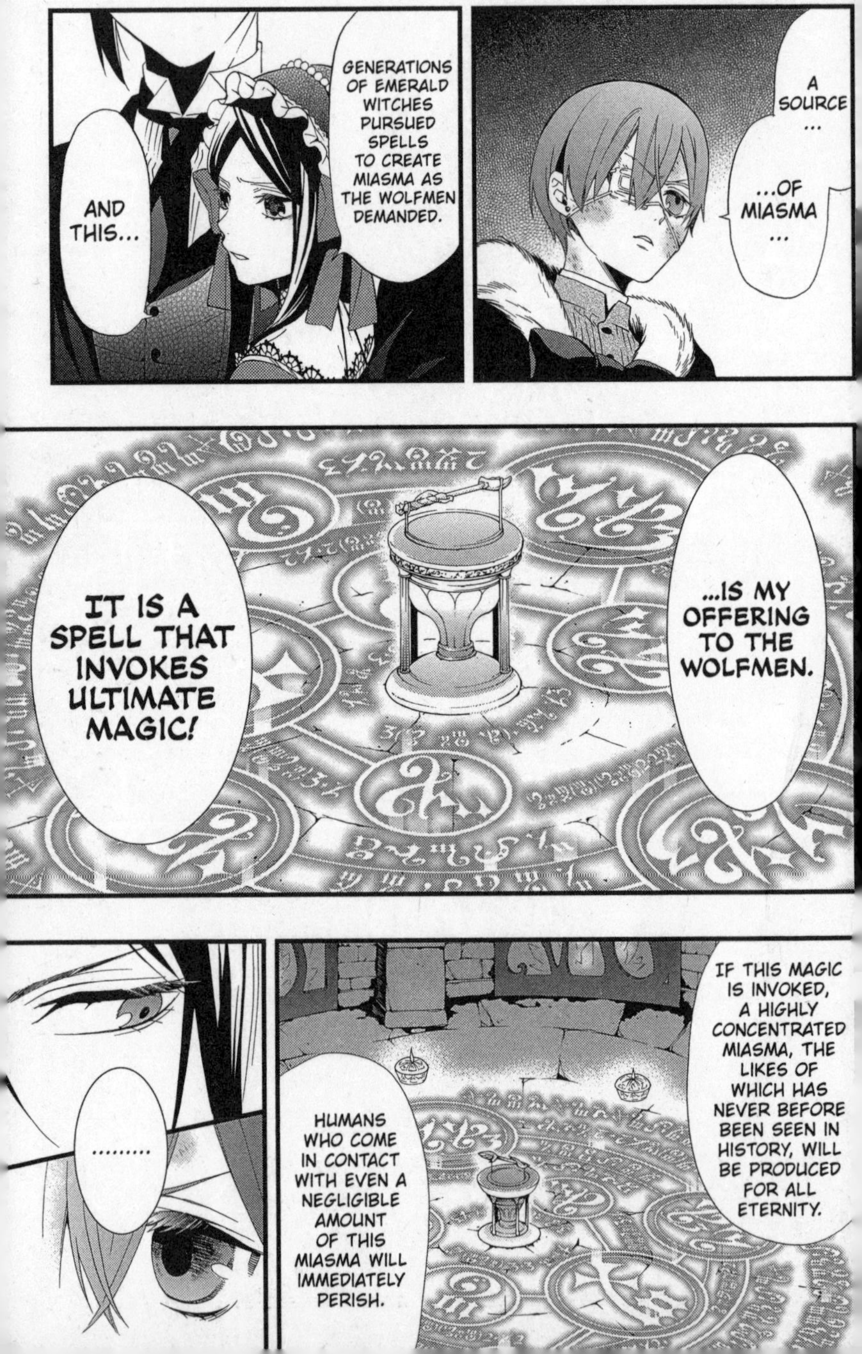
A SOURCE ...
...OF MIASMA ...
GENERATIONS OF EMERALD WITCHES PURSUED SPELLS TO CREATE MIASMA AS THE WOLFMEN DEMANDED.
AND THIS...
...IS MY OFFERING TO THE WOLFMEN.
IT IS A SPELL THAT INVOKES ULTIMATE MAGIC!
IF THIS MAGIC IS INVOKED, A HIGHLY CONCENTRATED MIASMA, THE LIKES OF WHICH HAS NEVER BEFORE BEEN SEEN IN HISTORY, WILL BE PRODUCED FOR ALL ETERNITY.
HUMANS WHO COME IN CONTACT WITH EVEN A NEGLIGIBLE AMOUNT OF THIS MIASMA WILL IMMEDIATELY PERISH.
....

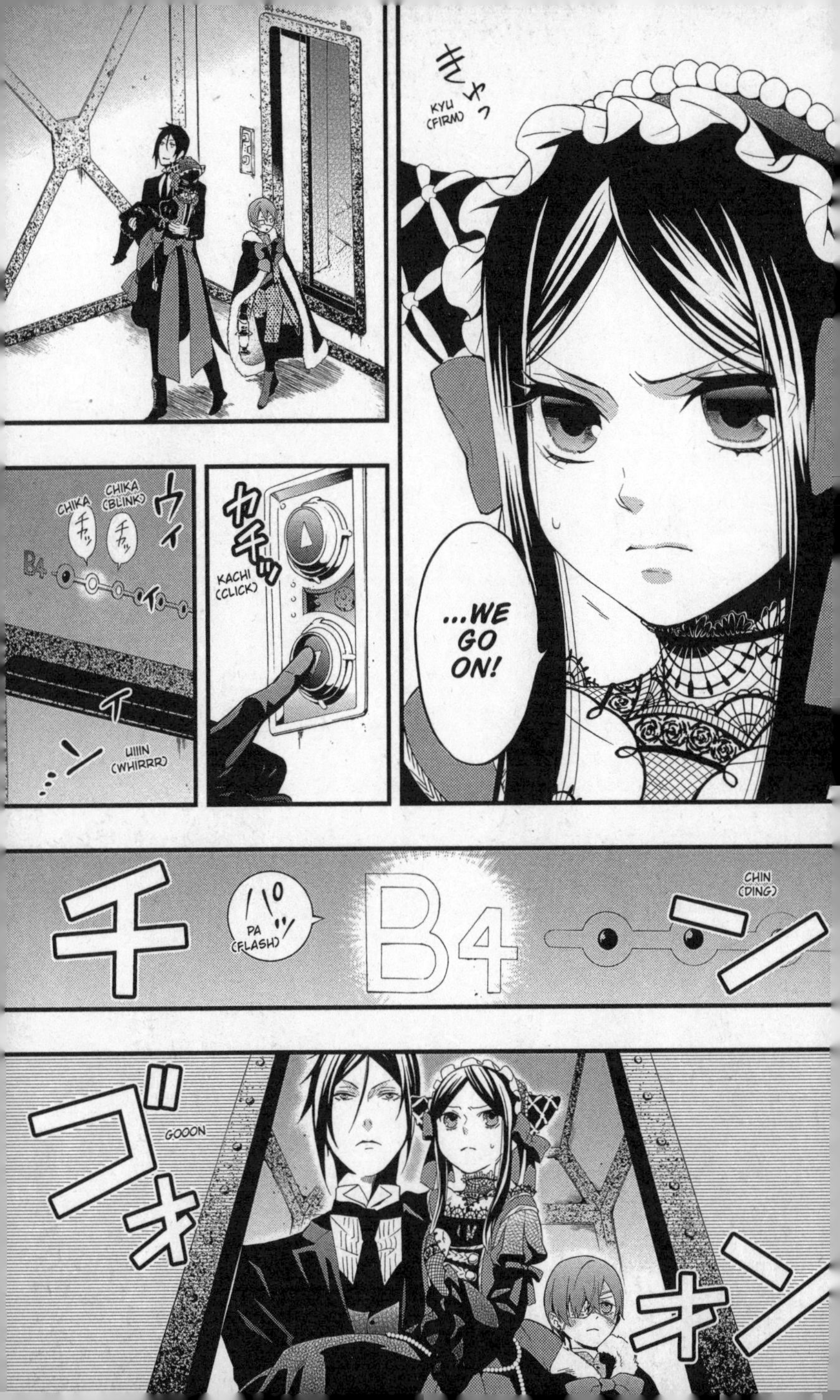

きゅっ
KYU (FIRM)
...WE GO ON!
カチッ
KACHI (CLICK)
チカッ
CHIKA (BLINK)
チカッ
CHIKA
B4
UIIIN (WHIRRR)
チーン
CHIN (DING)
B4
パッ
PA (FLASH)
ゴォォン
GOOON

OOOOO
(FWOOSH)

GI
(CREAK)

COME,
YOU TWO.

...!

HEY.

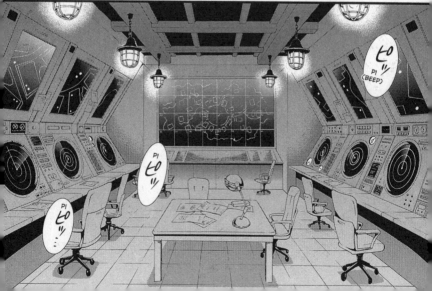

PI
(BEEP)

PI

PI

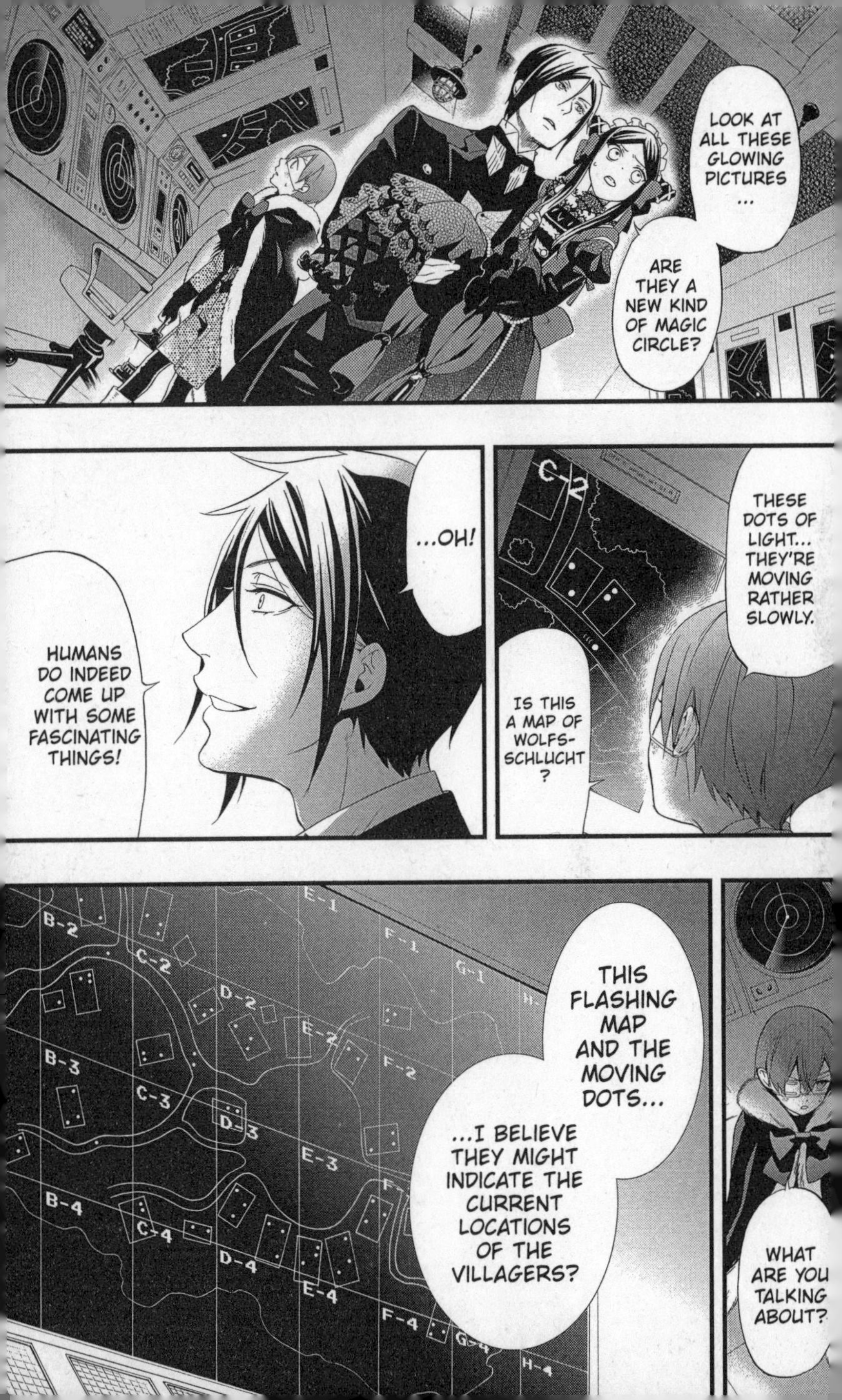
LOOK AT ALL THESE GLOWING PICTURES ...
ARE THEY A NEW KIND OF MAGIC CIRCLE?
THESE DOTS OF LIGHT... THEY'RE MOVING RATHER SLOWLY.
IS THIS A MAP OF WOLFS-SCHLUCHT?
...OH!
HUMANS DO INDEED COME UP WITH SOME FASCINATING THINGS!
WHAT ARE YOU TALKING ABOUT?
THIS FLASHING MAP AND THE MOVING DOTS...
...I BELIEVE THEY MIGHT INDICATE THE CURRENT LOCATIONS OF THE VILLAGERS?

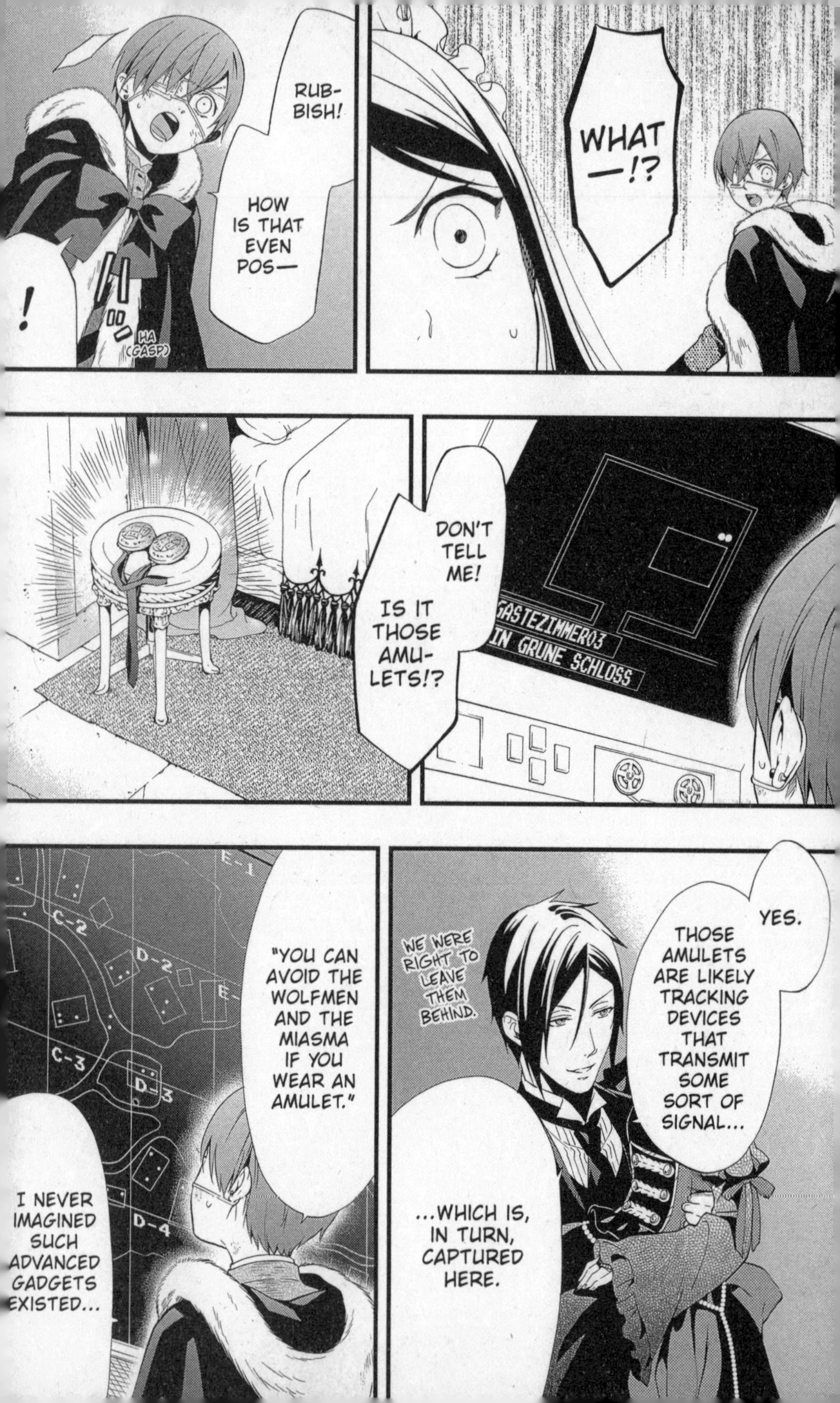
WHAT —!?
RUB-BISH!
HOW IS THAT EVEN POS—
!
HA (GASP)
DON'T TELL ME!
IS IT THOSE AMU-LETS!?
GASTEZIMMER03
IN GRUNE SCHLOSS
YES.
THOSE AMULETS ARE LIKELY TRACKING DEVICES THAT TRANSMIT SOME SORT OF SIGNAL...
WE WERE RIGHT TO LEAVE THEM BEHIND.
...WHICH IS, IN TURN, CAPTURED HERE.
"YOU CAN AVOID THE WOLFMEN AND THE MIASMA IF YOU WEAR AN AMULET."
E-1
C-2
D-2
C-3
D-3
D-4
I NEVER IMAGINED SUCH ADVANCED GADGETS EXISTED...

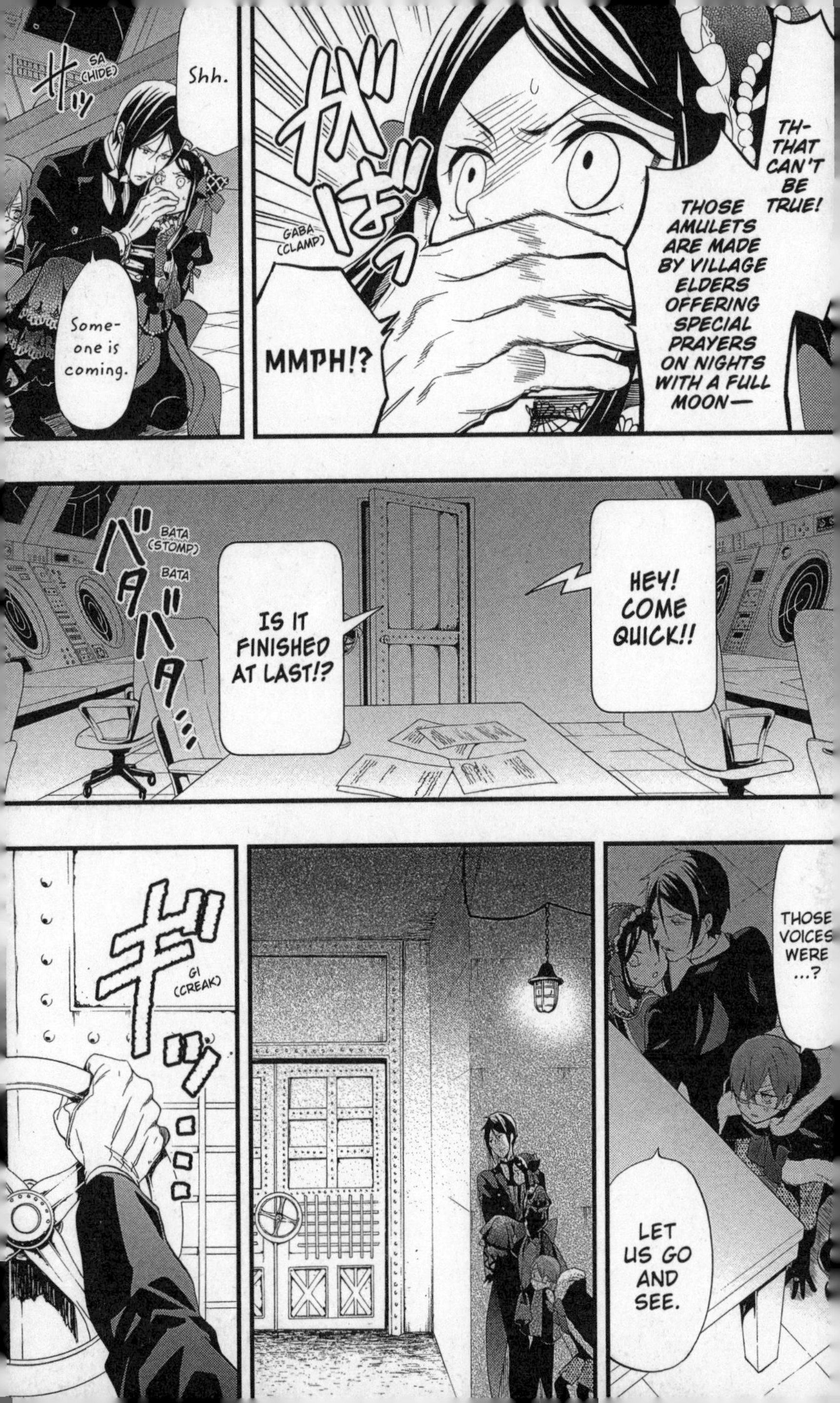
TH-THAT CAN'T BE TRUE! THOSE AMULETS ARE MADE BY VILLAGE ELDERS OFFERING SPECIAL PRAYERS ON NIGHTS WITH A FULL MOON—
GABA (CLAMP)
MMPH!?
SA (HIDE)
Shh.
Some-one is coming.
HEY! COME QUICK!!
IS IT FINISHED AT LAST!?
BATA (STOMP)
BATA
THOSE VOICES WERE ...?
LET US GO AND SEE.
GI (CREAK)

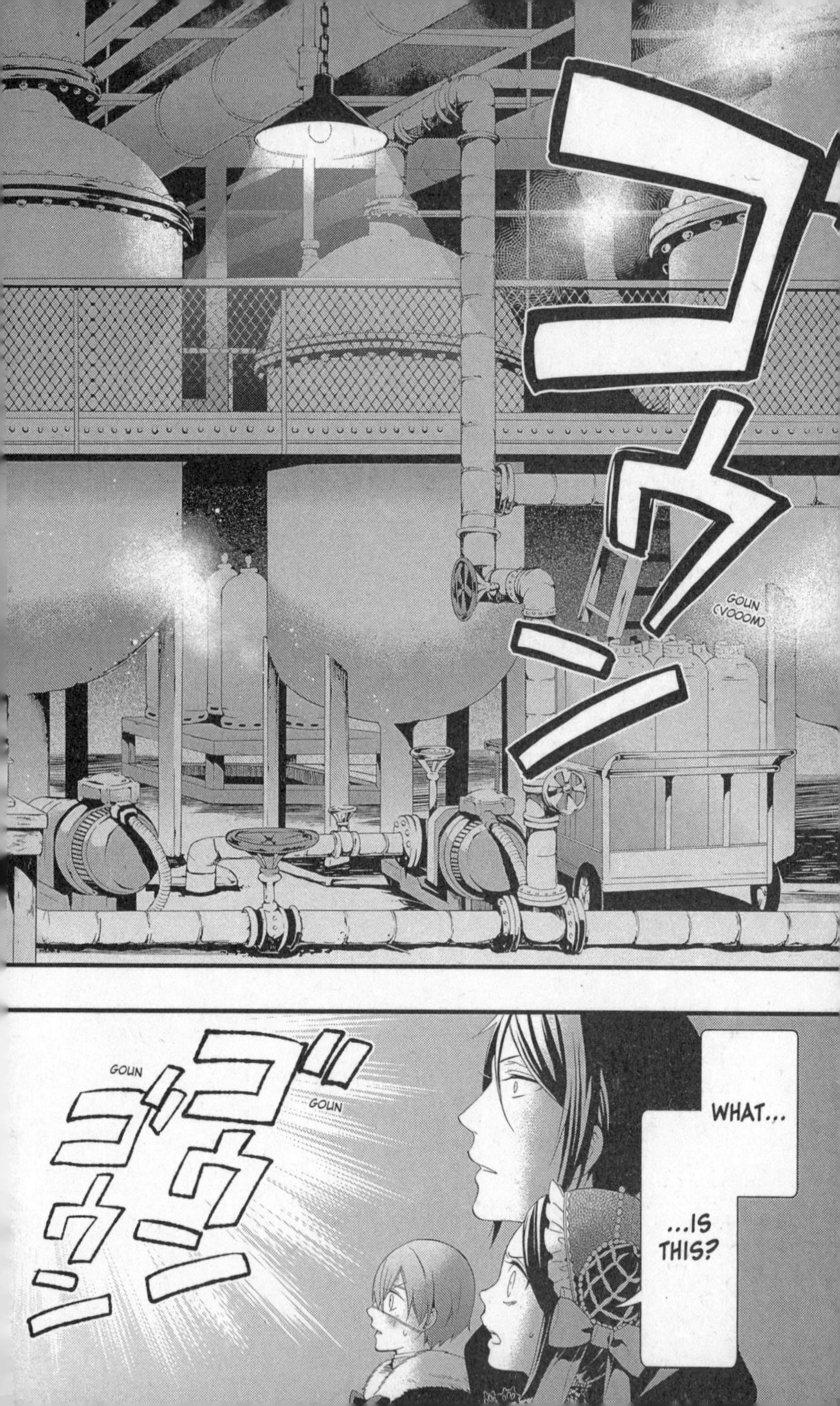
GOUN
(VOOOM)
WHAT...
...IS THIS?
GOUN
GOUN

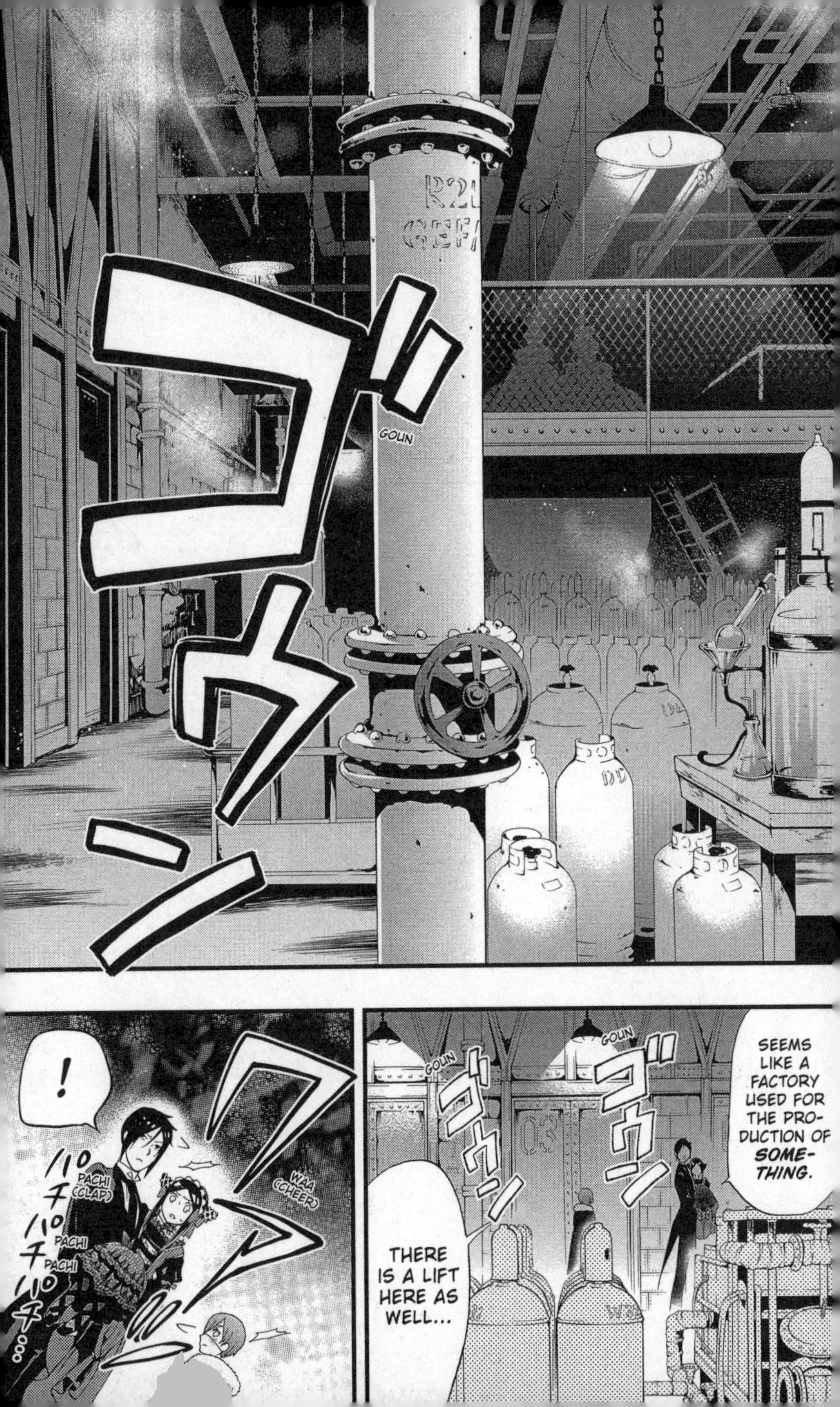

GOUN
GOUN
GOUN
SEEMS LIKE A FACTORY USED FOR THE PRODUCTION OF **SOMETHING**.
THERE IS A LIFT HERE AS WELL...
!
PACHI (CLAP)
WAA (CHEER)
PACHI
PACHI

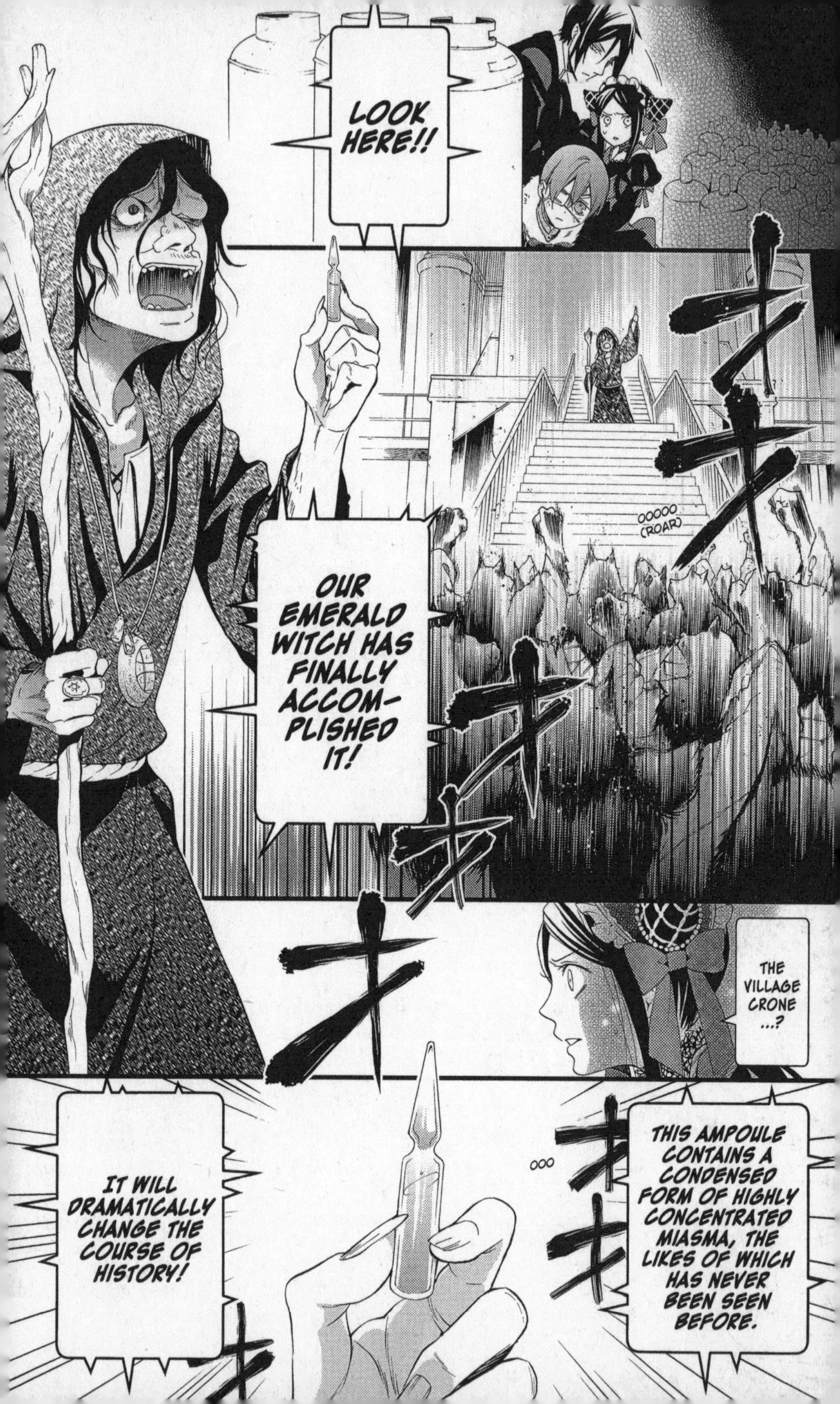
LOOK HERE!!
OOOOO (ROAR)
OUR EMERALD WITCH HAS FINALLY ACCOM-PLISHED IT!
THE VILLAGE CRONE ...?
THIS AMPOULE CONTAINS A CONDENSED FORM OF HIGHLY CONCENTRATED MIASMA, THE LIKES OF WHICH HAS NEVER BEEN SEEN BEFORE.
OOO
IT WILL DRAMATICALLY CHANGE THE COURSE OF HISTORY!

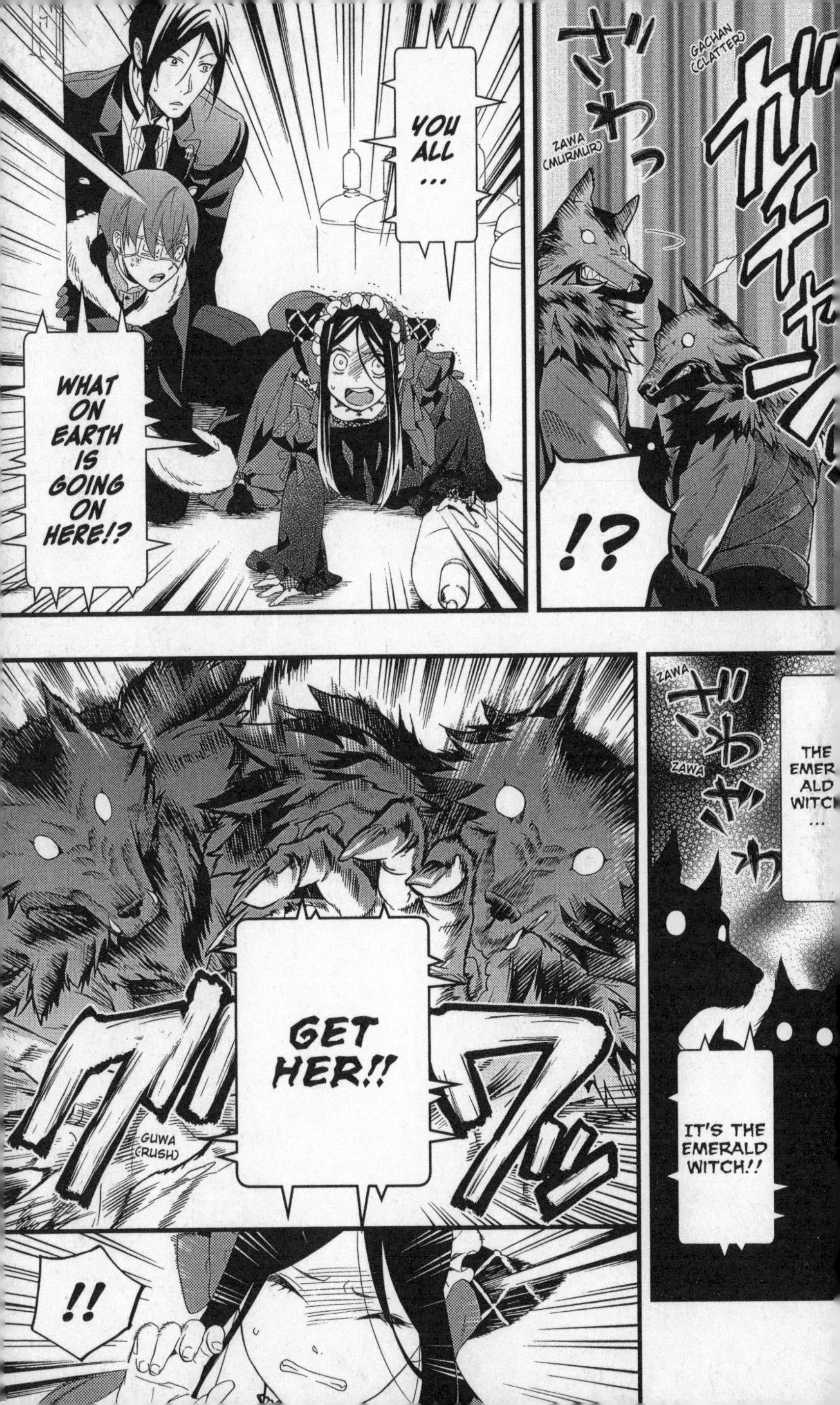
GACHAN (CLATTER)
ZAWA (MURMUR)
!?
YOU ALL ...
WHAT ON EARTH IS GOING ON HERE!?
ZAWA
ZAWA
THE EMERALD WITCH ...
IT'S THE EMERALD WITCH!!
GET HER!!
GUWA (RUSH)
!!

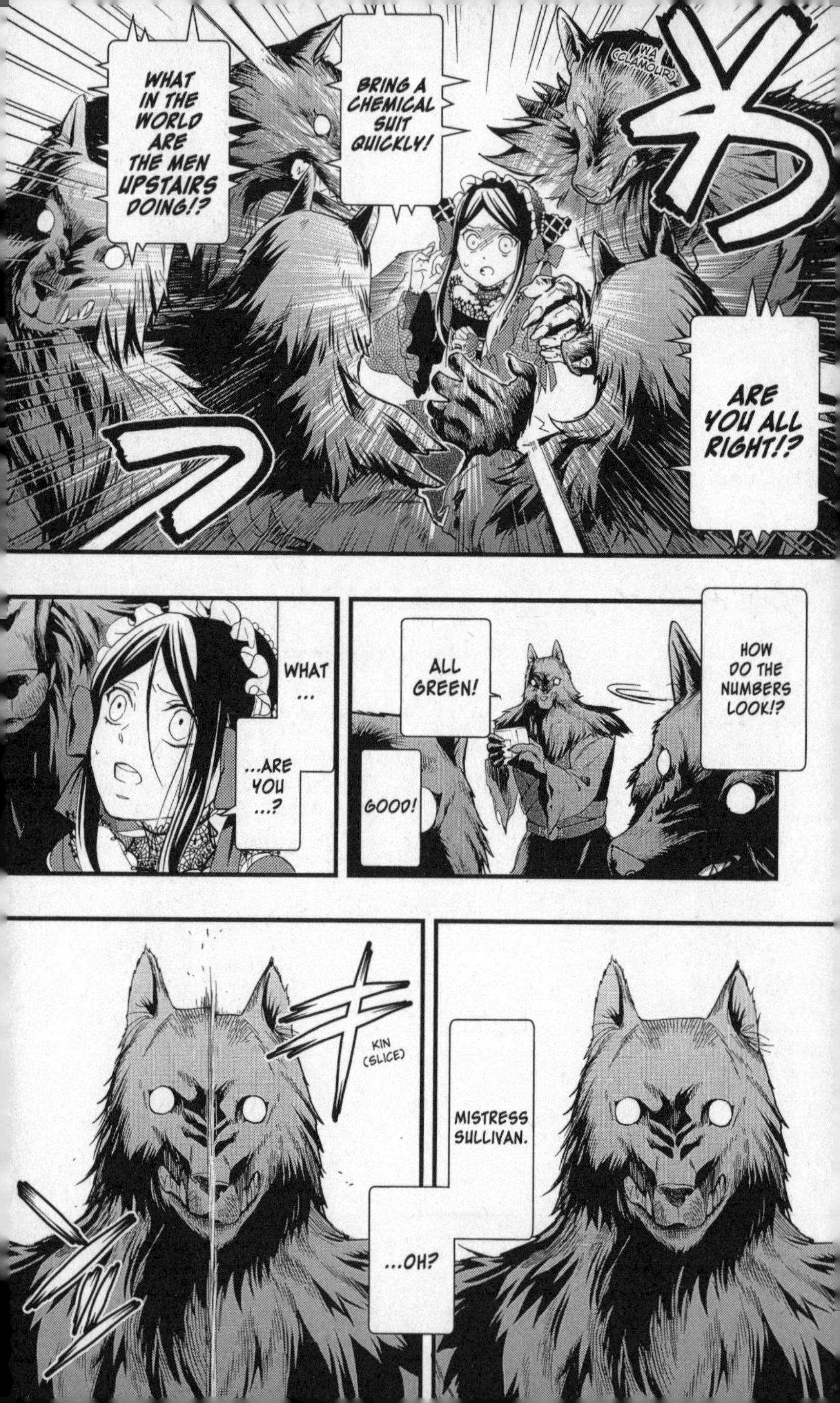
WA (CLAMOUR)
BRING A CHEMICAL SUIT QUICKLY!
WHAT IN THE WORLD ARE THE MEN UPSTAIRS DOING!?
ARE YOU ALL RIGHT!?
HOW DO THE NUMBERS LOOK!?
ALL GREEN!
GOOD!
WHAT ...
...ARE YOU ...?
MISTRESS SULLIVAN.
...OH?
KIN (SLICE)

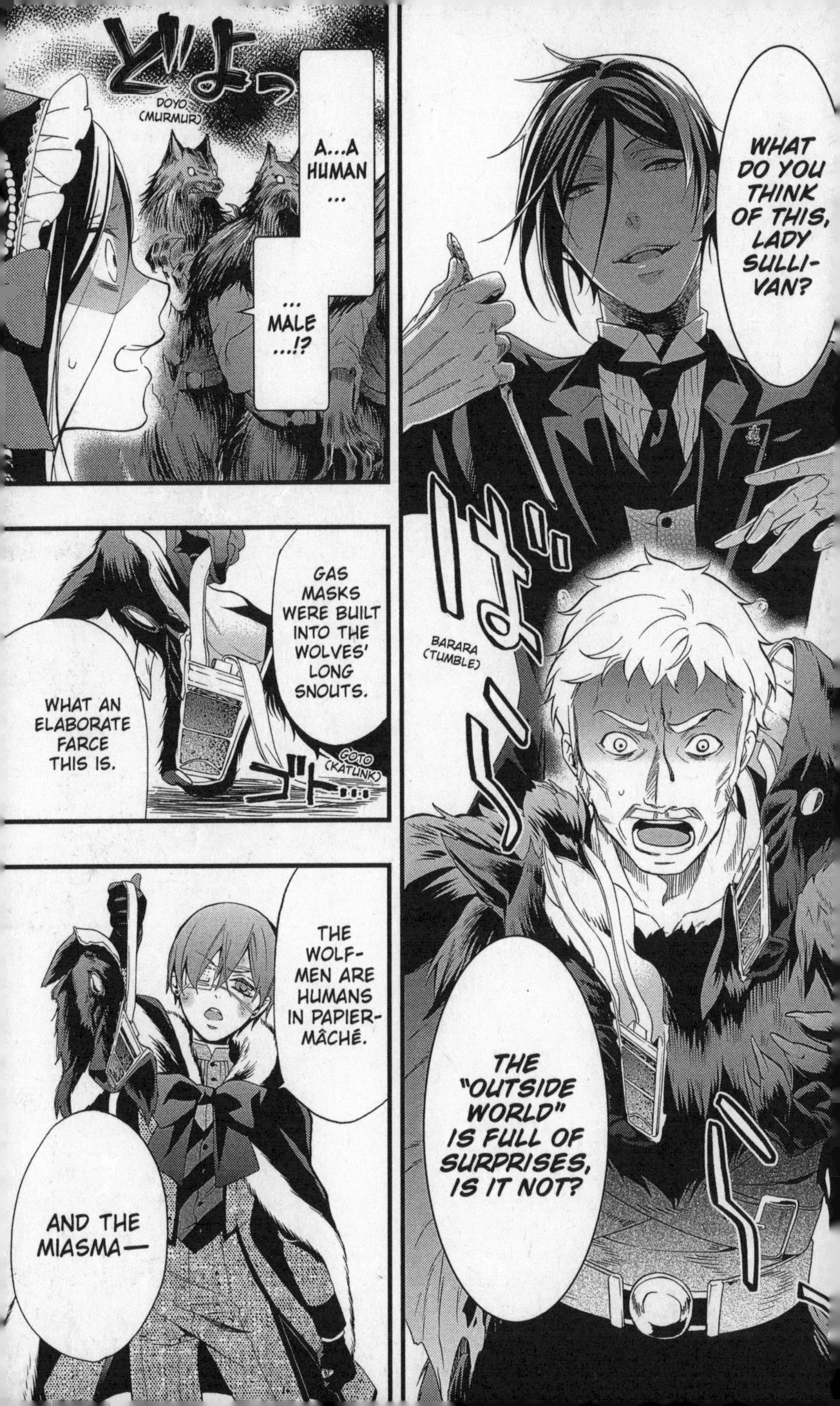
WHAT DO YOU THINK OF THIS, LADY SULLIVAN?
BARARA (TUMBLE)
THE "OUTSIDE WORLD" IS FULL OF SURPRISES, IS IT NOT?
どよっ
DOYO (MURMUR)
A...A HUMAN...
...MALE...!?
GAS MASKS WERE BUILT INTO THE WOLVES' LONG SNOUTS.
WHAT AN ELABORATE FARCE THIS IS.
GOTO (KATUNK)
THE WOLF-MEN ARE HUMANS IN PAPIER-MÂCHÉ.
AND THE MIASMA—

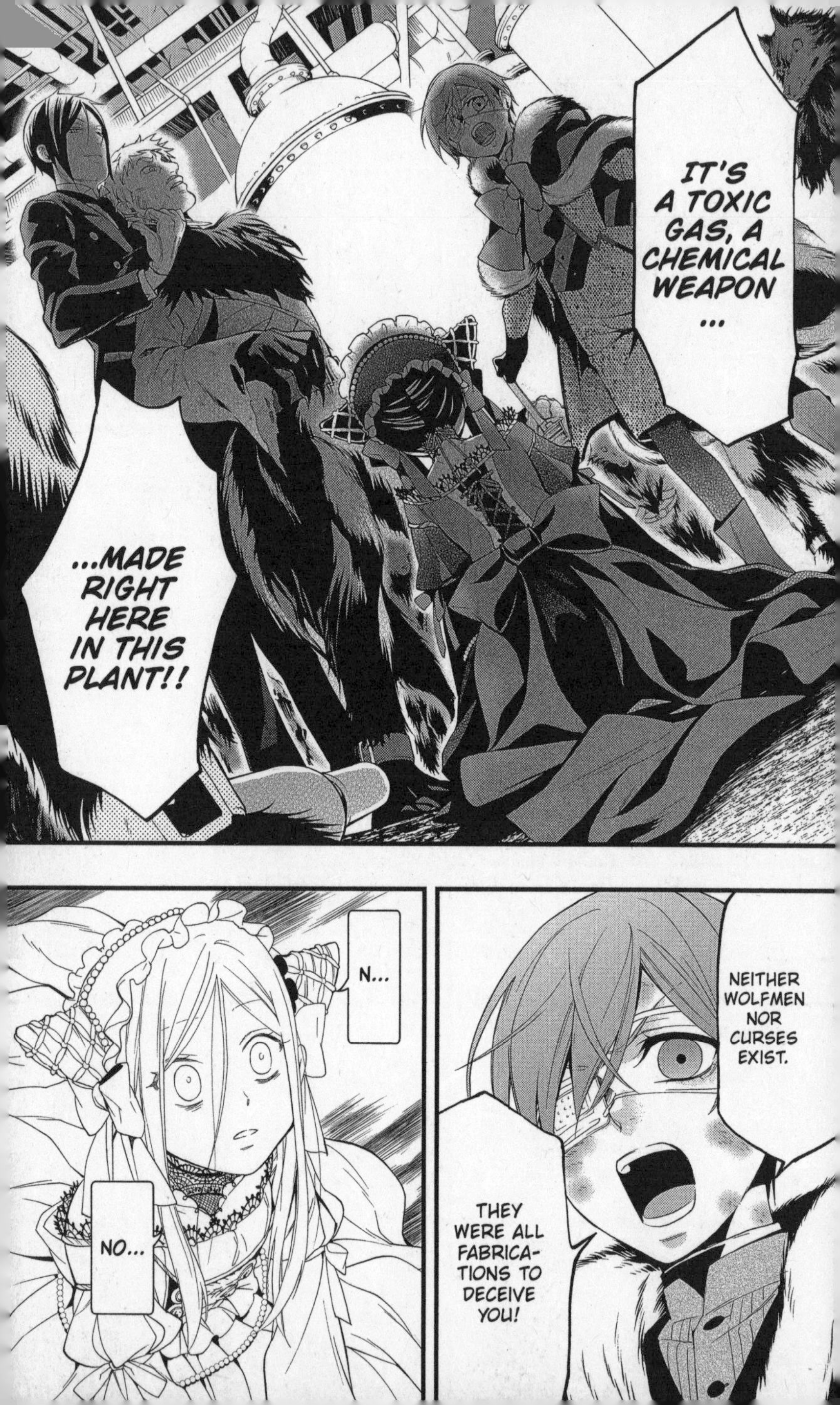

IT'S A TOXIC GAS, A CHEMICAL WEAPON ...
...MADE RIGHT HERE IN THIS PLANT!!
NEITHER WOLFMEN NOR CURSES EXIST.
THEY WERE ALL FABRICA-TIONS TO DECEIVE YOU!
N...
NO...

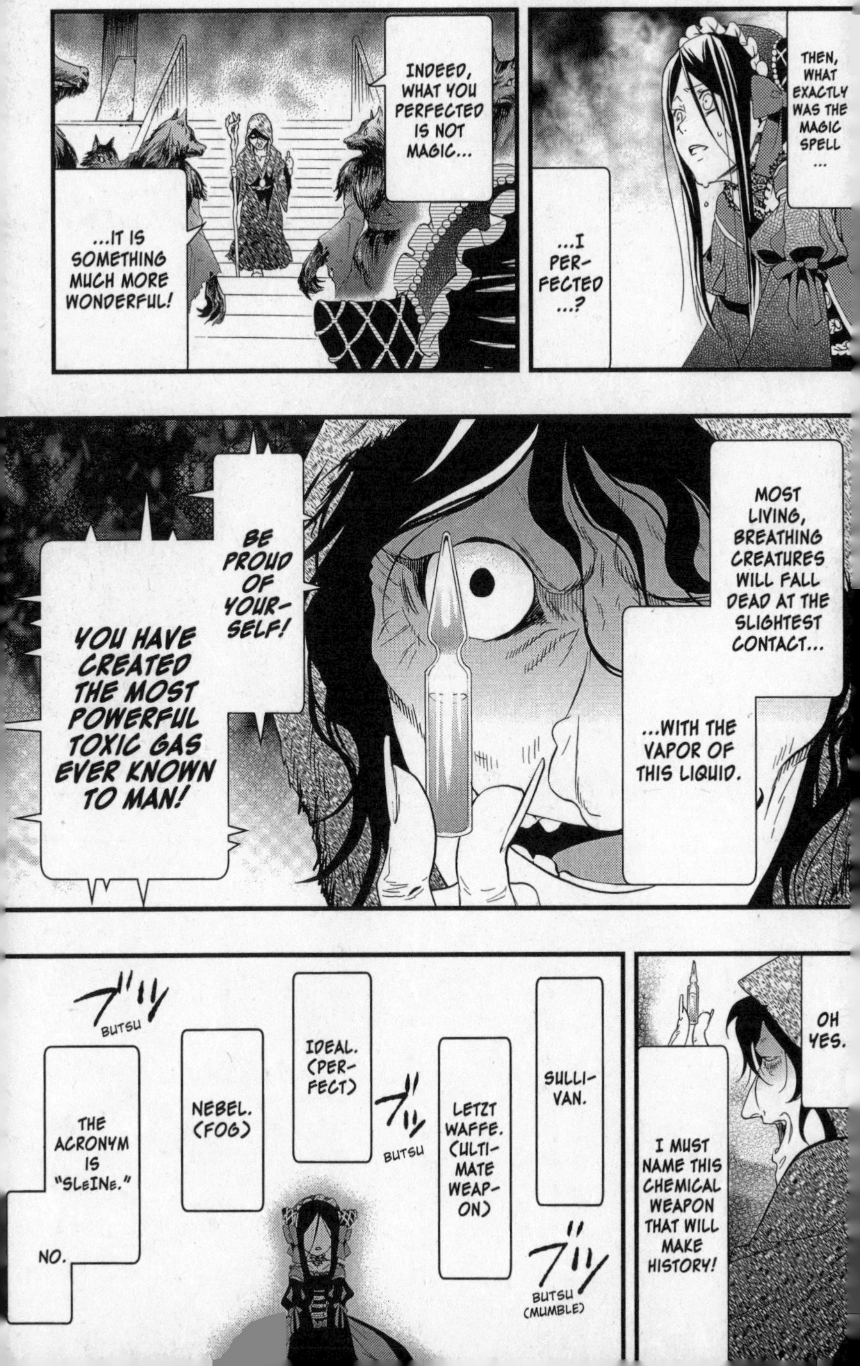
THEN, WHAT EXACTLY WAS THE MAGIC SPELL ...
...I PER-FECTED ...?
INDEED, WHAT YOU PERFECTED IS NOT MAGIC...
...IT IS SOMETHING MUCH MORE WONDERFUL!
MOST LIVING, BREATHING CREATURES WILL FALL DEAD AT THE SLIGHTEST CONTACT...
...WITH THE VAPOR OF THIS LIQUID.
BE PROUD OF YOUR-SELF!
YOU HAVE CREATED THE MOST POWERFUL TOXIC GAS EVER KNOWN TO MAN!
OH YES.
I MUST NAME THIS CHEMICAL WEAPON THAT WILL MAKE HISTORY!
SULLI-VAN.
ブツ
BUTSU (MUMBLE)
LETZT WAFFE. (ULTI-MATE WEAP-ON)
ブツ
BUTSU
IDEAL. (PER-FECT)
NEBEL. (FOG)
ブツ
BUTSU
THE ACRONYM IS "SLeINe."
NO.

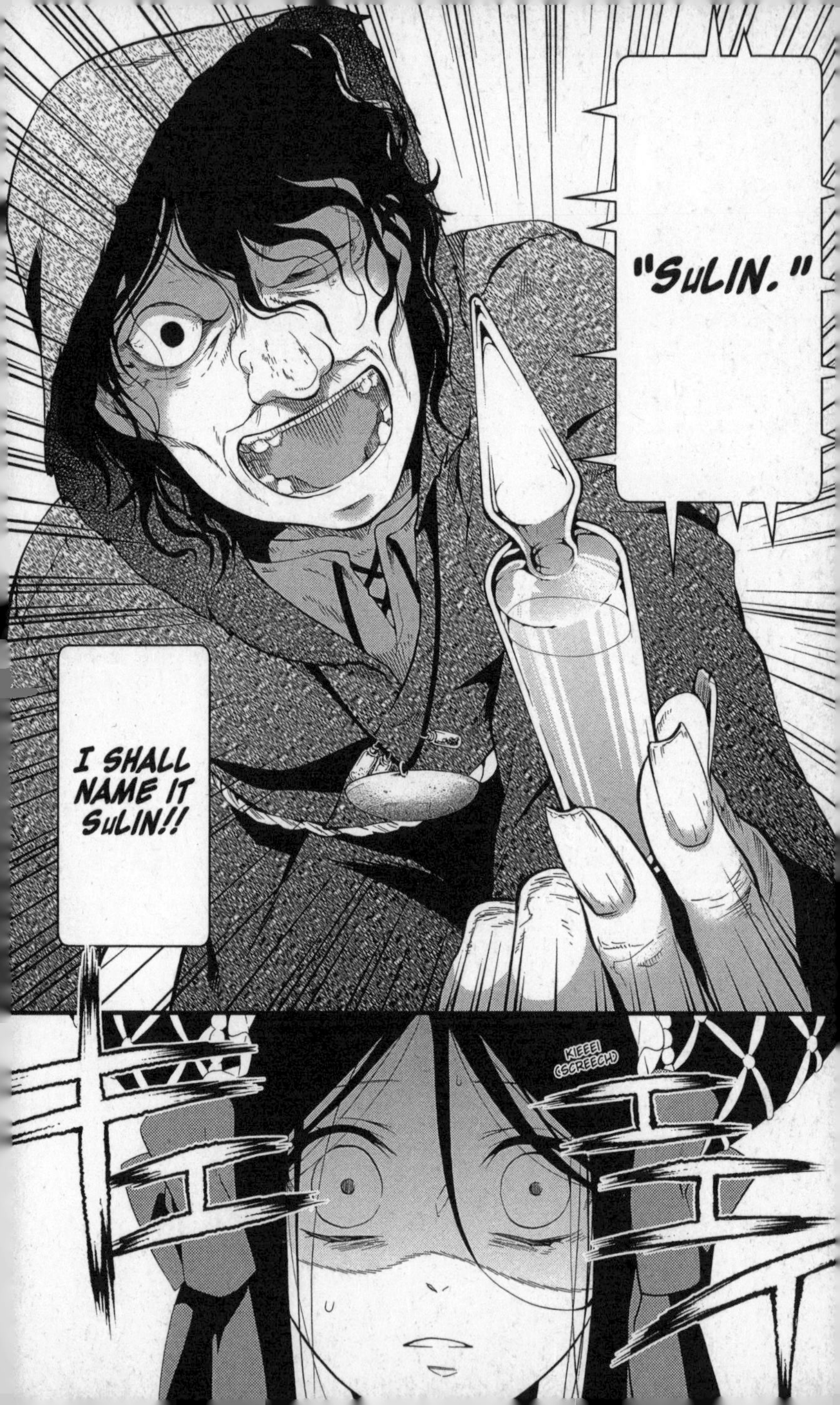
"SuLIN."
I SHALL NAME IT SuLIN!!
KIEEE! (SCREECH)

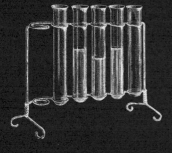

Black Butler

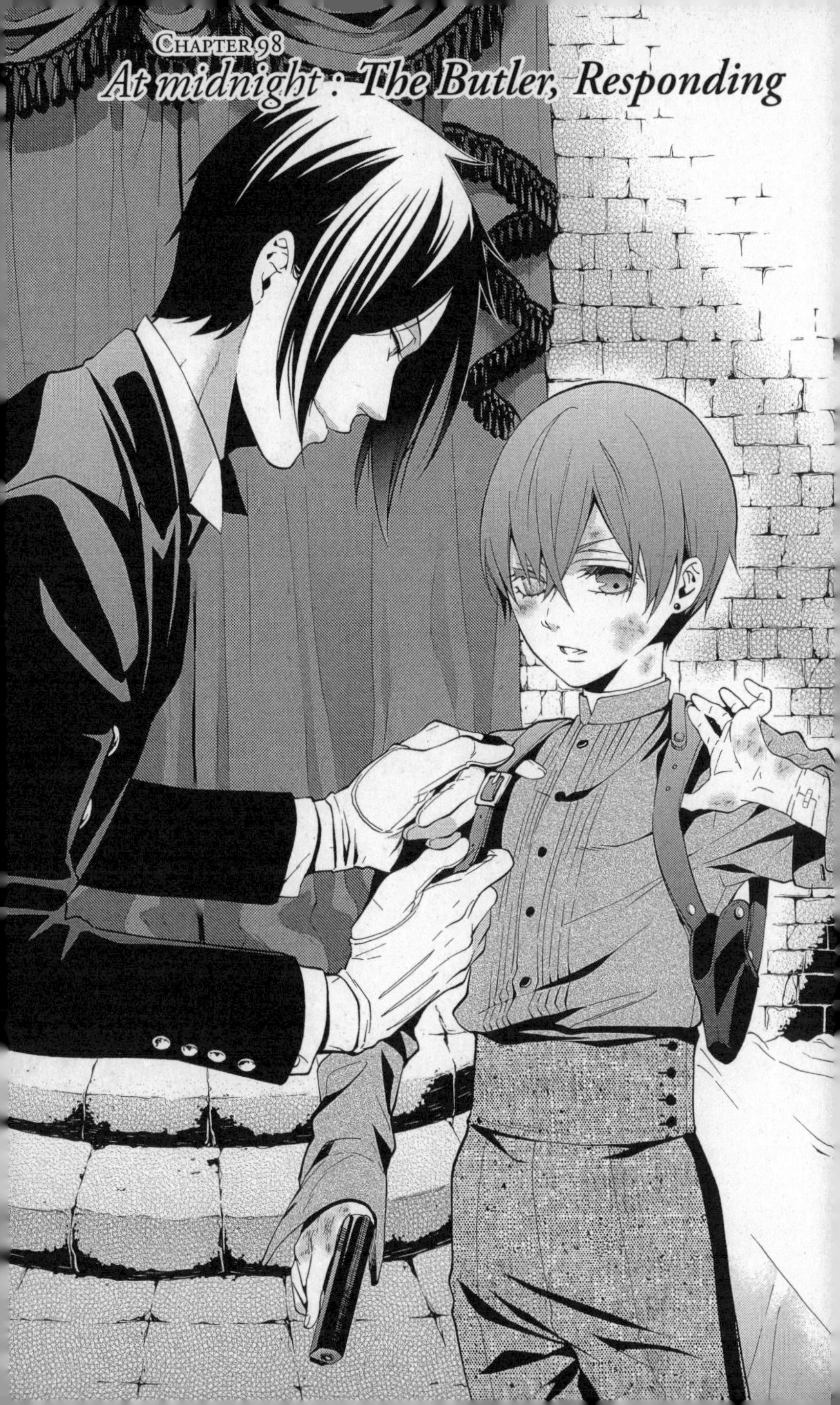
Chapter 98
At midnight : The Butler, Responding

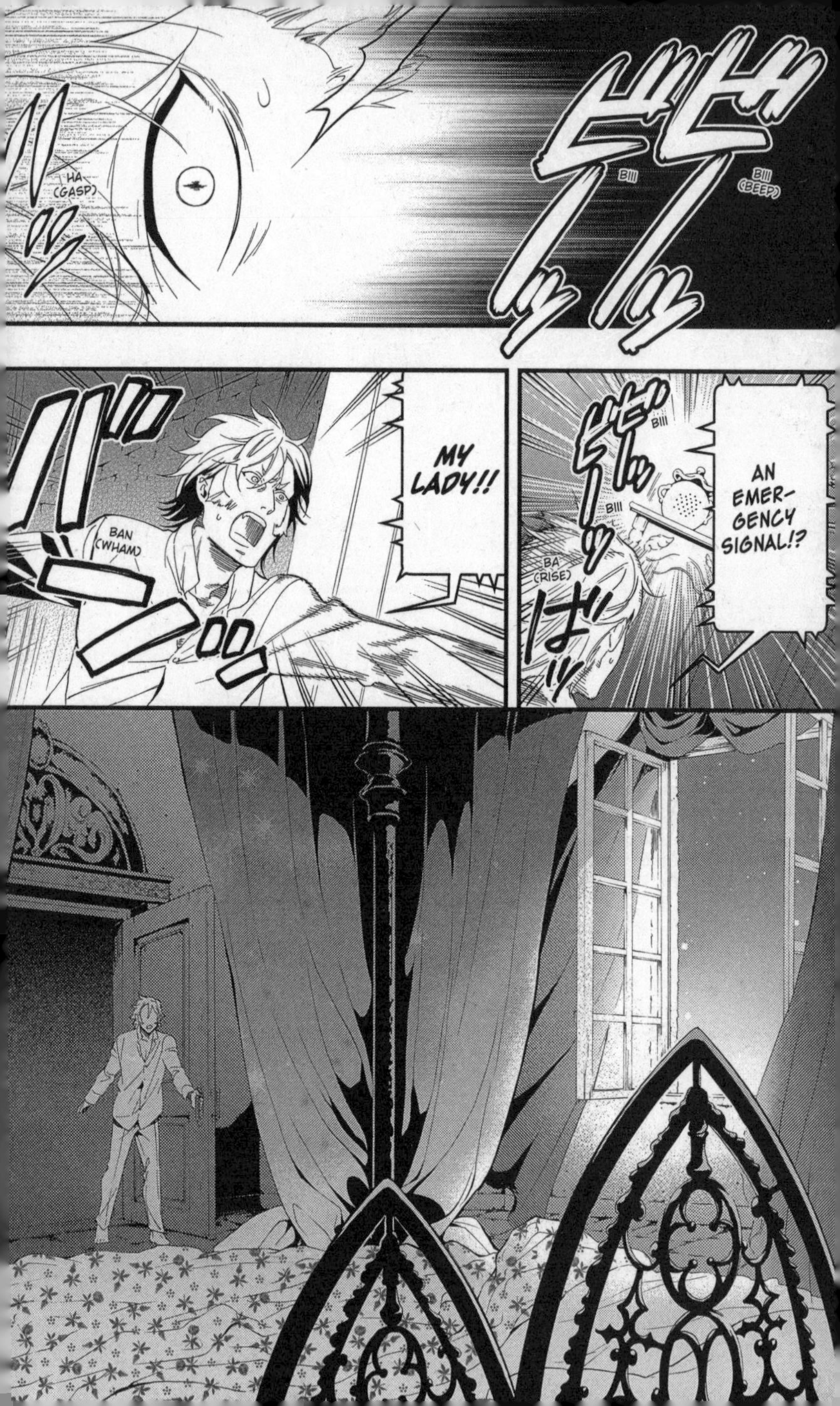

BIII
BIII
(BEEP)
HA
(GASP)
BIII
BIII
BA
(RISE)
AN EMERGENCY SIGNAL!?
MY LADY!!
BAN
(WHAM)

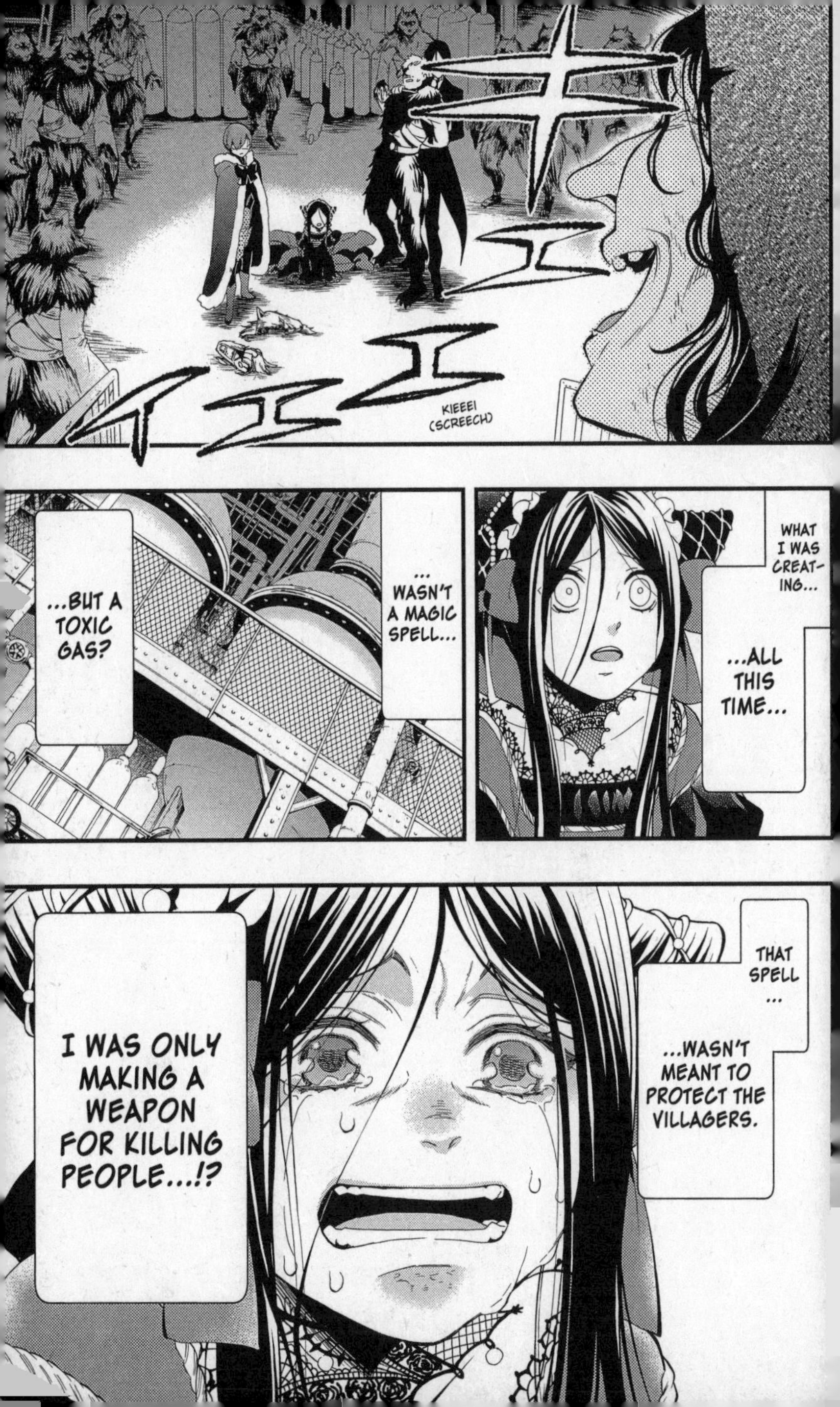
KIEEEI (SCREECH)
WHAT I WAS CREATING...
...ALL THIS TIME...
...WASN'T A MAGIC SPELL...
...BUT A TOXIC GAS?
THAT SPELL...
...WASN'T MEANT TO PROTECT THE VILLAGERS.
I WAS ONLY MAKING A WEAPON FOR KILLING PEOPLE...!?

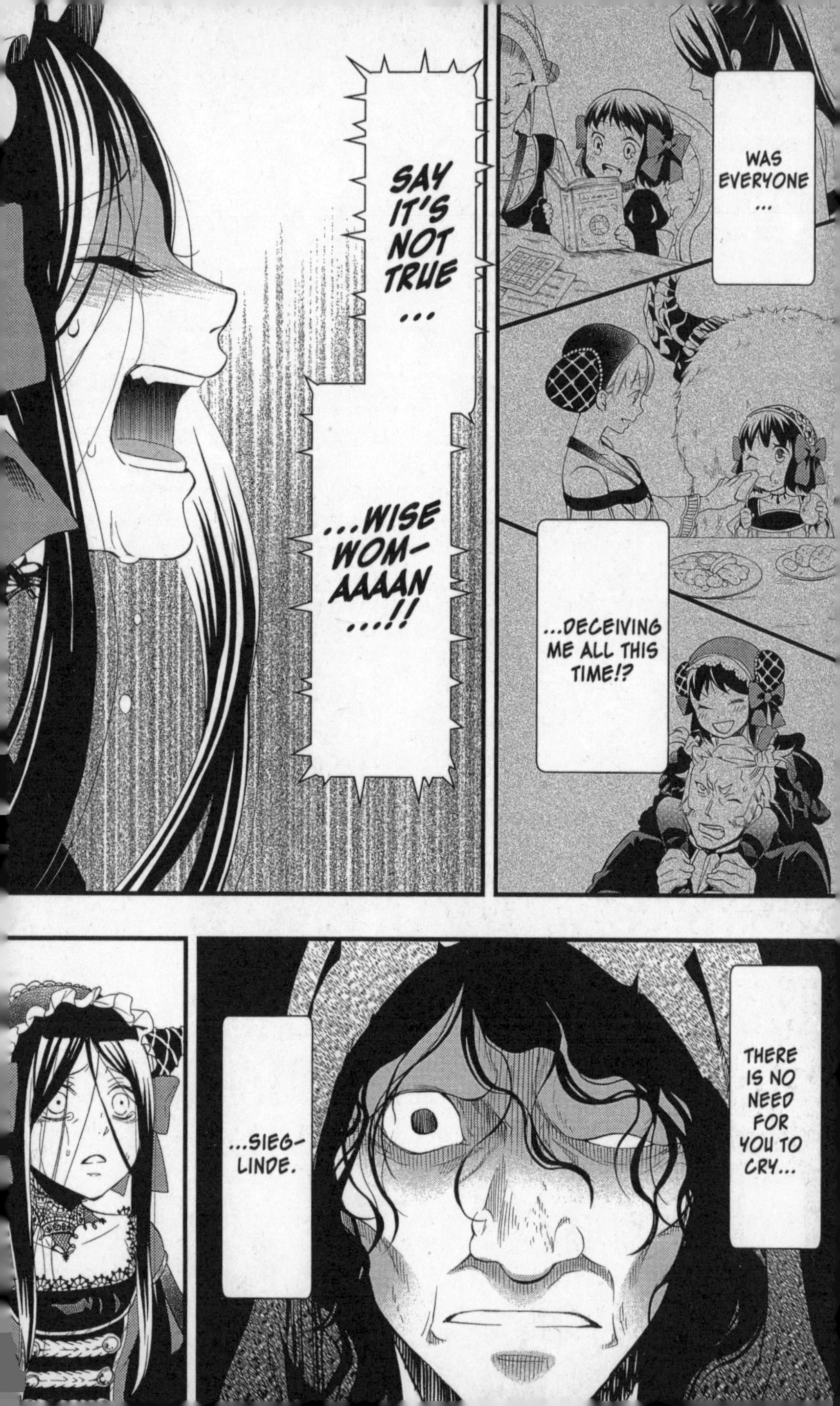
WAS EVERYONE ...
...DECEIVING ME ALL THIS TIME!?
SAY IT'S NOT TRUE ...
...WISE WOM-AAAAN...!!
THERE IS NO NEED FOR YOU TO CRY...
...SIEG-LINDE.

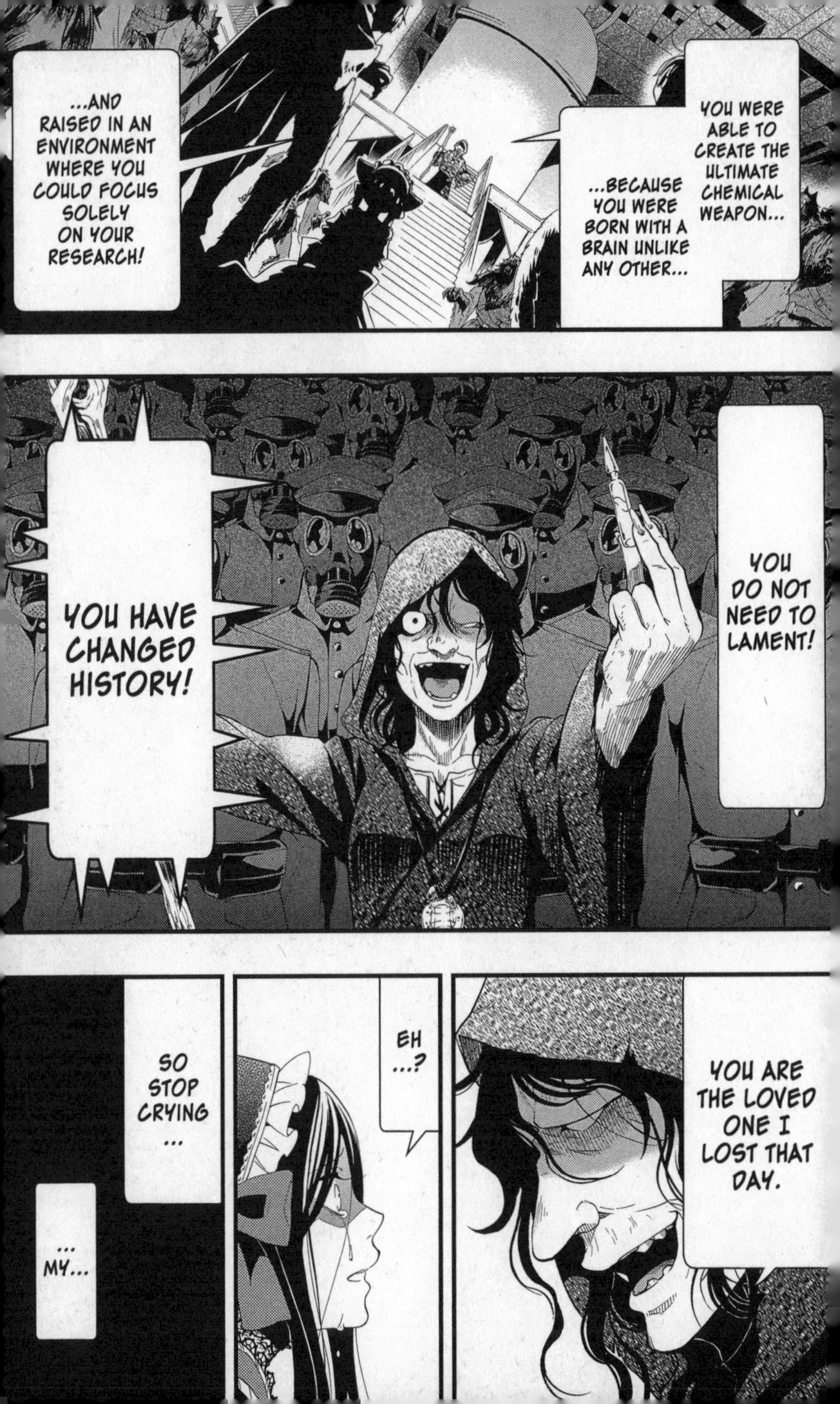
YOU WERE ABLE TO CREATE THE ULTIMATE CHEMICAL WEAPON...
...BECAUSE YOU WERE BORN WITH A BRAIN UNLIKE ANY OTHER...
...AND RAISED IN AN ENVIRONMENT WHERE YOU COULD FOCUS SOLELY ON YOUR RESEARCH!
YOU DO NOT NEED TO LAMENT!
YOU HAVE CHANGED HISTORY!
YOU ARE THE LOVED ONE I LOST THAT DAY.
EH ...?
SO STOP CRYING ...
... MY...

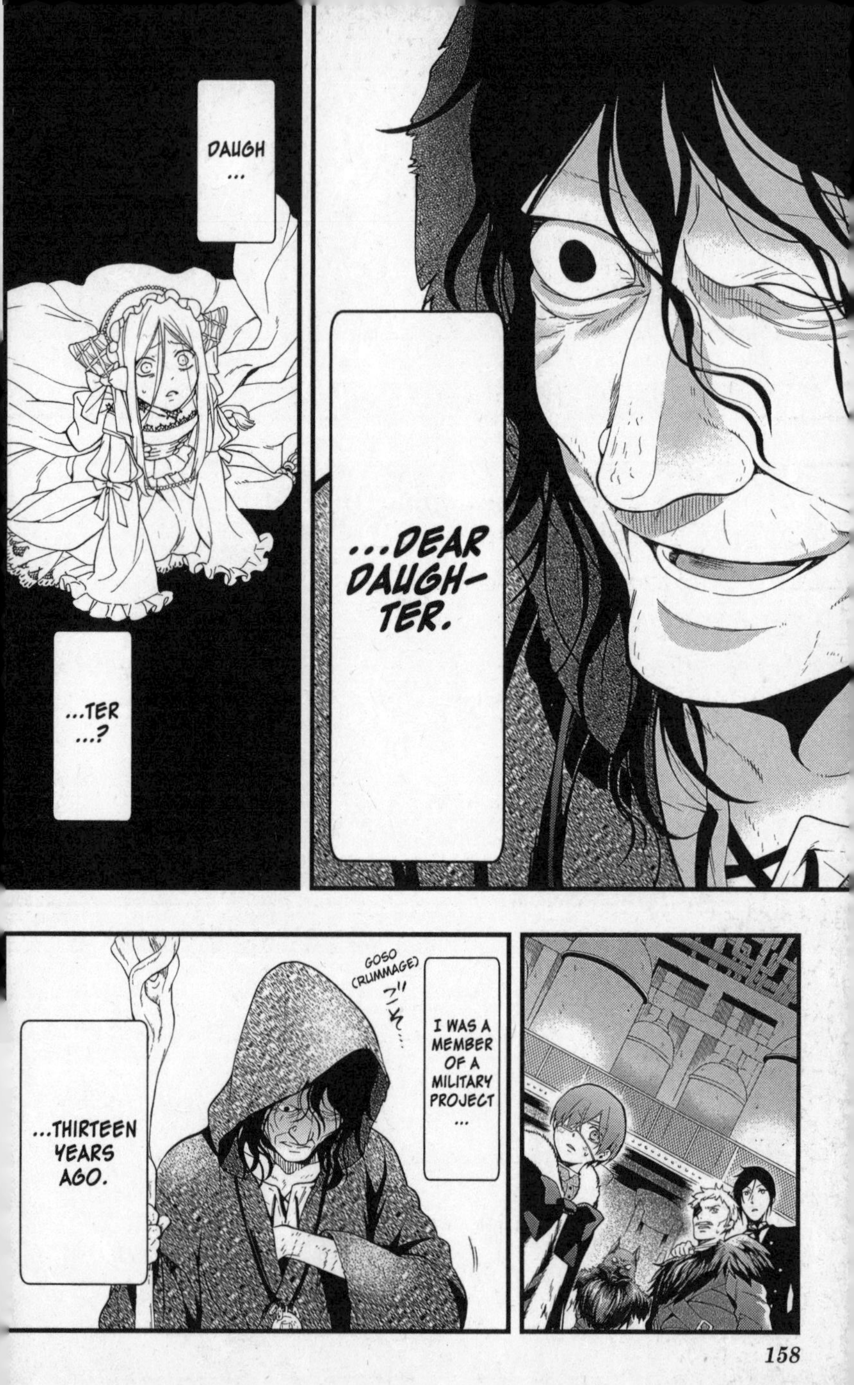
...DEAR DAUGHTER.
DAUGH ...
...TER ...?
I WAS A MEMBER OF A MILITARY PROJECT ...
GOSO (RUMMAGE)
...THIRTEEN YEARS AGO.

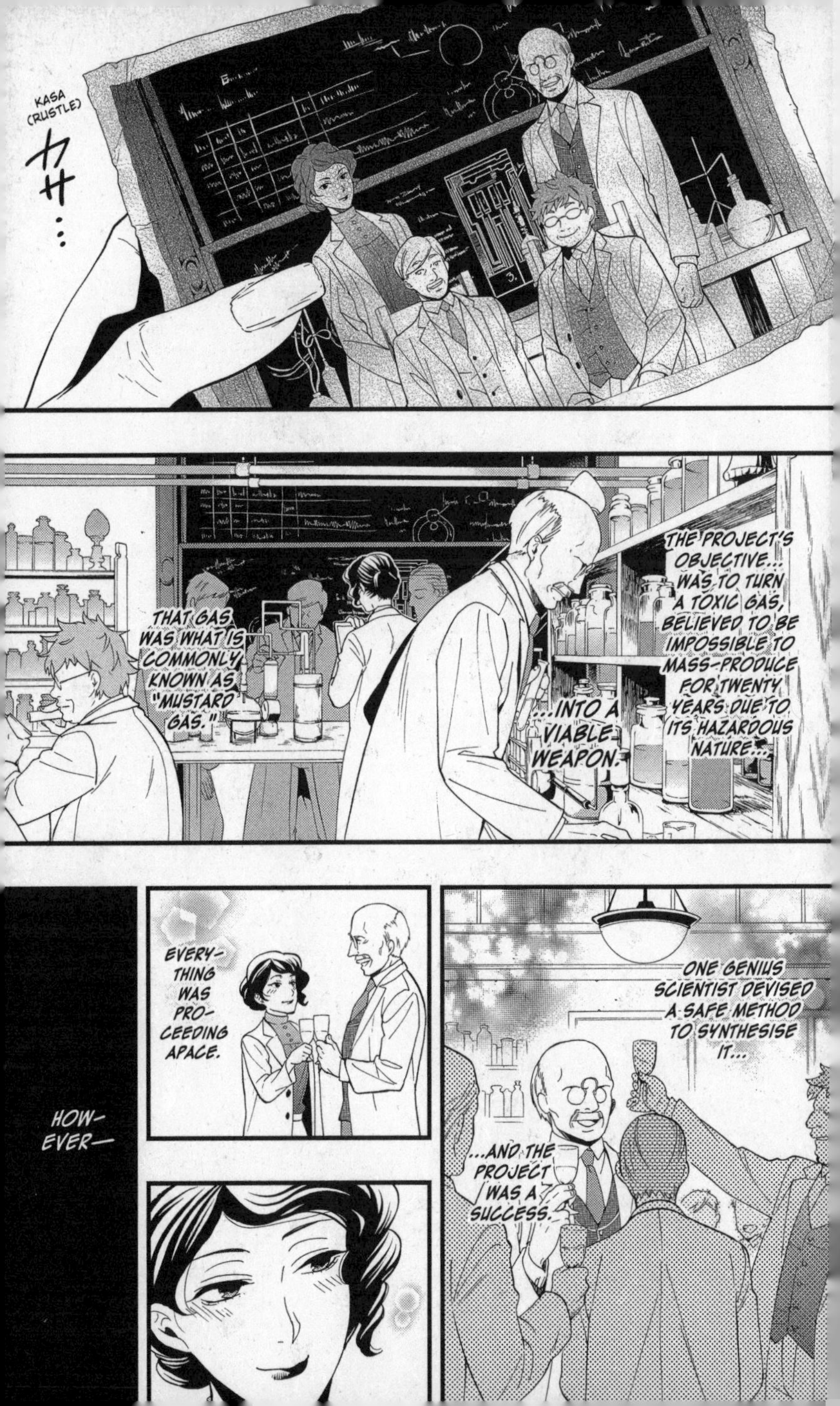
KASA (RUSTLE)
カサ…
THE PROJECT'S OBJECTIVE... WAS TO TURN A TOXIC GAS, BELIEVED TO BE IMPOSSIBLE TO MASS-PRODUCE FOR TWENTY YEARS DUE TO ITS HAZARDOUS NATURE...
...INTO A VIABLE WEAPON.
THAT GAS WAS WHAT IS COMMONLY KNOWN AS "MUSTARD GAS."
ONE GENIUS SCIENTIST DEVISED A SAFE METHOD TO SYNTHESISE IT...
...AND THE PROJECT WAS A SUCCESS.
EVERY-THING WAS PRO-CEEDING APACE.
HOW-EVER—

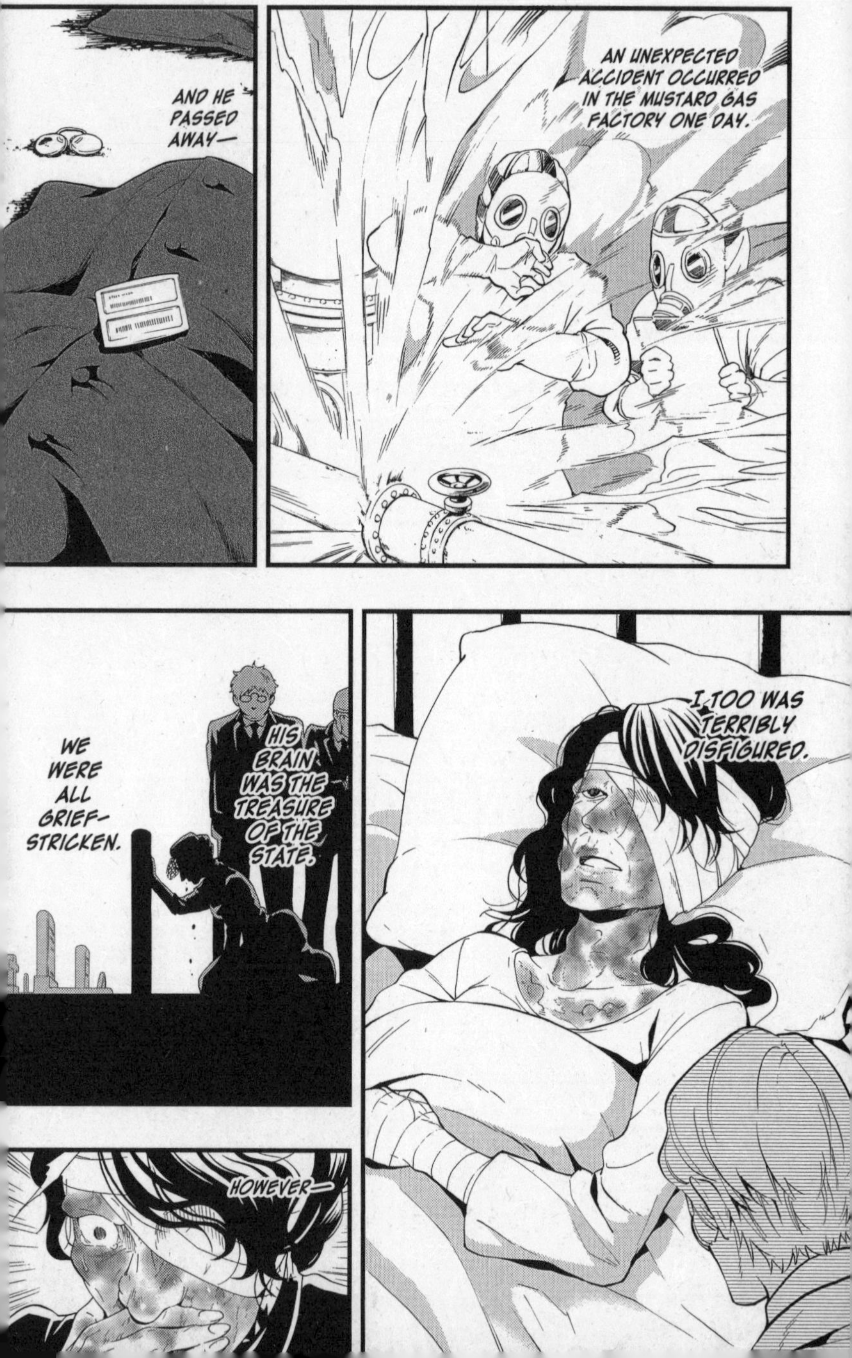
AN UNEXPECTED ACCIDENT OCCURRED IN THE MUSTARD GAS FACTORY ONE DAY.
AND HE PASSED AWAY—
I TOO WAS TERRIBLY DISFIGURED.
HIS BRAIN WAS THE TREASURE OF THE STATE.
WE WERE ALL GRIEF-STRICKEN.
HOWEVER—

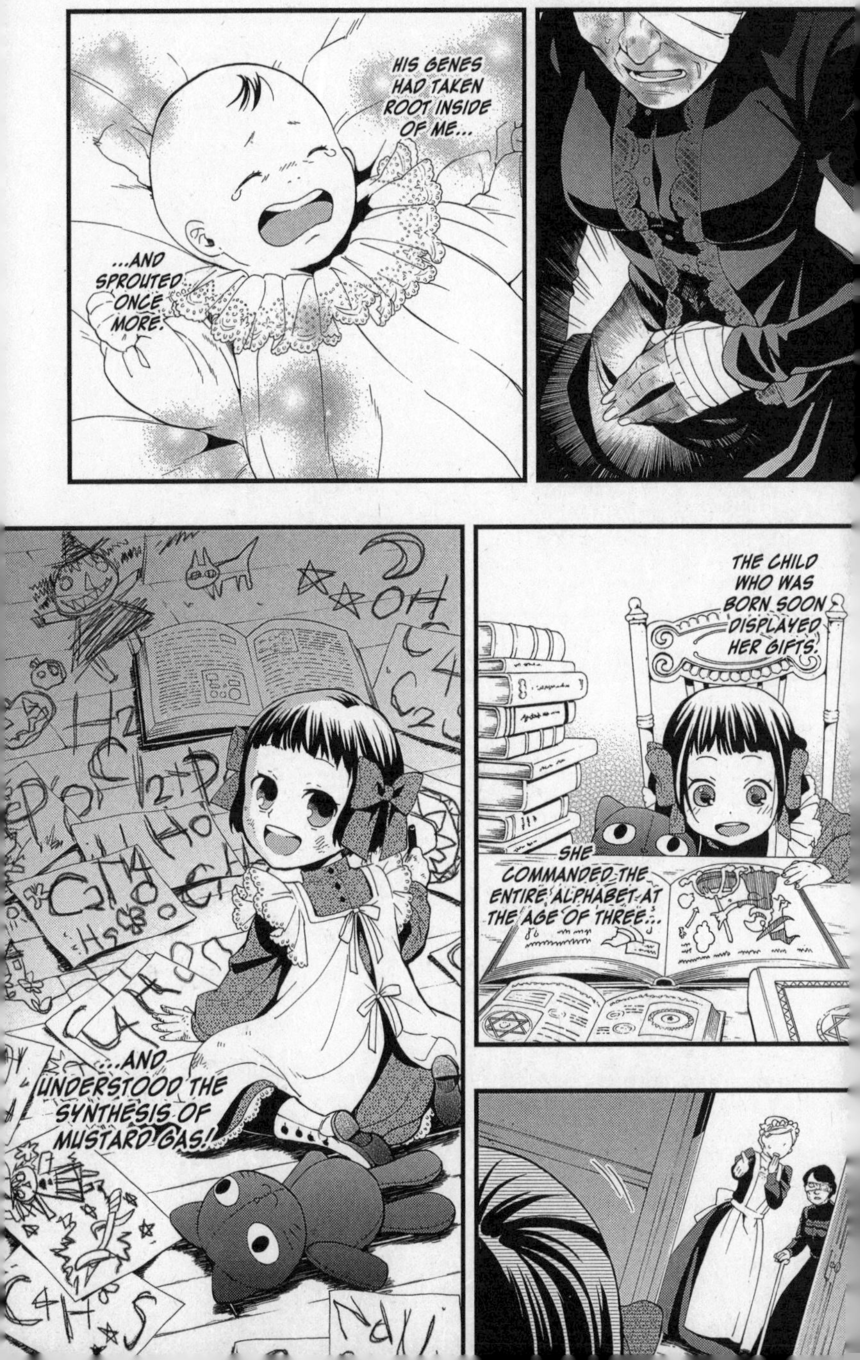
HIS GENES HAD TAKEN ROOT INSIDE OF ME...
...AND SPROUTED ONCE MORE.
THE CHILD WHO WAS BORN SOON DISPLAYED HER GIFTS.
SHE COMMANDED THE ENTIRE ALPHABET AT THE AGE OF THREE...
...AND UNDERSTOOD THE SYNTHESIS OF MUSTARD GAS!

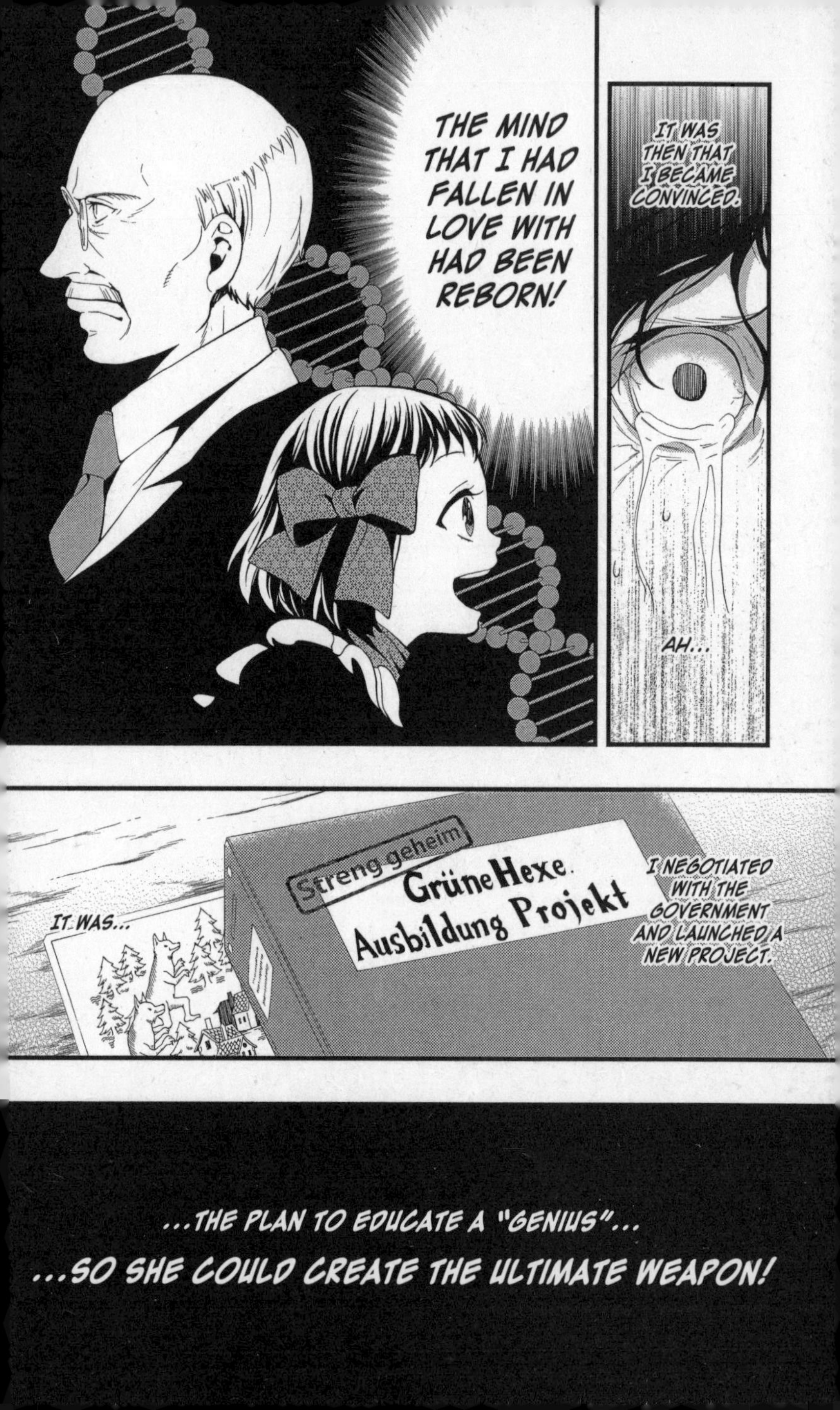
IT WAS THEN THAT I BECAME CONVINCED.
AH...
THE MIND THAT I HAD FALLEN IN LOVE WITH HAD BEEN REBORN!
I NEGOTIATED WITH THE GOVERNMENT AND LAUNCHED A NEW PROJECT.
Streng geheim
Grüne Hexe. Ausbildung Projekt
IT WAS...
...THE PLAN TO EDUCATE A "GENIUS"...
...SO SHE COULD CREATE THE ULTIMATE WEAPON!

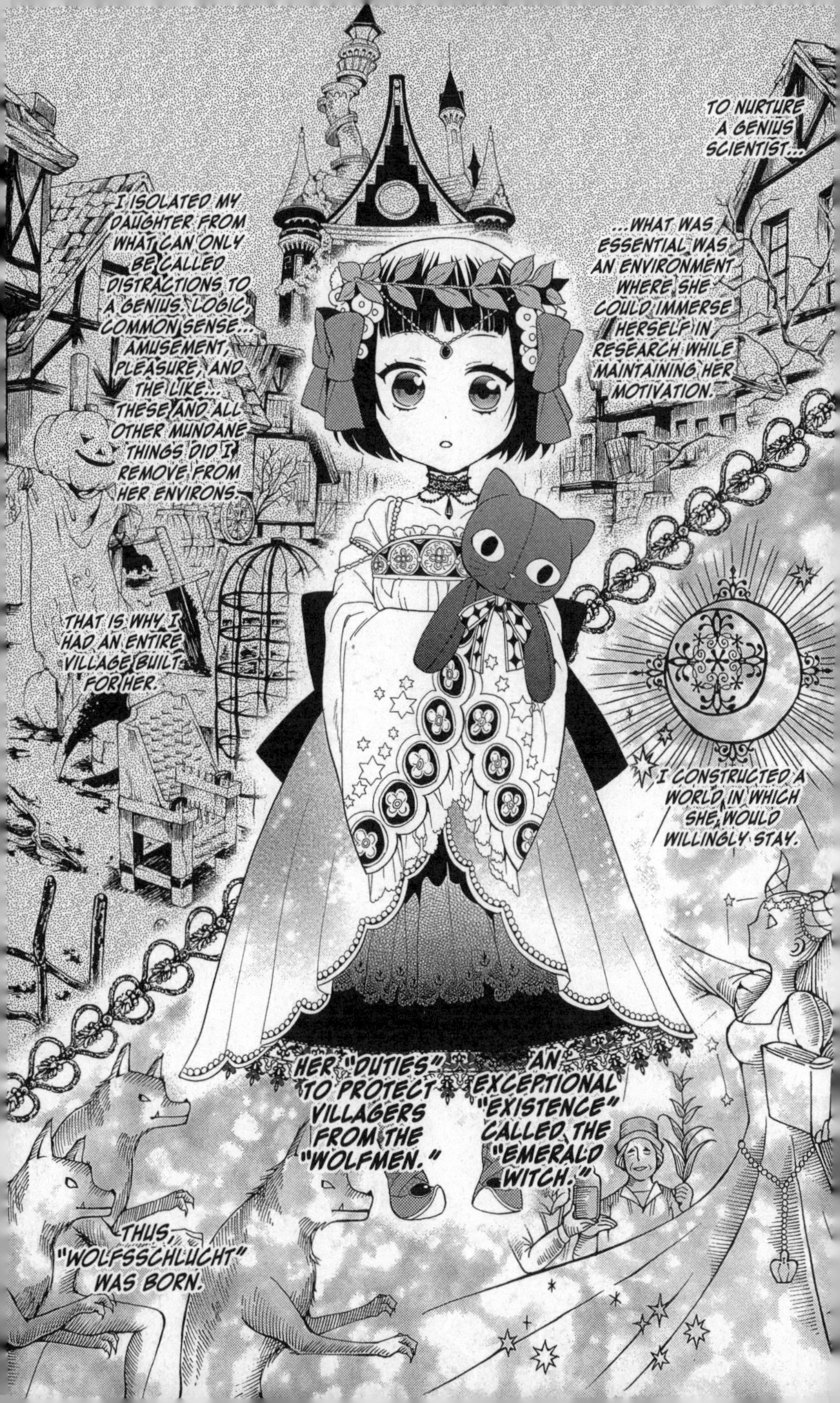
TO NURTURE A GENIUS SCIENTIST...
...WHAT WAS ESSENTIAL WAS AN ENVIRONMENT WHERE SHE COULD IMMERSE HERSELF IN RESEARCH WHILE MAINTAINING HER MOTIVATION.
I ISOLATED MY DAUGHTER FROM WHAT CAN ONLY BE CALLED DISTRACTIONS TO A GENIUS. LOGIC, COMMON SENSE... AMUSEMENT, PLEASURE, AND THE LIKE... THESE AND ALL OTHER MUNDANE THINGS DID I REMOVE FROM HER ENVIRONS.
THAT IS WHY I HAD AN ENTIRE VILLAGE BUILT FOR HER.
I CONSTRUCTED A WORLD IN WHICH SHE WOULD WILLINGLY STAY.
AN EXCEPTIONAL "EXISTENCE" CALLED THE "EMERALD WITCH."
HER "DUTIES" TO PROTECT VILLAGERS FROM THE "WOLFMEN."
THUS, "WOLFSSCHLUCHT" WAS BORN.

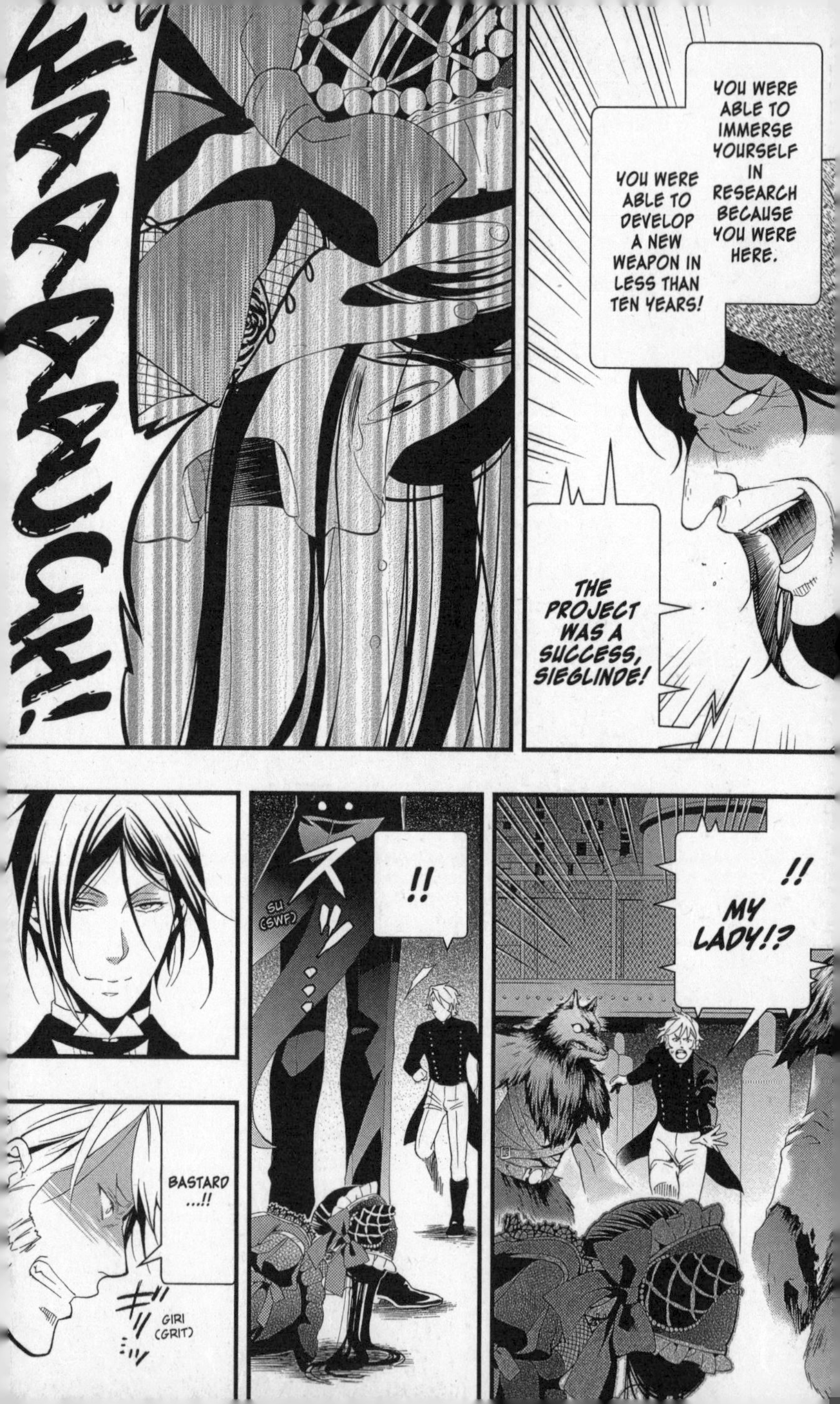
YOU WERE ABLE TO IMMERSE YOURSELF IN RESEARCH BECAUSE YOU WERE HERE.
YOU WERE ABLE TO DEVELOP A NEW WEAPON IN LESS THAN TEN YEARS!
THE PROJECT WAS A SUCCESS, SIEGLINDE!
WAAAAUUCH!
!! MY LADY!?
!!
SU (SWF)
BASTARD ...!!
GIRI (GRIT)

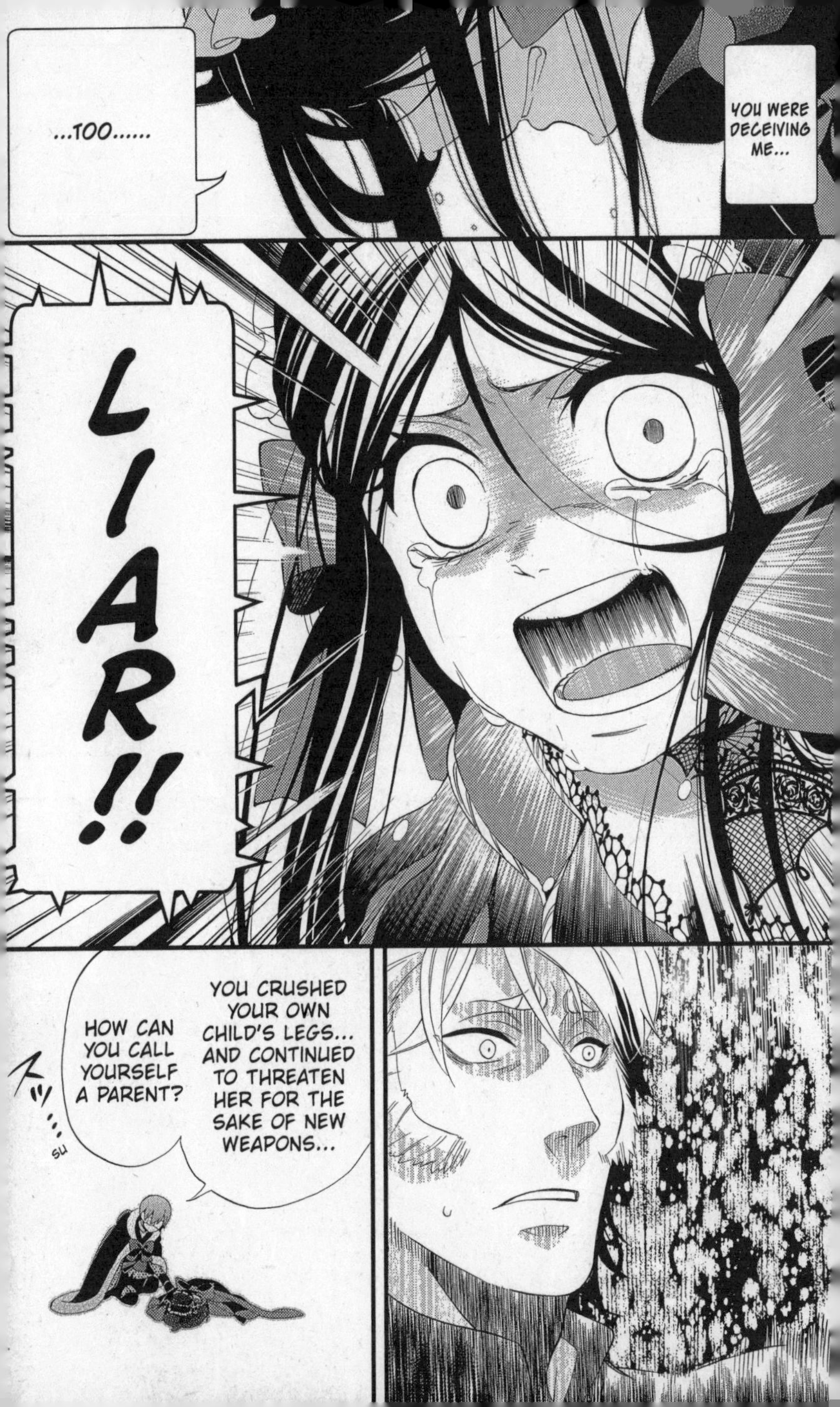
YOU WERE DECEIVING ME...
...TOO......
LIAR!!
YOU CRUSHED YOUR OWN CHILD'S LEGS... AND CONTINUED TO THREATEN HER FOR THE SAKE OF NEW WEAPONS...
HOW CAN YOU CALL YOURSELF A PARENT?
SU

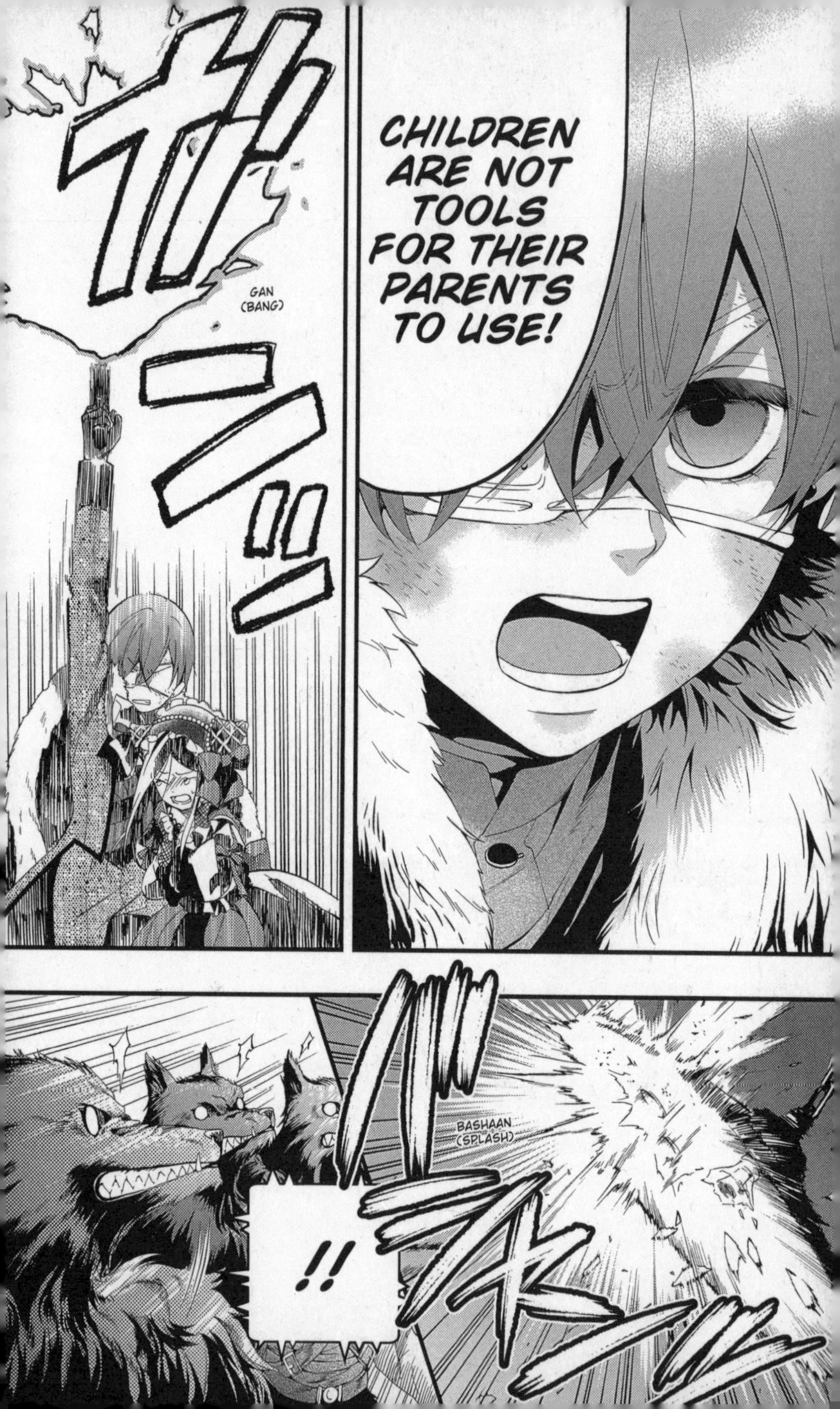
CHILDREN ARE NOT TOOLS FOR THEIR PARENTS TO USE!
GAN (BANG)
BASHAAN (SPLASH)
!!

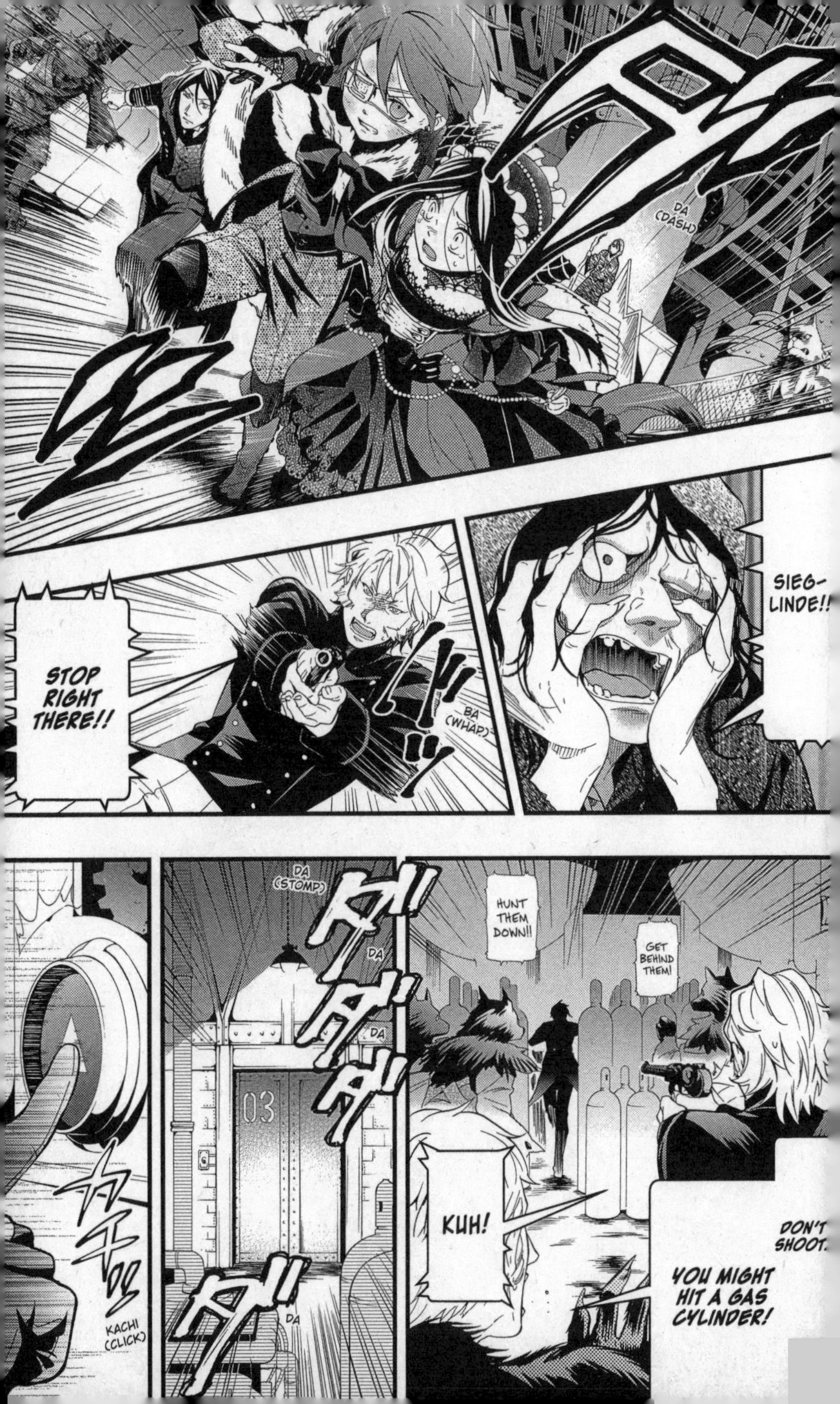
DA (DASH)
SIEG-LINDE!!
BA (WHAP)
STOP RIGHT THERE!!
HUNT THEM DOWN!!
GET BEHIND THEM!
DON'T SHOOT.
YOU MIGHT HIT A GAS CYLINDER!
KUH!
DA (STOMP)
DA
DA
DA
KACHI (CLICK)

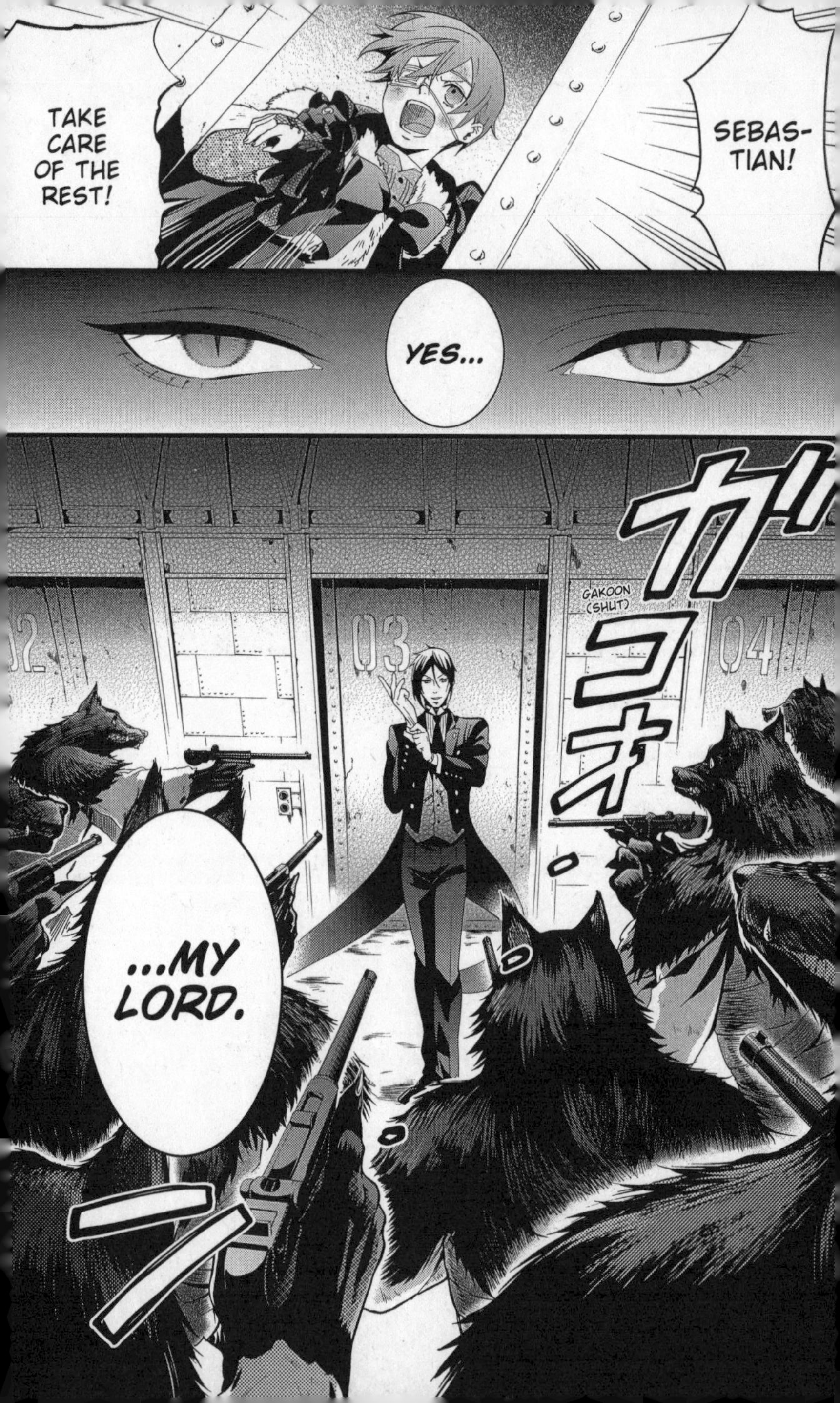
SEBAS-TIAN!
TAKE CARE OF THE REST!
YES...
GAKOON (SHUT)
...MY LORD.

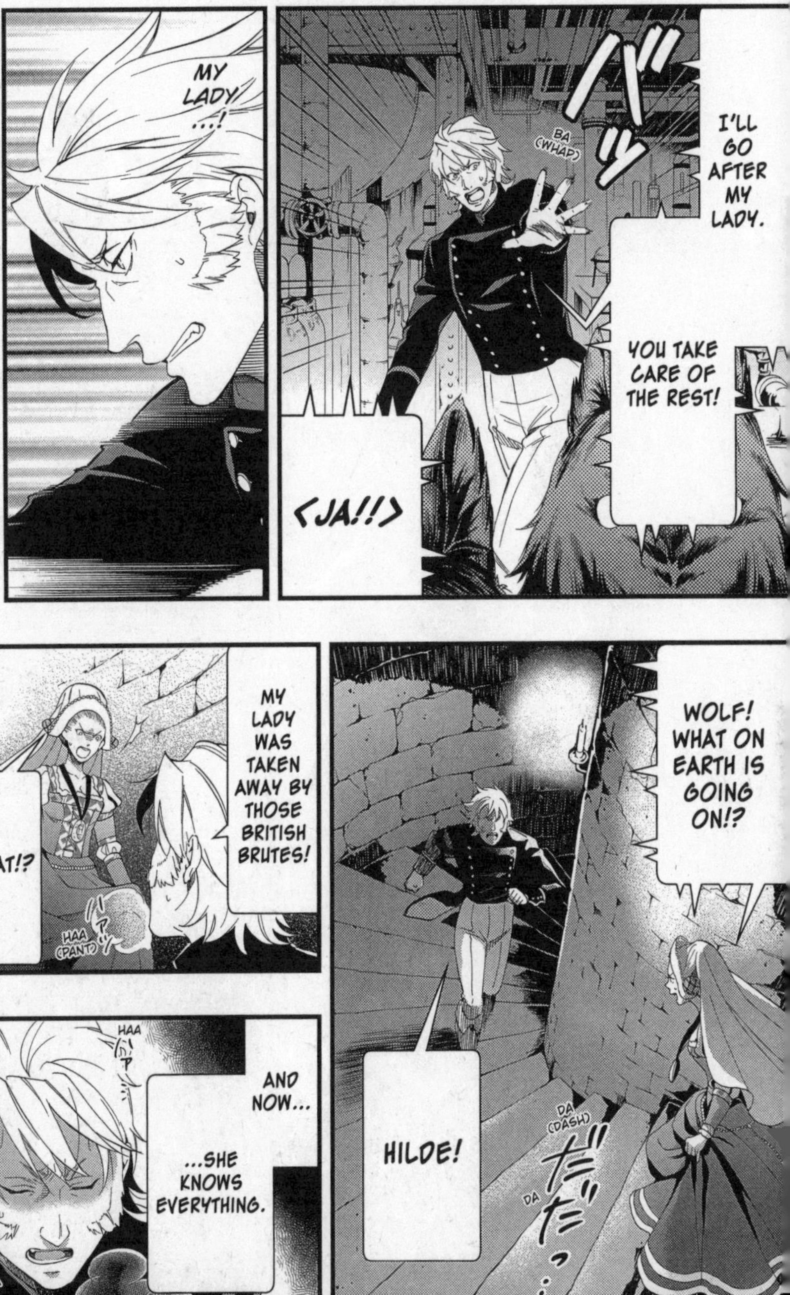
BA (WHAP)
I'LL GO AFTER MY LADY.
YOU TAKE CARE OF THE REST!
<JA!!>
MY LADY ...!
WOLF! WHAT ON EARTH IS GOING ON!?
HILDE!
DA (DASH)
DA
MY LADY WAS TAKEN AWAY BY THOSE BRITISH BRUTES!
WHAT!?
HAA (PANT)
HAA
AND NOW...
...SHE KNOWS EVERYTHING.
HAA

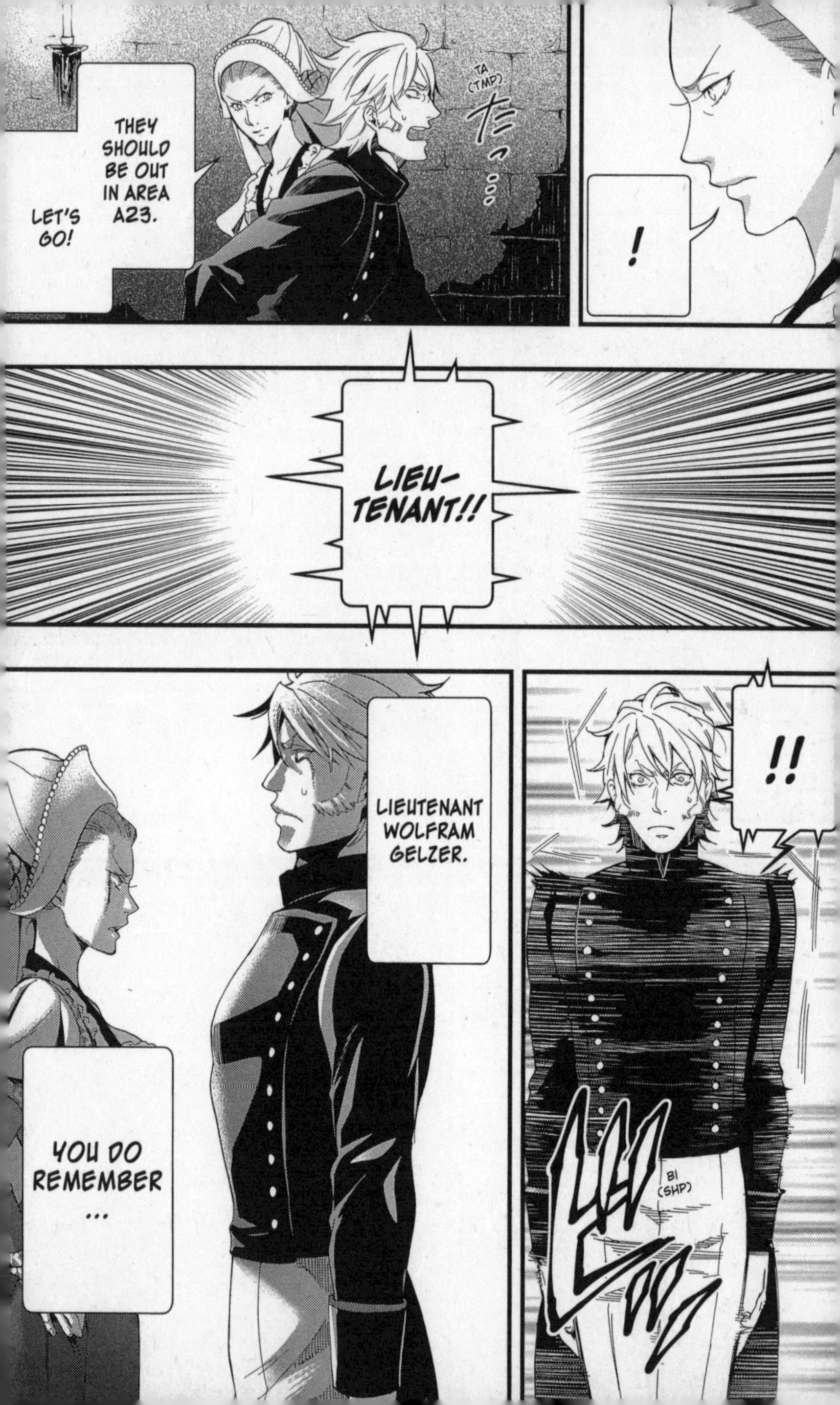
!
TA (TMP)
THEY SHOULD BE OUT IN AREA A23.
LET'S GO!
LIEU-TENANT!!
!!
BI (SHP)
LIEUTENANT WOLFRAM GELZER.
YOU DO REMEMBER ...

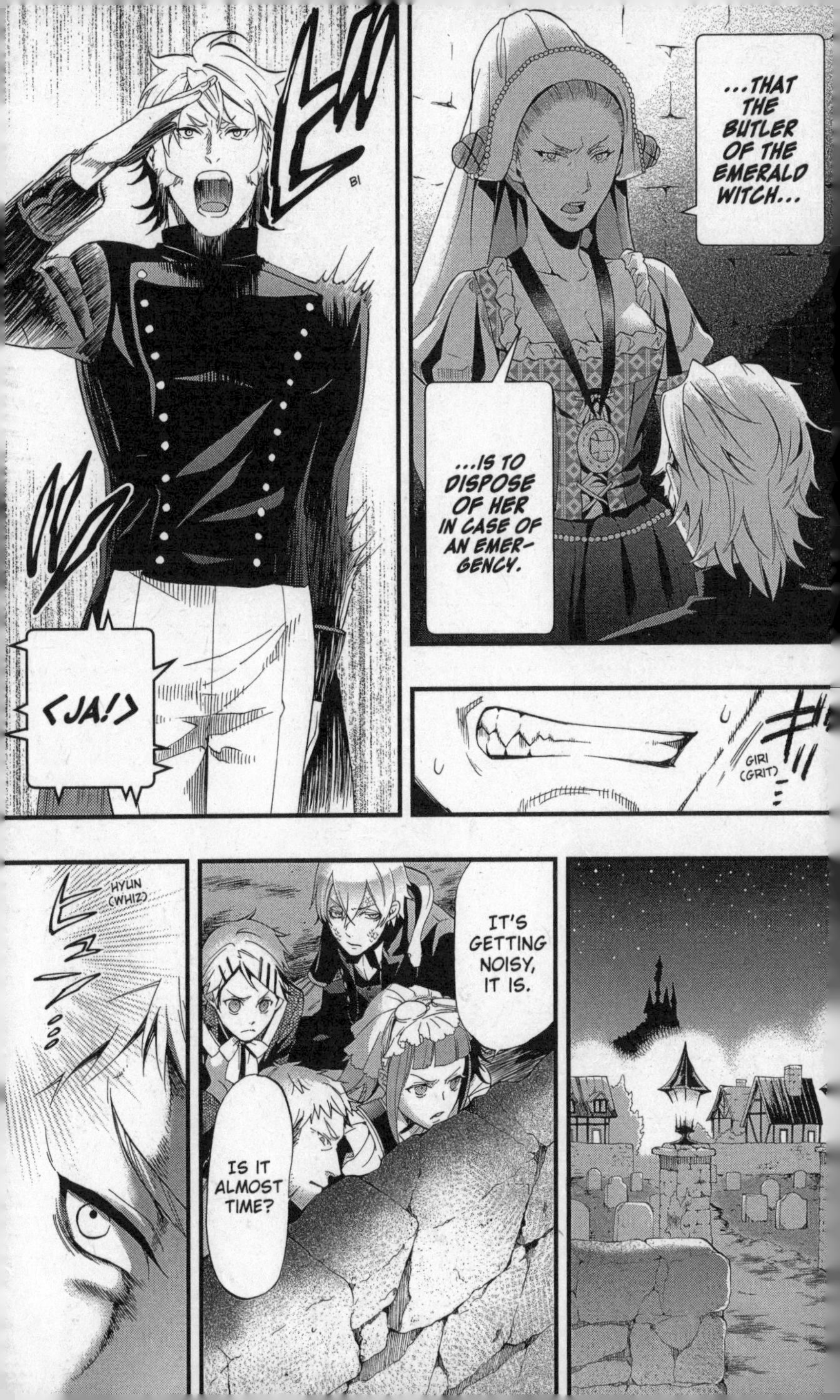

...THAT THE BUTLER OF THE EMERALD WITCH...
...IS TO DISPOSE OF HER IN CASE OF AN EMERGENCY.
GIRI (GRIT)
BI
<JA!>
IT'S GETTING NOISY, IT IS.
IS IT ALMOST TIME?
HYUN (WHIZ)

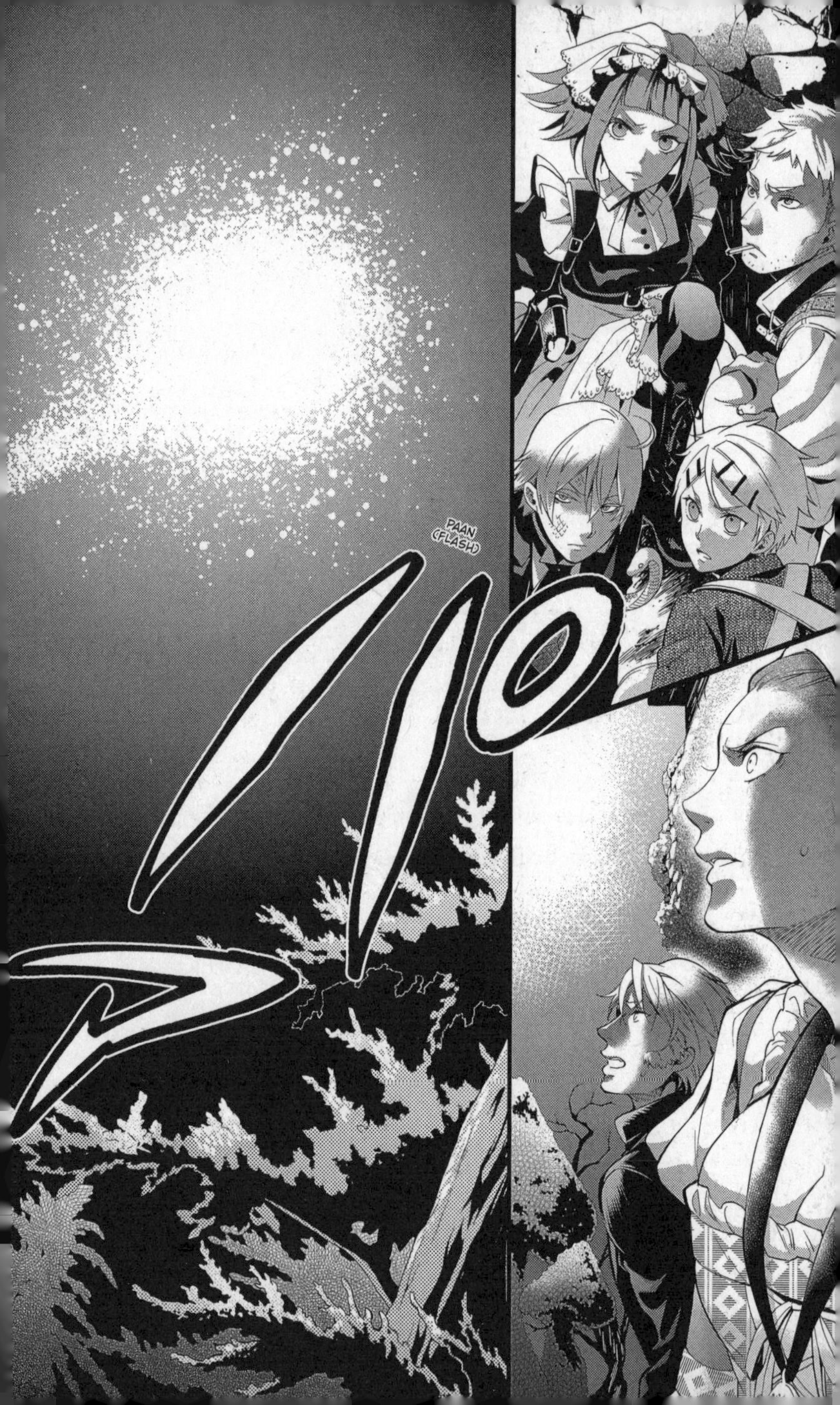
PAAN
(FLASH)

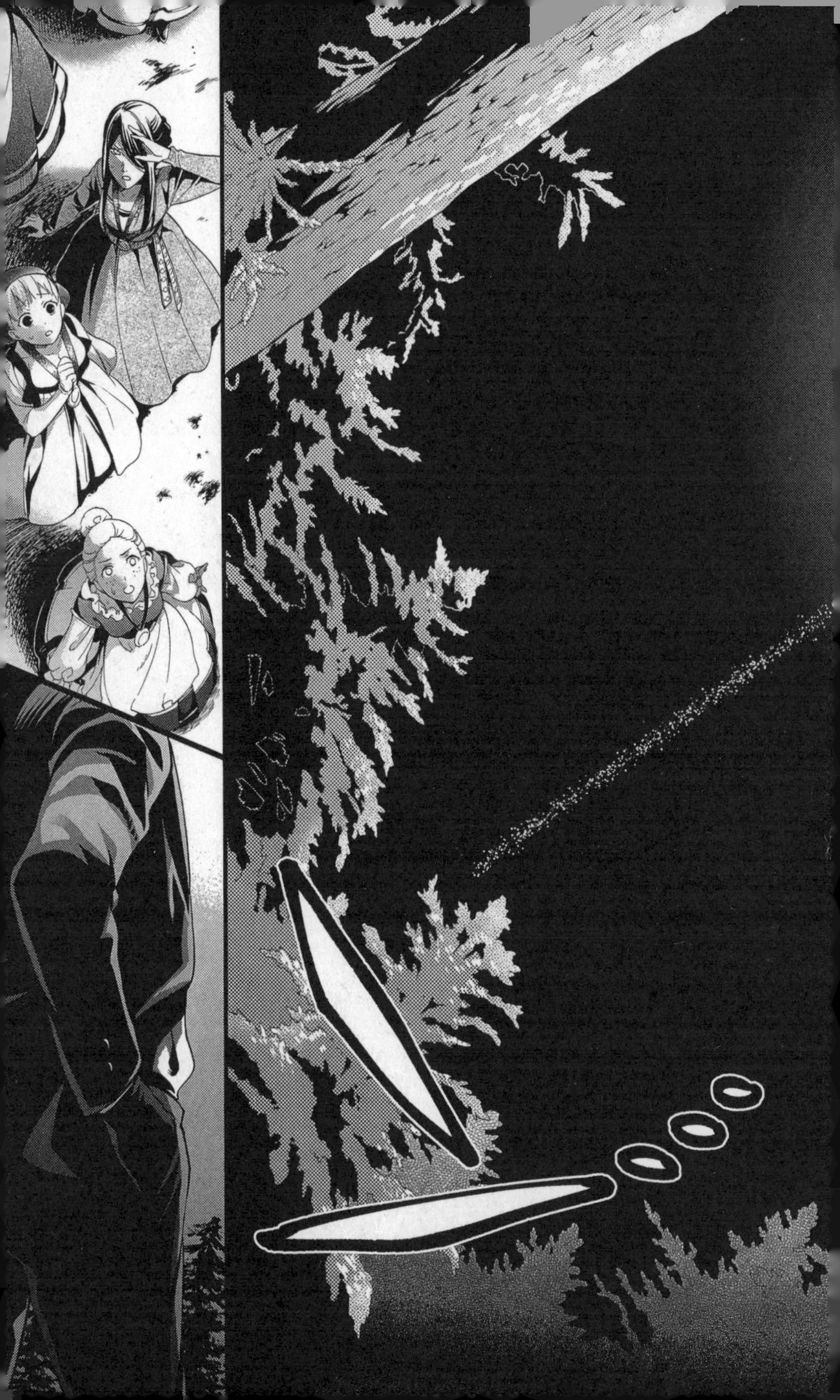

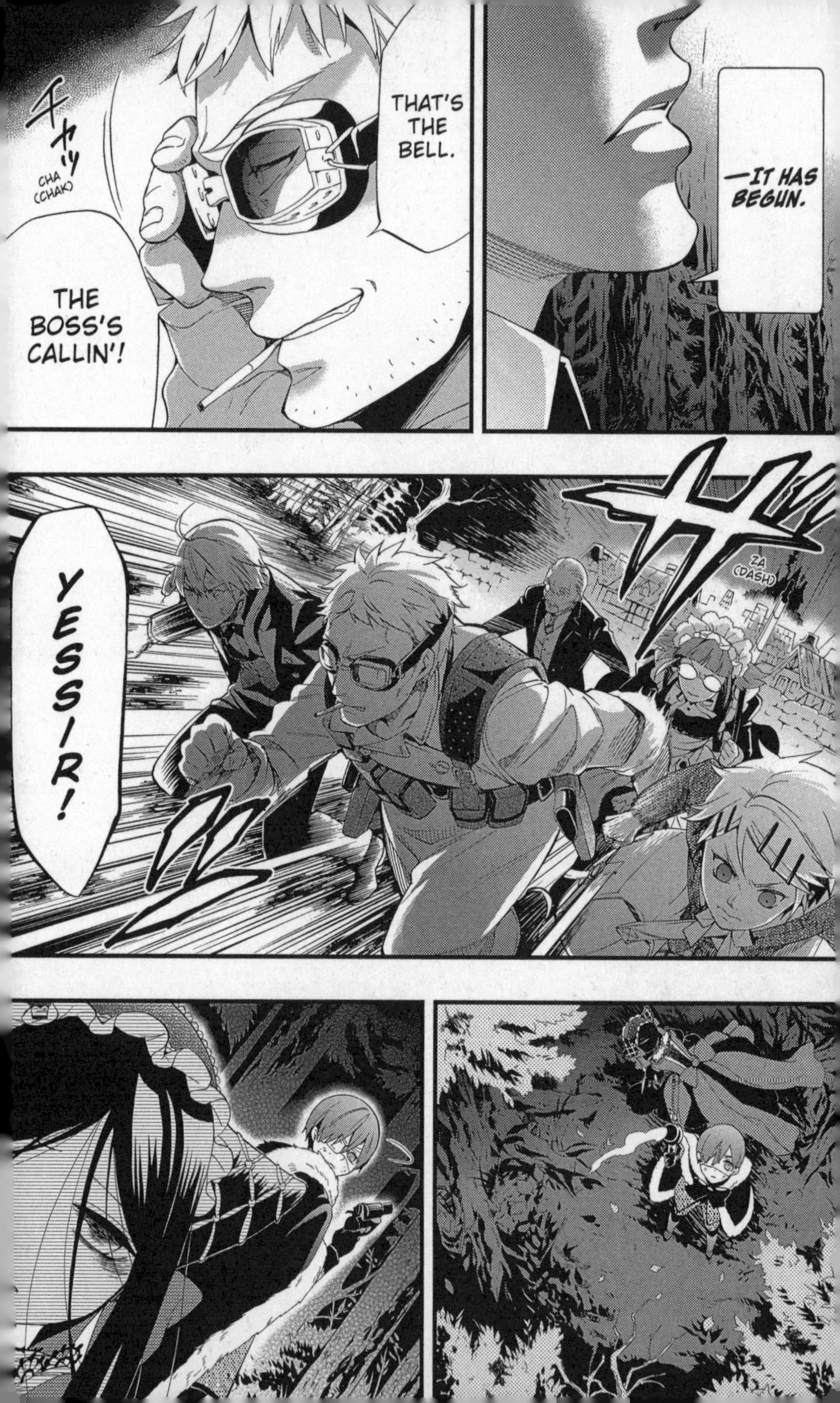

—IT HAS BEGUN.
THAT'S THE BELL.
チャッ
CHA (CHAK)
THE BOSS'S CALLIN'!
ザッ
ZA (DASH)
YESSIR!

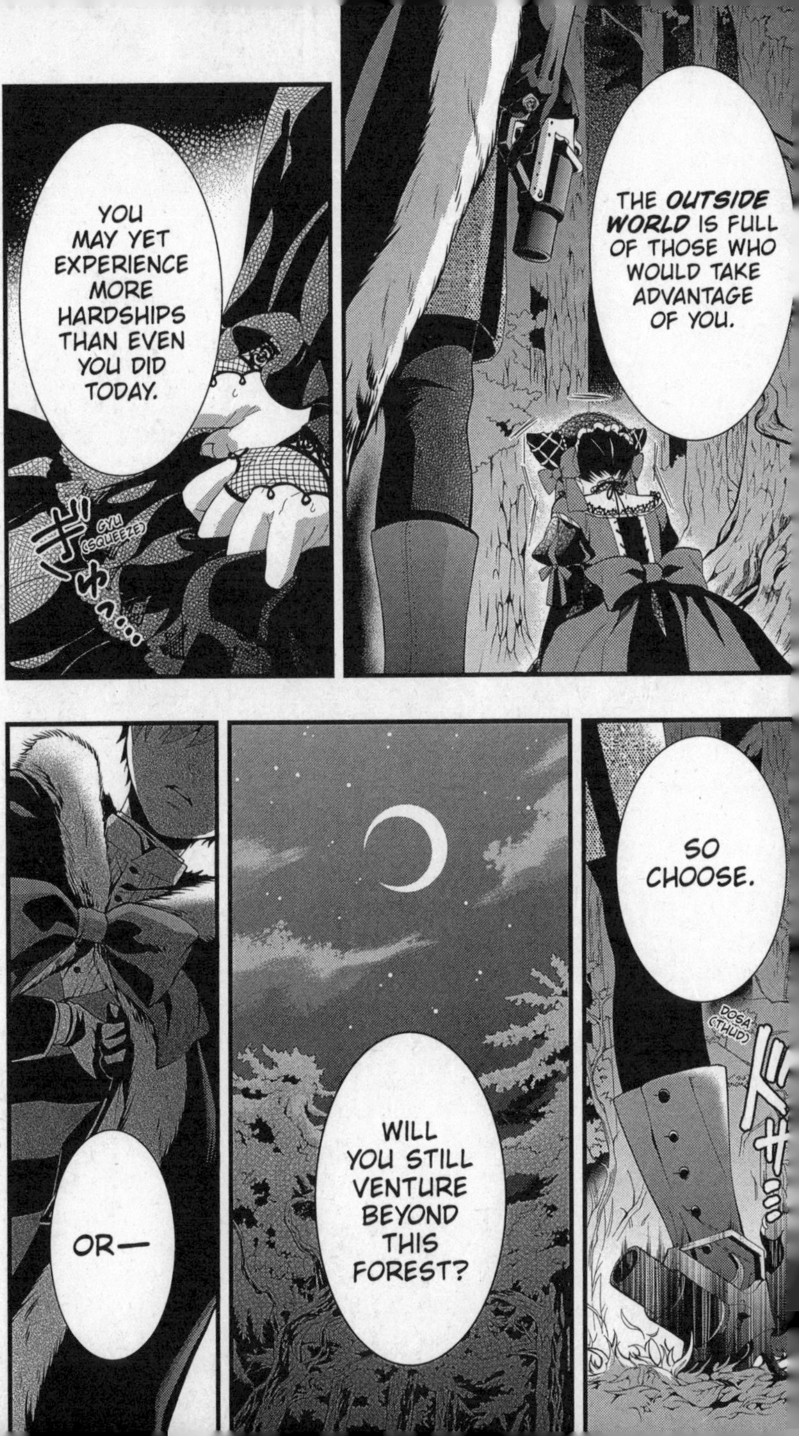
THE OUTSIDE WORLD IS FULL OF THOSE WHO WOULD TAKE ADVANTAGE OF YOU.
YOU MAY YET EXPERIENCE MORE HARDSHIPS THAN EVEN YOU DID TODAY.
GYU (SQUEEZE)
SO CHOOSE.
DOSA (THUD)
WILL YOU STILL VENTURE BEYOND THIS FOREST?
OR—

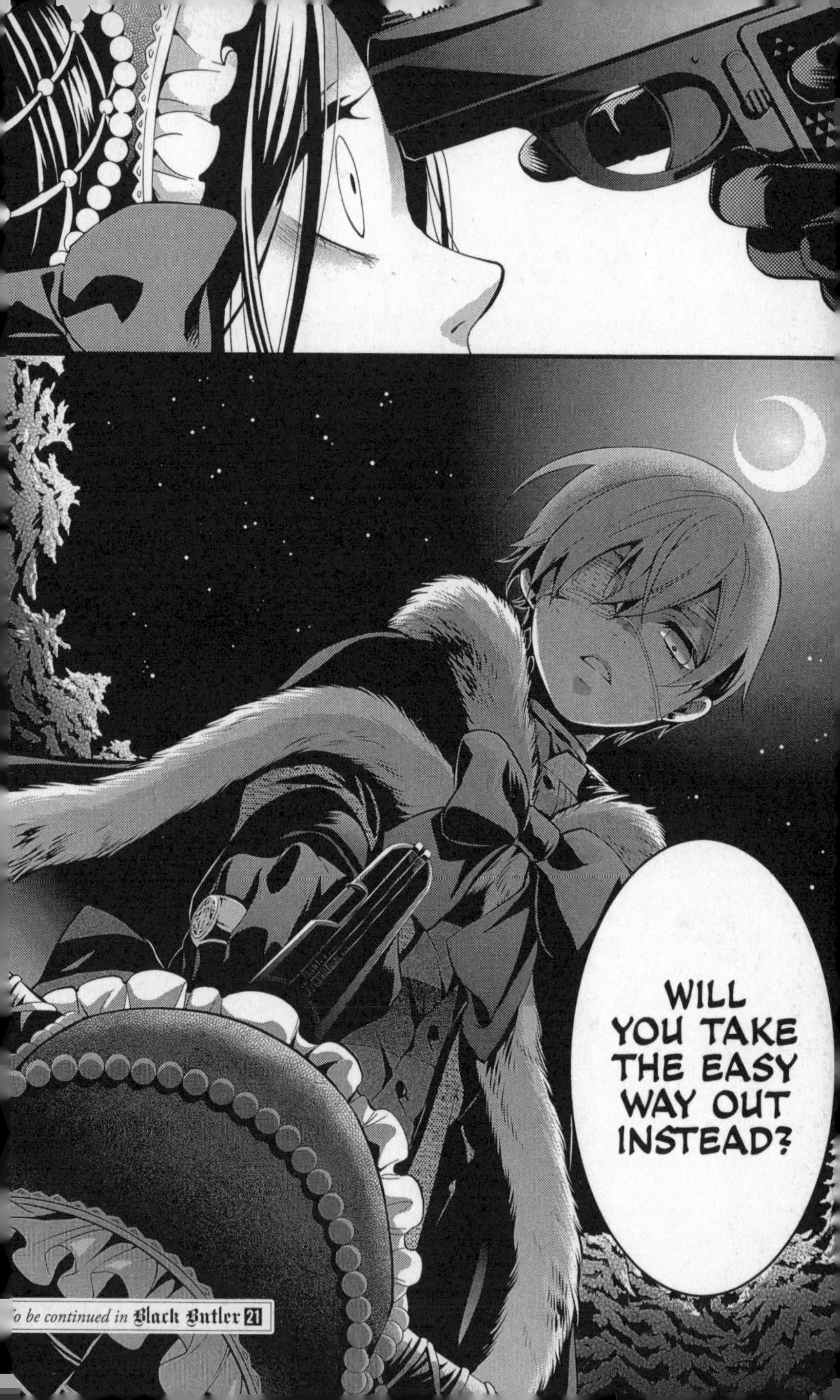
WILL YOU TAKE THE EASY WAY OUT INSTEAD?
To be continued in Black Butler 21

⤜ Black Butler ⤛

黒執事

❧ Downstairs

Wakana Haduki
7
Saito Torino
Tsuki Sorano
Chiaki Nagaoka
Asakura
*
Takeshi Kuma
*
Yana Toboso

❧

Adviser

Rico Murakami

*

Special Thanks

Akira Suzuki

and You!

Translation Notes

Page 29
Theban alphabet
The characters used in the magic circle are letters from the Theban alphabet. This mystical alphabet is also known as the Witches' Alphabet and has long been used to write spells and inscriptions. Though of uncertain origin, the script and alphabet came into prominence in medieval times.

Page 96
$C_4H_8Cl_2S$
The "ciphers" here are actually chemical formulas. The first formula, $C_4H_8Cl_2S$, is the chemical formula for mustard gas, a powerful chemical agent used in warfare. It was first used in this fashion by the German army in 1917 during World War I. The symptoms Ciel suffers following his trip to the Werewolves' Forest are those of mustard gas exposure. The chemical agent causes serious damage to the skin, eyes, and respiratory tract. When the gas comes into contact with the skin, it can cause redness and itching and eventually blistering, during which large yellowish pustules may erupt. If one's eyes are exposed for any significant length of time, temporary blindness may occur, often lasting upwards of ten days. When inhaled, the gas may cause the infected individual to bleed from the nose, in addition to other effects.

Page 96
NaOCl
NaOCl is the chemical formula for sodium hypochlorite, which is known to neutralise the effects of mustard gas when dissolved in water (aka household bleach). This solution can play a key role in the basic steps for mustard gas decontamination—flush eyes immediately with water; remove all exposed clothing and double-seal into plastic bags before washing the skin with soap and water (or 0.5% solution of sodium hypochlorite); avoid forcing the contaminated individual to vomit, instead have them drink milk or water if it can be kept down—and appear in the rite of purification performed by Lady Sullivan in Volume 19.

Page 120
"...a feast served on your naked body..."
This is a reference to *nyotaimori*, a form of sexual entertainment where food (usually sashimi and sushi) is served using a naked woman as the platter.

Page 140
Gästezimmer03, In Grüne Schloss
The German text on the monitor reads "Guest room 03, Emerald Castle."

Page 150
SuLIN
In Japanese pronunciation, Sullivan, the name from which SuLIN is derived, begins with "sari," so SuLIN is actually "sarin," a lethal nerve agent that can be weaponised. Even minimal exposure can cause victims to perish within minutes. Sarin was discovered in 1938 in Germany by scientists who were researching stronger pesticides. The compound was named after the discoverers—*S*chrader, *A*mbros, *R*üdiger, and Van der *Lin*de. The magic circle on page 110 contains the chemical structure of sarin ($C_4H_{10}FO_2P$) written in Theban script.

Page 162
Streng Geheim: Grüne Hexe Ausbildung Projekt
The German text on the binder reads "TOP SECRET: Emerald Witch Education Project."

Yana Toboso

AUTHOR'S NOTE

At last, we reach the twentieth volume of **Black Butler**! When I tell people that this series was originally scheduled to be just one volume long, they say, "No wayyy!"

So I hereby declare:
.If I had known this series was going to be more than ten volumes long, I wouldn't have used Roman numerals for the volume numbers!!!!!!

And so this is Volume 20 with thanks and gratitude.

BLACK BUTLER ⓴

YANA TOBOSO

Translation: Tomo Kimura • **Lettering: Alexis Eckerman**

KUROSHITSUJI Vol. 20 © 2014 Yana Toboso / SQUARE ENIX CO., LTD. First published in Japan in 2014 by SQUARE ENIX CO., LTD. English translation rights arranged with SQUARE ENIX CO., LTD. and Hachette Book Group through Tuttle-Mori Agency, Inc.

Translation © 2015 by SQUARE ENIX CO., LTD.

Yen Press
Hachette Book Group
1290 Avenue of the Americas, New York, NY 10104

www.HachetteBookGroup.com
www.YenPress.com

Yen Press is an imprint of Hachette Book Group, Inc. The Yen Press name and logo are trademarks of Hachette Book Group, Inc.

The publisher is not responsible for websites (or their content) that are not owned by the publisher.

First Yen Press Edition: July 2015

ISBN: 978-0-316-30501-3

10 9 8 7 6 5 4 3 2 1

BVG   3 1901 05419 1491

Printed in the United States of America